SALES
PROMOTION
MANAGEMENT

THE PRENTICE HALL SERIES IN MARKETING

Philip Kotler, Series Editor

S.C. Johnson & Son Distinguished
   Professor of International Marketing

Northwestern University

ABELL/HAMMOND	Strategic Market Planning: Problems and Analytical Approaches
COREY	Industrial Marketing: Cases and Concepts, 3rd ed.
GREEN/TULL/ALBAUM	Research for Marketing Decisions, 5th ed.
KEEGAN	Global Marketing Management, 4th ed.
KOTLER	Marketing Management: Analysis, Planning, Implementations, and Control, 6th ed.
KOTLER/ANDREASEN	Strategic Marketing for Nonprofit Organizations, 3rd ed.
KOTLER	Principles of Marketing, 4th ed.
LOVELOCK	Services Marketing: Text, Cases, and Readings
MYERS/MASSY/GREYSER	Marketing Research and Knowledge Development: An Assessment for Marketing Management
NAGLE	The Strategy and Tactics of Pricing: A Guide to Profitable Decision Making
QUELCH	Sales Promotion Management
RAY	Advertising and Communication Management
RUSSELL/VERRILL/LANE	Kleppner's Advertising Procedure, 10th ed.
STERN/EL-ANSARY	Marketing Channels, 3rd ed.
STERN/EOVALDI	Legal Aspects of Marketing Strategy: Antitrust and Consumer Protection Issues
URBAN/HAUSER	Design and Marketing of New Products

SALES PROMOTION MANAGEMENT

JOHN A. QUELCH
Graduate School of Business Administration
Harvard University

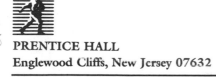

PRENTICE HALL
Englewood Cliffs, New Jersey 07632

LIBRARY OF CONGRESS
Library of Congress Cataloging-in-Publication Data

Quelch, John A.
    Sales promotion management / John A. Quelch.
    ISBN 0-13-788118-5
    1. Sales promotion—Case studies.   2. Design—Case studies.
  I. Title.
  HF5438.5.Q45   1989
  658.8'2—dc19

88-25278
CIP

Editorial/production supervision
and interior design: York Production Services
Manufacturing buyer: Margaret Rizzi
Cover design: Wanda Lubelska Design

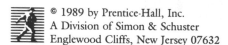 © 1989 by Prentice-Hall, Inc.
A Division of Simon & Schuster
Englewood Cliffs, New Jersey 07632

Printed in the United States of America

10 9 8 7 6 5 4 3 2 1

ISBN 0-13-788118-5

Prentice-Hall International (UK) Limited, *London*
Prentice-Hall of Australia Pty. Limited, *Sydney*
Prentice-Hall Canada Inc., *Toronto*
Prentice-Hall Hispanoamericana, S.A., *Mexico*
Prentice-Hall of India Private Limited, New Delhi
Prentice-Hall of Japan, Inc., *Tokyo*
Simon & Schuster Asia Pte. Ltd., *Singapore*
Editora Prentice-Hall do Brasil, Ltda., *Rio de Janeiro*

DEDICATED TO ALDEN G. CLAYTON

CONTENTS

PREFACE

Sales promotion expenditures by consumer goods and services marketers have increased dramatically during the past decade. An economic recession is likely to fuel this trend further, as consumers and distributors become increasingly price sensitive and demanding of promotional inducements from manufacturers to purchase their products. Sales promotion management is, therefore, likely to grow rather than diminish in importance in the years ahead.

This book is aimed at advanced students of sales promotion and at managers charged with developing or approving sales promotion programs who have progressed beyond the primer stage. It is not another introduction to sales promotion tactics. Written from the producer (rather than distributor) perspective, the book includes an introductory chapter and twelve case studies. The reader will complete the book with a more thorough understanding of the complexities of sales promotion and with an enhanced ability to make sales promotion management decisions.

The case studies are unique in that they cover a variety of consumer goods and services. Beyond consumer packaged goods, there are cases on soft goods, consumer services, and durables. The cases are grouped into four sections based on this classification of goods with each section being introduced by an overview article. Each case finds management grappling with one or more challenges in sales promotion—setting objectives and strategy, selecting promotion tactics, designing individual promotion events and integrated promotion calendars, organizing for effective implementation of promotions, and evaluating the results. Beyond the challenge of solving the managerial problems presented in each case, readers will find that most of them include substantial background information on sales promotion policies and programs that is generalizable to their own business situations.

The case studies are preceded by an introductory chapter that focuses on the issue of sales promotion design. While promotion design is only one aspect of sales promotion management, it has received scant attention. Discussions with managers indicate that they have more difficulty designing sales promotions than they do settling on sales promotion objectives and developing sales promotion strategies. The introductory chapter provides a framework that the reader can use to determine, first, the decisions that a manager must confront in designing any promotion and, second, what those decisions should be in light of the product characteristics and market circumstances with which the manager is dealing. The framework represents a synthesis of some seventy interviews with line marketing and sales managers and sales promotion staff specialists at the twelve case study sites and, as such, cuts across all classes of consumer goods and services.

Sales promotion is now established as an important and increasingly respectable element of the marketing mix. In particular, it is integral to both communications policy—since managers often have to make trade offs between advertising and promotion expenditures, and to pricing policy—since most sales promotions are by definition temporary price incentives. This book should give the reader insights on how sales promotions can be managed better within the context of overall marketing strategy.

ACKNOWLEDGMENTS

My interest in sales promotion began ten years ago when the Marketing Science Institute of Cambridge, Massachusetts, under the direction of Professor Stephen A. Greyser and Alden G. Clayton, included sales promotion as a priority on its research agenda. Since then, MSI has sponsored numerous academic research studies and conferences on sales promotion topics and continues to lead in this area. The encouragement and support of the MSI community of scholars and business executives have greatly assisted me in understanding more thoroughly the complexities of sales promotion.

Throughout the research effort that has culminated in this book, I have benefited from the counsel, collaboration and friendship of three colleagues: Professor Paul W. Farris of the Colgate Darden School of Business Administration, University of Virginia; Professor Scott Neslin of the Amos Tuck School of Business, Dartmouth College; and Dr. Christopher H. Lovelock. Their ideas and insights have been a continuing source of both stimulation and rigor. In addition, Professors Robert J. Dolan and Walter J. Salmon of the Harvard Business School faculty generously reviewed and critiqued several drafts of the introductory chapter to this book.

Thanks are also due to my research assistants during the past seven years, all of whom have been persuaded to write at least one case study on sales promotion. I thank Penny Pittman Merliss, Alice MacDonald Court, Neil Collins, Melanie D. Spencer, and Cynthia A. Bates for their diligence, professionalism, and good humor.

Taking one step back in the case writing process, I must acknowledge the many executives of the companies and organizations discussed in the case studies for the trust and time which made this book a reality. In similar vein, I gratefully recognize the financial support and encouragement for my case writing efforts furnished by the Division of Research at the Graduate School of Business Administration, Harvard University.

Finally, thanks to Whitney Blake at Prentice Hall, one of the best Marketing Editors in the industry, and to Thelma Prince for her customary professionalism in editing and proofreading the manuscript.

John A. Quelch
Boston, Massachusetts
January 1988

SALES
PROMOTION
MANAGEMENT

INFLUENCES ON SALES PROMOTION DESIGN

JOHN A. QUELCH

INTRODUCTION

Sales promotions are used by almost all consumer goods and services producers. Two recent examples are

☐ To persuade consumers to buy snowthrowers early and thereby even out consumer demand and reduce the company's inventory exposure, Toro ran a preseason promotion on selected snowthrower models in 1983 that offered a buyer a rebate if snowfall in his/her market area proved to be below average. Competitors were unable to match this promotion at short notice and Toro sales exceeded projections.

☐ When the product manager on Heinz ketchup, the leading brand, faced a strong challenge from Hunt's in the southern United States, he responded with higher deal allowances and higher value coupons than in the rest of the country where Heinz's share leadership was more secure.

Sales promotions are temporary incentives targeted at the trade (trade promotions), or at end consumers (consumer promotions).[1] While sales promotions generally aim to change purchase behavior, they vary in whether they attempt to persuade trade customers or end consumers to buy a product for the first time, to buy more, to buy earlier, or to buy more often.

In recent years, consumer goods and services marketers have increased their sales promotion expenditures significantly. By one estimate, promotion expenditures grew 304% between 1977 and 1985 to reach $99.4 billion, while advertising expenditures grew 231% to $54.0 billion during the same period (Bowman, 1985). Relatedly, the frequency and complexity of promotions and the variety of objec-

---

[1]Temporary incentives targeted at salespeople are also sometimes treated as promotions. They are, however, beyond the scope of this study.

tives they are called upon to address have also expanded. As a result, managers are increasingly searching for the most effective way to design individual promotion events.

Managerial rather than academic contributions on promotion design have focused on suggesting the appropriate types of promotion to achieve particular promotion objectives (Strang, 1976). In addition, Peckham (1973) and Ennis (1985), have independently tabulated conventional wisdom on the promotion objectives and tactics appropriate for high- versus low-share brands and for new versus established products.

Studies of sales promotion have only occasionally drawn inferences about optimal promotion design, though its importance is increasingly acknowledged (Hardy, 1986; McAlister, 1986). Those that have typically address only one or two aspects of the problem—usually timing concerns such as the frequency and duration of promotions and the depth of the discount rate—and only in packaged goods contexts. Issues such as whether a promotion should be run on one or all sizes in a product line or adjusted from one market area to another have received scant attention.

SALES PROMOTION STRATEGY

Sales promotions can improve producer profits because they permit price discrimination and because they can, in other ways, influence trade and consumer behavior.

Price discrimination.   Promotions permit producers to practice price discrimination, charging different prices to different consumers and trade accounts that vary in price sensitivity (Narasimhan, 1984). For example, a shoe mail order business sends a series of seven catalogs with progressively more generous promotion offers to new inquiries; once a consumer places an order, he or she receives no more catalogs in the sequence. Price discrimination also explains the use of coupons and price specials aimed at the more price-sensitive consumer who will make the effort to clip, save, and redeem coupons or search out a store offering a retail price special on his or her preferred brand. Designing promotions that enable more price-sensitive consumers and trade accounts to pay less usually generates more contribution than if one price is charged to all. Promotions also enable producers to practice price discrimination over time by adjusting to variations in demand and supply without changing list prices.

Trade behavior.   Temporary promotions encourage the trade to forward buy, reducing the probability of out-to-stocks on retail shelves and, in some cases, reducing the buffer stocks producers must hold.[2] Promotions also encourage the trade to provide temporary displays, price cuts, and/or advertising features that shift inventories to consumers who have lower holding costs (Blattberg, Eppen, and Lieberman, 1981) and may add excitement at the point-of-sale to the merchandising of mature and mundane products. By so doing, promotions can stimulate primary

---

[2]There are also negative consequences to forward buying for normal inventory that are noted below.

as well as selective demand and potentially lower unit production costs. Finally, promotions reduce the retailer's risk in stocking new products. As a result, more consumers are exposed faster to more new products than would otherwise be the case. Some of these consumers, induced by promotion to try a new brand, may become loyal repeat purchasers.

Consumer behavior. Temporary promotions can instill a sense of urgency in consumers, persuade them to stop comparing alternatives, and buy earlier, and maybe in greater quantities, than would otherwise have been the case.[3] For this reason, temporary promotions often produce greater sales responses than equivalent list price cuts (Beem and Schaffer, 1981). A second benefit is that promotions, such as coupons in free-standing newspaper inserts, can enhance the attention-getting power of advertising and convey brand benefit as well as price information. Promotions also convey brand information by stimulating trial use (Fornell, Robinson, and Wernerfelt, 1985; Levedahl, 1986). Finally, promotions enable producers to reach the deal-prone consumer and encourage him or her to switch. Buying on deal is thought to be used as a simple decision rule by many of today's time-pressured consumers and by those who derive psychological satisfaction from being smart shoppers, who take advantage of price specials and redeeming coupons.

A further advantage of sales promotion is that expenses are largely incurred on a variable cost, pay-as-you-go basis; in contrast, advertising requires an up-front investment that involves more financial risk. Thus, even if consumer advertising could, for example, induce the trade to provide incremental merchandising support, the use of sales promotion to achieve this objective might be preferable.

Notwithstanding these benefits, producers are concerned that temporary promotions have the following negative effects.

Decreasing brand loyalty. The objective of many sales promotions is to encourage brand switching and, thereby, to counter the franchise-building effects of competitive brands' advertising. Though other factors such as the proliferation of new product options have raised the consumer's probability of switching (Johnson, 1984), few managers deny that increasing promotion expenditures have diminished the strength of brand franchises and brand loyalties.

Increasing price sensitivity. Frequent price promotions make trade customers and consumers more price sensitive not just toward the brands on deal but toward all brands in a category. Consumers become unwilling to make any purchases unless on deal. And even brand-loyal consumers start timing their purchases to coincide with deals on their favorite brands.

Inadequate merchandising support. Trade accounts often claim promotion allowances without providing the incremental merchandising support required to qualify and, in addition, pocket allowances rather than pass them through to the

---

[3]The demand acceleration effects generated by temporary promotions may also be evident when a producer preannounces a list price increase.

consumer (Chevalier and Curhan, 1976; Curhan and Kopp, 1986). Competition for space in many channels is such that producers find themselves competing for a retailer's favor by dropping performance requirements or turning a blind eye to verification.

Forward buying and diversion.   Regardless of whether they provide extra merchandising support, many trade accounts respond to temporary promotions by buying in excess of normal inventory requirements as return on investment calculations dictate. Producers of well-known brands that can serve as traffic builders, that are non-perishable, and that incur low inventory holding costs relative to value are especially vulnerable. Forward buying causes peaks and troughs in factory shipments, induces an artificial seasonality in trade demand patterns, reduces the accuracy of production and logistics forecasts, and, consequently, increases manufacturing and distribution costs. Though forward buying can decrease retail out-of-stocks and give retailers more discretion as to when they promote, excess inventories that result also can be resold or diverted to other retailers at a price higher than the promotional purchase price but lower than the producer's prevailing price in other geographic areas.

Detracting from a quality image.   Some consumers may infer that a promoted item is not selling well, is about to be discontinued, or carries a list price that is artificially high relative to the product's quality. Such negative quality attributions seem more likely if promotions are not common to the category; if the promotion is unexpected by consumers as opposed to, for example, an annual year-end clearance sale of automobiles or fashion merchandise; if the promotion is communicated by the producer rather than the retailer; if consumers perceive interbrand differences; if the other elements of the marketing mix (such as the advertising, packaging, and distribution channels) do not testify to product quality; and if independent sources such as *Consumer Reports* give the product low marks.

Focusing management on the short term.   Because sales promotions can have an impact on short-term sales, they are extensively used by product managers who are on fast-track career paths and are driven by the emphasis of stock analysts and top management on quarterly financial results.

Sales promotion is a contributory rather than exclusive cause of each of these problems. Nevertheless, in designing sales promotion events, managers are becoming increasingly concerned about minimizing these negative effects.

SALES PROMOTION DESIGN

Managers understand clearly that their promotion design decisions are constrained by the role of promotion in their marketing strategies, by current and anticipated competitive promotion activity, and by the size of their promotion budgets. Managers also understand that the design must begin with the specification of an objective.

While the range of objectives is large (see Exhibit 1 for a listing), it is not our intent here to provide guidelines on the objectives product managers should pursue since our interviews indicated minimal confusion on this point. Rather, confusion arises once the objective has been set and the manager must determine what promotion will best produce the desired results.

Examination of the promotion planning process at several companies suggests

---

EXHIBIT 1 Promotion objectives for Brand X

I. *Consumer Target*
- ☐ To persuade *new category users* to try the category and Brand X in particular and thereby increase primary as well as selective demand.
- ☐ To persuade *existing category users* to include Brand X in their evoked sets and to try and/or switch to Brand X.
- ☐ To persuade *existing Brand X* users to
    - –continue to purchase Brand X and not to switch.
    - –increase their purchase frequency of Brand X.
    - –purchase now rather than later by overcoming reasons for postponement.
    - –adopt new uses for Brand X and so use more product, resulting in higher purchase quantities and purchases of larger sizes.
    - –purchase multiple units of Brand X to take them out of the marketplace for an extended time period.

II. *Trade Target*
- A. *Distribution*
    - ☐ To maintain or increase existing distribution, shelf facings, and shelf locations for Brand X.
    - ☐ To persuade existing outlets to stock additional open stock models and/or temporary promotional models of Brand X.
    - ☐ To persuade the trade to stock a complete line of a producer's products.
- B. *Support*
    - ☐ To persuade existing outlets to provide temporary price cuts, special displays, and advertising features for Brand X.
    - ☐ To provide retailers with an opportunity to increase in-store excitement and, thereby, to persuade them to promote Brand X aggressively in their stores.
    - ☐ To achieve secondary placements of Brand X near related items in stores where it already has distribution.
- C. *Inventories*
    - ☐ To increase the average trade account order size for Brand X.
    - ☐ To increase Brand X's share of trade inventories to preempt competition and motivate special merchandising support to sell them through.
    - ☐ To flush trade inventories of Brand X if they are excessive or if Brand X is being discontinued in favor of another item requiring shelf space.
- D. *Good Will*
    - ☐ To insulate the trade from consumer-price negotiation at the point-of-purchase (when Brand X is a durable good).
    - ☐ To insulate the trade from a temporary sales reduction that might be caused by an increase in the price of Brand X.

that, once the objective has been specified, there are three dimensions encompassing six issues that must be addressed in sequence in the design of any promotion:

I *Type*

☐   What *type* of promotion should be used to address the objective?

II *Scope*

☐   To which pack sizes or models should the promotion apply (*product scope*)?

☐   In which geographical markets should the promotion be offered (*market scope*)?

III *Tactics*

☐   When should the promotion be offered, when should it be announced, and how long should it last (*timing*)?

☐   What explicit or implicit *discount* should the promotion include?

☐   What *terms* of sale should be attached to the promotion?

Variations of this framework have been presented previously in Quelch (1983); Lovelock and Quelch (1983), and Quelch, Neslin, and Olson (1987). Below, we define each of the six design issues, state the options open to product managers, and draw some generalizations from practice that are applicable under all product-market circumstances.

I. TYPE

Issue #1: Type

Sales promotions are of two broad types: trade and consumer promotions. Trade promotions are temporary price incentives offered to the trade in the form of off-invoice allowances (deducted from producer invoices) or bill-back allowances (that producers pay when a trade account provides evidence of incremental merchandising support). Trade promotions also include temporary adjustments to merchandising programs such as early buy allowances and dating and stock balancing programs designed to encourage the trade to build inventories and stock the full line.

Types of consumer promotion include samples, price quantity promotions (such as price packs and bonus packs), coupons, rebates, premiums, sweepstakes, financing incentives, service contracts, and trade-in allowances. The variety of consumer and trade promotions can be usefully categorized along two dimensions: immediate versus delayed value and price cut versus added value:[4]

Immediate versus delayed value.   Immediate-value promotions reward the consumer at the time of purchase; delayed-value promotions such as frequent-flier offers reward the consumer sometime after purchase (in some cases

---

[4]These two dimensions were selected as most important from among a variety of criteria that can be used to distinguish one type promotion from another (see Farris and Quelch, 1983, chapter 7).

only after multiple purchases). The former have a more powerful impact, particularly in stimulating impulse purchases or brand-switching at the point-of-sale. Delayed-value promotions create a weaker but longer term impact, are often used to reward and reinforce the loyalty of existing consumers, and lend themselves to price discrimination because consumers must make an effort to take advantage of them. For example, in the case of a delayed value self-liquidating premium (such as a recipe book mailed to a consumer who sends in three cereal box tops and a three-dollar check), the consumer is made aware of the brand first when the offer is noticed, second each time a purchase proof is collected, third when the premium is applied for, fourth when it is received, and fifth each time it is used.

Price cut versus added value.   All promotions offer the consumer an extra incentive to buy but not always in the form of a direct reduction in the price of the promoted product. Rather than offering "the same for less," premiums, for example, offer "more for the same price." They represent an added value that is independent of the promoted product, a value to the consumer that is greater than the cost to the producer, and, if selected carefully, one that can reinforce the brand's current advertising theme rather than detract from its quality. Such consumer promotions tend to support the long-term strength of the brand franchise, while more price-oriented types of consumer promotions, especially price/quantity promotions, tend to erode it.

The following chart illustrates how various consumer promotions fit into this classification scheme:

	Immediate	Delayed
Price Cut	Retail price special Price pack	Coupon Rebate
Added Value	Bonus pack Gift-with-purchase	Mail-in premium Frequent-flier program

II. SCOPE

Issue #2: Product Scope

Product scope refers to the range of sizes, varieties, models, and products to which a particular promotion should be extended. Given increased price comparison shopping at the point-of-sale, the tendency to add line extensions under brand umbrellas rather than launch new brands, and the associated need to minimize cannibalization effects, the product scope decision is becoming increasingly important.

Some producers like Hartmann Luggage offer around fifty hardsided and softsided stockkeeping units (SKUs) in each of four price-fabric combinations under a single brand umbrella. In contrast, Procter & Gamble offers Ivory brand dishwashing liquid in only four sizes, though the company also markets the Joy and Dawn brands in the same four sizes with equivalent list pricing. Despite the variation in the number of SKUs, there are three key product scope questions applicable in both cases:

☐ Should promotions be run on the entire line or on individual items or, in Hartmann Luggage's case, on subgroups of SKUs (such as men's softsided luggage in one price-fabric combination)?

☐ If promotions are run selectively, should they be offered on the more or less popular items, the higher or lower price points?

☐ Should promotions be run on "in-line" open stock merchandise, or on "out-of-line" special pack merchandise especially made for that purpose?

During a year, a brand can run more than one promotion so management must assess the comparative effectiveness of running one or a few promotions covering multiple items versus multiple promotions on individual items. In either case, product scope decisions are likely to be influenced by trade, consumer, competitor, and sales force considerations such as the following:

☐ When different *classes* of *trade* tend to promote different models in the line, a line promotion can accommodate the preferences of all channels. Food stores, for example, promote medium sizes of toothpaste while mass merchandisers emphasize larger sizes.

☐ When different models are targeted at different *consumer segments,* it may be appropriate to promote models selectively. Cross elasticities among models and, therefore, cannibalization costs resulting from trade-ups and trade-downs will usually be lower under these circumstances, although this is not always the case.

☐ When different models in the line face different sets of *competitors,* promoting individual models may be preferable. For example, a producer may anticipate a competitive new product entry at a certain price point and run a promotion on the model in its own line that is most threatened in order to load dealer inventories ahead of the introduction. Confining the promotion to a single model can reduce the chances of it precipitating an all-out promotion war.

☐ *Sales force* capacity to present promotion offers to trade buyers is often limited. The producer of a broad line under a single brand umbrella may have to use multiple-item promotions because there are not enough promotion calendar slots to promote each model separately.

Issue #3: Market Scope

Should the same promotions be offered in all market areas? Toro, for example, promotes different lawn mower models in different regions at different times of year in response to climatic variations and local consumer preferences for particular models. In addition, Toro management believes that a national promotion program can be more easily discovered and selectively matched or beaten by competitors. Developing regional promotion programs adds a protective measure of complexity.

Although the regional tailoring of sales promotions is currently of considerable managerial interest, there are four principal problems to be considered:

☐ *Managerial Effort.* More management time is required to plan and present multiple programs to sales force management. A staff of regional merchandising managers may be needed to interface between headquarters and the field on regional adaptations of the promotion program. In addition, regional tailoring increases the number of separate deal events that have to be evaluated. Extra staff and computer facilities must be available.

☐ *Cost Effects.* Offering deals of different magnitude in different regions at the same time can complicate demand forecasting and production and logistics scheduling; safety stocks have to be larger as a result. When demand in excess of expectations in response to a regional deal requires that product be shipped in from a more distant plant, extra transportation and handling costs are incurred. In addition, advertising efficiencies may be reduced in companies accustomed to announcing promotions in their national advertising.

☐ *National Accounts.* Trade buyers at the headquarters of national chains often purchase for stores located in several market areas. Although store managers are still permitted some retail pricing flexibility, there is a trend toward centralization of merchandising decisions. Many trade accounts may, therefore, either not be receptive to a complex promotion program involving separate deals for different market areas or alternatively, place chain-wide orders in particular markets to take advantage of diversion opportunities.

☐ *Diversion.* The trade can divert merchandise bought on promotion in one market area to stores in another area if transportation costs are more than offset by the promotion discount. Diversion is especially common when short distances separate market areas with large populations.

III. TACTICS

Issue #4: Timing

Timing issues in promotion design concern when to promote, how far in advance to announce promotions, how long to promote, and how often to promote.

When to promote. Promotions are typically offered when trade inventories of the product category, brand, and/or specific models are either (a) below normal, the objective of the promotion then being to build inventories or (b) above normal, the objective then being to flush them. Retaliatory promotions closely following a competitor's are often unprofitable because trade pipelines are already loaded with the inventory of the competing brand.

The seasonality of consumer demand is an important influence on the timing of promotion activity. Products are subject to seasonal demand if their level of use is influenced by the weather, if they are subject to annual model changeovers, if they are often bought as gifts, or if they require extensive comparison shopping (meaning that purchases are greater during the major three-day shopping weekends).

When to announce.   Most producers preplan their temporary promotions as part of the annual marketing planning process. Those promotions that are not preplanned are usually implemented in response to unexpected competitive activity or to flush high inventories resulting from unexpectedly slow sales. The timing of some preplanned promotions, such as seasonal clearance sales of products subject to annual model changeovers, is known ahead of time to both consumers and the trade. In other cases, the timing of promotions may be negotiated by producer and retailer in advance as part of a seasonal merchandising program; advance planning improves the odds that adequate inventories will be on hand for the promotion and that competing chains will not be promoting the same product in the same week. As promotions become more complex and creative, and as producers try to tie their promotions in with store merchandising themes, such cooperative preplanning is becoming more prevalent.

Duration.   The appropriate duration of a promotion depends on the inter-purchase interval of target customers and how long it will take for a high proportion of them to be exposed to the promotion. Promotion duration must also take account of the need to avoid promotion overlaps so that a single product purchase cannot qualify for multiple promotion offers.

Frequency.   The appropriate frequency of promotions depends on the interest of the trade in featuring the product and the category, consumer deal proneness (especially if heavy users are more deal prone), the need to respond to unexpected competitive promotions with additional events, the number of slots on the sales force calendar, and the complexity and duration of events. If a producer runs two trade promotions in rapid succession, the second will generally be unprofitable even if it offers a higher discount rate because trade inventory increases in response to the first deal will not have been worked down. In addition, trade and consumer confusion is likely when promotions are so frequent that they overlap. According to one General Motors executive: "The frequency of our promotions may now be beyond a dealer's capacity to respond."

Issue #5: Discount Rate

Every producer promotion, whether it offers a straight price cut or an added value, represents implicitly or explicitly a discount from the normal price.[5] The depth of discount any brand should offer depends on:

☐   The threshold minimum, in absolute and/or percentage terms, which is required to attract the attention of the trade or target consumer to prompt the desired change in purchasing behavior.

---

[5]A special display with no reduction from normal shelf price can generate incremental retail sales and is sometimes viewed as a promotion.

- ☐ The proportion of purchases being sold through to the trade at normal list prices. The lower this figure, the less the credibility of list prices, and the deeper the discount that may be required. According to the CEO of a shoe manufacturer: "The trade wants to promote what is widely accepted at list price."
- ☐ Discount norms established for the category by other brands in the same price bracket.
- ☐ Fluctuations in input costs. When they soften, producers may respond not by lowering list prices but by increasing deal discount rates.
- ☐ Cost savings to the trade as a result of accepting the deal. For example, if pallet shipments of a promoted item result in direct product cost savings to the retailer, the necessary discount, all other things being equal, should be lower.

Issue #6: Terms and Conditions

Trade allowance terms may specify the timing of payment by the producer, the quantity of deal merchandise that a trade account may buy, and the nature and timing of the extra merchandising support to be provided. Terms may also be attached to consumer promotions; coupon expiration dates and rebate claim requirements are examples.

Trade allowance terms might ideally:

- ☐ Indicate that promotional allowances will be paid on a bill-back (rather than off-invoice) basis after evidence of performance is received.
- ☐ Specify the size and timing of incremental displays, feature advertisements, and price cuts to be provided by the trade.
- ☐ Limit trade accounts to one order and one shipment per promotion to reduce forward buying and diversion.
- ☐ Limit the quantity of promotion merchandise to a percentage of each account's open stock purchases to prevent the brand being stocked on an in-out basis by discount channels.

To this point, we have introduced six elements of promotion design and noted some generic factors that managers consider when making decisions on each of these issues. We next introduce three specific product-market factors that influence decisions on all six design elements.

INFLUENCES ON SALES PROMOTION DESIGN

This section describes three significant product-market factors that influence how product managers design their promotions. These factors, derived from field research, cut across all classes of consumer goods and services.

Consumer Involvement

Products and services can be classified according to how involved consumers are in purchase decision making. More involving products are typically more complex, higher priced, infrequently purchased items that carry considerable financial, social, or psychological risk. The number of product features and the range of product alternatives to be considered are usually high (the more involved consumer welcomes a broader choice), the products on the market may have changed significantly since the consumer's last purchase, and cascaded demand opportunities for accessories and service often further complicate matters. With the exception of emergency replacement purchases, the decision making and search process for high involvement products is typically extensive, often includes several store visits, and may involve several postponements before a purchase is finally made.

High-involvement decisions include purchases of durables and ego-intensive packaged goods like cosmetics. Low-involvement decisions include most purchases of low-ticket, frequently purchased, packaged goods. Some low-involvement categories are characterized by variety seeking; the consumer, out of boredom, indifference, or deal sensitivity, switches from one brand to another. Impulse purchasing is common in such categories. Other low-involvement categories, particularly commodities such as salt, are characterized by inertia; the consumer repeatedly buys the same item not out of loyalty but because the effort to search out the best price-quality value in the category is not seen to be worthwhile. Of course, involvement in a purchase decision is a matter of degree and may vary among consumers buying the same product or service.

Inventory Risk

Inventory risk to the trade takes two forms, the opportunity cost of out-of-stocks and the lost margin associated with residuals that cannot be sold to consumers at full price. Inventory risk is higher when aggregate consumer demand or the mix of demand is unpredictable, when producers restrict returns, when the purchase cycle cannot be easily accelerated, when holding costs are high, when supplementary stocks cannot be obtained expeditiously (due to offshore production or lack of producer back-up stocks) and consumers are unwilling to switch to alternatives, when prices are unstable, and in categories characterized by obsolescence, seasonality, and postponability.

The inventory risk associated with obsolescence varies from product to product. In the case of fresh baked goods, obsolescence is a function of the physical characteristics of the product; in the cases of cars and apparel, it is a means of stimulating primary demand and accelerating the replacement cycle. The extent to which residuals are devalued by new model introductions depends on how different the new are from the old.

Inventory risk is greater for seasonal products and services. When consumer demand is concentrated in particular time periods, the cost of out-of-stocks is greater because the consumer may not be in the market again until the next season. And when demand is unpredictable as well as seasonal, as in the case of snowthrowers, inventory risk is compounded. Postponability of the purchase also augments risk, especially when consumers postpone because of exogenous factors outside of the marketer's control.

The influence of inventory risk on promotion policy is mitigated if a producer enjoys forward channel control through exclusive distribution (automobiles), direct store delivery (fresh baked goods), or direct contact with the end consumer (airlines). Forward channel control gives producers of high-inventory-risk items access to more accurate and timely retail inventory data and, therefore, the ability to manage their inventories more tightly to minimize stock-outs and residuals. It also facilitates the use of more complex types of promotion.

Franchise Strength

A strong franchise typically enjoys (i) strong brand awareness and loyalty based on perceived superiority of benefit delivery, (ii) dominant market share in a category or in the relevant market segment, (iii) rising rather than declining brand and category growth trends (reflecting stage in the product life cycle), and (iv) an importance to the trade based on rate of turnover and contribution to total sales, direct product profits, or store image.

Franchise strength also depends on the intensity of competition in a category. Competitive intensity is, in turn, a function of variables such as the number of competitors, the closeness of competitors' market shares, the degree of differentiation and customer loyalty, new product turnover, and excess capacity (particularly if the cost structure is high fixed cost, low variable cost). The higher each of these variables is, the more intensive the competitive environment.

Strong franchises are viewed by the trade as attractive traffic builders that warrant special merchandising support. These brands may be used by consumers in making price comparisons among stores; as such, retailers sometimes subsidize the retail prices on these brands to achieve even lower retail price points than a mere pass through of producer allowances would warrant (Albion, 1983).

Exhibit 2 summarizes our findings regarding the relationships between the three product-market factors and the first two design dimensions: type and scope. Our field research yields a relationship statement in 16 of the 18 cells created by decomposing the design dimensions as follows:

I. Type	Price cut or added value	
	Immediate or delayed	
II. Scope	Product scope—	Multiple or selective
		More or less popular
		In-line or out-of-line
	Market scope—	National or regional

Only in the case of inventory risk and promotion type was the field research unable to yield a hypothesis that we can be confident of verifying in a subsequent large-scale empirical test. As indicated in Exhibit 2 and discussed below, the field research yielded relationship statements for 5 cells in which our a priori confidence of empirical verification is higher than for the other 11.

Similarly, Exhibit 3 summarizes our findings regarding relationships between the three product-market factors and the tactical promotion design elements: timing,

EXHIBIT 2 Relationship statements between product-market factors and promotion design elements: type and scope

Design Elements	Product-Market Factors	Involvement		Inventory Risk		Franchise Strength	
		High	Low	High	Low	High	Low
TYPE	TYPE						
	• Price Cut or Added Value	AV	PC			AV	PC
	• Immediate or Delayed	D	I			D	I
SCOPE	PRODUCT SCOPE						
	• Multiple or Selective	S	M/S	S	M	S	M
	• More or Less Popular	M	L	L/M	M	M	M
	• In-Line or Out-of-Line	O	I	I	O	O	I
	MARKET SCOPE						
	• National or Regional	N	R	R	N	N	R

KEY ☐ No relationship suggested by field research

◼ (light) Relationship with moderate a priori confidence

◼ (dark) Relationship with strong a priori confidence

discount rate, and terms. In four cells, the field research failed to yield a relationship statement. In eight cells, we have particularly strong a priori confidence in the proposed relationships. Five of these cells concern the influence of franchise strength on promotion tactics, the only relationships in the matrix that have been the subject of previous empirical research. Our confidence in these five relationship statements is enhanced by the convergence of our field research findings with the conclusions of prior research.

We now consider the relationships presented in Exhibits 2 and 3 and discuss how the three product-market factors influence each of the six elements of promotion design:

I. TYPE

Issue #1: Type

What types of promotion should be emphasized under different product market circumstances?

EXHIBIT 3   Relationship statements between product-market factors and promotion design elements: tactics

Design Elements / Product-Market Factors	Involvement		Inventory Risk		Franchise Strength	
	High	Low	High	Low	High	Low
TIMING						
• When to Promote: In- or Off-Season			I	I/O	I/O	O
• When to Announce: Early or Later	E	L	E	L	L	E
• Duration: Long or Short	L	S			S	L
• Frequency: High or Low	L	H			L	H
DISCOUNT RATE • Deep or Shallow	S	D	D	S	S	D
TERMS • Tight or Loose			T	L	T	L

(Left margin vertical label: TACTICS)

KEY ☐ No relationship suggested by field research

☐ Relationship with moderate a priori confidence

☐ Relationship with strong a priori confidence

☐ Relationship with strong a priori confidence consistent with prior empirical research

Involvement.   Producers of high-involvement products prefer not to offer straight price cuts since they can disrupt the price-feature logic of product lines, stimulate negative quality inferences by consumers, and encourage consumers to press dealer salespeople for additional discounts. As an alternative, producers such as Hartmann Luggage often prefer to target price-sensitive consumers with specially designed promotional models that are not part of the permanent product line.

Marketers of high-involvement products typically use straight price cuts only when the practice is common to a category or when the objective is to hook the consumer into an ongoing relationship with the producer as is the case, for example, with mass market cameras that require particular types of film. When straight price cuts are used, they are often limited to lower priced models in the line, particularly if the line extends to the premium end of the market. Major appliance producers, for example, have found that price cuts are more effective on lower priced models and delayed value rebates more effective on higher priced models. First, an equivalent percentage discount permits a larger rebate in absolute dollars to be offered on the higher priced model. Second, the purchaser of a higher priced model can afford to pay the full price and does not object to waiting for a rebate check from the producer, whereas the purchaser of a lower priced model usually prefers immediate cash savings off the sticker price.

Because high-involvement products are typically higher ticket items that often offer cascaded demand opportunities in the form of consumables (such as film for cameras), accessories (flash and lens attachments), and service, a wider variety of added value consumer promotions can be used than is available to the producer of low-involvement goods. These additional promotions offer low-interest financing, extended warranties, trade-in allowances, and price breaks on installation and delivery, all of which address barriers to purchase that might otherwise lead consumers to postpone buying. Cascaded demand opportunities permit the bundling of several items in consumer promotion offers that represent a decision-making convenience to the consumer, encourage the consumer to buy more than the core product at the time of the purchase, maximize the total value of the sale on items for which consumers are in the market infrequently, and help to establish a continuing relationship with the consumer.

Low-involvement products cannot typically exploit cascaded demand opportunities. They allocate a higher percentage of their promotion dollars to immediate-value promotions that deliver a price break at the point-of-sale, especially in the case of products susceptible to variety-seeking and impulse purchasing; price-quantity promotions that encourage the consumer to purchase multiple units; continuity promotions that induce consumers to stay loyal on successive purchase occasions; and promotions (such as sweepstakes and contests) that add excitement to the purchase process in categories that many consumers view as dull.

Franchise strength.   What promotion tactics should strong franchise brands use? Strong franchise brands tend to allocate a relatively higher percentage of their promotion dollars to value-added (more for the same price) promotions such as bonus packs that encourage consumers to use more product rather than price-off (same quantity for lower price) promotions which are more likely to focus the consumer's attention on the item price. When strong franchise brands do deliver straight price cuts, trade allowances are often preferable to consumer promotions such as coupons. Trade allowances on a strong franchise brand are more likely to be passed through to consumers than those on a weak brand. In addition, trade deals that occur unannounced to consumers and last for only a short time are likely to be taken advantage of by fewer of a strong brand's regular consumers than coupons that can be saved and redeemed as needed. As a result, the strong franchise brand may find that the proportion of promotion costs that reach consumers who would have purchased in the absence of promotions is lower for trade allowances than for coupons. Based on a coupon redemption study, Neslin and Clarke (1987) concluded: "High share brands can be at a disadvantage with respect to couponing and thus, from a profit standpoint, more coupon dollars should be allocated toward low share brands" (p. 31). Those marketers of strong franchise brands that do use discount coupons are increasingly trying to distribute them by direct mail to non-user households identified through market research.

Weak franchise brands have fewer options. Promotion tactics such as bonus and price packs, which require special trade handling that strong brands can force the trade to accept, are not available for weaker brands. Weak franchise brands allocate a relatively higher percentage of their promotion budgets to price promotions that provide an immediate price break to the consumer rather than added-value and delayed-value promotions that may not make sufficient impact. Weak franchise brands also typically concentrate limited promotional resources on one or a few types of promotion, participate in promotions with other brands that can jointly attract greater trade and consumer attention, and use simple promotion offers that can be communicated easily to the trade because a sales force selling brands with different franchise strengths will not be able to give weaker brands an equal amount of time to that given to the major brands.

Weak franchise brands try to emphasize consumer promotions over trade promotions because they ensure better pass through and permit benefit information to be delivered to consumers that can supplement or substitute for advertising. In many cases, however, weak franchise brands have to emphasize trade promotions just to maintain distribution.

II. SCOPE

Issue #2: Product Scope

What factors determine whether a brand should promote all items in the line or run promotions selectively on individual models? Should the promoted models be the faster moving, popular items or the slower moving, less popular items? And should they be open stock in-line items or especially produced out-of-line items?

Involvement. Producers of all but the most differentiated high-involvement products recognize a need to offer some limited price promotions but, given the need to preserve a quality image and the credibility of the pricing structure, the multiple price points that the lines cover, and the probable differences in competitive pressure at each level, they are less likely than producers of low-involvement packaged goods to offer price promotions across the entire product line.[6] For example, some luggage manufacturers prefer to offer promotions on especially de-

---

[6]The availability of a complete line at the point-of-sale is especially important to the producer of high-involvement items. It can help the selling process by facilitating trade-ups and the producer, if he can dominate the dealer's floor space, can convey an impression of company size, category dominance, and quality that may reassure the consumer. Producers of high-involvement items try to achieve full line stocking by using a variety of merchandising programs (including quantity discounts, dating, and stock balancing) that are part of the permanent pricing structure rather than temporary price promotions.

signed out-of-line merchandise that is different from the regular line and to offer out-of-line merchandise as gift-with-purchase and purchase-with-purchase promotions on in-line merchandise. Those promotions that are offered on in-line merchandise never apply across all four price-fabric combinations but, rather, to a selection of items (soft- or hard-sided) within a single price bracket. This approach focuses the attention of salespeople and dealers on specific items; the broader the line, the more important it is to give such directional assistance. In addition, a selective promotion approach permits a high proportion of the promoted items to be presented in consumer advertising without being so restrictive that opportunities to encourage multiple unit purchases of matched sets are foregone. Usually the lowest price-fabric combination is promoted to maximize the number of new consumers attracted to the franchise and to minimize cannibalization effects.

In low-involvement categories, such as cookies, which are subject to variety seeking, product managers may prefer to promote all items in the line at the same time to satisfy a broader range of consumer preferences and to achieve a stronger presence at the point-of-sale that can stimulate multiple-unit impulse purchases. However, many producers of low-involvement products do not promote all pack sizes of the brand at the same time. When consumer involvement is low, size loyalty is usually low: first, because the product formula is the same across all sizes; second, because the consumer's involvement with all aspects of the purchase decision including choice of size is low; and third, because consumers shop frequently for low-involvement products, the potential inconvenience to a consumer from buying a smaller size than usual is minimal. As a result, a deal-prone consumer will readily switch to whichever size is on promotion. In theory, therefore, producers of low-involvement brands should be able to successfully promote less popular sizes.

Inventory risk.   The influence of inventory risk on product scope design decisions depends on its source. Producers of high-inventory-risk items subject to seasonality usually selectively promote the more popular items in their lines during the peak periods of consumer demand in order to secure the best possible slots on retail promotion calendars. On the other hand, producers of high-inventory–risk items subject to obsolescence defensively promote the less popular items toward the end of the selling season to make way for replacement inventories.

Producers with forward channel control are especially able to promote selectively their less popular items because they have more precise and timely inventory data and can be more certain of achieving retail execution. For example, most automobile financing promotions only apply to models with inventories in excess of forecast. Likewise, the computers of major airlines can compare actual and expected bookings on each flight and suggest changes in the mix of seats available at different fares right up to departure time. However, in such forward control situations, the low cost of analyzing sales and inventory data and promoting in response to inventory risk can lead managers to be overly restrictive in the product scope of their promotions. As one airlines marketing manager commented: "If we use too fine a scalpel in our promotion policy, we risk making our fare structures too complex. The travel agent's job becomes harder and we risk confusing and upsetting consumers."

Producers of high-inventory-risk items should not attempt promotions of out-of-line merchandise. Such merchandise is likely to have even less seasonal carryover potential than in-line merchandise so any residuals will be subject to correspondingly steeper end-of-season discounts.

Franchise strength.   Strong franchise brands are better able to limit the number of items in their regular product lines that they promote to the trade. Though one might think that they would restrict promotion support to their slower movers, they do in fact promote the more popular sizes. For example, 10 of the 14 size-specific promotions on Procter & Gamble's Dawn, Ivory, and Joy dishwashing liquids in 1982 were run on the two most popular of the four sizes sold. There are three reasons for our, perhaps counterintuitive, finding that the popular sizes are promoted more often. First, the trade wants to use the more popular sizes as traffic builders; for that reason, even strong franchise brands prefer to emphasize a strength, not a weakness in their promotions. Second, an allowance on a popular item can help gain distribution for a new item in the line by increasing the rate of inventory turnover of the whole line. According to the General Electric product manager for ranges, a promotion on a fast-moving, mid-line model is more likely than an allowance on a new premium model to secure distribution for the latter. Third, weak franchise competitors are more likely to obtain distribution for their faster-moving popular sizes and tend to heavily promote them. Hence, share leaders, such as Crest in the toothpaste category, do not have to promote the less popular sizes in their lines as aggressively because they are often the only brands in these sizes stocked by retailers.

Because strong franchise brands have typically achieved high "ever-tried" levels in a category, their promotions focus less on trial and more on both retaining current users and trading them up to larger sizes. Hence, strong franchise brands are more likely to promote selectively the larger sizes in their lines. The four 1982 promotions on Dawn, Ivory, and Joy that were not on the two most popular sizes were on the largest size; no promotions were run on the smallest size.

Only strong franchise brands can hope to secure trade cooperation in promoting out-of-line merchandise. Similarly, the strength of Procter & Gamble's franchise in dishwashing liquids enables it to persuade most trade accounts to accept promotions in the form of price packs and bonus packs that they will not accept from weaker competitive manufacturers because of the special handling required. Though these special packs contain the same product formulation, they are the packaged goods equivalent of out-of-line merchandise. They ensure pass through of the promotion value to the end consumer, enable the company to allocate deal stock to each trade account according to the percentage of open stock purchased at list price, and facilitate the accurate forecasting of promotion costs.

Weak franchise brands are more likely to promote all items in their lines for three reasons.[7] First, average distribution penetration is typically lower and the

---

[7] Newly launched brands are sometimes an exception; they may selectively promote smaller sizes to stimulate trial purchases.

variation in distribution penetration among items in the line is higher than in the case of strong franchise brands. A line promotion permits a trade account to promote whichever size(s) it prefers to stock. Second, when no one size of a brand enjoys sufficient shelf movement to warrant special merchandising support, a producer may have to offer the trade allowances on the entire line to secure special support for one item. This approach helps to sustain multiple sizes in distribution. Third, weak franchise brands cannot command as much trade buyer attention in sales presentation; line promotions covering all sizes are appropriate because they are straightforward and easy to present.

Issue #3: Market Scope

What factors determine whether a promotion should be adjusted from one market to another?

Because they are attractive traffic builders yet promoted by producers less often, strong franchise brands (especially in low bulk to value categories such as toothpaste that are inexpensive to transport and store) are more subject to forward buying and diversion by the trade. As a result, differential deal policies—in timing, terms, or discount rates—from one region to another are harder to implement without leakage. Hence, even though strong franchise brands have the management resources to plan, execute, and evaluate regional promotions, they should avoid substantial and frequent intermarket differences in the timing and levels of their trade deals. They should, rather, follow the example of toothpaste producers and regionalize their promotional efforts through varying consumer promotion tactics and spot advertising.

Managers of strong franchise brands in high involvement categories such as consumer electronics are particularly cautious about varying trade deals by region on nationally distributed items. First, high proportions of their sales are to chains with national coverage. Second, consumers may do their own diverting by searching out outlets in remote markets to buy at the lowest possible prices. They would not invest this effort for low involvement products; in these cases it is left to the trade to bring the diverted product to the consumer.

On the other hand, strong franchise brands in service businesses that are immune from forward buying and diversion can tailor their promotions by market. Hertz, for example, is the leading car rental company nationally but is weaker in key Florida markets where several large, low-cost competitors such as Alamo focus on the dominant price-sensitive tourist segment rather than the service-sensitive business segment. Hertz runs different types of promotions incorporating more generous discounts in these markets.

The higher the inventory risk, the more incentive there is to tailor promotional activity by market. Such tailoring can induce trade accounts to accept more product and can reduce the producer's inventory risk when tailoring involves the promotion of different products in different markets. Time permitting, excess inventories of an item in one market can be moved to another market where that item is in heavier demand. For example, airlines shift capacity to routes serving Florida during spring break. As a result of such regional stock balancing, out-of-stocks and promotions to dispose of residuals can both be minimized.

III. TACTICS

Issue #4: Timing

What factors influence when to promote, when to announce a promotion, and how long and how often to promote?

When to promote.   When inventory risk stems from seasonality in the timing of consumer demand, it is essential that the producer secure space in trade promotion calendars in season and, preferably, at the front end, with a high impact promotion. In 1980, 84% of Toro's promotion expenditures for snowthrowers and lawn mowers were spent during seasonal demand peaks. Producers of strong franchise brands such as Toro are best able to secure retailer support when consumer demand is strongest, but they should be on guard against efforts by smaller producers to run promotions just before the peak selling period with the objectives of elongating the season, shifting consumer demand forward and benefiting from purchase acceleration by those consumers who will not anticipate or be able to wait for the promotion on the strong brand. The promotional launch for a new brand should also occur before rather than during a seasonal demand peak (when the trade will already have planned to feature the most popular established brands).

Some managers argue that since the trade will offer fewer price promotions in the off-season, only strong franchise brands can usually expect to benefit. Strong franchise brands (particularly in the case of services which cannot be inventoried) may use off-season promotions to even out demand. However, obtaining the retailer's attention during the off-season is sometimess easier for a smaller brand because there are fewer deals being offered.[8]

When to announce.   High-involvement products such as automobiles are often subject to annual model changeovers and may, therefore, announce their periodic clearance sales in advance. Since such sales are usually common to all brands in a category, they should not, unless advertised unusually aggressively, detract from the quality image of the brand. In addition, since the timing of such periodic sales is known to consumers in advance, the more deal sensitive cannot complain if they paid full price and did not postpone their purchases. Finally, these sales are typically communicated to consumers by the trade, so negative quality inferences are low because the consumer perceives the trade rather than the producer as the source of the discount.

When inventory risk is high, producers usually prenegotiate the timing of

---

[8]The wider use of direct product profit analysis that takes account of a product's movement and margin after direct products costs may reduce a retailer's willingness to promote smaller brands even during the off-season.

their promotions with trade accounts to ensure the availability of sufficient stocks. Producers of high-inventory–risk items who enjoy forward channel control, such as automobile producers, have more flexibility in timing their promotions and often delay notifying their dealers until the last moment so that the efforts of dealer salespeople will not diminish in anticipation of forthcoming promotions (Doyle and Saunders, 1985). When inventory risk is low, the producer does not need to communicate its promotion plans to the trade so far in advance.

Managers of weaker franchise brands and newly introduced items try to improve their chances of being featured by letting the trade know when they will be on promotion well in advance. Though constrained by the trade's lead times in merchandising planning, strong franchise brands try not to announce their deals far in advance or run their deals at the same times each year. Such unpredictability is more feasible for strong franchise brands because the trade will respond to deals on them even at short notice. Unpredictability in deal timing limits preemption by competitors, deal-to-deal buying by consumers, and both forward buying and diversion by the trade. On the other hand, the advantages of unpredictability have to be weighed against the costs. First, there may be particular weeks when, because of seasonal consumer demand patterns, the strong franchise brand especially wants to be featured by the trade; even if no promotion is announced in advance, the trade, based on past experience and common sense, will anticipate a deal. Second, production and logistics requirements can be better forecast if the deal is announced in advance and trade orders are received early.

Duration. Most managers agree that the length of consumer promotions should be sufficient to permit a high number of target consumers to be exposed to the offer and should, therefore, match the interpurchase interval of the product.

Because low-involvement products are frequently purchased, the duration of the deals offered to the consumer can be shorter. However, many trade deals run for sixty days or more when only one week of special merchandising support from nonexclusive retail accounts can reasonably be expected. In the absence of supplier-retailer preplanning of retail promotions in the channels for low-involvement products, lengthy trade promotions may be necessary to increase the chances of a retailer being able to slot the promoted product into its promotion calendar.

Because the interpurchase interval and consumer search time for high-involvement products are longer, there is a need for longer promotions to ensure that as many target customers as possible are exposed. Few automobile promotions, therefore, last for only a week. At the same time, because high-involvement product purchases are typically postponable, the duration of promotion offers must be limited to create some sense of urgency among consumers and accelerate their purchases to cater to the short-term perspective of the trade and to avoid promotion overlaps that might permit a single product purchase to qualify under multiple promotion offers. In addition, as one General Motors executive commented: "Promotions longer than two months do not make sense because our dealers operate on short time horizons. We might do better to offer one month promotions and extend them, if necessary, to attract a second wave of consumers who missed the initial offer."

Weak franchise brands are usually on deal for longer periods of time than strong franchise brands. There are three main reasons for this:

☐   The retailer will be more able to fit the small brand into its promotion program in a week when a promotion on a large share brand is not available. The retailer is predisposed to promote small brands to avoid increasing dependency on major brands but only in the absence of promotions on the majors.

☐   The producer sales force in a company with high- and low-share brands will be able to mention the low-share brands in presentations to trade accounts only sporadically. It is important that they be on deal whenever the salesperson has the chance.

☐   Small-share brands are often proportionately more dependent on purchases by deal-prone brand switchers than are large-share brands. Large-share brands enjoy disproportionately high shares of brand-loyal users (Raj, 1985).

Frequency.   Overly frequent retail price specials can detract from the quality of high-involvement products in the eyes of both trade and consumers. A further consequence may be deterioration in the perceived credibility of list prices. According to the marketing vice president for General Electric's Major Appliance Business Group: "When consumers lose confidence in the price-quality relationship in a category, they can become confused and postpone their purchases." Their confusion may have to be countered with additional dissonance-reducing advertising.

At the same time, producers of high-involvement products—notably household appliances—maintain a limited promotional presence on a continuing basis so that retail salespeople always have a model to present to the promotion-sensitive shopper. In addition, retail outlets then have no excuse for not pushing the line and the promotion-sensitive consumer is less likely to switch to another brand or postpone his or her purchase until the next periodic sale.

In low-involvement categories, there is less need for concern about the quality implications of frequently being on deal. First, deals are common even on premium brands of packaged goods. Second, there is less risk to the consumer buying an item on deal. Indeed, many deals are regarded by consumers as corrections to retail prices that are much higher than the level of interbrand differentiation would warrant. Third, there are far fewer special display opportunities in the typical supermarket than the number of packaged goods deals chasing them, so frequent trade promotions are necessary to increase the chances of securing some additional merchandising support.[9] Partly because they cannot secure as many retail features as they would like, most producers of packaged goods supplement their trade deal activity with consumer promotions dispersed throughout the year to permit the promotion-sensitive consumer to benefit from buying the product even when it is not available on retail special.

Strong franchise brands can be confident that, when they do promote, they will receive substantial incremental merchandising support from many retailers. The less

---

[9]As indicated in the later discussion of Discount Rate (issue #5), this same logic can also argue for deeper discount deals on low-involvement products.

often they promote, the more predictable the timing and strength of their promotion support by the trade will be. Too frequent promotions by large-share brands may result in "promotion meltdown," whereby one promotion following too closely behind another cannot achieve equally strong factory shipments. Small brands cannot be similarly confident of trade support and must, therefore, promote more often (or offer a larger discount) to achieve a proportionate number of features.

In competitively intense environments, the relative strength of even the strongest franchises is limited, so producers must be prepared to promote frequently and be able to administer complex promotion programs where several events may overlap. Since the timing of competitive promotions is less certain and less likely to be announced in advance, producers must reserve a higher proportion of the budget as a contingency to invest in unexpected promotion opportunities and counterattacks.

Issue #5: Discount Rate

What factors determine how deep a promotion discount should be as a percentage of an item's normal price?

Consumer involvement. Discount rates on high-ticket, high-involvement products, unless they are part of a clearance sale, should not typically be as deep as on low-involvement products for five reasons. First, a discount can be offered on a high-ticket item that is low in percentage terms but significant enough in absolute terms to attract consumer attention and influence purchase behavior. By contrast, low-priced items such as bar soap often have to be promoted in multiple unit packages to ensure that a coupon or retail discount of adequate value can be offered.

Second, many high-involvement brands offer multiple price-feature combinations to meet the needs of as many consumers as possible and so minimize the pressure to price promote particular models. Too deep a discount on any one of several models in the same product line can disrupt the pricing logic because the price gaps between models are so narrow. In contrast, most producers of low-involvement products offer one or, at most, two brands in a particular price-quality band rather than multiple price-feature combinations, so are not as constrained in their discounting by the possibility of disrupting the price logic of their product lines.[10]

Third, consumers are more likely to perceive differences between brands in high-involvement situations (Assael, 1984). Yet, product complexity increases the difficulty of making direct price comparisons. As a result, the pulling power of price in the decision-making process is mitigated.

Fourth, a deep discount on a high-involvement product may present so stark a contrast with the reference price represented by the normal retail price that the consumer questions the credibility of the reference price and lowers his or her quality expectations such that the product is no longer seen as an attractive

---

[10]However, producers of those low-involvement products offered in multiple package sizes have to be concerned with maintaining the price logic among them.

value at the promoted price. In contrast, consumers who buy frequently purchased, low-involvement packaged goods are more self-confident and less easily persuaded that a higher priced national brand is superior in quality, especially as private-label quality has improved with the maturation of technology. Deeper discounts may, therefore, be viewed as appropriate to close price gaps that are excessive relative to perceived quality differences.

Fifth, the price elasticity of demand for promoted low-involvement products is greater than for high-involvement products, first because more consumers perceive fewer interbrand differences and are, therefore, more willing to switch and, second, because they can easily afford to stockpile multiple units of low-ticket items in response to retail price specials. Despite the likelihood of post-promotion slumps in factory shipments, the prospect of large short-term sales increases in response to promotions motivates managers of low-involvement products to consider deeper discounts.

Inventory risk.   Given equally realistic list prices, high-inventory-risk items should typically be subject to steeper discounts than low risk items to compensate trade accounts for sharing the risk and to motivate them to stock the full line. In contrast, producers of low-risk items, particularly strong franchise brands, have to be concerned about trade accounts engaging in forward buying rather than buying too little; therefore, they do not need as deep discounts.

Items subject to obsolescence lose their value over time. If the timing of the obsolescence is predictable, as in the case of automobiles, the loss in value may be anticipated in progressively larger discounts as the date approaches. The contribution loss associated with this sequential discount process is typically less than if a single discount rate is used.[11]

In the case of items such as personal computers rendered obsolete unexpectedly by competitive new product introductions, a planned series of discounts is not possible unless a new product announcement precedes actual introduction. If this is not the case, there will be a sudden loss in value because, in a category characterized by rapid technological change, few consumers will be willing to purchase a technically obsolete product at any price. In such situations, a single deep discount swiftly implemented should help to clear stocks, perhaps before all consumers become aware of the new product.

Franchise strength.   Strong franchise brands need not usually offer discounts as deep as those offered by weaker brands for five reasons. First, because strong franchise brands turn faster at retail, are promoted less often, and have more traffic building power, a modest discount on a strong brand is more likely to stimulate a trade response and pass through of the savings to the consumer than a similar discount on a small brand. According to one Procter & Gamble brand manager: "The trade needs an extra incentive to push a weaker brand."

[11]Lazear (1986) has identified the factors determining the speed with which a retail price should be reduced.

Second, the ability of strong franchise brands to break even on overly generous promotions is limited. A leading brand such as Crest toothpaste with a 40% gross margin must sell 33% more volume than normal to break even on a 10% deal and twice normal volume to break even on a 20% deal. In addition, Crest must obtain this extra volume from the remaining 60% of the market. If Aqua-fresh, the number three brand, ran similar promotions, it would need to obtain far fewer incremental units from a larger portion of the market; deeper discounts, therefore, appear more likely to pay out on smaller brands.

Third, in setting a discount rate, the product manager should always consider the other brands in the category. A deep discount on a leading national brand may place it in the same price range as private labels or generics; if passed through, the deal may therefore attract—at great cost in terms of lost contribution from regular customers—customers who are extremely unlikely to repurchase the brand later on at regular list price (Shoemaker, 1977).

Fourth, heavy trade discounts on leading national brands are often not fully passed through to consumers. There are several reasons for this. First, the trade usually avoids pricing national brands at parity with its own private label products. Second, the trade will not pass through deal money beyond what is necessary to achieve attractive "psychological" retail price points (such as 99 cents). Indeed, a leading national brand can sometimes get away with a lower discount than that needed to achieve a critical retail price point if the trade is prepared to subsidize a further reduction for traffic-building purposes. Third, empirical evidence suggests that when a brand is discounted and featured in a special store display, the level of sales increase is not related to the depth of the discount over a wide range, especially in a product category with stable primary demand (Chevalier, 1975). Fourth, some trade accounts have responded to "deal clutter" by pricing all national brands in a category at the same everyday low price, irrespective of differing discount rates.

Fifth, purchase and use of a low-market-share brand is generally more risky to the consumer. The smaller brand must offer list price and deal discount levels at least equal to the value of the reduced risk associated with the safer brand. A strong franchise brand that is perceived as superior by consumers need not match competitive promotions with equivalent discounts. According to Keon's bargain value model of promotions (1980), consumers attracted by competitive promotions will switch back to the strong franchise brands without incentives being required to make them do so after they rediscover the relative inferiority of the alternatives.

In certain circumstances, larger brands may have to offer proportionately greater discounts:

☐   When a vicious spiral of move and counter-move results in a promotion war that disrupts the pricing structure of a product category and places the principal competitors in a "prisoner's dilemma" from which it is difficult to escape. The deeper the pockets of the competitors, the deeper the discounts may go, particularly if there is any prospect of a promotion war stimulating primary demand or of the market leaders capturing share from lesser competitors who lack the resources to match their discounts.

☐ When weak franchise brands, rather than offering price reductions from artificially inflated list prices on an almost continuous basis, instead roll back their prices to everyday low levels and offer minimal incremental deals.

Issue #6: Terms and Conditions

Franchise strength is the key determinant of whether a brand can require and enforce tight terms regarding the timing and nature of the incremental retail merchandising support needed to qualify for producer allowances. Strong brands are more likely to have the resources in money and manpower to check and enforce performance. In 1984, for example, Black & Decker began attaching performance requirements to all its off-invoice allowances. The percentage of qualifying units fell from 90 to 60 but Black & Decker's share of trade features held steady, indicating that the trade is interested in providing merchandising support for strong brands regardless of how tight their performance requirements are. Thus, under some circumstances, strong brands may choose to relax certain of the terms attached to their promotion offers. For example, the periods during which retailers must provide incremental merchandising support to qualify for allowances may be lengthened to reduce the likelihood that competing retailers will promote the same item in the same week and thereby reduce the profitability of the promotion to each.

In contrast, weaker brands cannot be as restrictive in their allowance terms if they hope to receive incremental trade support. Rather than specify no qualifying conditions, they should, however, aim for realistic ones. For example, a weak franchise brand is not likely to secure an end-aisle display but may be able to obtain an on-shelf price cut for four weeks combined with an obituary advertising feature; that is better than nothing.

Producers of high-inventory–risk items who enjoy forward channel control should be able to impose tighter performance requirements. For example, the terms of General Motors' low interest financing promotions in 1986 required consumers to take delivery of their cars before a specified date. They were effectively limited to the cars sitting on dealer lots unless they placed their orders at the start of the promotion period; further depreciation in the value of existing inventories was therefore minimized. The producers calculated that they could take a lower contribution loss in season than would have to be absorbed if the same cars became residuals at the end of the model year.

The relative importance of enforcing particular terms varies with product-market circumstances. For example, marketers of products with high inventory risk stemming from seasonal demand are especially interested in ensuring that they receive incremental merchandising support during key selling periods. Likewise, marketers of low-involvement products subject to impulse purchases stress obtaining additional displays while marketers of infrequently purchased, high-involvement products often emphasize feature advertisements to attract store traffic.

CONCLUSION

As sales promotion expenditures continue to grow, managers need help in sorting through an increasingly complex array of promotion options in order to design more effective promotions. However, conventional wisdom in this area has been limited to the type, timing, and discount rate of promotions for high- versus low-share brands and based exclusively on studies of packaged goods.

Using field research, we have specified six key elements in sales promotion design that are applicable across a wide range of consumer goods and services. We have identified three product-market factors that appear to influence managers' promotion design decisions. We then offered guidelines on promotion design decisions, given a brand's product-market circumstances. Finally, we have organized these relationships into a framework that managers can use to guide their promotion design decisions.

We must acknowledge the following limitations. First, the relationships proposed in Exhibits 2 and 3 have not yet been empirically verified. Second, the ways in which managers make trade-offs among the six design elements (for example, frequent shallow discount promotions versus a few deep discount promotions) need further exploration. Third, a better understanding is required about how the individual promotions designed by each product manager are integrated with the promotion plans of all the other products sold by the company or divisional sales force. In the typical consumer goods company, a headquarters sales merchandising department works with the marketing department to develop a single promotion calendar that delineates a balanced, attractive set of promotion offers for the sales force to present to trade buyers. The integration of product promotion plans must involve design trade-offs among brands.

Good promotion design is central to improving the productivity of sales promotion expenditures. Communication between product management, sales management, and sales promotion staff specialists is enhanced when all can buy into the same promotion design principles. In addition, a thorough promotion design framework can be the basis for evaluating the effectiveness of both individual promotions and product promotion plans. Finally, the results of the promotion design process are what the consumer and the trade buyer see in the marketplace and, as such, are certainly critical to the achievement of the marketer's promotion objectives.

REFERENCES

ALBION, MARK S., *Advertising's Hidden Effects*, Boston, MA: Auburn House, 1983.

ASSAEL, HENRY, *Consumer Behavior and Marketing Action*, 2nd ed., Boston, MA: Kent Publishing Co., 1984.

BEEM, EUGENE R. and H. JAY SHAFFER, "Triggers to Customer Action—Some Elements in a Theory of Promotional Inducement," Working Paper 81-106, Cambridge, MA: Marketing Science Institute, December 1981.

BLATTBERG, ROBERT C., GARY D. EPPEN, and JOSHUA LIEBERMAN, "A Theoretical and Empirical Evaluation of Price Deals for Consumer Nondurables," *Journal of Marketing,* 45 (Winter 1981), pp. 116–129.

BOWMAN, RUSSELL D., "Sixth Annual Advertising and Sales Promotion Report," *Marketing Communications,* August 1985, pp. 5–8.

CHEVALIER, MICHEL, "Increase in Sales Due to In-Store Display," *Journal of Marketing Research,* 12 (November 1975), pp. 426–431.

CHEVALIER, MICHEL and RONALD C. CURHAN, "Retail Promotions as a Function of Trade Promotions: A Descriptive Analysis," *Sloan Management Review* (Fall 1976), pp. 19–32.

CURHAN, RONALD C. and ROBERT J. KOPP, "Factors Influencing Grocery Retailers' Support of Promotion," Working Paper 86-104, Marketing Science Institute, July 1986.

DOYLE PETER and JOHN SAUNDERS, "The Lead Effect of Marketing Decisions," *Journal of Marketing,* 22 (February 1985), pp. 54–65.

ENNIS, F. BEAVAN, *Marketing Norms for Product Managers,* New York: Association of National Advertisers, 1985.

FARRIS, PAUL W. and JOHN A. QUELCH, *Advertising and Promotion Management,* Radnor, PA: Chilton Book Company, 1983.

FORNELL, CLAES, WILLIAM T. ROBINSON, BIRGER WERNERFELT, "Consumption Experience and Sales Promotion Expenditure," *Management Science,* 31:9 (September 1985), pp. 1084–1105.

HARDY, KENNETH G., "Key Success Factors for Manufacturers' Sales Promotions in Package Goods," *Journal of Marketing,* 50 (July 1986), pp. 13–23.

JOHNSON, TOD, "The Myth of Declining Brand Loyalty," *Journal of Advertising Research,* 24:1 (February–March 1984), pp. 9–14.

KEON, JOHN W., "The Bargain Value Model and a Comparison of Managerial Implications with the Linear Learning Model," *Management Science,* 11 (November 1980), pp. 1117–1130.

LAZEAR, EDWARD P., "Retail Pricing and Clearance Sales," *American Economic Review,* 76:1 (March 1986), pp. 14–32.

LEVEDAHL, J. WILLIAM, "Profit Maximizing Pricing of Cents-off Coupons: Promotion or Price Discrimination?" *Quarterly Journal of Business and Economics,* 24:4 (Autumn 1986) pp. 56–70.

LOVELOCK, CHRISTOPHER H. and JOHN A. QUELCH, "Consumer Promotions in Services Marketing," *Business Horizons,* 26:3 (May–June 1983), pp. 66–75.

MCALISTER, LEIGH, "The Impact of Price Promotions on a Brand's Market Share, Sales Pattern and Profitability," Cambridge, MA: Marketing Science Institute, 86-110, December 1986.

NARASIMHAN, CHAKRAVARTHI, "A Price Discrimination Theory of Coupons," *Marketing Science,* 3:2 (Spring 1984), pp. 128–147.

NESLIN, SCOTT A. and DARRAL G. CLARKE, "Relating the Brand Use Profile of Coupon Redeemers to Brand and Coupon Characteristics," *Journal of Advertising Research,* 27:1 (February–March 1987), pp. 23–32.

PECKHAM, JAMES O., Sr., *The Wheel of Marketing,* Chicago: A.C. Nielsen Co., 1973.

QUELCH, JOHN A., "It's Time to Make Trade Promotion More Productive," *Harvard Business Review,* 61:3 (May–June 1983), pp. 130–136.

QUELCH, JOHN A., SCOTT A. NESLIN and LOIS B. OLSON, "Opportunities and Risks of Durable Goods Promotion," *Sloan Management Review,* 28:2 (Winter 1987), 27-38.

RAJ, S.P. "Striking a Balance Between Brand 'Popularity' and Brand Loyalty," *Journal of Marketing,* 49 (Winter 1985), pp. 53-59.

SHOEMAKER, ROBERT W. and F. ROBERT SHOAF, "Repeat Rate of Deal Purchases," *Journal of Advertising Research,* 17 (April 1977), pp. 47-53.

STRANG, ROGER A., "Sales Promotion—Fast Growth, Faculty Management," *Harvard Business Review,* (July-August 1976), pp. 115-124.

IT'S TIME TO MAKE TRADE PROMOTION MORE PRODUCTIVE

JOHN A. QUELCH

Trade promotion is supposed to be a cooperative marketing activity. Manufacturers extend promotions, or deals, in the form of temporary price reductions to encourage retailers and wholesalers to increase purchase commitments and build inventories. The trade publicizes these price reductions to consumers, who then step up their purchases. Everyone along the line benefits.

Too often in recent years, though, the arrangement hasn't been working as planned. Manufacturers complain that the costs associated with trade promotions are rising too fast and that retailers and wholesalers are failing to deliver on such promises as special in-store displays, feature advertising mentions, and fully discounted consumer prices. The trade complains that manufacturers are being unreasonable in their expectations. Friction has replaced cooperation.

The following survey findings give an indication of the nature of the problems in trade promotions:

☐ Responding to a 1981 *Chain Store Age* survey, 76.4% of retailers state that they are being offered more promotions than the previous year; 22.2% report fewer deals.[1]

☐ An annual survey of managers in 65 consumer packaged goods companies indicated that 40% of the average 1980 marketing budget was spent on advertising, 35% on trade promotion, and 25% on consumer promotion.[2] Thus, trade promotions comprise a substantial segment of marketing expenses.

☐ Line managers with consumer packaged goods manufacturers responding to a 1981 *Progressive Grocer* survey ranked the total number of trade promotions and their frequency as 2 and 4 in a list of their most important problems; retail line managers ranked these as 30 and 27 respectively.[3] This suggests much disparity in the two groups' perceptions.

☐   In a 1981 survey, managers of marketing services in major consumer packaged goods companies cited "effective trade and consumer promotion" more frequently than any other issue as their biggest challenge.[4]

This study reviews ways to improve the productivity and design of trade promotion programs. The analysis and conclusions are based primarily on field interviews conducted during 1981 and 1982 with some 30 line marketing managers and sales promotion specialists. This article is written from the perspective of manufacturers of grocery products, health and beauty aids, and semidurable goods, but has obvious implications for other consumer goods producers.

DIMINISHING RETURNS

Trade promotions differ both in role and nature from the two other elements in a typical marketing budget—advertising and consumer promotions. Advertising generally communicates information about brand benefits to emphasize product identity and cement brand loyalty. It usually represents a long-term investment in future sales. Trade promotion, in contrast, is typically viewed as an easily executed means of boosting short-term sales. The emphasis is on price rather than brand benefits. Costs vary directly with unit sales and are therefore incurred on a pay-as-you-go basis at less financial risk than advertising costs. While the effectiveness of both advertising and trade promotion ultimately depends on the level of consumer response, trade promotion requires cooperation between the manufacturer and the trade.

Consumer promotion programs may emphasize either brand image, or price. Some, such as a sweepstakes or premium offer, communicate brand benefits directly to the consumer and require little retailer input. Others, such as manufacturers' price reductions and bonus packs, encourage consumers to sample a brand but do nothing to enhance its image.

When manufacturers offer trade promotions, they expect that the financing costs associated with taking on additional inventory will persuade retailers to provide special merchandising support to accelerate product movement. This might include passing the manufacturer's price reduction through to the consumer, featuring this price cut in store advertising, and displaying the product prominently. Manufacturers expect to obtain short-term increases in sales and market share as a result of this support.

But many executives interviewed indicate that trade promotions are no longer meeting these objectives. They mention four main failings:

1. Trade pressure for frequent promotion deals erodes consumer franchises of existing brands, adds to the expense of establishing new brands, and heightens consumer price sensitivity. (A 1981 Needham, Harper & Steers tracking survey found that 58% of women and 65% of men "try to stick to well-known brand names" compared to 74% and 80% in 1975.)[5] In some cases price reductions

increase neither market share nor total category demand of products.

2. A trade buyer often responds to promotion deals by purchashing only for normal inventory; because the discount compares favorably with inventory holding costs, the buyer could add to inventories without reducing standard ROI. Frequent discounts facilitate deal-to-deal purchasing that results in uneven factory shipments and increased production costs.

3. Trade buyers often take advantage of discounts but fail to provide merchandising support or pass price reductions through to the consumer even when required to do so by the terms of the transaction. (One study of supermarket purchasing and merchandising decisions found that of 992 deals accepted, 46% received no merchandising support and only one-third of total deal allowances were passed through to the consumer.)[6]

4. Some retailers respond to deals by purchasing above their own requirements and reselling or diverting the excess to other retailers at a profit. Diversion of low-bulk, high-margin health and beauty aids is especially widespread.

The severity of these problems varies from one product category to another, and, within a category, from one brand to another. But most managers interviewed consider that their trade promotion expenditures are rising at the same time as their productivity is declining.

A Changing Environment

In explaining these difficulties, managers in grocery-product manufacturing identify three problems. First, some managers emphasize the growing concentration of buying power of the grocery chains relative to that of the manufacturers. Chains can now use electronic scanning systems installed at checkout counters to determine which items should be stocked and promoted. Thus, they are no longer as dependent on manufacturers' salespeople to tell them which items to carry and in what quantity. In addition, retailers are increasingly concerned with protecting the market shares of their own private label and generic brands that have increased at the expense of national brands in many product categories.

A second problem, in the view of other managers, is that the pressure for trade promotions is an inevitable result of heightened retail competition stimulated by a depressed economy, increased consumer price sensitivity, and the emergence of new retail forms such as no-frills warehouse grocery stores. Moreover, the average supermarket at any given time is faced with 1,000 items offered on promotion but has the capacity to set up only about 50 end-of-aisle displays each week. Thus, there are simply too many promotion deals chasing a limited number of special in-store displays and feature spots in retailer advertising.

A third problem, say additional managers, is the manufacturers. These managers argue that manufacturers' salespeople and product managers are too wrapped up in the short term; often they attempt to meet year-end objectives by implementing fourth-quarter promotions that steal from future sales.

Manufacturers' Rationale

Despite increasing dissatisfaction with trade promotions, most manufacturing executives don't consider eliminating this marketing technique and reducing list prices across the board a feasible alternative.

For one reason, promotion deals provide them with the flexibility to adjust to temporary variations in demand and supply and to attract more price-sensitive, less brand-loyal consumers without changing list prices. Moreover, deals allow them to maintain higher list prices than otherwise, thereby protecting their gross margins in the event of any federal price controls.

Many manufacturers, however, would like to reduce their trade promotion expenditures. But those companies that have tried sudden dramatic reductions have experienced unpleasant repercussions. Even large, powerful manufacturers have sustained big market share losses from such efforts—Pillsbury on cake mixes, Philip Morris on 7Up, and Gorham on silver flatware—because wholesalers and retailers retaliated. The trade may respond to trade promotion cutbacks by cutting feature activity on the brand, refusing to carry the full product line, reducing the number of shelf facings, or declining to carry a weak brand sold by the same manufacturer.

Once a product category or an individual brand becomes associated with heavy trade promotion in the minds of manufacturer salespeople, wholesale and retail buyers, and consumers, the situation is hard to reverse. Only if management is prepared to accept a dramatic drop in sales volume is a sudden cutback in trade promotion feasible. A gradual shift of marketing expenditures from trade promotion to consumer promotion and, later, to advertising is less likely to cause sales force resentment or trade retaliation.

Manufacturers can ward off trade pressure for more promotion deals for their premium-priced national brands. One method is the introduction of "fighting brands," such as Colgate-Palmolive's Value Brands and Procter & Gamble's Summit line of paper products priced as much as 20% below the major advertised national brands. Another is comparative advertising of national brands with private labels, such as Charmin bathroom tissue and Ivory dishwashing liquid, to justify their higher prices. Manufacturers can also withdraw or regionalize their weak-selling brands when the cost of maintaining them in nationwide distribution is the offer of deals on their stronger brands.

HOW TO IMPROVE PROMOTION MANAGEMENT

Because promotion touches many functions in the organization—advertising, sales, production, and finance—managers must commit themselves to improving productivity in this area. The interviews and evaluations lead us to conclude that the commitment must focus on encouraging managers, first to view trade promotions as an integral element of marketing strategy and, second, to improve their design.

Changing the Managerial Orientation

As an initial step in improving promotion management and productivity, managers should evaluate the ability of marketing personnel to handle trade promotions and consider expanding training in this area. This involves assessing the qualifications of in-house sales promotion staff to review brand promotion plans, of product managers to design and execute promotions, and of salespeople to tailor presentations to individual trade accounts and advise buyers on inventory management.

As a part of sales force evaluation, managers should consider changing performance measures. One possibility is shifting to a system that considers profit contribution as well as quantity of cases sold. At PepsiCo, for example, the bonus component of a salesperson's compensation package is based not only on achieving volume targets but also on deal and distribution cost targets negotiated between marketing and sales force managers.

Another method is to set detailed promotion-related objectives for salespeople, particularly those who service stores as well as headquarters accounts. Some manufacturers offer bonuses if a brand's share of feature advertising in a salesperson's territory exceeds the brand's market share and has grown over the preceding period.

Finally, product managers and the sales force can be placed on different time periods for performance measurement purposes to avoid pressure on manufacturing and distribution capacity during the fiscal year's fourth quarter. Lever Brothers, for example, assesses the performance of each of its six regional sales organizations on a different calendar year.

A second step in changing managerial orientation is to recognize that the marketing strategies required for trade accounts differ. To tailor promotion and merchandising efforts, managers must understand each major customer's marketing strategy. This is especially important because the grocery trade is increasingly segmented. There are warehouse stores that purchase most of their merchandise on deal discounts and food emporiums that stress quality and assortment over price.

Salespeople must also understand how the buyers at each trade account are evaluated. Many retailers emphasize deal-to-deal buying and inventory loading and assess their buyers solely on average margins achieved. It can be more useful to evaluate on the basis of ROI, where deal discounts are traded off against inventory-carrying costs.

The manager with a good understanding of an account will make more effective presentations and obtain more merchandising support for his brands. Some manufacturers design optimal purchase plans to maximize the ROI of key individual trade accounts based on their forthcoming promotion calendars.

Finally, managers should determine which accounts are not providing the required merchandising support for the allowances they claim. Procter & Gamble, for one, restricts allowances on purchases of company products by warehouse stores. These do not usually advertise specific items or maintain shelf displays regularly so that special merchandising support is rarely given. Interestingly, Procter & Gamble's action is supported by many supermarket chains that compete with warehouse stores and themselves furnish merchandising support for promotion deals. Few manufacturers realize how much respect they can earn from the trade by legitimately enforcing their performance requirements.

Improving Promotion Design

The effectiveness of trade promotions can be increased if product managers spend more time on promotion design. They need to identify and develop promotion objectives consistent with a brand's long-term strategic aims. They must also design promotions in the light of the consumer-buying process for the product. Promotions for impulse items, for example, should focus on gaining additional display space at the point-of-purchase.

To develop profitable promotions, managers should consider the following issues:

Product range.   All sizes in a brand line should be promoted together only when no particular size enjoys sufficient shelf movement to warrant special merchandising support or when individual wholesalers and retailers are themselves pushing different sizes. The trade tends to respond to an across-the-board promotion deal by giving special merchandising support to the one size that is most profitable to them. Product managers should consider promoting their larger sizes more often than smaller ones to accelerate in-home product use and permanently trade consumers up to large-size items.

The complexity of the decision lies in the number of stockkeeping units that comprise the brand. For example, the Hartmann Luggage Company manufactures a multitude of separately priced, hard-sided and soft-sided luggage items. Most of these are made in four fabrics and in men's and women's styles. Should Hartmann promote its entire line, its higher- or lower-priced stock or its more or less popular items? Should it promote the entire range in a single fabric line at the same time or a single size in all four fabrics? Or is the Hartmann quality image such that promotions cheapen the brand and should be avoided altogether?

A brand's trade promotion activity should not be developed piecemeal but should be planned on an annual basis. For example, a product manager of one frozen food brand implemented a balanced portfolio of trade promotion offers during 1980 for the twelve packings (six flavors in two sizes) in his line. He made six trade promotion offers—three at low discount rates on the most popular items and three at higher discount rates on items with growth potential. He divided the offers between the individual-serving size and the larger family-serving size. The brand's profitability rose 45% over the previous year.

Market scope.   When a brand's market share, competitive activity, sales force pressure, retail environment, or trade and consumer responsiveness to promotion offers vary from one marketplace to another, it is inadvisable to offer a single trade promotion program in all market areas. But product managers who design regional trade promotion strategies should keep in mind several limitations to this approach. Because extensive efforts are required not only to plan such programs but also to present them to sales force managements, only the largest companies can afford them. Regional marketing programs also add to distribution costs and trade buyers for national chains do not welcome the complexity of different deal offers for different market entities.

Discount rates. In setting the discount rate, a product manager should consider how much additional volume is required to break even, whether the discount is so deep it attracts customers who are unlikely to buy again at regular list price, and whether the trade will pass the entire discount through to the consumer.

To avoid self-destructive promotion deal wars, product managers should not automatically match or exceed the discount rates offered by competing brands. Leader brands, in particular, should have discount rates below the norm and just above the threshold necessary to stimulate trade interest. However, an unusual competitive threat may require a more aggressive approach. To discourage the eastward advance of Procter & Gamble's Folger's coffee, General Foods offered deep discounts on Maxwell House. P&G retaliated with even heavier spending. The profitability of the Maxwell House division fell sharply, but did General Foods have any option except to discount? Under certain circumstances, promotion deal wars are unavoidable. (General Foods and P&G were able to sustain their deal war partly because each gained market share at the expense of weaker national and regional brands that could not support an equivalent level of deal activity.)[7]

Timing. The primary timing issues are when, how often, and how long to promote. The timing of deals should not be predictable so that wholesalers, retailers, and consumers will not be able to coordinate their purchase cycles with them.

The frequency and duration of trade promotion offers depend heavily on a brand's importance to the trade. A high-share brand in a high-volume category should be able to get great merchandising support from many trade accounts even if promoted infrequently for only two or three weeks at a time. Such a brand may also be able to command support for an off-season deal. Deals for a low-share brand in a low-volume category should probably be offered more often and for longer periods. It will then be available whenever a trade account has a promotion slot that cannot be filled with a more attractive brand.

Terms. To decide the details of allowances for any trade promotion offer, the product manager should first rigorously define merchandising performance requirements. For example, the size, location, and timing of both feature advertisements and in-store displays can be specified and related to a sliding scale of allowances for different levels of performance.

Next, the product manager should incorporate multiple options to cater to the different promotion preferences of various classes of wholesalers and retailers. Salespeople and trade buyers can discuss which option is best for each retail account.

Finally, the manager should monitor current trends in the terms of allowances. These include linking off-invoice allowances to minimum purchase requirements, limiting accounts to one order per promotion, avoiding split shipments in all but the most seasonally sensitive product categories, and reducing the number of free goods allowances requiring retailers with scanning systems to post additional computer records.

Integrated promotions.   To encourage trade buyers to increase their purchases and schedule special merchandising support, trade promotions should run concurrently with consumer promotions. For example, a widely advertised cash refund offer with a sweepstakes built around a theme relevant to store merchandisers can often stimulate special store displays for the promoted brand or product line.

MAKING INFORMED DECISIONS

To effectively plan future promotions, managers must be able to evaluate past campaigns in detail. To do that, certain key questions must be answered, including the following:

What are the effects, both short- and long-term, of trade promotions on brand sales, market share, and profits?

What are the design features of profitable trade promotions?

What mix of trade promotions over the course of the annual promotion plan makes most sense?

What is the optimal allocation of marketing expenditures among trade promotion, consumer promotion, and advertising?

To begin to answer these questions, management needs descriptive information, including internal data on factory shipments, promotion activity, price changes, and external data on warehouse withdrawals by the trade, retail shelf movement, store penetration, feature advertising and display support by the trade, and competitor prices. Display activity is harder to monitor than advertising features because expensive store visits are required. Moreover, unless store observations are taken each week, special displays lasting just seven days may be overlooked.

Manufacturers should also consider developing decision support systems for promotion evaluation and planning. At Chesebrough-Pond's, for example, factory shipments, warehouse withdrawals, retail sales, and other data for each brand size are merged into a common data base organized by retail account. As a result, marketers can conduct analyses at various levels of aggregation—by brand size, by individual account, by class of trade, by size of account, and by sales territory. In addition, product managers use a simulation model which can compute the profit impact of past promotions, in total or by account, and project the profit impact of proposed programs.

Managers should also aim to understand the effects of a promotion on buying behavior—particularly purchases by such groups as brand switchers, "deal-prone" consumers who tend to buy whatever brand is on sale, and loyal users who would have been prepared to pay the regular price. Such questions can be considered through a study of the diary or scanner system purchase records of consumer panels. Some companies analyze data in selected markets in conjunction with shipment and account sales data.

Too often, companies reduce the value of trade promotion as a marketing tool by excessive use. The trade as well as manufacturers must realize that if the same national brands are nearly always "on special," consumers will become skeptical.

Manufacturers have to counter this erosion of trade promotion productivity. They can gradually reduce trade promotion expenditures, shifting funds to consumer promotion and advertising that will support brand franchises. In addition, they can increase the productivity of trade promotion expenditures by improving promotion management, promotion design, and promotion evaluation. In either case, effective leadership is essential for successful implementation.

REFERENCES

1. *Chain Store Age,* September 1981, p. 32.
2. Donnelley Marketing, *Third Annual Survey of Promotion Practices,* July 1981, p. 2.
3. "48th Annual Report of the Grocery Industry," *Progressive Grocer,* special issue, April 1981.
4. Temple, Barker & Sloan, Inc., "Findings of Marketing Services Survey of U.S. Packaged Goods Manufacturers," September 1981, p. 9.
5. Reported in Bill Abrams, "Brand Loyalty Rises Slightly, But Increases Could be a Fluke," *Wall Street Journal,* January 7, 1982, p. 23.
6. See Michel Chevalier and Ronald C. Curhan, "Retail Promotion as a Function of Trade Promotion: A Descriptive Analysis," *Sloan Management Review.* Fall 1976, p. 19.
7. See "FTC Judge OKs GF Defense vs. Folgers," *Advertising Age,* February 8, 1982, p. 6.

CHESEBROUGH-POND'S INC.: VASELINE PETROLEUM JELLY

JOHN A. QUELCH
PENNY PITTMAN MERLISS

On September 2, 1977, Mary Porter was appointed product manager for Vaseline petroleum jelly (VPJ) and given three weeks to prepare the 1978 budget for the brand.[1] To project 1978 sales and profits she would have to develop a marketing plan that specified the level and nature of three types of marketing expenditures: advertising, consumer promotion, and trade promotion. Porter decided to begin by analyzing VPJ's marketing strategy over the previous five years, with particular emphasis on the nature, effectiveness, and profitability of its sales promotions.

COMPANY BACKGROUND

Vaseline petroleum jelly was the first product sold by the Chesebrough Manufacturing Company, founded by Robert Chesebrough in 1880. Chesebrough, who sold lamplighting oil, had frequently visited the oil fields of Pennsylvania, where he heard about a miraculous black jelly that formed on the rods of the oil pumps. He successfully duplicated this "rod wax" in his laboratory, lightened its color, and used a then unproven marketing technique—distribution of free samples—to introduce the product.

At the same time another entrepreneur, Theron Pond, distilled an improved kind of witch hazel from a native American shrub and sold it as a "pain-destroying and healing remedy." This product launched the Pond's Extract Company, which by the 1920's had become the leading U.S. marketer of popularly priced skin creams and cosmetics. Pond's also owed much of its early success to a marketing innovation: it was the first company to advertise with endorsements by socially prominent women.

In 1955 the two companies combined to form Chesebrough-Pond's Inc. (CPI), and Wall Street analysts hailed it "the marriage of the aristocrats." The new firm expanded through diversification. During the fiscal year that ended December 31, 1976, CPI's six divisions recorded after-tax profits of $54 million on net sales of $747 million.

The Health and Beauty Products (HBP) Division, which accounted for 22% of CPI's 1977 sales, marketed VPJ. Although HBP's 1976 sales of $163 million were second only to those of the international division, HBP's five-year average growth rate of 9.3% was the second lowest among CPI's divisions. The HBP Division also marketed Cutex nail care products, Pond's creams, Q-Tips cotton swabs, and Vaseline Intensive Care moisturizing products.

THE MARKET FOR PETROLEUM JELLY

Executives at HBP described petroleum jelly as "a household staple" used by over 90% of the population, but noted that both level and frequency of use varied substantially. A consumer survey indicated that heavy users were either women aged 45 years or older who viewed petroleum jelly as a multifunctional skin-care product or mothers who used petroleum jelly for baby care and did not consider it appropriate for their own skin care. Other results from this survey are reported in Exhibit 1.

Petroleum jelly sales to the consumer market at manufacturers' prices were estimated at $25 million in 1976, of which Vaseline petroleum jelly claimed a 90% share. (VPJ was also sold to institutions—hospitals, other medical facilities, and some industrial buyers. Porter was not responsible for these sales.) Direct competitors with VPJ were private label petroleum jellies, which sold primarily in 16-oz. jars at prices 30% below VPJ's through mass merchandisers such as K mart. The Vaseline product did not appear to be losing share to these private labels, none of which was manufactured by CPI. It also competed in the broader skin-care market with special purpose products, such as hand lotions and moisturizing creams.

Vaseline petroleum jelly was available in two forms, pure and carbolated; both were packaged in several sizes of jars and tubes. Carbolated VPJ was a specialized first aid product with an active ingredient. It was priced higher than pure VPJ and distributed primarily through drugstores. It was almost never featured at a discount by the trade and was not advertised separately. For several years carbolated VPJ had accounted for a stable 7% of VPJ dollar sales to consumers.

Factory shipments of each size of pure VPJ from 1974 through 1977 are reported in Exhibit 2. More than half of VPJ's ounce volume was sold in the popular 3.75- and 7.50-oz. jars.

EXHIBIT 1   Results of VPJ consumer survey

During March 1977 personal interviews were conducted with 500 female heads of households who qualified as users of petroleum jelly (on the basis of having used petroleum jelly during the previous month). Sixty percent of those approached qualified.

☐   90% of petroleum jelly purchasers last bought VPJ. When asked to name a brand of petroleum jelly, 97% mentioned VPJ; 23% recalled recently seeing or hearing VPJ advertising.

☐   51% of heavy users were aged 18 to 34 years, and three-quarters of this group had a child under 4 years in their households. (Households using petroleum jelly at least once a day were considered heavy users; those using it less than twice a week were "light-using" households.)

☐   Heavy users made on average six purchases of petroleum jelly per year, whereas light users made on average only one purchase per year.

☐   86% of respondents considered the size of petroleum jelly last bought their "regular" size. Heavy users were more likely than light users to purchase larger-size jars.

☐   35% of respondents reported making their last petroleum jelly purchase in a food store, 30% in a drugstore, and 30% in a mass merchandise or discount store. Light users (46%) and users from households with a child under 4 years (44%) were more likely to have made their purchases in food stores.

☐   33% of heavy users and 46% of light users could not recall the price paid for the last jar of petroleum jelly they purchased.

☐   70% of respondents agreed strongly with the statement "petroleum jelly is economical."

☐   20% of respondents reported having more than one jar of petroleum jelly in their households.

☐   86% of respondents stated that they kept a jar of petroleum jelly in the bathroom; 34% mentioned the bedroom, 6% mentioned the kitchen, and 2% mentioned the garage, basement, or workshop.

☐   The average quantity of petroleum jelly applied varied significantly by use from 3.1 g (sunburn) and 2.1 g (baby use) to 0.3 g (removing makeup) and 0.1 g (chapped lips). Share of total usage occasions also varied by use: 1% (sunburn), 4% (baby use), and 12% (chapped lips).

☐   The number of households using petroleum jelly was 15% lower in winter than summer. However, among user households, frequency of use was 25% higher in winter.

☐   For all except household uses (such as preventing rust and lubricating hinges), both the incidence and frequency of use were higher among females than males.

Source: Company records

DISTRIBUTION AND PRICING

Vaseline petroleum jelly was distributed primarily through grocery, drug, and mass merchandise stores; these accounted for 85% of Vaseline's ounce volume. Sales through variety stores and other outlets accounted for the remainder. However, VPJ distribution varied by size among the major channels (as shown in Exhibit 3); the 15-oz. jar, for example, was sold primarily through drugstores and mass merchandisers. Distribution penetration was high for the brand as a whole; in 1977 VPJ was carried in at least one size by 92% of grocery stores and 96% of drugstores.

All HBP products were sold by the same 130-person sales force. Salespeople focused on "headquarter accounts" rather than individual retail outlets. At least once a month HBP salespeople visited buyers at the head offices of food, drug, variety store, and mass merchandising chains as well as buyers for wholesalers representing

EXHIBIT 2 Pure VPJ factory shipments by size, 1974–1977 (thousands of dozens)

Size (oz.)	1974	1975	1976	1977*
1.75 (jar)	1,069.5	873.6	1,012.5	849.6
	(100)†	(82)	(95)	(79)
3.75 (jar)	997.7	973.2	1,137.5	1,116.1
	(100)	(98)	(114)	(112)
7.50 (jar)	540.8	544.4	773.2	628.3
	(100)	(101)	(143)	(116)
12.00 (jar)	216.7	186.3	192.7	157.5
	(100)	(86)	(89)	(73)
15.00 (jar)	249.8	227.1	292.1	293.1
	(100)	(91)	(117)	(117)
1.00 (tube)	114.2	104.3	120.2	106.7
	(100)	(91)	(105)	(93)
3.75 (tube)	47.7	34.2	41.6	33.3
	(100)	(72)	(88)	(70)
Total	3,236.4	2,943.1	3,569.8	3,184.6
	(100)	(91)	(110)	(98)
Equivalent units‡	543.6	504.5	626.9	562.3
	(100)	(93)	(115)	(103)

Source: Company records

*1977 sales estimated as of July 31.

†Numbers in parentheses are indices based on 1974 factory shipments by size (base = 100).

‡One equivalent unit = 3.6 million oz.

EXHIBIT 3 Pure VPJ jar sales volume by outlet type, May–June 1977 (equivalent ounce basis)

Jar size (oz.)	Outlet type			
	Grocery	Drug	Mass merchandiser	Total
1.75	6%	3%	0.2%	9%
3.75	18	7	2.0	28
7.50	16	8	5.0	29
12.00	8	3	2.0	13
15.00	5	11	6.0	21
Total	53%	32%	15.0%	100%

Source: Company records

Note: To be read, "Of the 85% of VPJ ounce sales through the three principal channels of distribution, 6% were 1.75-oz. jars sold through grocery stores."

independent retailers in each class of trade. During 1976 chain purchases accounted for 45% of VPJ dollar sales to the consumer market.

Salespeople were compensated by a combination of salary and bonus based on achievement of volume quotas. Sales force management and HBP division executives negotiated quarterly volume quotas for each brand. In addition, they established a calendar of consumer and trade promotions for each brand, reflecting its need for sales force support and the number of promotion events the sales force could present to the trade at one time. Porter believed that the sales force viewed VPJ as a mature, unexciting brand that required frequent price promotions to stimulate trade interest. Salespeople often pressed for such promotions toward the end of each quarter to help achieve their quotas.

Prices for VPJ were approved by the division general manager, whose key aim was profit improvement. (Exhibit 4 lists factory and suggested retail prices as of July, 1977.) The suggested prices allowed retailers who purchased direct from CPI a 40% margin, but actual retail prices were often 10% lower, particularly in grocery stores and mass merchandise outlets. In 1974 escalating petroleum costs required price increases ranging from 37% on the 15-oz. size to 70% on the 1.75-oz. size. Annual price increases between 1975 and 1977 had added a further 18% to manufacturer prices. Variable manufacturing costs for VPJ were expected to rise by 5% in 1978.

MARKETING EXPENDITURES

The three principal areas of VPJ marketing expenditures were advertising, consumer promotion, and trade promotion. Sales force expenses were treated as division overhead and not allocated among brands. Brand budgets for VPJ from 1975 through 1977 are summarized in Exhibit 5.

EXHIBIT 4   Pure VPJ price list, July 1977

Size (oz.)	Suggested retail price (SRP)	SRP per ounce	Suggested wholesale price (SWP)	SWP per ounce	Manufacturer's selling price (MSP)	MSP per ounce	MSP per dozen
1.75 (jar)	$0.57	$0.33	$0.403	$0.230	$0.342	$0.195	$4.10
3.75 (jar)	0.79	0.21	0.558	0.149	0.473	0.126	5.68
7.50 (jar)	1.19	0.16	0.840	0.112	0.713	0.095	8.56
12.00 (jar)	1.59	0.13	1.122	0.094	0.953	0.079	11.44
15.00 (jar)	1.69	0.11	1.193	0.080	1.013	0.068	12.16
1.00 (tube)	0.69	0.69	0.487	0.487	0.413	0.413	4.96
3.75 (tube)	1.25	0.33	0.883	0.235	0.750	0.200	9.00

Note: Suggested retail prices allowed retailers a 40.0% margin on direct purchases from the manufacturer and a 29.4% margin on purchases from wholesalers. Suggested wholesale prices allowed wholesalers a 15.1% margin on purchases from the manufacturer.

EXHIBIT 5   VPJ Brand Budgets, 1975–1977 ($000)

	1975	1976	1977*
Gross sales†	$17,792 (100%)	$22,491 (100%)	$22,938 (100%)
Variable manufacturing costs	8,616 (48%)	10,618 (47%)	10,572 (46%)
Gross margin	9,176 (52%)	11,873 (53%)	12,366 (54%)
Advertising‡	1,590 (9%)	2,410 (11%)	2,123 (9%)
TV: Network	1,280	1,526	1,720
Spot	97	586	
Print: Magazine	44	141	62
Sunday supplement		38	45
Newspaper			97
Consumer promotion	137 (1%)	448 (2%)	330 (1%)
Trade promotion	1,810 (10%)	2,468 (11%)	2,202 (10%)
Total marketing expenditures	3,537 (20%)	5,326 (24%)	4,655 (20%)
Profit before SG&A expenses, overhead, and taxes	$5,639 (32%)	$6,547 (29%)	$7,711 (34%)

Source: Company records

*Revised budget as of July 31, 1977. By September 1977 it appeared that these estimates would closely match actual results.

†Before deductions of off-invoice and base contract allowances; includes sales of both pure and carbolated VPJ.

‡Includes production costs and public relations expenditures as well as media costs.

Advertising

The primary objective of VPJ advertising through the 1970s was to increase sales by suggesting new product uses. Earlier brand advertising had concentrated almost exclusively on baby care, but in 1972 the message began to include VPJ's versatility as a skin-care product for adults and children (see Exhibit 6). Some HBP executives believed that VPJ advertising should present product uses beyond skin care; others thought that emphasizing VPJ's usefulness as a shoe-shining aid or hinge lubricant might cause some consumers to stop using it for skin or baby care.

Bimonthly VPJ advertising expenditures showed substantial period-to-period fluctuations (see Table 1). Porter believed these indicated a lack of sustained commitment to advertising as well as management's tendency to cut fourth-quarter advertising expenditures to meet annual profit targets.

Media selection showed greater consistency. Network television was the principal medium for VPJ advertising; print media were used primarily to announce VPJ consumer promotions. Both electronic and print media advertising rates rose on average 15% annually between 1974 and 1977.

EXHIBIT 6   1977 VPJ 30-second television commercial (titled "Year Round")

1. LITTLE GIRL: Whatcha doin' Mom?
2. MOM: Helping prevent diaper rash with Vaseline Petroleum Jelly.
3. (SFX: BABY) Wouldn't change Lisa without it.
4. LITTLE GIRL: Whatcha doin' sis?
5. SIS: Taking off eye make up with
6. Vaseline Petroleum Jelly.
7. Good for the dry skin on these rough spots too.
8. LITTLE GIRL: What're you doin' Mr. Adams?
9. MR. ADAMS: I got a little burn. I am soothing it,
10. with Vaseline Petroleum Jelly.
11. ANNCR: (VO) In all seasons, for all reasons ...
12. ...do it with Vaseline Petroleum Jelly.

Source: William Esty Company, Inc., N.Y., N.Y.

TABLE 1   Index of bimonthly measured media advertising for VPJ, 1974-1977

	1974	1975	1976	1977
January–February		83	78	113
March–April		64	103	92
May–June	100	36	39	102
July–August	108	114	128	97
September–October	49	100	132	
November–December	42	11	136	

Source: Company records

Note: (Base: May–June 1974 = 100.) Figures not adjusted for media cost inflation.

Consumer Promotion

Historically, VPJ brand management had spent little money on consumer promotion. During 1973 only one consumer promotion (a 10-cent coupon) was run; in 1974, none occurred. In 1975, however, three events were run: a free glass jar packaged with the 7.5-oz. VPJ, a 10-cent cross-ruff coupon[2] packed in two million boxes of Procter & Gamble's Ivory Snow, and a 50-cent refund offer for two VPJ proofs of purchase.

1976 VPJ events.   Consumer promotion expenditures continued to increase during 1976; that year marked four events, each coinciding with a promotion to the trade.

1. *February:* A two-dollar cash refund offer involving VPJ and four other HBP brands was announced in the February issues of *Family Circle* and *Ladies' Home Journal* and in full-page, four-color Sunday newspaper supplement advertisements on February 15 (see Exhibit 7). Consumers could also learn of the offer at the point of purchase through four-color riser cards for end-aisle and cut-case displays and shelf talkers including refund applications, which were shipped to retailers with each case of VPJ.[3]

2. *April:* To coincide with National Baby Week, one dollar's worth of coupons for five HBP brands used in baby care (including a 15-cent coupon for any size VPJ) were carried inside 4.65 million boxes of Kimbies disposable diapers. Coupons for Kimbies were carried by two participating HBP brands.

3. *June:* A shrink-wrapped twin pack of two 3.75-oz. jars of VPJ, with a label encouraging consumers to keep one jar in the kitchen and the other in the bathroom, was preticketed with a retail price of 99 cents. The pack also included a 50-cent refund offer for proofs of purchase from two 3.75-oz. jars. The twin pack was shipped only in cases of three dozen, to encourage the trade to feature it in special displays. (Exhibit 8 shows merchandising flyer.)

4. *September:* An eight-page "programmed learning" advertisement was run in *Reader's Digest* (October 1976) to educate consumers about skin care and the uses of VPJ, Vaseline Intensive Care lotion, and Vaseline Intensive Care bath beads. The reader could answer a "skin test" on a mailable pop-up card which doubled as an entry to the Vaseline Soft-to-Touch sweepstakes. Sweepstakes prizes, such as fur coats and cashmere sweaters, all emphasized the soft-to-touch theme. The sweepstakes was an attention-getting overlay to a $1.50 cash refund offer for a proof of purchase from each of the three

[2]A cross-ruff coupon is carried either on or inside the package of a non-competitive brand. It is used when the target markets of the sponsor and carrier brands are similar.

[3]Riser cards are attention-getting signs placed above a special display. Cut-case displays are shipping cartons that could double as store display units when cut to shape by store personnel; these allow retailers to display a product without unpacking it. Shelf talkers are small signs attached to the front of the shelf on which the product is regularly stocked.

EXHIBIT 7   1976 Newspaper and magazine advertisement for $2 cash refund promotion

EXHIBIT 8   1976 Merchandising flyer for VPJ twin-pack promotion

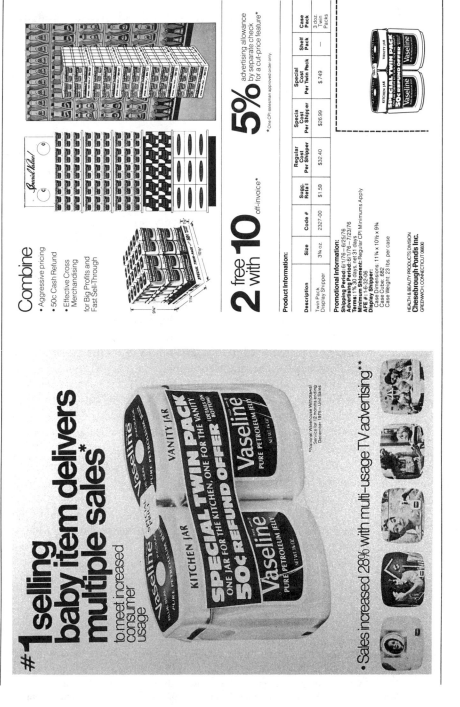

#1 selling
baby item delivers
multiple sales*

to meet increased
consumer
usage

* Sales increased 28% with multi-usage TV advertising**

*National Warehouse Withdrawal
Service for 12 months ending
December 1975—Uni Sales

Combine
- Aggressive pricing
- 50¢ Cash Refund
- Effective Cross Merchandising

for Big Profits and
Fast Sell-Through

2 free
with 10
off-invoice*

5%
advertising allowance
by separate check
for a cut-price feature*

*One CPI salesman approved order only

Product Information:

Description	Size	Code #	Sugg. Retail	Regular Cost Per Shipper	Special Cost Per Shipper	Special Cost Per Twin Pack	Shelf Pack	Case Pack
Twin Pack Display Shipper	3¾ oz.	2327-00	$1.50	$32.40	$26.99	$.749	—	3 doz. Twin Packs

Promotional Information:
Shipping Period: 6/1/76 – 6/25/76
Advertising Period: 6/1/76 – 7/23/76
Terms: 1% 30 days, net 31 days
Minimum Shipment: Regular CPI Minimums Apply
AFF # 1-6-32-06
Display Shipper:
Case Dimensions: 11¾ x 10½ x 9¾
Case Cube: 682
Case Weight: 23 lbs. per case

HEALTH & BEAUTY PRODUCTS DIVISION
Chesebrough-Pond's Inc.
GREENWICH, CONNECTICUT 06830

participating brands. The offer was also advertised through riser cards and shelf talkers at the point of purchase (see Exhibit 9).

The principal costs to VPJ for these events are summarized in Exhibit 10. For multiple-brand promotions, costs were allocated according to each brand's share of coupon or proof-of-purchase redemptions.

1977 VPJ events.   Consumer promotion expenditures for VPJ were cut by one-quarter in 1977; only three promotion events were implemented.

1. *February:* A Swiss Army multipurpose knife was offered as a self-liquidating premium[4] on the labels of 7.5-oz. jars of VPJ. The knife, a $21.00 retail value bought by CPI for $10.00, was offered to consumers for $10.50 plus one VPJ front label. The 50-cent difference between purchase and selling prices covered handling. Costs of $18,000, however, were incurred for point-of-purchase display materials and 1,500 knives used as dealer loaders.[5]

2. *April:* A 25-cent coupon for large sizes of three HBP brands, including VPJ (15-oz.), was printed on packages of the 24-oz. size of Vaseline Intensive Care bath beads. To encourage multibrand displays at the point of purchase, a self-liquidating premium which doubled as a dealer loader was also offered and advertised in women's magazines. Because redemption of the on-pack coupons would be delayed until purchasers had used up the contents of the boxes, HBP managers believed an additional purchase incentive was necessary to stimulate special trade merchandising activity. Thus, in selected markets, a newspaper advertisement delivered 65 cents worth of coupons on the three participating brands (including a 15-cent coupon toward a 15- or 12-oz. jar of VPJ). In other markets newspaper advertising featured a one dollar cash refund for proofs of purchase on two of the three brands.

3. *September:* A two-page advertisement in *Reader's Digest* (October 1977) and a similar advertisement in Sunday newspaper supplements delivered 50 cents worth of coupons on three Vaseline brands, including a 10-cent coupon for VPJ. These advertisements, along with riser cards and shelf talkers at the point of purchase, also announced a $40,000 sweepstakes. To encourage potential entrants to find in-store Vaseline displays, the ads indicated that official entry forms and instructions were available at the point of purchase.

---

[4]A self-liquidating premium requires consumers to send cash as well as proof of purchase. The cash amount covers handling, mailing, and the cost of the premium, which is usually offered at 30% to 50% below normal retail price.

[5]A dealer loader is a sample of a premium displayed at the point of purchase until the end of the promotion, when it usually becomes the property of the store or department manager.

EXHIBIT 9 1976 Merchandising flyer for $1.50 cash refund promotion

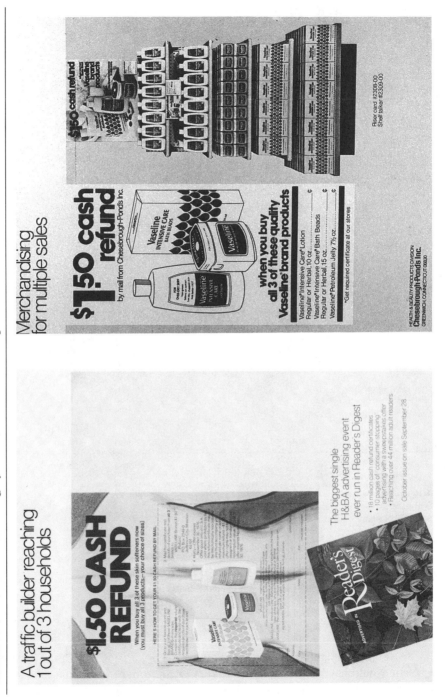

EXHIBIT 10   Costs to VPJ of 1976 consumer promotions

1. *January:* Allocated Cost to VPJ: $129,000

	Circulation (million)	% Response	Number of responses	Cost per response	Total cost (five brands)
Sunday supplement	30.00	0.7	210,000 ⎫	$2.25* ⎫	$599,625
Magazines	14.50	0.2	29,000 ⎪	⎪	
Point-of-purchase materials	2.75	1.0	27,500 ⎭	⎭	
21,000 riser cards					$27,225
60,000 shelf talkers					$15,375

2. *April:* Allocated Cost to VPJ: $56,620

	Face value	Circulation (million)	Redemption rate %	Number of redemptions	Cost per redemption	Total cost (VPJ only)
Coupon redemption	15 cents*	4.65	4.0	186,000	21.05 cents*	$39,150
Coupon artwork and printing						$14,300
Package flagging and coupon insertion						$3,170

3. *June:* Cost to VPJ: $82,150

	Circulation (no. of twin packs)	% Response	Number of responses	Cost per response	Total cost (VPJ only)
Refund offer	1,260,000	7.0	88,200	75 cents*	$66,150
Special packaging					$16,000

4. *September:* Allocated Cost to VPJ: $141,200

	Circulation (million)	% Response	Number of responses	Cost per response	Total cost (three brands)
Reader's Digest	18.0	0.5	90,000 ⎫	$1.75* ⎫	$315,000
Point-of-purchase materials	4.5	2.0	90,000 ⎭	⎭	
30,000 riser cards					$27,000
75,000 shelf talkers					$13,000
Sweepstakes prizes, judging, handling					$54,000

Source: Company records

*Includes face value of coupon or refund plus handling charges

FUTURE CONSIDERATIONS

After reviewing the consumer promotion history, Porter wondered how much latitude she would have in planning the 1978 VPJ consumer promotions. She thought division management would again wish to include VPJ in several multiple-brand promotions. She suspected, however, that these were of most benefit to the weaker participants and that her consumer promotion dollars might be better spent on events exclusive to VPJ.

Timing the promotions was another problem. Some HBP managers believed consumer promotions should coincide with trade promotions. Others thought they should be launched between trade promotions, arguing that promotions should be spread more evenly to avoid wide demand fluctuations, which hampered efficient production and inventory control.

Porter realized that she first had to define her objectives for consumer promotion. Some HBP executives favored it to stimulate short-term sales. Others argued that indiscriminate use of premiums, coupons, and sweepstakes further increased consumer price sensitivity and that consumer promotions were valuable only when they reinforced the brand's advertising image.

Trade Promotion

In general practice, trade promotions temporarily offered merchandise to the trade at a discount from the regular list price. Porter characterized how trade buyers usually responded to a manufacturer's limited-time trade promotion offer:

> They weigh the financial incentive of buying an above-normal quantity of the product at a discount against the financing costs associated with the additional inventory. Of course, they can minimize these costs—and make the manufacturer happy—by accelerating the product's movement off the shelves. To do this, they have to pass all or part of our incentive on to the consumer as a retail price cut. To achieve the greatest sales increases, they should feature the price cut in store advertising and set up a special in-store display.

Manufacturers used a variety of trade promotion allowances. Case allowances on products ordered during the promotion period offered either a reduction from list price on the invoice to the trade (for example, 10% off invoice) or free goods with a specified minimum purchase (for example, one case free with purchase of ten). Because manufacturers could not legally control retail prices, they had no assurance that case allowances would be fully or partially passed on to consumers as retail price reductions. (Many manufacturers, including CPI, sometimes permitted their trade accounts to take merchandise ordered during the promotion period in two shipments. Thus, the second shipment might arrive after the promotion and be sold at the manufacturer's regular suggested retail price.)

Additional merchandising allowances, also paid on a per-case basis, were sometimes offered. For example, a 10% allowance might be offered if the trade featured the product at a price discount in its consumer advertising. Or a special allowance might be offered to stores that set up end-aisle or off-shelf displays of prescribed size during the promotion period. Unlike off-invoice allowances,[6] these were only paid after the manufacturer received evidence of performance, such as an affidavit, advertising tear sheet, or display photograph.

---

[6]Off-invoice and free-goods allowances are deducted from the bill sent to the trade. Merchandising allowances are paid on a "bill back" basis by separate check.

In addition to case and merchandising allowances, manufacturers sometimes offered a *base contract* to the trade, by which any account buying a minimum quantity of the product received a percentage discount. A 5% base contract discount was offered on all VPJ orders over $75.

Past VPJ events.   Given VPJ's dominance in its category, Porter was surprised to discover that over 70% of 1976 factory shipments were sold to the trade on promotion. The 1977 marketing plan outlined three objectives for VPJ trade promotion:

1. Stimulate cut-price feature advertising and displays, especially on larger sizes.
2. Reinforce and expand distribution of larger sizes of all trade channels.
3. Limit erosion of distribution of smaller sizes.

PORTER'S ANALYSIS

Porter summarized the terms of timing of VPJ trade promotions from late 1972 through mid-1977 (see Exhibit 11). She noted that a trade promotion had been offered on at least one size during every quarter of each year. Duration of the offers varied widely, with some lasting as long as 60 days (in contrast to most retailers, who featured brands through price advertising and special displays for one week only). With one exception, VPJ's trade promotions were national, not tailored to particular regional or city markets.[7] Porter noted that the average level of trade promotion discounts seemed to have increased over the five years. In addition, she observed that since 1973 price increases often coincided with trade promotions, complicating evaluations of their impact.

Three questions came to Porter's mind as she reviewed the VPJ trade promotion history.

1. How extensive was inventory loading during the promotional period? Trade buyers, who could often predict the timing of a brand's trade promotion offers, could deliberately let inventory run down in anticipation of a promotion, buy heavily during the promotion period, then let orders drop again. This produced peaks and valleys in the flow of factory shipments and an artificial seasonality of demand. Porter had noted a fall-off in VPJ shipments before and after most promotions. Could HBP be selling at a discount VPJ volume that the trade would buy anyway to meet normal consumer demand?
2. Just how much merchandising support was VPJ receiving at the retail level? Comparative data on the extent of feature advertising for petroleum jelly and three other product categories, reported in Exhibit 12, suggested that

---

[7]By law, different trade promotion offers could be made at the same time in different market areas, but in any given market area an equivalent offer had to be made on a proportional basis to all competing retail outlets. Major supermarket and drug chains and mass merchandisers generally preferred that manufacturers offer the same trade promotion in all market areas.

the trade did not view VPJ as a traffic builder. Further, most VPJ trade promotions involved case allowances. Should the proportion of performance-based allowances be increased, and, if so, could performance requirements be enforced?

3. How effective were across-the-line promotions? Traditionally, VPJ had used line promotions across all sizes to encourage retailers to stock more than one size. However, the company typically required retailers to feature only one size in a tiny "obituary" newspaper ad to take an advertising allowance on their purchases of all VPJ sizes.

RESEARCH EVIDENCE

During 1976 VPJ factory shipments had increased 22% over 1975. Unit sales to consumers had risen 11%. During the first half of 1977, however, factory shipments and consumer sales were 11% and 2% lower than the equivalent 1976 figures. Some HBP executives suggested that heavy VPJ promotion during 1976 had overstocked the trade, the consumer, or both. To address this issue and the broader question of how much advertising, consumer promotion, and trade promotion expenditures each contributed to VPJ sales and profit performance, two research studies had been commissioned.

The first report, prepared by John Dennerlein, CPI's special projects manager, with the assistance of an independent consulting firm,[8] estimated incremental sales and contribution generated by VPJ trade promotions over a five-year period. A series of computer models estimated what the normal monthly factory shipments of each VPJ size would have been without each trade promotion, and then compared these figures with actual shipments. Similarly, the contribution from actual sales at the promotion price could be compared with the contribution normal sales would have provided at full price. The calculations of incremental unit sales and contribution took account of lost sales at full price before and after, as well as during, each promotion period.

The results of Dennerlein's investigation are presented in Exhibits 13 and 14. Exhibit 13 reports the net incremental contribution associated with each VPJ trade promotion from 1972 through June 1977, broken down by size. Dennerlein also plotted factory shipments, incremental unit sales, retail inventories, and consumer sales over time for each VPJ size. As an example, his chart for the 7.5-oz. VPJ is presented as Exhibit 14.

Dennerlein concluded that VPJ trade promotions were profitable and were "the major factor behind year-to-year changes in VPJ sales." He believed that VPJ trade promotions, especially when they coincided with consumer promotions, not only stimulated the trade to build inventories but also increased consumer sales. Dennerlein opposed any significant transfer of VPJ money from trade promotion to advertising.

[8]SPAR (Sales Promotion Analysis Reporting), a commercial service of Pan-Eval Data Inc.

EXHIBIT 11 VPJ trade promotion history, 1972–1977

Year	Duration	Sales days promoted	Consumer promotion activity	1.75 oz.	3.75 oz.	7.50 oz.	12.00 oz.	15.00 oz.	Comments
1972	9/1–10/15	29	none	—	—	5% OI staple 10% OI M/C	5% OI staple 10% OI M/C	5% OI staple 10% OI M/C	OI = off-invoice. A staple or standard case contained one dozen units. A master case (M/C) was a prepacked mix of sizes, usually including six dozen units.
1973	1/2–2/13	31	none	5% OI staple 10% OI M/C + 5% OI on choice of one size	5% OI staple 10% OI M/C + 5% OI on choice of one size	5% OI staple 10% OI M/C + 5% OI on choice of one size	5% OI staple 10% OI M/C + 5% OI on choice of one size	5% OI staple 10% OI M/C + 5% OI on choice of one size	
	5/1–6/30	43	none	5% OI (SE and SW regions only)	5% OI	5% OI	—	—	
	9/4–11/2	46	10-cent coupon on any size VPJ	7% + 5% OI on choice of one size	7% + 5% OI on choice of one size	7% + 5% OI on choice of one size	7% + 5% OI on choice of one size	7% + 5% OI on choice of one size	
1974	2/1–3/15	29	none	10% OI + 10% ad	—	10% OI	10%	10%	
	5/1–6/14	31	none	10% OI + 10% ad	—	10% OI + 10% ad	—	—	
	8/1–9/13	31	none	1 w/11	1 w/11	1 w/11	1 w/11	1 w/11	An additional 10% discount given to accounts showing evidence of feature advertising support for the brand. One case provided free for every 11 ordered.
	11/1–12/13	28	none	—	10% OI	—	—	10% OI	

Year	Dates	No.	Promotion						Terms
1975	1/2–2/14	31	Container pack premium with 7.50-oz. size	1 w/11	—	—	—	1 w/11	
	3/10–4/18	32	10-cent cross-ruff coupon with P&G Ivory Snow; multibrand	—	—	1 w/11 or 2 w/10 on choice of one size	1 w/11 or 2 w/10 on choice of one size	1 w/11 or 2 w/10 or choice of one size	
	6/2–6/27	21	none	—	1 w/11 + 10% ad	—	—	—	
	9/2–9/30	21	50-cent refund offer 2 VPJ proofs of purchase	1 w/11	—	2 w/10	—	—	
	11/3–12/12	27	none	—	2 w/10 + 10% ad choice of one size	—	—	2 w/10 + 10% ad choice of one size	
1976	1/5–2/27	41	$2 refund offer; multibrand	1 w/11	1 w/11	2 w/10	1 w/11	1 w/11	5% ad allowance for feature ad on any one size.
	4/5–4/30	21	15-cent cross-ruff coupon with Kimbies; multibrand	—	—	2 w/10 on choice of one size	2 w/10 on choice of one size	2 w/10 on choice of one size	Only one order permitted during promotion period. 10% ad allowance for ads featuring all three promoted brands.
	5/14–6/25	38	50-cent refund offer for 2 VPJ proofs or purchase	2 w/10 on twin pack + 5% ad	—	—	—	—	
	8/2–9/24	43	Reader's Digest sweepstakes; $1.50 refund offer and sweepstakes; multibrand	1 w/11 + 5% ad	1 w/11 + 5% ad	2 w/10 + 5% ad	1 w/11 + 5% ad	1 w/11 + 5% ad	Bonus 5% ad allowance for ads featuring all three promoted brands.

EXHIBIT 11 (continued) VPJ trade promotion history, 1972-1977

Year	Duration	Sales days promoted	Consumer promotion activity	1.75 oz.	3.75 oz.	7.50 oz.	12.00 oz.	15.00 oz.	Comments
1976 (cont.)									
	10/4-11/11	30	none	—	12% OI	—	—	—	Display allowance of $3 per retail outlet for an end-aisle, off-shelf display of all three brands (minimum 15 dozen per display).
	10/4-12/13	50	none	—	—	—	—	15% OI	
1977	1/3-2/25	40	Swiss Army knife self-liquidating premium	—	—	10% OI	—	—	5% ad allowance if knife featured in advertising.
	4/4-4/29	20	25-cent coupon for 15-oz. VPJ; multi-brand	—	10% OI on choice of one size + 5% ad	—	—	10% OI on choice of one size + 5% ad	Display allowance of $3 per retail outlet for displays of two out of three promoted brands (minimum 15 dozen per display).
	5/2-5/27	21	none	—	—	2 w/10	—	—	
	6/6-6/24	22	none	—	10% OI on twin-pack	—	—	—	

Source: Company records

EXHIBIT 12   Food trade's advertising support for petroleum jelly and other packaged goods

	A Ads (>3 in.)*		B Ads (1–3 in.)*		C Ads (<1 in.)*		Total		Average no. of ads per account per year
	No.	%	No.	%	No.	%	No.	%	
Petroleum Jelly									
VPJ	—	—	3	7.0%	39	93.0%	42	100%	2.63
Private label	—	—	—	—	6	100.0	6	100	0.37
Category									
Laundry detergents	109	10.1%	517	48.1%	449	41.8%	1,075	100%	67.00
Bar soaps	18	3.9	249	53.3	200	42.8	467	100	29.00
Hand lotion	2	1.2	25	14.7	143	84.1	170	100	11.00

Source: Company records, based on 1975 Majers data for three major metropolitan markets. Majers, an independent market research firm, monitored grocery, drug, and mass merchandiser newspaper advertising support for a wide variety of products.

Note: Of the 42 VPJ ads counted, 2 were for the 1.75-oz. size; 12 for the 3.75-oz. size; 20 for the 7.50-oz. size; 6 for the 12-oz. size; and 2 for the 15-oz. size.

* Ads are grouped by size in newspaper column inches. For example, a C ad would be one column wide and less than one inch long. In a large newspaper advertisement featuring many brands offered by a supermarket, a C ad (also known as an obituary ad or line mention) might consist of a single line giving the brand name and unit price. An A ad, in contrast, would usually appear in very large type and include a picture.

A second study, conducted by the CPI market research department, measured the efficacy of VPJ advertising expenditures. It found weak correlations between quarterly VPJ advertising expenditures and factory shipments, retail inventories, and consumer sales. The researchers noted that consumer sales had declined during the first half of 1977, even though media advertising expenditures were almost 50% higher than during the equivalent period in 1976.

THE PROBLEM

These findings and the sales results of first-half 1977 had prompted HBP Division executives to reduce VPJ media advertising expenditures for the second half of 1977 to around $700,000, compared with $1.4 million during the same period in 1976. Porter opposed this cut. "If anything," she commented, "the 1976 promotion pumped so much VPJ into the pipeline that advertising ought to have been increased." She wanted to develop a 1978 television advertising campaign that stressed VPJ's versatility and to increase advertising expenditures at the expense of trade promotion. (Four finished commercial executions of a new television advertising campaign could be developed at an approximate cost of $200,000.) She admitted, however, that "the HBP Division's traditional orientation toward push rather than pull marketing would

EXHIBIT 13 Estimates of trade participation and net incremental contribution (or loss) associated with VPJ trade promotions, 1972–1977

Promotion period		Sales days promoted	Estimated trade participation					Incremental contribution (or loss) by size					Total net incremental contribution (or loss)
Year	Duration		1.75-oz.	3.75-oz.	7.50-oz.	12.00-oz.	15.00-oz.	1.75-oz.	3.75-oz.	7.50-oz.	12.00-oz.	15.00-oz.	
1972	9/1–10/15	29	—	—	75%	55%	60%	—	—	$29,133	$27,246	$56,870	$113,249
1973	1/2–2/13	31	55%	65%	70	50	55	$14,522	$58,982	36,770	31,471	32,682	174,427
	5/1–6/30	43	55	70	75	—	—	14,054	21,795	61,066	—	—	96,915
	9/4–11/2	46	55	65	70	55	55	38,496	68,334	54,191	24,970	60,730	246,721
1974	2/1–3/15	29	—	—	75	55	60	—*	—*	26,204*	28,306	56,335	110,845
	5/1–6/14	31	55	—	70	—	—	11,146*	—*	24,973*	—*	—a	36,119
	8/1–9/3	31	55	65	70	55	55	(43,388)	25,881	(15,644)	43,808	24,533	30,190
	11/1–12/13	28	—	75	—	—	70	—*	8,562	—*	—*	54,615*	63,177
1975	1/2–2/14	31	55	—	75	—	—	(90,623)	—	23,148	—	—	(67,475)
	3/10–4/18	32	—	—	85	65	75	—	—	46,934	39,894	49,182	136,010
	6/2–6/27	21	—	75	—	—	—	—	(18,334)	—	—	—	(18,334)
	9/2–9/30	21	55	75	75	—	—	(13,219)	—	27,652	—	—	14,433
	11/3–12/12	27	—	75	—	—	70	—	(31,115)	—	—	29,509	(1,606)
1976	1/5–2/27	41	80	90	95	80	80	32,984*	21,921*	159,265*	50,669*	65,902	330,741
	4/5–4/30	21	—	85	90	75	80	—	—	8,939	(2,651)	15,693	28,581
	5/14–6/25	38	70	80	85	70	75	—	89,887	—	—	—	89,887
	8/2–9/24	43	70	80	85	70	—	48,863	59,310	102,004	40,103	41,278	291,558
	10/4–11/11	30	—	90	—	—	—	—	(39,570)	—	—	—	(39,570)
	10/4–12/13	50	—	—	—	—	85	—	—	—	—	26,932	26,932
1977	1/3–2/25	40	—	—	85	—	—	—*	—*	124,248*	—*	—*	124,248
	4/4–4/29	20	—	90	—	—	85	—	51,642	11,094	—	99,763	151,405
	5/2–5/27	21	—	—	90	—	—	—	—	11,094	—	—	11,094
	6/6–6/24	22	—	85	—	—	—	—	32,136	—	—	—	32,136
1972–77	Average	32	59	78	79	62	70	871	26,879	47,998	31,535	47,233	86,160

Source: SPAR research commissioned by CIP.

Note: To be read: The trade promotion running from September 1 through October 15, 1972, generated a net incremental contribution of $29,133 on sales of the 7.50-oz. size, and a total net incremental contribution of $113,249.

* A list-price increase on the designed size occurred simultaneously with the promotion.

EXHIBIT 14 Factory shipments, incremental unit sales, retail inventories, and consumer sales for 7.5-oz. VPJ, 1972–1977

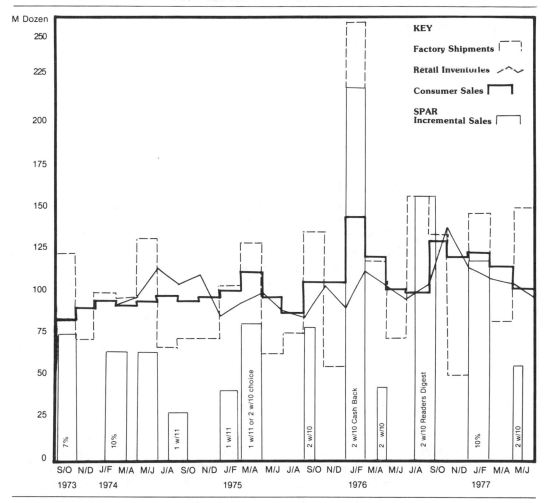

Source: Company records

make this proposal tough to sell." She also expected resistance from the HBP sales force and the trade.

As she began to plan the brand budget, Porter learned that the division had scheduled several significant new product launches for the second half of 1978. Profits from established brands such as VPJ would cover the substantial marketing expenses for these introductions. Accordingly, the HBP general manager informed Porter that her 1978 VPJ budget should show a profit, after advertising and promotion expenses, at least 10% greater than the current 1977 estimate of $7.7 million.

PROCTER & GAMBLE CO. (B)

JOHN A. QUELCH
ALICE MACDONALD COURT

It was June 1982, and Charles Garner had been brand assistant on H-80 for six months. H-80 was the code name for a new light-duty liquid detergent[1] (LDL) scheduled for introduction into test market at the end of 1982 by the Packaged Soap and Detergent Division (PS&D) of the Procter & Gamble Co. (P&G). The H-80 Brand Group had been hard at work developing the H-80 first-year marketing plan. Under the guidance of Kate Jones, the brand manager, overall volume objectives and marketing support levels had been determined and marketing support had been appropriately divided between introductory advertising and promotion. As brand assistant, Garner had responsibility for developing all promotion plans for H-80. His task over the next few weeks was to formulate a detailed Year I national sales promotion plan from which a test market plan for a limited geographical area could be derived.

COMPANY BACKGROUND

By 1981, the Procter & Gamble Co. operated in 26 countries. As indicated in Exhibit 1, sales totaled $11.4 billion, of which 70% were made in the U.S. P&G manufactured 90 consumer and industrial products in the United States, including three of the leading LDL brands, Ivory Liquid, Dawn, and Joy. The company also sold the leading brands in 14 of the other 24 consumer product categories in which it competed.

The company comprised nine major operating divisions organized by type of product: Packaged Soap and Detergents, Bar Soap and Household Cleaning Products, Toilet Goods, Paper Products, Food Products, Coffee, Food Service and Lodging Products, and Special Products. Each division had its own brand management (called Addvertising), Sales, Finance, Manufacturing, and Product Development line management groups. These groups reported to a division manager who had overall

---

[1]LDLs are defined as all mild liquid soaps and detergents designed primarily for washing dishes.

EXHIBIT 1   Consolidated statement of earnings for fiscal years ended June 30 (in millions of dollars except per-share amounts)

	1981	1980
Income		
Net sales	$11,416	$10,772
Interest and other income	83	52
	11,499	10,824
Costs and expenses		
Cost of products sold	7,854	7,471
Marketing, administrative, and other expenses	2,361	2,178
Interest expense	98	97
	10,313	9,746
Earnings from operations before income taxes	1,186	1,078
Income taxes	518	438
Net earnings from operations (before extraordinary charge)	668	640
Extraordinary charge—costs associated with the suspension of sale of Rely tampons (less applicable tax relief of $58)	(75)	—
Net earnings	$ 593	$ 640
Per common share		
Net earnings from operations	$8.08	$7.74
Extraordinary charge	(.91)	—
Net earnings	$7.17	$7.74
Average shares outstanding: 1981—82,720,858 1980—82,659,861		
Dividends	$3.80	$3.40

Source: Company records.

profit and loss responsibility. The divisions used centralized corporate staff groups for advertising services,[2] distribution, and purchasing.

The Advertising Department was organized on the brand management system. The responsibility for planning and directing the marketing effort for each brand was assigned to a brand group that typically included a brand manager, an assistant brand manager, and one or two brand assistants. This group planned, developed, and directed the total marketing effort for its brand. In developing its marketing

[2]Advertising services include the following specialized staff departments: TV Commercial Production, Media, Copy Services, Art and Package Design, Market Research, Field Advertising, Market Systems and Computer Services, Promotion and Marketing Services, and Advertising Personnel.

plans, the brand group worked closely with other departments within their division, with specialists in the advertising services staff groups, and with the advertising agency[3] assigned to their brand. Exhibit 2 presents the PS&D Division Advertising Department's organizational chart.

LIGHT-DUTY LIQUID DETERGENTS

The LDL industry recorded factory sales of $850 million and volume of 59 million cases in 1981.[4] The average U.S. consumer had 1.5 LDL brands at home at any one time, used 0.6 fluid ounces of product per sinkful of dishes, and washed an average of 12 sinksful each week. The average purchase cycle was three to four weeks. LDL consumption increases resulting from the growing number of U.S. households[5] were partly offset by the increased penetration of automatic dishwashers (ADWs) as ADW households used one-half less LDL than non-ADW households.[6] Based on these trends, P&G executives projected category volume growth of 1% per year over the next five years.

The market could be conceptually divided into three major segments on the basis of product benefit. The performance segment, accounting for 35% of category volume, included brands providing primarily a cleaning benefit; the mildness segment, accounting for 37% of category volume, included brands providing primarily the benefit of mildness to hands; and the price segment, accounting for 28% of category volume, included brands whose primary benefit was lost cost.[7] Three companies sold almost 75% of LDLs, with P&G holding a 42% share[8] of the market, Colgate-Palmolive Company a 24% share, Lever Brothers, the U.S. subsidiary of Unilever, a 7% share.[9] The remaining 27% of the market consisted mainly of generic and private label brands. A higher proportion of the marketing budgets of P&G LDLs was allocated to advertising and a lower percentage to promotion than was the case for either Colgate or Lever LDLs. Colgate and Lever sold an estimated 75% of their LDL volume to the trade on deal compared to about half for P&G.

---

[3]P&G retained 10 leading advertising agencies to work with the brand groups on the development and execution of advertising strategy.

[4]Volume is measured in P&G statistical cases, each containing 310 ounces.

[5]Household growth was a better indicator of LDL volume than population growth, as research indicated LDL household consumption varied only slightly with the number of people in the household. There were over 79 million households in the United States in 1983.

[6]ADW households still used LDL for pots and pans and small cleanups.

[7]Price brands were sold to retailers for an average of $7.50/statistical case versus $17.00/statistical case for the premium-priced mildness and performance brands.

[8]Share of the market is defined as share of statistical case volume.

[9]In 1981, U.S. sales of Colgate-Palmolive Company were $5.3 billion and U.S. sales of Lever Brothers were $2.1 billion.

EXHIBIT 2 PS&D division partial organization chart—Fall 1981

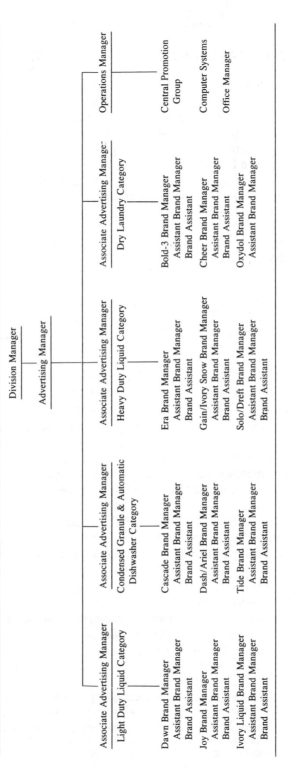

Division Manager

Advertising Manager

Associate Advertising Manager

Light Duty Liquid Category

Dawn Brand Manager
Assistant Brand Manager
Brand Assistant

Joy Brand Manager
Assistant Brand Manager
Brand Assistant

Ivory Liquid Brand Manager
Assistant Brand Manager
Brand Assistant

Associate Advertising Manager

Condensed Granule & Automatic
Dishwasher Category

Cascade Brand Manager
Assistant Brand Manager
Brand Assistant

Dash/Ariel Brand Manager
Assistant Brand Manager
Brand Assistant

Tide Brand Manager
Assistant Brand Manager
Brand Assistant

Associate Advertising Manager

Heavy Duty Liquid Category

Era Brand Manager
Assistant Brand Manager
Brand Assistant

Gain/Ivory Snow Brand Manager
Assistant Brand Manager
Brand Assistant

Solo/Dreft Brand Manager
Assistant Brand Manager
Brand Assistant

Associate Advertising Manager

Dry Laundry Category

Bold-3 Brand Manager
Assistant Brand Manager
Brand Assistant

Cheer Brand Manager
Assistant Brand Manager
Brand Assistant

Oxydol Brand Manager
Assistant Brand Manager

Operations Manager

Central Promotion
Group

Computer Systems

Office Manager

PROMOTION OF P&G's ESTABLISHED LDL BRANDS

P&G's three brands in the LDL category, Joy, Ivory Liquid, and Dawn, together accounted for 30% of the dollar sales volume and profit of the PS&D Division. While each of the three brands was a different formulation which offered a distinct benefit to appeal to separate consumer needs, they were all marketed similarly. The percentage breakdown of marketing expenditures between advertising and promotion for the three brands is indicated in Table 1.

In general, the brand managers spent about half of each LDL's marketing budget in advertising, with the balance in promotion. Competitive brands allocated about 40% of their marketing budgets to advertising.

TABLE 1   Advertising/consumer promotion/trade promotion dollar splits for P&G's LDL brands

	1977	1978	1979	1980	1981	1982
Ivory Liquid	48/42/10	54/38/8	54/36/10	54/35/11	50/40/10	55/37/8
Dawn	N/A	N/A	58/31/11	51/39/10	46/42/12	51/40/9
Joy	55/36/9	51/41/8	48/42/10	55/34/11	50/39/11	60/30/10

Ivory Liquid was the leading brand in 1981 with a 15.5% share of the LDL category. Because Ivory had the highest trial levels in the category, the brand's primary sales promotion strategy was continuity of purchase combined with a secondary objective of stimulating trial among younger women and heavy LDL users.[10] Ivory had reduced its promotion frequency from eight four-week events in 1972 to six events in 1982. Only 20% of Ivory's promotion budget was allocated to trade allowances. Despite merchandising performance requirements tied to these allowances, it was difficult to ensure that the funds were passed through to the consumer in the form of retail price cuts.

The remaining 80% of Ivory's promotion budget was allocated to consumer promotion. About two-thirds of Ivory's promotion events were price packs,[11] which were intended to encourage continuity of purchase by current brand users. Such price packs accounted for 30% of Ivory's total yearly volume. The remaining one-third of consumer promotions were coupon offers supported by trade allowances. The brand used couponing to stimulate trial. Exhibit 3 summarizes Ivory Liquid's 1981 and 1982 promotion plans, as well as the plans proposed for 1983.

Dawn was introduced nationally in 1976 as a performance brand. In two years Dawn rose to the number two position in the LDL category and by 1981 held a 14.1% market share. Dawn had captured about 70% of its volume from non-P&G

---

[10]Ivory Liquid's current customers tended to be both slightly older than the average and lighter LDL users (defined as consumers who washed seven sinksful of dishes or less per week).

[11]A price pack was defined as a specially produced retail package announcing a temporary reduction from the standard retail price. For example, "30¢ off the regular retail price." The average percent reduction to the consumer was 10%–20%.

EXHIBIT 3 Ivory promotion calendars: 1981–83

	January	February	March	April	May	June	July	August	September	October	November	December
1981	20¢ off mailed coupon *plus* $1.30/case trade allowance	48 oz. 30¢ off price pack *plus* 22 oz. $1.30/case trade allowance			32 oz. 20¢ off price pack	22 oz. $1.30/case trade allowance		32 oz. 20¢ off price pack *plus* 20¢ BFD coupon on any size		20¢ off free standing insert coupon *plus* $1.30/case trade allowance		
1982	48 oz. Harlequin Romance book on-pack premium *plus* $1.30/case trade allowance	32 oz. 20¢ off price pack			22 oz. 13¢ off price pack	32 oz. 20¢ off price pack			20¢ free standing insert coupon *plus* $1.30/case trade allowance			32 oz. 27¢ off price pack
Proposed 1983	20¢ off BFD coupon on any size *plus* $1.80/case trade allowance	22 oz. 20¢ off price pack			32 oz. 27¢ off price pack		22 oz. 20¢ off price pack		20¢ free standing insert coupon *plus* $1.80/case trade allowance		48 oz. 40¢ off price pack	

Note: (1) Coupons were redeemable on any package size.

(2) Per case allowances are quoted in terms of statistical cases.

brands, with the remaining 30% cannibalized equally from Ivory and Joy. Dawn's rapid growth was attributed to its unique benefit as the superior grease-cutting LDL in the category. Dawn's sales promotion strategy was trial-oriented with two-thirds of Dawn's promotion events being trial-oriented couponing events supported by trade allowances, while the remaining one-third were price packs. Exhibit 4 summarizes Dawn's 1981, 1982, and 1983 promotion plans. The brand manager believed that Dawn's success was due to its distinctive grease-cutting benefit. He therefore tried to design consumer promotion events that emphasized this benefit at the same time as they provided an economic incentive to the consumer.

Joy ranked third in the LDL category with a 12.1% market share in 1981. Its product benefit was to deliver "shiny dishes." Joy had the lowest trial level of P&G's three LDLs. To strengthen Joy's appeal, an improved "no-spot" formula was scheduled for national distribution by September 1982. The new formula caused water to "sheet" off dishes when they were air drying, leaving fewer spots than other brands. In addition, the improved formula reduced the cost of goods sold by about $3 million per year. The brand manager hoped to increase Joy's volume by 10% with the introduction of Joy's improved product. Marketing expenditures were to be increased modestly with emphasis on trial-oriented consumer promotion events. Approximately half of Joy's promotions were trial-oriented couponing events supported by trade allowances and prepriced events.[12] The balance of events were price packs. Exhibit 5 summarizes Joy's 1981, 1982, and 1983 promotion plans.

The PS&D promotion planning calendar comprised 13 four-week promotion events. Each LDL participated in at least five events annually. While the brand groups occasionally planned regional promotion variations to facilitate testing of a new promotion idea or strengthen promotion support in a weak performance area, they generally planned national sales promotions. The brands generally avoided the simultaneous promotion of two or more of the company's LDLs whenever possible in order to avoid fragmenting the attention of the sales force and the trade. In addition, there was concern that some trade buyers might respond by promoting only one of P&G's LDLs and ignore the others. However, some sales managers believed that promoting all three LDLs together would lessen cannibalization among the brands by minimizing the consumer switching resulting from promotion and argued that such line promotions would be attractive to the trade since such promotions would include high-volume brands. The PS&D Division organized one or two divisional promotion events each year involving three to ten brands, often including one or more LDLs.[13]

---

[12]A prepriced pack was defined as a specially produced retail package that had the retail price marked on the label before it was delivered to the retail store. P&G generally used prepriced packs to promote smaller LDL sizes to stimulate trial. The average percent reduction to the consumer was 30%–50%.

[13]Such divisional promotion events typically included a sweepstakes or contest combined with case refund offers and coupons.

EXHIBIT 4 Dawn promotion calendars: 1981–83

	January	February	March	April	May	June	July	August	September	October	November	December
1981	32 oz. 20¢ off price pack		22 oz. 13¢ off price pack		32 oz. $1.30/case trade allowance		22 oz. 13¢ off price pack		48 oz. 30¢ off price pack	32 oz. 20¢ off price pack		
1982	20¢ PCH* coupon *plus* $1.30/case trade allowance		32 oz. 20¢ off price pack		22 oz. 13¢ off price pack		48 oz. 30¢ off price pack			22 oz. 20¢ off price pack	32 oz. $1.30/case trade allowance	
Proposed 1983	20¢ PCH coupon *plus* $1.80/case trade allowance		32 oz. 27¢ off price pack		20¢ free-standing insert coupon *plus* $1.80/case trade allowance		20¢ free-standing insert coupon *plus* $1.80/case trade allowance			22 oz. 20¢ off price pack		20¢ free-standing insert coupon *plus* $1.80/case trade allowance

*Coupon distributed along with Publisher's Clearing House mailing.

69

EXHIBIT 5 Joy promotion calendars: 1981-83

	January	February	March	April	May	June	July	August	September	October	November	December
1981	32 oz. 27¢ off price pack	32 oz. 20¢ off price pack		22 oz. 13¢ off price pack		20¢ free-standing insert coupon *plus* $1.30/case trade allowance		22 oz. 13¢ off price pack	20¢ free-standing insert coupon *plus* $1.30/case trade allowance		32 oz. 20¢ off price pack	
1982		48 oz. two 40¢ cross-ruff* coupons distributed in 171 oz. Cheer laundry detergent *plus* 22 oz. 13¢ off price pack		32 oz. 20¢ off price pack		22 oz. 13¢ off price pack		20¢ free-standing insert coupon *plus* $1.30/case trade allowance		48 oz. 40¢ off price pack	20¢ mailed coupon *plus* $1.30/case trade allowance	
Proposed 1983		20¢ free-standing insert *plus* $1.80/case trade allowance		22 oz. 20¢ off price pack		12 oz. 49¢ prepriced pack			22 oz. 20¢ off price pack		20¢ mailed coupon *plus* $1.80/case trade allowance	

*Two coupons good on the next purchase of Joy, distributed in specially marked boxes of Cheer laundry detergent.

THE DEVELOPMENT OF H-80

H-80 was a high-performance LDL that combined suspended nonabrasive scrubbers[14] with a highly effective detergent system to provide superior cleaning versus other LDLs when used full strength on tough baked-on foods and parity cleaning versus other LDLs when diluted with water for general dishwashing. The scrubber system represented a distinctive new product benefit and was the first major technological innovation in the category since the introduction of Ivory Liquid.[15] The H-80 formula was completely homogenous and did not require shaking.

The PS&D Division began work on this innovation in response to a 1980 Dishwashing Habits and Practices Study that revealed that 80% of U.S. households scour and scrub their dishes at least once a week with an average household scouring four times a week. This research also revealed that the removal of burnt or baked-on foods was considered the toughest cleaning job by more consumers than any other dishwashing task and that most consumers did not view their current LDL as sufficiently effective for such tough cleaning jobs. Based on this research, the Advertising Department concluded that a consumer need existed for a high-performance LDL.

The Product Development Department (PDD) began work on this project in early 1981. An H-80 brand group was established to guide the development process and test marketing of the brand. By mid-1981, they had developed a technological breakthrough and a formula that they believed would fulfill the existing consumer need. Successful laboratory and in-home use testing was completed by the end of 1981.

H-80 emerged from the development process as a rich green opalescent liquid that felt slightly gritty to the touch. The liquid was thicker than that of other LDLs and H-80's herbal fragrance was completely unique within the category. The package was bright green and shaped like an arrowhead. The label carried an endorsement from the American Fine China Guild that read, "Safe for all fine china."

Based on the results of pretest market research[16] conducted to project H-80's potential market share, the brand had recommended a market share objective of 11%. The pretest market research projected H-80's market share to reach 13% by the end of Year I. However, given the aggressive competitive environment of the LDL market, the brand group had thought it prudent to set a conservative objective for H-80. The brand group projected H-80's national volume and share as indicated in Table 2.

Planned capital investment of $20 million for H-80 was below the average for a new P&G product. The cost structure of P&G's existing LDL brands, summarized in Exhibit 6, was applicable to H-80. The brand group estimated that P&G would have to spend at least $60 million on a 12-month introductory marketing plan for

[14]The scrubbers were made from the biodegradable shells of microscopic sea organisms.

[15]Ivory Liquid's formula included a detergent with a patented molecular structure that prevented the roughness and cracking that exposure to other detergents caused to human skin.

[16]P&G uses a proprietary technique for simulating test markets and predicting market shares.

TABLE 2   H-80 projected sales

Year	LDL market projections (000,000 cases)	H-80 estimated market share	H-80 estimated market volume (000,000 cases)	H-80 estimated sales* ($000,000)
1982	59.4	—	—	—
1983	59.8	7%	4.2	$ 71.4
1984	60.1	11	6.6	112.2
1985	60.8	11	6.7	113.9

*H-80 carload cost of a statistical case was $17.00. See Table 3.

H-80. While this did not meet the 36-month marketing payout objective generally sought by a new PS&D product (see Exhibit 7), the brand believed a longer payout was justified because of the low capital investment required. However, the payout picture was further clouded because of the likelihood that some of H-80's volume would be cannibalized from current P&G LDLs. Based on current market shares, only about 60% of H-80's volume would be net extra for the PS&D Division. If this occurred, it would lengthen payout for the division considerably.

P&G management was fully aware that H-80 was a risky venture. P&G's current market share of over 40% made cannibalization a virtual certainty and suggested a limited marketing investment to generate an attractive payout. Conversely, establishment in the increasingly competitive LDL category suggested the need for substantial marketing investment. An added element of risk was the revolutionary nature of the H-80 product, which contained a mild abrasive. Acceptance of this would require that consumers be educated and persuaded to modify current usage habits, a formidable task. Nevertheless, company management supported H-80 because it was an innovative product which met a real consumer need. The company had had outstanding successes with similar risky innovations in the past such as Pampers, Crest, and Bounce, although other innovations had failed. P&G attempted to limit risk by test marketing new products and only expanding distribution of those which proved to have high consumer appeal in the marketplace, and thus a high

EXHIBIT 6   Cost structure for an established LDL brand (%)

Cost	51%
Distribution	7
Selling and general administration	10
Marketing expenditures	20*
Profit	12
Total	100%

Source: Company records

*Includes advertising, trade, and consumer promotion expenditures.

EXHIBIT 7   H-80 marketing payout schedule (millions of dollars)

	Year I	Year II	Year III	Year IV
Revenue	$71.4	$112.2	$113.9	$113.9
Expenses:				
Marketing (20% of sales after Year I)	60.0	22.4	22.8	22.8
Cost of goods, distribution, and SG&A (68% of sales)	45.2	76.2	77.5	77.5
Total expenses	105.2	98.6	100.3	100.3
Profit/(loss)	$(33.8)	$13.6	$13.6	$13.6
Cumulative profit/(loss)	$(33.8)	$(20.2)	$(6.6)	$7.0

likelihood of success. Further, initial test market failures were frequently modified, retested successfully, and later expanded to national distribution.

The brand managers on P&G's established LDLs also expected some cannibalization, but projected that their brands' losses would be less than proportional to their market shares. As shown in Exhibit 8, Ivory Liquid and Joy expected to lose only 75% and 80%, respectively, of their proportionate losses, since their benefits would not compete directly with those of H-80.[17]

When the brand managers on Ivory, Dawn, and Joy were asked how they might change their brand marketing plans in light of the introduction of H-80, all three indicated that they would not increase their spending, but that they would formulate their promotion plans more defensively. Specifically, all three said they would plan to run strong offers designed to encourage consumers to stock up before H-80's introduction, then use trial-oriented couponing events following H-80's introduction to regain lost users.

Based on P&G LDL category experience, the brand group expected the following distribution by size two months after H-80's introduction: 70% distribution in

EXHIBIT 8   LDL market share projections (% of LDL market volume)

	Without H-80			With H-80			
Year	Ivory Liquid	Dawn	Joy	Ivory Liquid	Dawn	Joy	H-80
1982	15.5%	14.7%	12.2%	15.5%	14.7%	12.2%	—
1983	15.5	15.0	12.3	14.7	14.0	11.4	7.0%
1984	15.5	15.5	12.4	14.2	13.9	11.1	11.0
1985	15.5	15.9	12.5	14.2	14.3	11.2	11.0
1986	15.5	16.5	12.7	14.2	14.9	11.4	11.0

[17]Proportionate loss is defined as a loss of sales proportionate to market share. For example, Ivory's 1983 share was expected to be 15.5%. If Ivory lost its fair share of H-80's 11% of the market, it would lose 15.5% × 11% = 1.7 share points.

stores representing 90% of total grocery volume on 48 oz., 85% on 32 oz., 90% on 22 oz., and 75% on 12 oz.[18] To maintain these distribution levels, Garner believed the brand had to promote all sizes of H-80 in the first year.

P&G did not advertise a new brand until it had achieved 70% distribution, which the brand group expected H-80 to achieve six weeks after introduction. H-80's media plan would give the brand LDL category leadership media weights for the first six months of its introductory advertising campaign. The average media weight for the major advertised LDL brands was 300 gross rating points (GRPs)[19] every four weeks. H-80 planned 450 GRPs during weeks 6–18, 375 GRPs during weeks 19–31, and 300 GRPs during weeks 32–52. The Brand and Advertising Agency expected this media campaign would achieve a 65% consumer awareness of H-80's advertising by three months after introduction.

The H-80 advertising strategy aimed to convince consumers that H-80 was an outstanding dishwashing liquid for cleaning tough-to-remove foods from dishes. Advertising would be targeted at female heads of larger households aged 18–35. Consumer research had revealed that H-80 had the most well-defined target audience of any of the LDLs. The research also suggested that H-80's target audience should be the heavy LDL user.[20]

Total cost for the 12-month media plan would be $18 million. In addition, promotion costs were expected to be $37 million and miscellaneous marketing expenses $5 million (including point-of-sale display material and $500,000 to produce television commercials).

H-80 introductory year advertising/promotion split would be 40%/60%, similar to the company average for a new brand. Thereafter, the brand manager's objective was to have at least 50% of marketing support in advertising.

H-80 would be available in four sizes and at prices equivalent to those of P&G's established LDL brands, as indicated in Table 3.

TABLE 3   H-80 sizing and pricing

Size	No. items/ actual case	No. items/ statistical case*	Manufacturer's carload item price	Estimated average retail price	Estimated % of volume per size†
48 oz.	9	6.5	$2.53	$2.99	10%
32 oz.	12	9.7	1.70	2.04	30
22 oz.	16	14.0	1.21	1.46	45
12 oz.	24	25.8	0.70	0.84	15

* A statistical case equals 310 ounces.

† Statistical cases.

[18]While the PS&D sales force only serviced 27% of grocery stores accounting for 75% of grocery sales volume, additional distribution could be achieved through grocery wholesale distributors that serviced smaller grocery stores.

[19]One gross rating point is achieved when one advertising exposure reaches 1% of the advertiser's potential audience. Gross ratings points can be calculated as the product of media reach times exposure frequency.

[20]A heavy LDL user washes 12 or more sinksful of dishes per week.

PROMOTION ISSUES FOR H-80

P&G's introduction of Dawn in 1976 was considered very successful. Dawn's introductory promotion plan, outlined in Table 4 with 1982 updated costs, helped Dawn to achieve a market share equivalent to that required by H-80.

TABLE 4   Dawn's year I introductory promotion plan

Month	Event	Cost in 1982 ($000,000)	Number of average weeks of year I volume per promotion event*
2 & 3	$2.70/statistical case trade allowance on all sizes	$ 1.8	8
	6 oz. sample mailed to 50% of households	30.3	—
4	22 oz./13¢ off price pack	1.2	10
6	32 oz./20¢ off price pack	1.0	10
8	48 oz./30¢ off price pack	0.3	13
10	22 oz./13¢ off price pack	1.2	10

*For example, eight weeks worth of total Year I volume of all sizes would be sold with the initial trade allowance, and ten weeks worth of total Year I volume on the 22-oz. size would be sold with the second event (13¢ off price pack).

With this introductory promotion program, Dawn had achieved the market share growth detailed in Table 5.

TABLE 5   Dawn's year I market share growth

	Month						Total year I
	1–2	3–4	5–6	7–8	9–10	11–12	
Percent of total year I share	30	80	100	120	130	140	100

Garner realized that he would probably not be able to achieve the same results for H-80 if he simply copied the Dawn plan. When Dawn was introduced, there was little couponing in the LDL category. However, by 1982, most major LDL brands distributed coupons frequently, and as Exhibit 9 shows, research indicated that coupons were widely used by consumers. Also, the LDL competitive environment was becoming more intense with the expansion of Sunlight by Lever Brothers in 1982. While it was still too early to tell how successful Sunlight would be with its national expansion, Sunlight had achieved an 11% share in the test market after only 12 months.

Sunlight's introductory promotion plan had been much more aggressive than the Dawn plan. It involved ten promotion events, including a $2.70/statistical case

EXHIBIT 9   Consumer use of manufacturers' coupons

Question: How often do you use a manufacturer's coupon when you purchase a dishwashing liquid?

| | By year | | | By 1981 usage patterns | | |
	1979	1980	1981	Heavy (+12 Sinksful/ week)	Medium (7–12 Sinksful/ week)	Light (1–7 Sinksful/ week)
Almost always	22%	25%	28%	28%	26%	24%
About half the time	17	18	18	18	19	18
Just occasionally	44	42	40	40	43	44
Never	16	14	13	13	12	13
No answer	1	1	1	1	—	1

Source: Company research

Note: To be read, for example: In 1979, 22% of all respondents who had washed some dishes by hand in the past seven days claimed that they used a manufacturer's coupon almost always when they purchased a dishwashing liquid.

trade allowance for months one–three in support of a free 5 oz. sample size plus a 15¢ coupon mailed to 50% of all households, three coupon events (one 20¢ free-standing insert coupon,[21] one 20¢ magazine coupon, and one 25¢ Best Food Day coupon),[22] three preprice events (on 12 oz., 22 oz., and 32 oz. sizes), a 6 oz. trial size, and two trade allowance promotions (one on the 48 oz. size and one on the 22 oz. size). The cost of Sunlight's Year I promotion plan was estimated at $75 million on a national equivalent basis.

Another key issue Garner faced was how to minimize H-80's cannibalization of P&G's other LDLs. As Garner examined the 1981, 1982, and 1983 promotion schedules for Ivory, Dawn, and Joy, he pondered when and how often H-80 should be promoted. He wanted to avoid the simultaneous promotion of two or more of the company's LDLs. However, given the limitation of 13 promotion periods, H-80 would have to be promoted alongside another LDL on at least some occasions.

Garner also wondered what promotion mix would be most effective for the H-80 introduction. Price packs and coupons seemed to be the most commonly used promotion vehicles in the category and recent P&G research, summarized in Table 6, indicated that these vehicles were liked and used by consumers.

However, the same research also indicated that a trial size represented the best purchase incentive for a consumer who had never tried a brand (see Table 7).

[21]A free-standing insert coupon was a coupon and ad preprinted on heavy paper and inserted loose into a newspaper or magazine.

[22]A Best Food Day coupon was a coupon run in a newspaper on the day that paper ran editorial material on food. This was also the edition in which most retail grocers placed their retail advertisements; hence the most advantageous day for grocers and manufacturers to run coupons.

TABLE 6   1981 Consumer ratings and use of promotion devices
(Index: highest rated/used device = 100)

| | Coupons | | Price pack | Premiums | | Refund/ rebate | Trial size | Bonus pack | Sweep- stakes |
	Mfr.	Store		Pack	Mail				
Percent liking very much/ fairly well	95	85	100	75	46	74	90	90	46
Percent used past three months	97	87	100	51	30	56	61	74	44

Source: Company research.

Note: These ratings were based on general consumer preferences rather than preferences within the LDL category.

Garner wondered if the less frequently used types of consumer promotion in the LDL category, such as premiums, mail-in refunds, or sweepstakes, could enable H-80 to attract the trade's attention and cut through the clutter of competitive promotions. He was particularly interested in the ability of free mail-in offers to achieve sampling of new users as reported in the independent industry research study presented in Exhibit 10.

Independent of the types of promotion event scheduled, Garner believed on the basis of LDL category experience that the following percentages of incremental trial would be achieved with each subsequent promotion.

Event I   —All reach is incremental trial.
Event II —Assume one-half of reach is incremental trial.
Event III —Assume one-quarter of reach is incremental trial.
Event IV —Assume one-quarter of reach is incremental trial.
Event V —Assume one-quarter of reach is incremental trial.

Garner predicted that he would have to achieve about a 40% trial level to support an 11% share based on results of previous introductions of products with similar usage profiles.

TABLE 7   1981 Consumer ratings and use of promotion devices
(Index: highest rated/used device = 100)

| | Coupons | | Price pack | Premiums | | Refund/ rebate | Trial size | Bonus pack | Sweep- stakes |
	Mfr.	Store		Pack	Mail				
Brand never used	46%	37%	29%	37%	17%	27%	100%	35%	13%

EXHIBIT 10   Effectiveness ratings of premiums and sweepstakes by manufacturers who sell through supermarkets

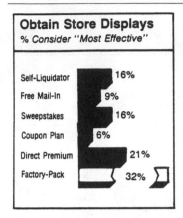

Obtain Store Displays
% Consider "Most Effective"

Self-Liquidator	16%
Free Mail-In	9%
Sweepstakes	16%
Coupon Plan	6%
Direct Premium	21%
Factory-Pack	32%

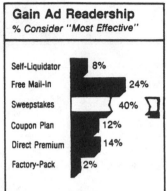

Gain Ad Readership
% Consider "Most Effective"

Self-Liquidator	8%
Free Mail-In	24%
Sweepstakes	40%
Coupon Plan	12%
Direct Premium	14%
Factory-Pack	2%

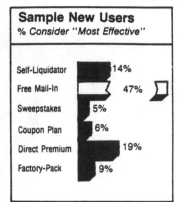

Sample New Users
% Consider "Most Effective"

Self-Liquidator	14%
Free Mail-In	47%
Sweepstakes	5%
Coupon Plan	6%
Direct Premium	19%
Factory-Pack	9%

Good Will, Old Users
% Consider "Most Effective"

Self-Liquidator	20%
Free Mail-In	22%
Sweepstakes	7%
Coupon Plan	15%
Direct Premium	22%
Factory-Pack	14%

Sell-In To Dealers
% Consider "Most Effective"

Self-Liquidator	7%
Free Mail-In	8%
Sweepstakes	19%
Coupon Plan	13%
Direct Premium	31%
Factory-Pack	22%

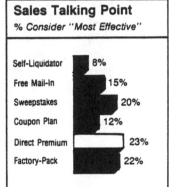

Sales Talking Point
% Consider "Most Effective"

Self-Liquidator	8%
Free Mail-In	15%
Sweepstakes	20%
Coupon Plan	12%
Direct Premium	23%
Factory-Pack	22%

Get Shelf Attention
% Consider "Most Effective"

Self-Liquidator	16%
Free Mail-In	19%
Sweepstakes	16%
Coupon Plan	4%
Direct Premium	10%
Factory-Pack	35%

Repeat Purchases
% Consider "Most Effective"

Self-Liquidator	23%
Free Mail-In	10%
Sweepstakes	6%
Coupon Plan	27%
Direct Premium	16%
Factory-Pack	18%

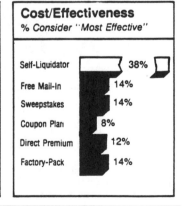

Cost/Effectiveness
% Consider "Most Effective"

Self-Liquidator	38%
Free Mail-In	14%
Sweepstakes	14%
Coupon Plan	8%
Direct Premium	12%
Factory-Pack	14%

Source: *Incentive Marketing,* December, 1981.

SALES PROMOTION ALTERNATIVES

Trade Allowances

Sales had advised Garner that a $2.70/statistical case trade allowance on all sizes in months 1–3 was necessary to stimulate initial stocking, in-store displays, and feature advertising by the trade. Garner also wondered whether a second trade promotion allowance event was necessary because of the competitive environment. He believed it would be most effective as a fourth event. Sales had informed him that an allowance below the current $1.80/statistical case used on the other P&G LDLs would be insufficient to generate trade support.

Sampling

Sampling was considered by P&G as the most effective trial-producing promotion device. Garner considered only mailed samples, as door-to-door delivery of samples by specially recruited crews was more expensive.

Garner worked with the Manufacturing Department to develop mailed-sample costs for various sizes, as shown in Exhibit 11. He was aware of P&G research indicating that too small a sample might not permit sufficient use to develop consumer interest in the product. He wondered which size would generate the most efficient and effective trial levels for H-80.

Couponing

While Dawn's introductory plan had not included any couponing, Garner felt that he should consider this promotion vehicle given its broad usage within the current LDL category and apparent appeal to consumers. He examined the costs and redemption

EXHIBIT 11   Mailed sampling costs per sample unit for H-80

Sample size	Delivered* cost/unit	% Usage†	% of consumers that use sample who repurchase
6 oz. miniature bottles	$.75	85%	50%
3 oz. miniature bottles	$.53	75	40
1.5 oz. miniature bottles	$.41	65	35
Two .75 oz. foil packets	$.31	40	30

*Includes mailing costs as well as manufacturing costs.

†Usage and repurchase rates vary by size.

estimates by distribution vehicle (see Exhibit 12) and by coupon value (see Exhibit 13) for five types of coupon programs:

☐ Coupons for H-80 alone could be mailed selectively to members of the target audience. The impact and redemption rate would be high because there would be no coupons for other brands in the mailing that might reduce consumer attention to H-80. However, this couponing method was expensive.

☐ Coupons for H-80 could be co-op mailed with other product coupons. Co-op couponing had slightly less impact but was considerably less expensive since delivery costs were shared with other brands. Such co-op mailings were organized by outside agencies. As a result, the timing of deliveries was fixed in advance and only one LDL brand could participate in any one coupon drop. The only available delivery times open to H-80 in the test market were three months and seven months following introduction.

☐ Free-standing newspaper insert (FSI) coupons offered Garner more flexibility in timing. The redemption rates for FSI coupons were strong but coupon theft and misredemption could also be high (particularly if the FSI was inserted in newsstand issues).

☐ Coupons distributed through the Best Food Day editions of local newspapers offered both low-cost delivery and flexibility in timing and in geographical coverage. There was, however, a greater potential for a new brand like H-80 to be lost among the many coupons run in newspapers. Also, the redemption rate was low and misredemption was high.

☐ Magazine coupons also offered low delivery costs and could be targeted at specific consumer groups. However, the potential to tie in with specific retailer feature dates did not exist. In addition, the redemption rate was low.

Special Pack Promotions

Garner considered four types of special packs: trial-size packs, prepriced packs, price packs, and bonus packs. Sales had advised that special packs should not be run until at least the second half of Year I, since the trade was reluctant to buy a special pack until a new brand was established to avoid carrying dual inventories of regular pack and special pack. However, if a new brand were introduced with a special pack, the trade would not need to carry dual inventories. A cost comparison by value/size and vehicle is shown in Exhibit 14.

A trial size would offer the consumer a low-risk, low-cost method of trying H-80. Because the consumer paid for the trial-size package, the cost to P&G per trial was lower than a sampling program.

A prepriced pack would also offer the consumer a low-risk, low-cost method of trying H-80, similar to a trial size. Usually, a prepriced pack was offered on the smallest salable size, in this case the 12 oz. size.

Price packs were widely used in the LDL category. Price packs were generally regarded as an effective promotion vehicle to retain current users and encourage

EXHIBIT 12 Theoretical couponing economics—20¢ coupon good on any size*

	Mail			Free-standing insert				
	Single brand	Basic co-op†	Extended co-op‡	Single brand	Full-page co-op	⅖ page co-op	Best Food Day	Magazine (on page)
Number distributed	40MM	24MM	45MM	44MM	38MM	38MM	58MM	58MM
Distribution cost/M§	$110.00	$16.45	$14.00	$37.50	$12.05	$5.05	$9.20	$5.70
Total distribution cost	$4,400,000	$395,000	$630,000	$1,650,000	$458,000	$182,000	$478,000	$319,000
Estimated % redemption	11.6%	11.6%	10.6%	7.6%	5.7%	5.1%	3.1%	2.6%
Number coupons redeemed	4,640M	2,784M	4,770M	3,344M	2,166M	1,938M	1,612M	1,456M
Total redemption costs‖	$1,322.4M	$793.4M	$1,357.5M	$953.0M	$617.3M	$552.3M	$459.4M	$415.0M
Grand total costs	$5,722.4M	$1,188.2M	$1,989.5M	$2,603.5M	$1,075.3M	$744.3M	$937.4M	$734.0M
Estimated % misredemption	10%	10%	10%	25%	25%	25%	25%	10%
Number households reached with product	4,174M	2,506M	4,293M	2,508M	1,625M	1,454M	1,209M	1,310M
Total cases moved	422M	253M	434M	257M	167M	149M	124M	132M
Cost per household reached	$1.37	$0.47	$0.46	$1.03	$0.66	$0.51	$0.78	$0.56
Cost per case moved	$13.56	$4.70	$4.58	$10.13	$6.44	$5.00	$7.55	$5.56

*Chart based upon average redemption data. Assume a new P&G LDL brand would redeem 50% higher due to strong advertising, product news, and high household category penetration.

† A coupon mailing involving at least ten noncompeting brands. Redemption rates were stable regardless of the number of brands.

‡ Extended coverage version of basic co-op coupon mailing.

§ Includes coupon production and preparation costs as well as cost of mailing.

‖ Includes trade and clearinghouse handling fees totalling 8.5¢ per coupon as well as amount of coupon.

EXHIBIT 13   Approximate relationship of redemption rate to
LDL coupon value (indexed to 20¢ value)

Coupon vehicle	Coupon value					
	20¢	25¢	35¢	50¢	$1.00	Get one free
Mail—Single brand	100	110	125	150	200	250
—Co-op	100	110	125	150	200	250
FSI co-op	100	110	125	150	200	250
Best Food Day	100	110	125	150	200	250
Magazine	100	110	125	155	200	250
On-pack	100	110	125	150	200	N/A
Cross-ruff (advertised on pack of another brand)	100	110	125	150	200	N/A

repeat purchase. The trade often set up special displays of price packs which could stimulate impulse purchases. Garner, however, wondered if a price pack would be good at generating trial for H-80.

Bonus packs offered low-cost distribution of free product but were not regarded as a strong trial device since they did not reduce the financial risk of trial to the consumer who had never used the product. However, bonus packs were considered an excellent means of promoting continuity of usage and offered a strong purchase incentive to the consumer who had purchased and liked the product before. Garner wondered if a bonus pack promotion would be effective in the second half of the introductory year.

Refunds

P&G did not usually use refund offers on a new brand because the economic benefit to the consumer was not immediately delivered and the value of the device in stimulating trial was questionable. However, Garner wondered if a high-value refund supported by point-of-purchase display material could generate significant trade and consumer interest. He also wondered if a refund requiring multiple purchases would be an effective continuity device if used in the second six months of H-80's first-year promotion plan. Garner analyzed the company's experience with refunds over the past three years (see Exhibit 15 for a refund fact sheet) and found that P&G distributed 30% of their refund offers through print, 27% through point-of-sale display material, 5% in- or on-pack, and 38% through divisional group promotions that used a combination of all three distribution methods plus television advertising.

Premiums

Premiums were believed useful in attracting attention at the point-of-sale and could offer excellent in-store display support, thereby stimulating impulse purchases. There were four major methods of premium distribution and types.

EXHIBIT 14   LDL special pack promotions

Type:	Trial size (6 oz.) product miniature	Prepriced size (12 oz.)	Bonus pack (32 oz.) oversize	Price pack cents off
Value:	Consumer price/bottle	Consumer price/bottle (savings off retail price)	% Free product	% of Normal retail
High	$.19	$.39 (50%)	25% (8 oz.)	30%
Medium	$.29	$.49 (40%)	15% (5 oz.)	20%
Low	$.39	$.59 (30%)	10% (3 oz.)	10%
Cost:				
High value	36¢/unit	Savings off retail price times number units/stat. case plus 50¢/stat. case manufacturing and trade handling	$6.10/stat. case	Cents off times number units/stat. case plus 50¢/stat. case manufacturing and trade handling
Medium value	29¢/unit		$5.00/stat. case	
Low value	22¢/unit		$4.25/stat. case	
Amount of promoted volume sold per event	4.7MM bottles	13 weeks business for 12 oz.	10 weeks business for 32 oz.	10 weeks business for 22 and 32 oz.; 13 weeks for 12 and 48 oz.

Note: All four types of promotion would be accepted by stores representing 70% of all commodity volume (ACV).

On-/in-pack premiums were attached to or packed in the product container and were offered free with the purchase of the promoted brand. These premiums made a strong impact on the shelf and often encouraged the trade to display the product off-shelf because of their irregular size. In-pack premiums were considered good trial-generating devices. However, the costs of extra packaging and of the premiums themselves could be significant. In addition, trade acceptance was estimated at only 30%–50% of all commodity volume because of inventory and shelf space problems (due to irregular size) as well as the risk of pilferage.

Near-pack premiums were displayed on the shelf next to or near the promoted product. Most near-pack premiums were free with the designated purchase but in the case of salable or price-plus near-packs the consumer was asked to pay a token sum. While near-packs offered more flexibility in the size of the premium a manufacturer

EXHIBIT 15   Refund facts—industry experience

I. *Factors that Influence Refund Response Rates*
  1. Method of distribution.
  2. Proof-of-purchase requirement/difficulty in obtaining proofs.
  3. Actual value of refund; value relative to price.
  4. Length of promotion.
  5. Design/appeal of offer and ad.
  6. Whether store coupon used with refund offer.
  7. Consumer interest in product/size of brand's consumer franchise.
  8. Whether single choice or variable offer.
  9. Whether refund in cash, check, or coupon.
  10. Brand's retail availability.
  11. Whether offer advertised via media or trade, or publicized in refund columns and newsletters.

II. *Typical Response Patterns*

		$1.00	$1.00	$1.00
Refund value				
Purchase requirements		1 22-oz. size	2 22-oz. size	3 22-oz. size
Consumer outlay for purchases		$1.50	$3.00	$4.50
% Savings on 22 oz. size		67%	33%	22%
Estimated Reponse as % of Offers Distributed				
Print		.9%	.5%	.3%
Point of sale		5.4	3.0	1.8
Direct mail		3.6	2.0	1.2
In-/on-pack other brand		8.2	4.5	2.7
In-/on-pack own brand		12.7	7.0	4.2

III. *Estimated Fulfillment Costs**

	Number distributed			
Print	44MM	$ 530,000	$300,000	$175,000
Point-of-sale	3MM	220,000	120,000	75,000
Direct mail	25MM	1,200,000	670,000	400,000
In-/on-pack other brand	6MM	660,000	360,000	220,000
In-/on-pack own brand	6MM	1,020,000	560,000	335,000

*Fulfillment costs include the $1.00 refund itself plus 34¢ return for handling. In addition to the fulfillment costs, assume $70M to $150M for display material/sales aids and/or $300M to $500M for print advertising; 3¢ per unit for in-/on-pack distribution carried by own brand, no extra package cost if carried by other brand, and $16.45/M for distributing direct mail offers via multibrand co-op.

could choose, they were hard to control as retailers often found it difficult to ensure that consumers made the purchases necessary to qualify to receive the premium.

A free-in-mail premium was mailed to the consumer when she or he sent the company the purchase requirements. Such offers were easily executed but did not provide an immediate benefit to the consumer. Self-liquidating premiums were delivered through the mail much like free mail-ins, but the consumer was required to send money as well as one or more proofs-of-purchase to cover the cost of the premium, handling, and mailing. The cost of such premiums to the consumer was between 30% and 50% lower than the regular retail price. Response rates were, however, quite modest. Exhibit 16 presents a company fact sheet comparing typical premium costs.

EXHIBIT 16   Objectives and costs of LDL premiums

	Marketing objectives				
Type of premium	Trial	Repeat purchase	Obtain in-store displays	Increase advertisement readership	Copy/product reinforcement
Self-liquidator			X	X	X
Partial liquidator by mail		X	X	X	
Free-in-mail for multiproofs		X	X	X	X
Free in mail for one proof	X		X	X	X
Near-pack—in store	X		X		X
On-/in-pack—in store	X		X		X

Type of premium	Typical item	Offer structure	National cost of promotion
Self-liquidator	Hair dryer	$9.00 plus 1 proof of purchase	$ 200,000
Partial liquidator	Hair dryer	$2.00 plus 4 proofs of purchase	400,000
Free-in-mail	Hair dryer	Free for 6 22 oz. proofs of purchase	2,200,000
Near-pack	Coupon holder	Free with one 22 oz.	950,000
On-/in-pack	Playing cards	Free with one 22 oz.	950,000

Note: Cost estimates include the premium itself, display materials and offer fulfillment. In the case of completely or partially self-liquidating premiums, they reflect offsetting revenue from consumers.

Sweepstakes/Contests

P&G was scheduled to run a group promotion four months following the introduction of H-80. Company research had revealed that smaller brands achieved good results behind group promotions because of the high distribution and display support these offers stimulated among the trade. However, Garner wondered if a new brand might get lost among P&G's established brands. See Exhibit 17 for an example of an upcoming group promotion. Garner estimated the cost of participating in a group FSI sweepstakes promotion would be about $50,000 and that it would achieve about a 2% response rate for H-80. Most brands participating in an offer of this type would also include a coupon in the FSI advertisement for the sweepstakes.

CONCLUSION

As Garner prepared to write the details of H-80's Year I national promotion plan in the format shown in Exhibit 18, he considered several things. How should he

EXHIBIT 17 P&G group sweepstakes promotion

Enter the SAIL FOR Savings

1st Prize **2nd Prize** **3rd Prize**

One (1) 13-day cruise for two on the luxury schooner Fantome PLUS $5,000 cash (approximate retail value $11,300.00).*

Five (5) 6-day cruises on the Flying Cloud (approximate retail value $3,200.00 per trip).*

2,000 L.L. Bean Boat and Tote™ Bags (approximate retail value $10.00).

*The First and Second Prizes include transportation to and from Freeport, Bahamas where the cruises originate.

Name _____
Address _____
_____
City _____
State _____
Zip Code _____
Telephone _____

OFFICIAL RULES—NO PURCHASE NECESSARY

1. Each entry you submit must be accompanied by one of the following:

   a. Any retail store ad dated between August 1, 1982 and September 30, 1982 which includes an ad for any one of these fine Procter & Gamble products:

Dash   Oxydol   Gain   Era   Bounty

White Cloud* or Charmin   Folger's Ground Roast or Flaked Coffee   Instant High Point   Ivory Liquid

   *Available only in limited areas.

   Circle the name of the product and its picture (if a picture is included in the ad) and circle the date printed on the ad.
   OR

   b. A plain piece of 3" x 5" paper on which you have handprinted or typed the name of any one of these fine Procter & Gamble products: Dash, Oxydol, Gain, Era, Bounty, White Cloud, Charmin, Folger's Ground Roast or Flaked Coffee, Instant High Point, Ivory Liquid.

2. Mail one of the above along with an Official Entry Form or plain piece of 3" x 5" paper on which you have handprinted your name and address. Mail your entry to: Sail For Savings Sweepstakes, P.O. Box 4036, Blair, NE 68009.

3. Retail ads submitted must be dated between August 1, 1982-September 30, 1982. Any printed retailer ad is acceptable — newspaper ads, in-store circulars, etc. You do not need to send the complete retail ad — only that portion which shows the participating brand and the date is necessary.

4. Enter the Sail For Savings sweepstakes as often as you wish, but each entry must be mailed separately in a hand addressed envelope no larger than 4⅛" x 9½" (#10 envelope). Entries must be postmarked between August 3, 1982-October 14, 1982, and received by October 22, 1982.

5. Winners will be determined in a random drawing conducted by D.L. Blair, an independent judging organization, whose decisions are final. All prizes will be awarded, limit one prize per name and address. Winners will be notified and prizes delivered by mail by approximately December 31, 1982.

6. One (1) First Prize of a 13-day cruise for two on the luxury schooner Fantome plus $5,000 cash (approximate retail value $11,300.00); five (5) Second Prizes of 6-day cruises for two on The Flying Cloud (approximate retail value $3,200.00 per trip) and 2,000 Third Prizes of L.L. Bean Boat and Tote™ Bags (approximate retail value $10.00) will be awarded. The First and Second Prize winners will also receive transportation to and from Freeport, Bahamas where the cruises originate. The cruise package includes meals while on board. All cruises awarded as First or Second Prizes must be completed by September 1, 1983; dates of departure are subject to availability.

7. This sweepstakes is open to residents of the United States, eighteen years or older at time of entry, except employees of Procter & Gamble and their advertising, judging, and promotion agencies, and the families of each. Void via participation at retail stores in Wisconsin and wherever prohibited by law. All federal, state, and local laws and regulations apply. Taxes, if any, are the sole responsibility of the prize winner. The odds of winning a prize will depend upon the number of entries received by October 22, 1982. Limit one prize per name and address. No substitution for prizes.

8. For a list of prize winners, send a separate, stamped, self-addressed envelope to: Sail For Savings Sweepstakes Winners' List, P.O. Box 4151, Blair, NE 68009.

Form No. 664-6172 528HXM

EXHIBIT 18 H-80 national sales promotion plan

Event	Timing												Number of average weeks volume	Cost
	January	February	March	April	May	June	July	August	September	October	November	December		
Stocking allowance														
$/physical case														
Trade allowance														
$/statistical case														
Sampling														
6 oz.														
3 oz.														
1.5 oz.														
2 × 0.75 oz.														
Couponing														
Mail—Single														
—Co-op														
—Extended														
FSI —Single														
—Full page co-op														
—2/3-page co-op														
BFD														
Magazine														
Special pack														
Price pack														
Bonus pack														
Trial size														
Refund														
Print														
Point-of-sale														
Direct mail														
In-/on-pack self, other														
Premium														
On-/in-pack														
Near-pack														
Free-in-mail														
Self-liquidator														
Partial liquidator														
Group promotion														

split his promotion dollars between trade and consumer promotions during the first year? How much of his brand should he plan to sell to the trade on deal? What promotion events should he recommend? How many times should he promote H-80 in its first year? Was the Dawn plan strong enough to work in the more competitive LDL environment H-80 faced? Would he be able to gain more leverage with the trade if he promoted H-80 with the other LDLs or would this hurt his brand? Which potential overlaps with the other LDLs should he most try to avoid?

BEECHAM PRODUCTS U.S.A. (A)

JOHN A. QUELCH
MELANIE D. SPENCER

In October, 1984, Susan Edwards, director of brand management, and Chris Weglarz, brand manager for Aqua-fresh toothpaste, were preparing for a brand group meeting on the 1985–86 media and promotion plan. Because Beecham's fiscal year began on April 1, the date of November 30, 1984, was set for completion of the plan.

Edwards noted that increased levels of media and promotion spending had been required in recent years to maintain an Aqua-fresh market share of approximately 12%, the level achieved in 1980, one year after the Aqua-fresh product introduction. The major factor in the rise of promotional expenditures was ever-increasing competitive spending on trade deals. Some members of the brand group questioned the level of trade promotion expenditures and argued that reallocating some trade promotion funds to consumer promotions would result in market share increases.

New information to assist in formulating the 1985–86 plan was available to the brand group. Using consumer toothpaste purchase data provided by scanner panels, the effectiveness of various promotional vehicles had been evaluated by Information Resources, Inc. (IRI).

COMPANY BACKGROUND

Thomas Beecham's study of the medicinal properties of herbs began in 1828 at the age of eight when he started work as a shepherd to augment his family's income. By the age of 20, Beecham was selling his herbal remedies throughout England. He became firmly established in the early 1850s as a "Chemist, Druggist and Tea Dealer." Among Beecham's accomplishments was the formulation of Beecham's Pills, a remedy for the common cold. This medicine became increasingly well known as Beecham first distributed the pills through mail order, then developed a national marketing program. By 1859, the product was sold from Africa to Australia.

Beecham was committed to customer satisfaction through product quality. This commitment was evident in his reservations about the power of advertising:

> It is possible, by plausible advertising, set forth in an attractive style, to temporarily arrest the attention of a certain number of readers, and induce them to purchase a particular article. But it is a more difficult matter to ensure their continued patronage. Unless the advertised article proves to be all that is claimed for it, not only do the purchasers discontinue its use, but warn others against it as a thing to be avoided.

Beecham believed in tailoring his products to the markets in which they were being sold. For example, when the company introduced Beecham's Pills in the United States, they were sweetened to appeal to American tastes. This philosophy also applied to the sales force. Beecham required that export salespersons speak the languages of their customers.

Growth continued through acquisition as well as international market expansion. Early acquisitions included Macleans, makers of a popular brand of toothpaste, and County Perfumery, which produced Brylcreem, the leading men's hairdressing in the United Kingdom. Brylcreem later spearheaded Beecham's expansion into the United States, becoming the best-selling men's hairdressing in the United States by 1960.

Encouraged by Brylcreem's success, Beecham made further acquisitions including S.E. Massengill (1971), a Tennessee-based producer of pharmaceuticals and feminine hygiene products, and the Calgon consumer products business (1977), which marketed well-known brands such as Cling-Free fabric softener, Sucrets sore throat lozenges, and Calgon water conditioner. The Calgon acquisition tripled the size of Beecham's U.S. consumer products business. In 1982, Beecham acquired the J.B. Williams division of Nabisco Brands, which marketed the leading U.S. iron supplement, Geritol.

By 1984, the Beecham Group, Ltd. had become a $2.5 billion consumer products and pharmaceutical company with headquarters in the United Kingdom. Beecham Products U.S.A., the U.S. consumer packaged goods division of Beecham Group Ltd., manufactured and marketed 17 brands, including Aqua-fresh, Massengill, Cling-Free, Calgon, Geritol, and Sucrets. The division's sales were $400 million in 1984.

Marketing within the division was organized around the classic product management system. Directors of brand management reported to the vice president of marketing. Each director of brand management was responsible for two to four brand management groups. The marketing vice president reported directly to the president of the division, making the chain of command relatively short and facilitating quick decision making.

PRODUCT CATEGORY HISTORY

Tooth powder was introduced in the United States in 1899. Similar in consistency to baking soda, tooth powder had to be combined with water before use, either by dipping a wet toothbrush into the powder or by forming a paste that could then be applied to the teeth. The procedure tended to be time consuming and messy.

In 1936, three brands of toothpaste were introduced: Squibb, Colgate, and Pepsodent. The next milestone occurred in 1955 when fluoride was incorporated into toothpaste formulas to aid in tooth decay prevention. Crest, introduced by Procter & Gamble Co. in 1955, was the first toothpaste to include fluoride. The therapeutic value of brushing with a fluoride toothpaste earned Crest the first American Dental Association (ADA) seal of approval.

Brands such as Crest and Colgate, which emphasized fluoride content and cavity prevention, were targeted at families with young children. These products developed strong brand loyalty. Many children, whose parents had purchased a particular product for its decay prevention continued to use the same brand as adults.

During the late 1960s and early 1970s, many new toothpaste brands were introduced, some of which emphasized cosmetic rather than therapeutic benefits. Ultra-Brite (1967), manufactured by Colgate-Palmolive, and Close-Up (1970), made by Lever Brothers, for example, focused on the whitening and breath-freshening properties of toothpaste. Advertising for these brands targeted a new audience, the teenager and young adult, who were beginning to make their own purchasing decisions, and emphasized the "sex appeal" of white teeth and fresh breath. Next came Aim, introduced by Lever Brothers in 1973. Like Close-Up, Aim was a gel, but since it contained fluoride, it was positioned as a therapeutic brand.

Through the late 1970s, the toothpaste category averaged volume growth of only 2% per year.

THE AQUA-FRESH INTRODUCTION

Prior to introducing Aqua-fresh nationally, Beecham conducted a test market in four cities. Aqua-fresh's market share objectives ranged from 8–9%. The product was positioned as a cosmetic brand with advertising emphasizing breath-freshening benefits with the tag line "Oceans of Freshness." The results were disappointing, with the product achieving only a 4% market share during the test period.

Research in the late 1970s had shown that two-thirds of U.S. households purchased both cosmetic and therapeutic brands, with different members of the household using different brands. Beecham, therefore, repositioned the brand as Double Protection Aqua-fresh, offering both breath-freshening and cavity-prevention benefits to the consumer. To communicate visually these dual attributes, the toothpaste combined a white paste component and an aqua gel component that gave the product a striped appearance. The toothpaste was awarded the American Dental Association (ADA) seal of approval because of its proven ability to fight cavities. Only five dentrifice brands were allowed to carry ADA seals on their cartons and in their advertising at that time: Aqua-fresh, Crest, Colgate, Aim, and Macleans. Beecham tested Aqua-fresh's new positioning in two markets in New York and Texas, with market share objectives of 10% and 12%, respectively. The achievement of their market share objectives resulted in a decision to launch Aqua-fresh nationally.

In January 1979, Beecham began a regional roll-out of Aqua-fresh in the

EXHIBIT 1   Toothpaste market size and competitive brand shares

	A.C. Nielsen retail sales data: 1980–84*				
	1980	1981	1982	1983	1984 (est.)
Aqua-fresh	12.9%	11.9%	11.6%	11.5%	11.4%
Crest	35.4	36.2	35.1	35.2	32.9
Colgate	17.8	18.4	22.5	22.4	23.6
Aim	10.2	9.5	9.5	9.7	9.1
Total market (thousands of dozens)	60,464	63,082	65,886	71,848	73,793
Retail $MM	$868	$974	$1,055	$1,130	$1,177
	SAMI warehouse withdrawal data: 1982–84†				
Aqua-fresh			12.1%	12.0%	12.2%
Crest			35.2	35.8	43.1
Colgate			22.9	22.8	23.3
Aim			10.0	9.0	8.6
Total market (thousands of dozen cases)			39,749	42,697	41,586

*A.C. Nielsen numbers included sales of food stores, drug stores, and mass merchandisers.

†SAMI measured product withdrawals from food chain warehouses only.

western third of the United States. Aqua-fresh was the first major new brand in the product category since Aim.

To stimulate trial of Aqua-fresh, Beecham undertook one of the largest sampling programs ever implemented in the industry. The weight of Aqua-fresh advertising during the introduction was also unprecedented. Mothers of teenagers were selected as the primary target market because management believed that teens, more than other consumers, faced the conflict between cosmetic and therapeutic benefits. Double Protection Aqua-fresh was believed especially appropriate for families with mothers concerned about cavity protection and with teens who insisted on a toothpaste that freshened breath. Advertising and promotion expenditures in the year following the introduction were $21.7 million and $23.1 million respectively. Crest, the market leader, and Aim, the number three brand, substantially increased promotions and advertising in response to the Aqua-fresh introduction, while Colgate, the number two brand, showed little reaction.

By the end of 1979, Aqua-fresh had established a nationwide market share of 12%, drawn proportionately from the three major competitors, Crest, Colgate, and Aim. Aqua-fresh achieved the number three share position in the category, with a higher share than Aim. Exhibit 1 shows Nielsen and SAMI[1] market share trends for the years following the Aqua-fresh introduction.

[1]The A.C. Nielsen Company monitored retail sales by brand/size in a sample of retail outlets nationwide. Selling Areas Marketing Inc. (SAMI), a division of Time Inc., monitored the rate of product withdrawals from trade warehouses.

Aqua-fresh, like its major competitors, was packaged in five tube sizes: 1.4 oz., 2.7 oz., 4.6 oz., 6.4 oz., and 8.2 oz. Each size of each brand was considered an "item." The percent of Aqua-fresh's 1984 volume by size was as follows:

	1.4 oz.	2.7 oz.	4.6 oz.	6.4 oz.	8.2 oz.
% volume distribution by size	7%	13%	20%	35%	25%

The percent of volume by item was similar for the other major brands, except that Crest and Colgate tended to sell a greater proportion of their volume in the smaller sizes. Manufacturer list prices of all the major brands were comparable.

The Aqua-fresh launch began a new era in dentrifrice marketing. What historically had been a stable, predictable product category became increasingly volatile and competitive. When Aqua-fresh was introduced, 25 items accounted for 80% of sales volume in the category. By 1984, 40 items accounted for 80% of toothpaste sales volume following introductions of several new flavors and gels by the market leaders.

PRODUCT CATEGORY DEVELOPMENT AFTER THE AQUA-FRESH INTRODUCTION

The first new product introduction after Aqua-fresh occurred in January 1981 when Procter & Gamble launched Advanced Formula Crest. Advertising implied that Advanced Formula's new fluoride gave consumers therapeutic benefits superior to those of its competitive brands. The product was presented to the trade at the same price as a one-for-one substitution for original Crest. The number of items in the category remained the same.

In the fall of 1981, Procter & Gamble, Colgate, and Lever Brothers all introduced new flavors. Crest Gel was the third flavor of Crest toothpaste (Crest Mint had been introduced in 1955) and increased the number of Crest items from 10 to 15. Colgate Gel and Aim Mint flavors doubled the number of items for each brand from 5 to 10. The gel introductions were the result of research showing that sweeter gels appealed to a younger audience. Colgate had identified that its users were older and, therefore, developed the gel to appeal to a younger market segment. Crest already had an image as a therapeutic brand for children. In the heavy advertising and promotion war that followed these introductions, Colgate gained market share as its new gel attracted younger users. Crest, however, lost share; its new gel simply cannibalized sales of its other two formulas.

To carry the ADA seal of acceptance, toothpaste manufacturers had to have their advertising claims cleared by the ADA. During 1981, the Aqua-fresh brand attempted to clear a plaque[2] claim with the ADA. Beecham research had shown that the three most important therapeutic attributes to consumers were: "Helps prevent cavities," "Contains fluoride," and "Helps remove plaque." The research

[2]Plaque is a sticky film on the teeth that can lead to gum disease and cavities if not removed.

also indicated that Aqua-fresh had not yet established the reputation for therapy that Crest, Colgate, and Aim had. Despite the dual-benefit positioning, Aqua-fresh users often liked the brand for its taste and breath freshening rather than for its fluoride/cavity prevention properties. Given the results, the brand group believed the plaque claim would improve Aqua-fresh's therapeutic image. However, the claim was refused by the ADA. The ADA refused to allow any dentifrice manufacturers to make the plaque claim at that time. They later established guidelines for clinical testing that would allow manufacturers to test and clear plaque claims.

Nevertheless, with the Crest Gel, Colgate Gel, and Aim Mint introductions in the fall of 1981, the brand group felt it had to reposition Aqua-fresh to address more consumer needs. Hence, in November of 1981, Beecham began shipments of new "Triple Protection Aqua-fresh" with an "even cleans stained film" claim added to the cavity prevention and breath-freshening attributes. At that time, this was as close as the ADA would allow to a plaque claim. Consumer research had indicated that stain removal was important to consumers and clinical research proved that Triple Protection Aqua-fresh was effective at cleaning stains. Triple Protection Aqua-fresh had three stripes, red, aqua, and white.

The new product was presented to the trade as a one-for-one substitution for the existing line. Because of the Crest Gel, Colgate Gel, and Aim Mint (15 items) introductions, Aqua-fresh's share of total shelf space declined. Nevertheless, after an initial share decline in January and February of 1982, the new formula helped Aqua-fresh regain and maintain market share at 11.5%, despite heavy competitive promotion and advertising support. Exhibit 2 lists the trial-generating consumer promotions fielded for each of the new brand items during their first six months.

DISTRIBUTION

Beecham Products U.S.A. employed a direct sales force which was responsible for achieving sales volume targets and implementing promotions in specific geographical regions.

Aqua-fresh was sold primarily through three channels: food stores, drug stores, and mass merchandisers. Table 1 shows Aqua-fresh and product category sales and

TABLE 1   Toothpaste sales (millions of dozens)

Aqua-fresh	1981/82	1982/83	1983/84
Food	4.8	4.8	5.2
Drug	1.6	1.6	1.8
Mass merchandiser	1.1	1.4	1.3
Total	7.5	7.8	8.3

Category	1981/82	1982/83	1983/84
Food	40.0	42.2	43.6
Drug	14.8	13.5	15.0
Mass merchandiser	9.0	11.7	13.7
Total	63.8	67.4	72.3

EXHIBIT 2 Six-month promotion activity for 1981–82 toothpaste introductions

Crest Gel 11/81–4/82	Colgate Gel 11/81–4/82*	Aim Mint 10/81–3/82	Triple Protection Aqua-fresh 1/82–6/82
25-cent mailed coupon, 12/81	10-cent FSI coupon, 11/81	25-cent FSI coupon, 10/81	Trial floor stand, 2/82
Trial floor stand, 1/82	25-cent FSI coupon, 1/82	15-cent magazine coupon, 11/81	15-cent FSI coupon, 2/82
25-cent on-pack coupon, 3/82	Mailed samples and 10-cent coupon, 1/82	15-cent FSI coupon, 12/81	12-cent mailed coupon, 4/82
	25-cent FSI coupon, 2/82	2 15-cent mailed coupons, 1/82	3 12-cent BFD coupons, 5/82
	20-cent mailed coupon, 3/82	Trial floor stand, 1/82	Trial floor stand, 6/82
	1.4 oz. trial floor stand, 3/82	15-cent FSI coupon, 2/82	
	15-cent FSI/BFD coupon, 4/82	25-cent FSI coupon, 3/82	
	25-cent in-store coupon		

*FSI = free-standing insert; BFD = Best Food Day.

EXHIBIT 3   Distribution of four toothpaste brands, 1983–84

| | Food stores—% ACV* | | | | |
| | Tubes | | | | |
	1.4 oz.	2.7 oz.	4.6 oz.	6.4 oz.	8.2 oz.
Aqua-fresh	36.3	80.9	81.4	82.8	63.9
Crest	38.0	83.4	85.8	87.2	71.3
Colgate	41.4	80.9	83.8	85.6	64.7
Aim	15.2	67.7	78.2	81.6	52.5
	Drug stores—% ACV*				
	Tubes				
	1.4 oz.	2.7 oz.	4.6 oz.	6.4 oz.	8.2 oz.
Aqua-fresh	67.7	71.1	84.8	80.5	59.1
Crest	83.0	73.1	89.1	93.9	68.7
Colgate	79.5	69.4	88.6	90.7	67.2
Aim	49.7	57.4	81.5	85.7	52.4
	Mass merchandisers—% of stores				
	Tubes				
	1.4 oz.	2.7 oz.	4.6 oz.	6.4 oz.	8.2 oz.
Aqua-fresh	53.3	69.3	80.7	97.0	82.3
Crest	44.0	73.0	74.7	99.3	96.3
Colgate	48.7	66.3	82.7	98.7	83.3
Aim	26.3	62.3	74.7	98.3	76.3

*ACV = all commodity volume

Aqua-fresh distribution penetration by channel from 1981 to 1984 in millions of dozens:[3]

Exhibit 3 shows Beecham fiscal year 1983/84 percentage ACV distribution by size for each channel.[4]

Food stores accounted for 60% of category dollar sales in 1984. Historically, health and beauty aid (HBA) products had been a small part of most food stores' business; however, a trend toward larger HBA sections in food stores developed in the early 1980s as they sought to emphasize higher margin merchandise. Food stores began to treat toothpaste as a loss leader to generate consumer traffic. As

---

[3]In 1983–84, the average number of ounces of toothpaste per unit sold was 6.04 (total), 5.84 (food), 6.0 (drug) and 6.65 (mass merchandiser).

[4]An item with 70% ACV (all commodity volume) in grocery stores was distributed in stores that accounted for 70% of the sales through all grocery stores.

a result, food stores became more demanding regarding promotional offers from manufacturers. Most food stores tended to stock three sizes of each major brand flavor. Reflecting the number of items pressing for limited shelf space, many food stores did not carry weaker brands.

Drug stores, on the other hand, relied on HBA products as a major source of sales. For this reason, drug stores stocked most brands and sizes of toothpaste. However, they were also pressing for promotional offers to give them an edge in competing with the food stores. Drug stores considered toothpaste an important traffic builder that could lead to the sale of other higher margin products. They, therefore, gave brands feature advertising support, maintained an average of four items per brand flavor, and realized lower margins on toothpaste than food stores, passing promotional savings through to the consumer. Drug stores accounted for 20% of category sales.

Mass merchandisers accounted for 20% of category sales volume and carried an average of four items per brand flavor. Because they typically offered the consumer an "everyday low price," trade promotions were not as important for mass merchandisers. Mass merchandisers featured toothpaste less frequently than food or drug stores, but when a feature was run, it usually generated greater percentage sales increases than a feature in either of the other two channels.

Beecham's sales force was smaller than those of the category leaders, Procter & Gamble and Colgate-Palmolive. Therefore, Aqua-fresh distribution was better in the larger chains and in regions of the country where such chains were predominant. Sales to the trade in New York City, for example, were complicated by the high number of small, independent supermarkets. The sales force was also too small to devote much time to setting up displays. Therefore, the Aqua-fresh brand team relied heavily on prepacked display pieces that could be handled easily by retailers.

As competition in the toothpaste category became fiercer and item proliferation put pressure on the shelf space available to any single brand in the category, the salesperson's job became more challenging. The sales force had to handle complex Aqua-fresh promotional calendars and monitor multiple competitive trade promotions at any one time. Adding shelf space for Aqua-fresh became increasingly difficult. Sales management developed new sales pitches to defend Aqua-fresh's shelf space. For example, the organizer, shown in Exhibit 4, focused on Aqua-fresh's contribution per item compared to the contribution per item of competitive brands with broader product lines.

AQUA-FRESH MARKETING

Brand management relied on advertising, trade promotion, and consumer promotion to market Aqua-fresh. Exhibit 5 shows media and promotion spending in dollars and as a percentage of sales for Aqua-fresh and the other major brands for 1979/80 through 1983/84. Brand management estimated that 70% of Aqua-fresh, Aim, and Colgate sales volume was shipped to the trade on deal; the corresponding figure for Crest was 60%.

EXHIBIT 4   Aqua-fresh trade organizer

A Category that Draws the Consumer
Dentifrice Dollar Volume

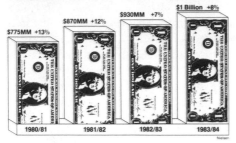

$775MM +13% | $870MM +12% | $930MM +7% | $1 Billion +8%

1980/81   1981/82   1982/83   1983/84

Nielsen

- ☐ Over last four years category has grown dramatically.
    Dollar Volume up 30% = 5.5 million cases.
- ☐ Aqua-fresh, Colgate, and Crest have accounted for nearly all of the category's growth.
- ☐ 7 of the top 10 HBA items are toothpastes— Aqua-fresh, Colgate, and Crest draw the consumer. (Progressive Grocer)
- ☐ Nearly 100% household penetration—every consumer is a potential sale.

Aqua-fresh®
#1 share/SKU

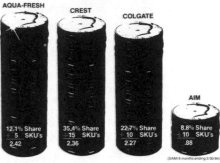

AQUA-FRESH | CREST | COLGATE | AIM

12.1% Share ÷ 5 SKU's 2.42 | 35.4% Share ÷ 15 SKU's 2.36 | 22.7% Share ÷ 10 SKU's 2.27 | 8.8% Share ÷ 10 SKU's .88

(SAMI 6 months ending 3/30/84)

- ☐ Aqua-fresh #1 seller per SKU, outselling Crest and Colgate. Outsells Aim 3 to 1.
- ☐ By flavor, Aqua-fresh is vying for the #1 position with a 12.1% share.
- ☐ Aqua-fresh sales are about equal to Crest Regular and Colgate Regular.

Aqua-fresh®
is #1 in Inventory Turns

AQUA-FRESH—10.8 Turns/Year

CREST—9.5

COLGATE—9.3

AIM—7.1

Aqua-fresh turns this much faster

13%
16%
52%

Aqua-fresh returns your investment faster than any brand in the category—in fact, 52% faster than Aim.

Aqua-fresh inventory turns nearly 11 times a year—with 2% 30 terms, you sell Aqua-fresh before you pay for it!

Fast turns + unsurpassed terms = Best Profit Return—Aqua-fresh

Aqua-fresh®
IS #1 IN MAKING MONEY
Annual Profit Return Per Inventory Dollar Invested

Aqua-fresh   AQUA-FRESH $2.48

Crest   CREST $2.19

Colgate   COLGATE $2.14

Aim   AIM $1.63
    (Based on Average Profit Margin—Nielsen)

REACT TO THE FACTS

- ☐ Aqua-fresh delivers more profit than Crest, Colgate and Aim.
- ☐ Aqua-fresh share of inventories is too lean in proportion to category shares.
- ☐ Aim inventories are too fat in proportion to category shares.
- ☐ Aqua-fresh out-of-stocks cost you money—
    Consumer delays purchase or
    Buys a brand with shorter terms of sale

SOLUTION: Carry all 5 Sizes
    Make Aqua-fresh share of inventory = share of sales

EXHIBIT 4   (continued)

Aqua-fresh®

#1 with your Promotion Dollars

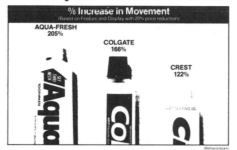

% Increase in Movement
(Based on Feature and Display with 20% price reduction)

AQUA-FRESH 205%

COLGATE 166%

CREST 122%

(Behaviorscan)

▢ Aqua-fresh sells better on promotion than Crest or Colgate

▢ Promoting a toothpaste is a consumer draw provided the brand you use is recognized by the consumer.

▢ *Feature and display Aqua-fresh to get the most out of your promotion dollars.*

▢ It's easier and more profitable to promote Aqua-fresh

Aqua-fresh	1 SKU/size
Crest	3 SKU's/size
Colgate	2 SKU's/size
Aim	2 SKU's/size

Aqua-fresh®

Best Return Comes from Feature and Display

Based on 20% Price Reduction	% Increase in Movement	WEEKLY MOVEMENT
		CS
Price Reduction	+47%	CS
Price Reduction + Feature	+186%	CS
Price Reduction + Feature + Display	+843%	CS

Based on 30% Price Reduction	% Increase in Movement	WEEKLY MOVEMENT
		CS
Price Reduction	+85%	CS
Price Reduction + Feature	+260%	CS
Price Reduction + Feature + Display	+1,087%	CS

$ _____

Aqua-fresh®

Sells the Consumer

Advertising:

▢ Reaching 90% of all households

▢ 588 GRP's a month

▢ 16 commercials/week

Consumer Promotion:

▢ 24 million 20¢ mailed coupons week of 9/30/84

Action Plan:

54-132AF   BEECHAM PRODUCTS, Pittsburgh, PA 15230   Printed in U.S.A.

EXHIBIT 5   Estimated advertising and promotion expenditures by brand

Category media spending
(millions of dollars)

	1979/80		1980/81		1981/82		1982/83		1983/84		1984/85	
	$MM	% Sales	$MM	% Sales	$MM	% Sales	$MM	% Sales	$MM	% Sales	$MM	% Sales
Aqua-fresh	$21.7	27%	$20.7	25%	$19.5	23%	$24.5	21%	$22.9	18%	$21.6	16%
Crest	25.8	9	29.4	13	48.4	18	36.9	11	37.0	10	31.0	10
Colgate	18.1	13	17.0	15	27.7	20	26.1	12	30.0	13	28.0	12
Aim	15.7	19	15.5	25	21.3	33	17.6	19	19.5	18	18.0	20

Category promotion spending
(millions of dollars)

	1979/80		1980/81		1981/82		1982/83		1983/84		1984/85	
	$MM	% Sales	$MM	% Sales	$MM	% Sales	$MM	% Sales	$MM	% Sales	$MM	% Sales
Aqua-fresh	$23.1	28%	$13.9	17%	$17.4	21%	$20.6	18%	$29.9	24%	$30.8	23%
Crest	28.1	10	31.8	14	31.1	12	36.1	11	65.1	17	55.4	14
Colgate	19.4	14	24.8	22	41.0	29	40.6	19	44.3	18	52.1	18
Aim	10.5	13	12.9	21	19.1	29	15.4	17	24.8	23	16.9	17

Aqua-fresh promotion spending
(thousands of dollars)

	1980/81	1981/82	1982/83	1983/84	1984/85
Price packs	$ 7,278	$ 4,642	$ 9,349	$12,512	$12,829
Trade merchandising allowances	4,088	8,984	8,273	9,590	10,353
Trial events and other	2,569	3,731	3,009	7,787	7,620
Total	$13,935	$17,357	$20,631	$29,889	$30,802

100

Advertising

Aqua-fresh spent its advertising dollars primarily in television. Television spots focused on the brand's attributes physically represented by the toothpaste's stripes. Exhibit 6 presents a storyboard from a typical triple protection Aqua-fresh commercial. The major objectives of Aqua-fresh advertising were to promote awareness of the brand, communicate product benefits, and emphasize ADA approval. In 1984, brand management estimated that a 17% share of voice was necessary to maintain Aqua-fresh's market share. They projected 1984–85 advertising expenditures of $21.6 million on sales of $134 million or 8.4 million dozens.

Trade Promotions

Manufacturers often offered a trade promotion or temporary price discount on a product for a specified period of time to boost short-term sales. The allowance was often dependent on the retailer providing merchandising support (retail price cut, feature advertisement, and/or special display) for the product during the promotion period. Although increased short-term sales and consumer trial might be generated, trade promotions rarely resulted in sustained sales volume and market share increases. Manufacturers encouraged the trade to accept promoted product packed in displays or floor stands to maximize sales.

In 1980, trade promotion expenditures by packaged goods manufacturers in the United States were estimated at $6.5 billion, with health and beauty aids trade promotions alone accounting for $3.3 billion of this total.[5] Trade allowances for toothpastes since 1980 had increased in step with manufacturer price increases, keeping the dead net, the unit cost to the trade after all allowances, at roughly the same level.[6] The result was more money for retailers and escalating trade promotion expenditures by manufacturers.

Aqua-fresh trade promotions frequently included allowances with merchandising requirements. Trade promotion was considered so important to the brand that one manager characterized the marketing planning process as follows: "First we figure the trade promotion spending required to be competitive; then, we add the media cost; then, whatever is left goes for trial events." The amount of the allowance and therefore the dead net cost varied depending on the size of the item on deal and the brand group's projections of expected competitive offers. The objective was to offer dead nets which were comparable to those of its major competitors. Proof of merchandising performance, such as an advertising tear sheet or a picture of a display, was necessary before Beecham paid a merchandising allowance.

Aggressive promotion was necessary to ensure merchandising support for the brand and to retain distribution of as many stockkeeping units (SKUs) as possible.

[5]Reported in Paul W. Farris and John A. Quelch, *Advertising and Promotion Management* (Radnor, PA: Chilton Book Company, 1983).

[6]The dead net cost was the cost of an item to the retailer after all allowances had been subtracted from the manufacturer's price.

EXHIBIT 6   Aqua-fresh television advertisement

FATHER: What's this...

a space age toothpaste!

MOTHER: No! It's our Aqua-fresh with a brand new see-through top.
TEEN: I can see its Triple Protection Formula!
MOTHER: Only Aqua-fresh has it.

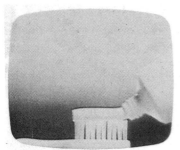

(VO): The maximum fluoride protection of the leading paste...

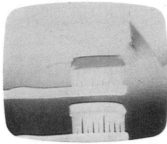

all the breath freshener of the leading gel...

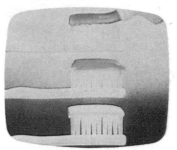

and gentle cleaners that even remove stained film...

SFX: SWOOSH
concentrated in one complete toothpaste.

MOTHER: And tests prove mothers prefer Aqua-fresh to the other leading brands

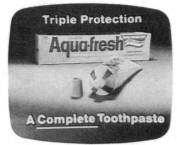

ANNCR (VO): Triple Protection Aqua-fresh. A complete toothpaste.

During periods of competitive introductions of new items, promotional expenditures to the trade were critical to sustaining shelf space. The 1983/84 shares of retailer feature advertising in the toothpaste category obtained by Aqua-fresh and the other major brands by type of distribution channel are shown in Table 2.

TABLE 2 Shares of retailer feature
advertising of toothpaste

	Food	Drug/mass merchandiser
Aqua-fresh	14%	11%
Crest	17	17
Colgate	24	24
Aim	13	13

The Crest brand was supported by regular trade promotions on key sizes plus Procter & Gamble's Cooperative Merchandising Agreement (CMA). The CMA enabled retailers to accrue a 10 cents–50 cents allowance per statistical case on Procter & Gamble products. A retailer could receive these allowances if it provided special merchandising support. Allowances earned on one product could be applied to the merchandising of any other product sold by Procter & Gamble's Health and Personal Care Division. The CMA helped to ensure Procter & Gamble of distribution of its weaker products. A further benefit was that Procter & Gamble did not have to sell Crest consistently at a high discount to gain merchandising support for the brand. Colgate offered a similar program. Beecham did not offer a CMA. Instead, Beecham offered the trade more lucrative bonus allowances tied to specific promotions. This gave Beecham tighter control over expenditures and greater assurance of extra merchandising performance for specific events.

Consumer Promotions

Consumer promotions typically aimed either to switch users of competitive brands to the promoted product or, secondarily, to reward current users. Aqua-fresh brand management used three types of consumer promotion: price packs, coupons, and trial sizes to generate trial of Aqua-fresh. Trial was viewed as an important objective as the brand was relatively new and consumer research showed that most consumers who tried Aqua-fresh preferred it to the other leading brands.

Price packs, with a standard price reduction (for example, "20 cents off") printed on the package were frequently run on the 4.6, 6.4, and 8.2 oz. sizes of Aqua-fresh, Colgate, and Aim. Retailers were paid the amount of the price reduction and were therefore obligated to pass the reduction on to the consumer. Promotions on the 8.2 oz. size offered the advantage of taking purchasers out of the market for a longer period. In 1984, Aqua-fresh price pack values on the 8.2 oz. size were 35 cents, while Aim and Colgate offered 40 cents and 30 cents respectively. Twin packs or "buy-two-get-one-free" offers were frequently fielded on the 6.4 oz. size to take the consumer out of the market for an even longer time. Crest combined a banded pack with an on-pack premium, offering two packs banded together with free Lego building blocks to stimulate sales to families with small children. All manufacturers fielded trade promotion offers in conjunction with price packs to ensure maximum retail merchandising support.

Price packs were known to generate heavier-than-normal retail sales especially when supported by extra merchandising effort by the trade in the form of end-aisle displays and feature advertisements. Price packs were preferred over trade promotions alone since the value of the promotion was typically passed through to the consumer in the form of a lower price rather than pocketed by the retailer. Some retailers, however, especially those that pursued an everyday low price strategy,[7] were resistant to price packs. Price packs typically required special handling. A new UPC number had to be coded into store computer systems. Trade resistance prompted Procter & Gamble to curtail Crest price-pack promotions in the spring of 1983, apparently in an effort to improve the company's relations with the trade. The other manufacturers offered trade accounts off-invoice allowances as alternatives to price packs. These allowances were less attractive than price-pack offers and, therefore, accounted for a small portion of promoted volume.

While price packs permitted regular users to stock up on inventory during a price-pack promotion, coupon promotions required a consumer to have a separate coupon for each unit purchased. Price packs were considered by some to detract more than coupons from a brand's image and to make consumers less willing to purchase a product at its regular price. On the other hand, a coupon was physically separated from the package. The timing and duration of a price-pack promotion were critical to its impact. If a nonuser were in the middle of a purchase cycle during the short (usually one week) period of a store's price-pack promotion, the price incentive would be less likely to motivate trial and the consumer would be missed. Coupons, on the other hand, permitted the consumer to choose the timing of the purchases but were not always effective in generating special merchandising support from retailers because of the extended period of the offer.

Aqua-fresh offered some coupons to stimulate trial. Consumer trial was particularly important to the brand as blind home-use tests had shown that consumers significantly preferred Aqua-fresh to the other major brands. Aqua-fresh coupons were distributed either through the mail, in the Best Food Day (BFD) sections of newspapers, or as a part of a free-standing-insert (FSI) in Sunday newspapers. Research had demonstrated that direct mail couponing generated higher redemption rates among triers; however, this method was also more expensive in terms of cost per thousand coupons distributed. Exhibit 7 shows planned coupon costs for the 1984–85 fiscal year.

A trial-size offer of 1.4 oz. tubes prepriced at 39 cents was also used to stimulate brand trial. Retail inventory turnover for the trial size was high versus the normal rate. Retailers could achieve higher than normal margins on trial sizes. They were shipped in prepacked displays that required little special handling. Because of the high margins, the high turnover, and the minimal handling requirements, retailers

---

[7]"Everyday low price" retailers used their promotion allowances to offer consistently low prices on the same items from one week to the next, as opposed to advertising very low sale prices on a different set of "hot specials" each week.

EXHIBIT 7   1984–85 Aqua-fresh coupons*

1. 20¢ Free-standing insert:	
Distribution (43MM × $2.25/M)	$ 98M
Printing	30M
Redemption (43MM × 3.1% × $.30)†	400M
Total cost	$ 528M
Circulation	30MM
Cost per thousand delivered	$17.60
2. 20¢ BFD coupon	
Distribution (45MM × $1.95/M)	$ 88M
Redemption (45 × 2.8% × $.30)	378M
Total cost	$ 466M
Circulation	45MM
Cost per thousand delivered	$10.36
3. 20¢ Mailed coupon	
Distribution (23.9MM × $6.00/M)	$ 143M
Printing	12M
20¢ redemption (23.9MM × 5.5% × $.30)	395M
Total cost	$ 550M
Circulation	23.9MM
Cost per thousand delivered	$23.02
4. 20¢ Mailed coupon	
Distribution (30MM × $9.75/M)	$ 293M
20¢ redemption (30MM × 8.0% × $.30)	720M
Total cost	$1,013M
Circulation	30MM
Cost per thousand delivered	$33.77
Total year: Four coupons	
Cost: $528M + $466M + $550M + 1,013M =	$2,557M
Coupons delivered: 30MM + 45MM + 23.9MM + 30MM =	128.9MM
Weighted average cost per thousand delivered	$19.84

*National coupons drops only. Some regional coupons were also fielded in defense against regional competitive activity.

†Handling each redeemed coupon, regardless of value, cost 10 cents.

found this type of promotion particularly attractive. In addition, regular brand users were unlikely to purchase trial sizes because they were too small.

As the toothpaste product category became increasingly competitive, trade and consumer promotion grew in importance. As one manager said:

> Since Aqua-fresh is the third leading brand, trade promotion expenditures are important to ensure that the trade will continue to stock our product. But Aqua-fresh can't afford to escalate trade promotions to get additional merchandising support because the competition will meet the increase and we will have accomplished nothing.

MARKET RESEARCH

A market research study was conducted to measure the effect of the introduction of Triple Protection Aqua-fresh on consumer attitudes and usage. The study, conducted in February 1983, had the additional objectives of measuring the effect of the Triple Protection introduction on the brand's therapeutic image and the impact of the Crest Gel and the Colgate Gel introductions.

Brand management concluded that the introduction of Triple Protection Aqua-fresh and the competitive gels had not substantially changed the unaided awareness, past four-week usage, or retention levels of the major brands. There were, however, modest improvements in the therapeutic image of Aqua-fresh and in the Aqua-fresh trial rate. While brand management believed that changes in advertising to emphasize Aqua-fresh's ADA seal of approval and therapeutic attributes could further improve the brand's therapeutic image, there was no agreement as to the best way to stimulate additional trial of the brand. Some managers believed that a nationwide sampling program would produce the best results, but others thought that trial sizes would be more cost effective. One manager was convinced that in-store displays were the key to stimulating new trial of Aqua-fresh and advocated increased spending for trade promotions. However, none of the managers could prove that one method was more effective than another.

BEHAVIORSCAN RESEARCH

Beecham executives decided to use BehaviorScan® research from Information Resources, Inc. (IRI)[8] to evaluate the effectiveness of various types of promotion. IRI had developed a system of tracking consumer purchasing behavior for most products sold through grocery and drug stores. This system used Universal Product Code (UPC) scanners to record information on the purchases of selected panels of about 2,500 households in eight U.S. markets.

The households in the eight consumer panels were randomly selected. Each was given an I.D. card to present to the store cashier upon checkout. This I.D. card signaled the computer to record the purchase data in the file of the appropriate panel member. IRI randomly selected members of each panel to receive prizes as an incentive for continued cooperation. Because of the minimal work required of panel members, about 70% of consumers who were asked to be on a panel accepted, giving IRI a representative sample of consumers in each market.

IRI's eight markets were selected on the following criteria:

1. Each market had to be large enough to provide meaningful results but small enough to be manageable since IRI had to arrange to provide UPC scanners to retailers in the area.

2. Residents had to do at least 95% of their grocery shopping in the market area.

---

[8]See "Information Resources, Inc. (A)," Harvard Business School case 9-583-053.

3. Markets in which a large proportion of all commodity volume was accounted for by a few major chains rather than a variety of small independent stores were preferred.

4. Each market had to be served by a newspaper with high readership so that newspaper advertising could be controlled and monitored.

5. Markets had to have cable television to permit control and monitoring of television advertising.

6. Markets had to be demographically similar to the U.S. average.

7. The boundaries of the market had to be clear and spillover of media from adjacent markets had to be minimal.

Because of these restrictions, some critics claimed that the BehaviorScan results were not representative of purchasing patterns in the United States. They cited the size and isolation of the markets as problems for products whose strongest markets tended to be urban areas. Most BehaviorScan markets were also located in "C" counties, or counties with lower measured buying power that, consequently, had lower coupon distribution. Consequently, to test coupons in BehaviorScan markets, distribution levels to those markets had to be increased.

In addition to tracking consumer purchases, IRI also monitored consumer and trade promotion activity and in-store merchandising for each brand. This allowed IRI to report information on competitive activity. The effectiveness of different types of promotions and merchandising could also be assessed by relating this information to consumer purchasing patterns.

By using BehaviorScan research, Aqua-fresh brand management hoped to resolve the following issues:

1. What was the relative value of trade and consumer promotions in increasing sales, market share, and consumer brand loyalty?

2. Should promotion dollars be shifted from price packs to couponing or other trial events?

3. Which consumer promotions were most effective in stimulating trial?

Given these objectives, Beecham first purchased toothpaste data from IRI's *Marketing Fact Book.* This book, compiled quarterly and annually, summarized BehaviorScan data for over 150 product categories. The book reported brand sales, market shares, volume per purchase occasion, number of purchases in a specified period, average retail prices, and the percentage of volume purchased on deal by the trade. The *Marketing Fact Book* also provided information on competitive brand purchases by households purchasing Aqua-fresh and the percentage of volume purchased by consumers on promotion. This information is reported in Exhibit 8; Exhibit 9 shows the *Marketing Fact Book* report on trade promotions in the toothpaste category.

IRI was commissioned by Beecham's market research department to conduct three customized studies for Aqua-fresh brand management. These measured brand loyalty, the effectiveness of different types of consumer promotions on trial and

EXHIBIT 8 Competitive sets among buyers of selected products*
(% of category volume and ranking)

| | Total households | | Aqua-fresh | | Colgate | | | | Crest | | | | Aim | |
| | | | | | Gel | | Paste | | Gel | | Paste | | | |
	Rank	%	Rank	%	Rank	%	Rank	%	Rank	%	Rank	%	Rank	%
Crest Paste	1	27.8	2	17.5	3	14.6	2	16.2	2	25.2	1	46.8	2	17.3
Colgate Paste	2	13.6	4	8.8	2	16.5	1	40.2	4	6.9	3	9.0	5	8.0
Crest Gel	3	12.9	3	9.4	4	9.4	5	6.3	1	32.9	2	12.0	4	8.6
Aqua-fresh	4	10.0	1	29.5	5	8.4	4	6.4	3	7.9	4	7.2	3	10.7
Colgate Gel	5	7.9	6	7.7	1	27.7	3	10.4	5	6.5	6	5.3	6	7.8
Aim	6	7.7	5	8.6	6	6.4	6	5.1	6	6.3	5	5.7	1	28.1

*Read as follows: In the case of the Aqua-fresh column, of those households who purchased Aqua-fresh, 17.5% of their annual toothpaste volume purchased was Crest Paste, which ranked as the second highest brand volume purchased. Among total households, Aqua-fresh had a 10% volume share.

Percent of volume purchased via price deal*
(index vs. total category purchases)

| | Total households | | Aqua-fresh | | Colgate | | | | Crest | | | | Aim | |
| | | | | | Gel | | Paste | | Gel | | Paste | | | |
	Deal	Index	Deal	Index	Deal	Index	Deal	Index	Deal	Index	Deal	Index	Deal	Index
Total category	26.8%	100	30.9%	100	31.1%	100	31.2%	100	28.6%	100	29.0%	100	32.8%	100
Aqua-fresh	28.3	106	28.3	92	38.6	124	40.7	130	31.3	109	32.9	113	35.5	108
Aim	26.8	100	33.2	107	36.7	118	39.0	125	28.4	99	32.0	110	26.8	82
Colgate total	28.5	106	36.8	119	28.6	92	28.1	90	31.7	111	32.1	111	39.3	120
Gel	28.6	107	37.2	120	28.6	92	26.7	86	33.6	117	32.9	113	39.4	120
Paste	28.5	106	36.5	118	28.7	92	28.5	91	29.8	104	31.6	109	39.2	120
Crest total	28.8	107	34.1	110	32.8	105	35.1	113	28.5	100	28.6	99	37.5	114
Gel	28.6	107	31.5	102	30.7	99	32.2	103	28.6	100	27.2	94	36.4	111
Paste	28.9	108	35.6	115	34.1	110	36.3	116	28.4	99	28.9	100	38.1	116

Source: IRI *Marketing Fact Book*.

Note: Read as follows: In the case of the Aqua-fresh column, of those households who purchased Aqua-fresh, 30.9% of their annual toothpaste volume was purchased on price deal, 28.3% of their Aqua-fresh volume was purchased on deal, 33.2% of their Aim volume was purchased on deal, etc.

*Price deals included store coupons, manufacturer coupons, price packs, and/or features.

EXHIBIT 9 Beecham IRI *Marketing Fact Book* toothpaste results: 1984

Base measures for response to 10% price change	% Vol. change	Rank*
Price increase	−14.5	39
Price reduction	18.7	62
Price reduction with ad feature only	54.6	91
Price reduction with store display only	52.8	109
Price reduction with both ad and display	95.1	108
Synergy for ad and display combined†	6.4	90

Summary of model brands included in the analysis	Share	
	Min	Max
Total Aqua-fresh toothpaste	9.4	15.0
Total Colgate Gel toothpaste	5.6	9.6
Total Colgate Regular toothpaste	10.2	19.7
Total Ultra-Brite toothpaste	2.2	4.8
Total Aim toothpaste	6.0	10.4
Total Close-Up toothpaste	3.3	11.7
Total Check	0.8	2.1
Total Crest Gel toothpaste	9.6	17.0
Total Crest Mint toothpaste	9.3	13.0
Total Crest Regular toothpaste	11.0	15.8

These brands accounted for 88.3% of category volume.
35,444 Observations in the analysis
Average brand share was 8.9%

Derived measures for response to 10% price reduction	% Vol. change	Rank
Difference with:		
Ad feature vs. price reduction only	35.9	91
Store display vs. price reduction only	34.1	111
Ad and display vs. price reduction only	76.4	110

Ratio measures:	Ratio	Rank
Ad feature to price reduction only	2.92	90
Display only to price reduction only	2.82	110
Ad and display to price reduction only	5.08	104
Feature only to display only	1.03	16
Feature and display to feature only	1.74	104
Feature and display only	1.80	70

Data summary by promotion type	Percentages		Average % price reduction
	Volume	Observations	
No ad feature or display	71.0	82.2	6.8
Ad feature only	10.9	7.4	12.5
Store display only	11.8	7.9	11.9
Ad feature and store display	6.4	2.5	17.7

* Indicates toothpaste's rank out of the 116 product categories reported in the *Marketing Fact Book*. For example, in the case of a 10% price increase, there were 38 product categories where the price increase would have resulted in less than a 14.5% decrease in volume.

† To measure the synergy between ad and display in combination, the "feature only" and "display only" effects were subtracted from the combination of "ad and display" (95.1 − 52.8 − 54.6 = −12.3). The price effect, 18.7, was then added back to arrive at a synergy of 6.4.

repurchase, and the effect of merchandising allowances on brand sales. Four BehaviorScan markets were included in the analysis: Pittsfield, Massachusetts; Marion, Indiana; Eau Claire, Wisconsin; and Midland, Texas.

Data used in the brand loyalty analysis were collected from February 1, 1981 to October 31, 1982. Households purchasing each of the four main toothpaste brands were divided into three groups: (1) low loyalty (the brand accounts for 40% or less of the household's total toothpaste consumption); (2) medium loyalty (the brand accounts for 40% to 70% of the household's total toothpaste consumption); (3) high loyalty (the brand accounts for more than 70% of the household's total toothpaste consumption). Detailed findings of the research are presented in Exhibit 10. Based on the results, Aqua-fresh brand management concluded:

☐ Aqua-fresh and Aim, the newer major brands, enjoyed less loyalty than Crest and Colgate, the older, larger share brands.

☐ Households with low brand loyalty were more likely than households with high brand loyalty to purchase toothpaste on deal and/or with a coupon.

EXHIBIT 10   Brand loyalty in toothpaste category

	1983*			
	Aqua-fresh	Colgate	Aim	Crest
% of households buying brand one or more times	18.6	25.6	12.9	40.8
Share of category	11.3	21.3	7.3	39.4
Total no. of oz. of toothpaste purchased per year per household	36.3	36.9	39.7	34.0
Total no. of oz. of brand purchased per year per household	12.0	16.7	11.4	19.4
Brand loyalty (% of total oz. purchased that were specific brand)	34.1	45.3	28.7	51.0
Distribution of loyalty among purchasers				
A. *% of Brand Buyers*				
Low loyalty (40% of less of cat. req.)	57.1	44.2	59.1	27.5
Medium loyalty (40% to 70% cat. req.)	17.1	21.3	19.1	19.9
High loyalty (70%+ of cat. req.)	25.8	34.5	21.8	52.6
	100.0	100.0	100.0	100.0
B. *% of Brand Volume*				
Low loyalty (40% or less cat. req.)	39.9	23.7	43.8	14.6
Medium loyalty (40% to 70% cat. req.)	23.7	24.7	25.6	18.1
High loyalty (70%+ of cat. req.)	36.4	51.6	30.6	67.3
	100.0	100.0	100.0	100.0
C. *% of Brand Bought on Deal* (by each group)				
Low loyalty (40% or less cat. req.)	37.4	37.0	31.2	33.6
Medium loyalty (40% to 70% cat. req.)	30.4	33.6	20.8	32.1
High loyalty (70%+ of cat. req.)	25.4	25.0	15.7	22.5
	31.9	29.9	23.8	25.8

*Timing: 1983 = 11/1/82–10/30/83.

☐   Households with low brand loyalty tended to be "loyal" to a set of brands rather than to a single brand. They purchased whichever brand in the set was on deal at the time they were in the market.

The analysis of trial promotion effectiveness covered a mailed sample, a 12 cent free-standing insert coupon (FSI), three 12-cent Best Food Day (BFD) coupons (fielded and analyzed as one event), price packs, and a 39-cent prepriced 1.4 oz. trial size. The study focused on trial among new users, defined as those households who had not purchased Aqua-fresh within the 24 weeks preceding each promotion and repurchase among both new users and current users. Exhibit 11 summarizes the results of the analysis. The major conclusions were:

☐   Trial-size and coupon events reached a greater percentage of new users, at 60% and 47% respectively, than did price-pack promotions, at 36–41%. For perspective, 35% of nonpromoted open stock purchases were made by new users. (Even with the high level of trials on open stock, brand management believed that promotions to stimulate trials were necessary for Aqua-fresh because of competitive promotions and Aqua-fresh's relatively low level of brand loyalty.)

☐   Price packs were the most cost-efficient trial events, generating revenues of 13 cents to 39 cents (depending on the size of the promoted item) per new user generated versus one-sixteenth cent for the trial-size event and 3 cents for coupons. (These values did not take account of repeat business and the strength of the revenue stream generated by a given event.)

☐   The 1.4 oz. trial size produced the highest level of new user repurchase within 12 weeks and, along with the 12-cent BFD coupon, generated higher levels of repurchase within 24 weeks than did the FSI coupon or the price packs. However, because the BFD coupons were fielded over a four-week period, many of the coupon repurchases might have been made with a second coupon.

☐   Aqua-fresh purchases tended to be limited to a single tube. Consumers did not typically make multiple purchases of Aqua-fresh when it was on promotion.

The third study by IRI analyzed the impact of price changes and retailer merchandising on the sales of Aqua-fresh, Crest, Colgate, and Aim during the 78-week period from July 26, 1982 to January 22, 1984. Findings from the research are presented in Exhibit 12. Brand management concluded the following:

☐   The degree of consumer loyalty exhibited by a brand was inversely proportional to the brand's promotion sensitivity. Aqua-fresh and Aim displayed a higher level of sensitivity to trade merchandising than Crest or Colgate.

☐   Given that Aqua-fresh fielded ten promotion events annually and that an average trade account featured and/or displayed Aqua-fresh during 10.3% of the weeks, the average trade account appeared to be providing merchandising support for half of the promotion events.

EXHIBIT 11 BehaviorScan trial promotion effectiveness analysis'

1. Promotion efficiency by type of promotion

	1.4 oz. Trial size	12¢ Coupons* FSI + BFD	Price packs		
			4.6 oz.	6.4 oz.	8.2 oz.
Average no. of households purchasing	4,162M	1,867M	1,192M	2,518M	1,842M
% new users†	60%	47%	41%	39%	36%
Average no. of new users	2,497M	877M	488M	982M	663M
Revenue from equivalent events‡	$ 245M	$ 355M	$1,212M	$ 997M	$1,516M
Less cost of equivalent events	$ 206M	$ 328M	$1,149M	$ 820M	$1,258M
Net revenues:					
Total	$ 39M	$ 27M	$ 63M	$ 177M	$ 258M
Per purchase	$0.009	$0.014	$0.053	$0.070	$0.140
Per new user purchase	$0.016	$0.031	$0.129	$0.180	$0.389

*FSI = free-standing insert in newspaper; BFD = Best Food Day section of newspaper.

†New users were defined as those households who had not purchased Aqua-fresh within the 24 weeks preceding the promotion.

‡Equivalent events indicate that revenues and costs were calculated as if the same promotion had been national in scope.

2. Net revenue from Aqua-fresh coupons

	12¢ FSI	12¢ BFD	20¢ FSI	20¢ BFD	20¢ Mailed
Average no. of households purchasing	1,281M	2,453M	2,155M	1,296M	2,870
% new users	49%	46%	55%	54%	57%
Average no. of new users	628M	1,128M	1,185M	700M	1,636M
Revenue from equivalent events	$ 395M	$ 315M	$ 580M	$ 622M	$1,202M
Less cost of equivalent events	$ 356M	$ 300M	$ 528M	$ 619M	$1,143M
Redemption rate	2.7%	2.4%	3.1%	2.8%	8.0%
Net revenue:					
Total (thousands of dollars)	$ 39M	$ 15	$ 52	$ 3	$ 59
Per purchase	$0.030	$0.006	$0.024	$0.002	$0.021
Per new user purchase	$0.062	$0.013	$0.044	$0.004	$0.036

3. Aqua-fresh new user repeat purchase*

Among new buyers: percent repeat within	12¢ FSI 10-81	12¢ BFD 5-82	1.4 oz. Trial 4-83	30¢† 6.4 oz. 4-83	15¢† 4.6 oz. 5-83	35¢† 8.2 oz. 5-83	30¢† 6.4 oz. 7-83	15¢† 4.6 oz. 9-83
12 weeks	13%	19%	33%	24%	15%	21%	17%	17%
24 weeks	19	43	36	29	31	30	23	25

*Read as follows: Among new buyers who first purchased Aqua-fresh with the 12¢ FSI coupon delivered 10-81, 13% purchased Aqua-fresh again within 12 weeks and 19% within 24 weeks.

†Price pack

EXHIBIT 12   BehaviorScan price and promotion sensitivity analysis

1. Increase in total brand sales by type of promotion

	20% Price cut	20% Price cut + display	20% Price cut + feature ad	20% Price cut + display + feature ad
Aqua-fresh	50%	122%	113%	152%
Crest	45	91	70	122
Colgate	52	105	106	166
Aim	45	154	155	198

2. Effect on sales of a competitive 20% price reduction

	% Change in volume			
20% Price reduction	Aqua-fresh	Crest	Colgate	Aim
Aqua-fresh	—	−3%	−3%	−7%
Crest	−9%	—	−5	−18
Colgate	−5	−5	—	−6
Aim	−5	−2	−6	—

3. Toothpaste promotion sensitivity*

	% of Weeks with feature or display	% of Brand volume moved by feature and display	Index of % volume moved to % weeks with feature and display	% of Brand volume purchased by households with low brand loyalty
Aqua-fresh	10.3%	17.9%	174	30.9%
Crest	21.4	27.4	128	14.6
Colgate	12.9	20.7	160	23.7
Aim	8.2	16.8	205	43.8

*Read as follows: For Aqua-fresh, 17.9% of brand volume was sold when brand was featured or displayed. Aqua-fresh had feature or display support during 10.3% of the weeks measured.

4. Increase in Aqua-fresh sales by promotion type*

Price change	No feature or display	Price pack only	Display	Feature	Feature and display
—	—	—	41%	48%	210%
−10%	24%	28%	50	59	336
−15	40	51	102	128	590
+20	47	71	186	186	843

*Read as follows: for a 10% price reduction, sales of the 6.4 oz. regular size increased 24% with no feature or display, 28% if the 10% reduction was delivered via a price pack, 50% with display support, 59% with feature support, and 336% with feature and display support.

(Exhibit 12 continues)

EXHIBIT 12 (continued)

5. Effect of Aqua-fresh price pack on sales

	4.6 oz.	6.4 oz.	8.2 oz.
Price pack value	$0.15	$0.30	$0.35
% Price reduction	9%	16%	15%
Sales increase from:			
"On-shelf" price cut only	18	61	45
Price pack with same price cut	20	76	75

□   All types of trade merchandising increased Aqua-fresh sales, with the combination of feature advertising, special off-shelf displays, and price reductions generating tremendous increases over normal retail sales during weeks when there was no special merchandising support.

□   The more generous price packs appeared to be very effective in increasing short-term sales volume for Aqua-fresh.

CONCLUSION

When the Aqua-fresh brand group met to discuss the 1985–86 media and promotion plan, there was disagreement on what actions were indicated by the BehaviorScan research. The brand manager believed the findings indicated that the combination of price packs and trade promotion should continue to be the major component of the plan. Another manager felt that the research supported couponing as the principal method of stimulating consumer trial. Still others favored sampling and argued that price packs did not reach sufficient new users and gave current users an unnecessary price break. Edwards asked each team member to review the promotion plans for 1983–84 and 1984–85 (see Exhibits 13 and 14) and develop a 1985–86 promotion spending plan for their next meeting the following week.

EXHIBIT 13   Aqua-fresh 1983–1984 national promotion plan*

Period	Event	Merchandising allowance	Handling allowance	Dead net unit price	Total cost ($000)
I	8.2 oz. 35¢ price pack† ($4.20/dozen)	$3.55	$.25	$1.40	$2,003
II	6.4 oz. 30¢ price pack ($3.60/dozen)	4.40	.25	.99	3,840
	20¢ mailed coupon	—	—	—	550
III	4.6 oz. 15¢ price pack ($1.80/dozen)	1.00	.25	.96	1,237
IV	2.7 oz. 10¢ price pack ($1.20/dozen)	.20	.25	.75	572
V	8.2 oz. 35¢ price pack ($4.20/dozen)	3.00	.25	1.43	1,894
	20¢ FSI coupon	—	—	—	528
	Mail-in umbrella premium (free with 4 proofs of purchase)	—	—	—	576
VI	2.7 oz. 10¢ price pack ($1.20/dozen)	.20	.25	.75	650
VII	6.4 oz. 30¢ price pack ($3.60/dozen)	1.00	.25	1.10	3,134
VIII	8.2 oz. 35¢ price pack ($4.20/dozen)	4.45	.25	1.35	2,186
	1.4 oz. prepriced trial-size floor stand	2.70	.25	.27	1,655
IX	4.6 oz. 15¢ price pack ($1.80/dozen)	.65	.25	.99	686
	20¢ mailed coupon	—	—	—	1,092
X	6.4 oz. 30¢ price pack ($3.60/dozen)	1.05	.25	1.20	2,495

*Does not include $3,000M in consumer sampling efforts such as programs like Gift Pax, samples to college students and newlyweds, $1,000M in miscellaneous trade promotion expenditures, including allowances for military sales and nontraditional channels of distribution, and $2,800M in regional defensive promotions for Aqua-fresh. These factors explain differences in total promotion costs between Exhibits 5 and 13.

†Merchandising and handling allowances are included here in the calculation of total Aqua-fresh price pack costs, but were excluded from the price pack cost data on Exhibit 5 which covered only the actual value of the price packs.

EXHIBIT 14 Aqua-fresh 1984–1985 promotion plan*

Period	Event	Merchandising and handling allowance	Dead net unit price	Total cost ($000)
I	6.4 oz. 30¢ price pack ($3.60 dozen)	$1.35	$1.10	$2,946
II	8.2 oz. 35¢ price pack ($4.20/dozen)	3.40	1.43	1,970
	20¢ FSI coupon	—	—	528
III	4.6 oz. 15¢ price pack ($1.80/dozen)	.90	.99	1,221
	Inflatable raft premium ($4.50 + 2 proofs)	—	—	203
IV	2.7 oz. 10¢ price pack ($1.20/dozen)	.10	.71	715
V	6.4 oz. $1.00 price pack– twin pack ($6.00/per half dozen)	.80	1.04	4,325
	20¢ mailed coupon	—	—	550
VI	1.4 oz. prepriced trial- size floor stand	2.95	.26	1,103
VII	4.6 oz. 15¢ price pack ($1.80/dozen)	.90	.99	1,067
	Shower massage premium ($9.95 + 3 proofs)	—	—	94
	20¢ mailed coupon	—	—	1,013
VIII	8.2 oz. 35¢ price pack ($4.20/dozen)	4.00	1.40	2,069
IX	6.4 oz. 30¢ price pack ($3.60/dozen)	4.80	.99	4,205
	20¢ BFD coupon	—	—	466
X	2.7 oz. 10¢ price pack ($1.20/dozen)	.12	.75	630

*Does not include sampling, tests of new promotions, or promotions which were regional only.

GENERAL ELECTRIC COMPANY: CONSUMER INCANDESCENT LIGHTING

JOHN A. QUELCH

In December, 1982, William Frago, general manager of the Consumer Marketing and Sales Department within General Electric (GE) Company's Lamp Products Division (LPD), was preparing to meet with Gary Rogers, LPD vice president and general manager, to discuss the 1983 operating plan for GE's consumer incandescent lighting (light bulb) business. Both Frago and Rogers had recently assumed their positions.

The discussion was to review three strategic alternatives proposed by different constituencies within the LPD to deal with GE's long-term share decline. First, the marketing programs section argued for an increased advertising program and shift in trade spending from off-invoice purchase allowances to bill-back advertising performance allowances. This plan had been tested in late 1981 and had begun to be implemented in early 1982. However, increased advertising spending and some promotion events were opposed by Consumer Sales and the Incandescent Lamp Department (ILD) and were on hold pending review by Frago and Rogers. Second, the Consumer Sales force believed LPD should attempt to gain more new distribution in rapidly expanding channels such as mass merchandisers and discount chains. Third, ILD strongly believed LPD should invest resources to improve its cost position and utilize excess capacity to manufacture private-label light bulbs. There was a strong feeling in ILD that light bulbs were a commodity and that a more favorable cost and price position was the secret to long-term success. There was a great deal of internal dissent in each of these groups as to which course of action should be pursued.

Despite improved performance in 1982, several issues were still debated by LPD executives. Some believed that the light bulb was a push product and that increasing national advertising expenditures at the expense of promotion allowances was risky. They argued that GE would have to narrow further its price premium over competitive light bulbs if it was to gain market share. Others argued that the current price premium could be sustained by a strong national advertising campaign to build preference for GE light bulbs. Some members of this group did not support LPD's decision to make private-label product.

THE LAMP PRODUCTS DIVISION

General Electric achieved a record $26.5 billion in outside sales in 1982. John F. Welch, Jr., GE's CEO, summarized his views on GE's strategic direction in a letter to shareholders in the 1982 annual report:

> Whether it's bringing new technologies and services to the marketplace or revitalizing our strong core businesses, we want GE to be a place where the bias is toward action—a high-spirited world-class enterprise that uses the resources of a large company and that moves with the agility of the youngest and smallest. The last decade has seen a dramatic shift in our business mix—from the old to the new, from relatively mature businesses to those in their high-growth stages. . . .
>
> While our shift to high technology has been significant, we have also been upgrading our core businesses. During 1982, there were strong cost improvement efforts and major plant and equipment expenditures to increase productivity and assure the competitiveness of these important traditional businesses.

In 1982, GE's businesses were grouped into product sectors. The Consumer Products Sector, which included the Lighting Business Group (LBG), accounted for 22% and 13% of GE's 1982 revenues and net earnings, down from 25% and 21%, respectively, in 1980. LBG's sales were 15% of the sector total in 1982, but LBG's return on investment had slipped 7% from 1979. The LBG comprised three divisions, one of which, the Lamp Products Division, was principally responsible for the manufacture and sale of lighting products to end consumers. Commercial, industrial, and OEM sales were handled by the other divisions. The LPD accounted for 48% and 52% of LBG's revenues and earnings in 1982.

The LPD manufactured and sold eight distinct product lines to consumers: consumer incandescent, consumer fluorescent, automotive, holiday, photographic, battery, wiring devices, and outdoor. Consumer incandescent products accounted for 54% of LPD sales in 1982. The GE consumer incandescent line included 1,300 stockkeeping units (SKUs) manufactured in six plants.

As shown in the organization chart (Exhibit 1), responsibility for the consumer incandescent business was shared between the general managers of the Incandescent Lamp Department and the Consumer Marketing and Sales Department. Product line managers in the Lamp Department were primarily responsible for cost analysis, sales forecasting, production scheduling, capacity planning, and working with Research and Development on new products. Product marketing managers in the Marketing Department were primarily responsible for developing advertising and promotion programs and exploring product improvements and line extensions. The two de-

EXHIBIT 1   Lamp products division: 1982 organization chart

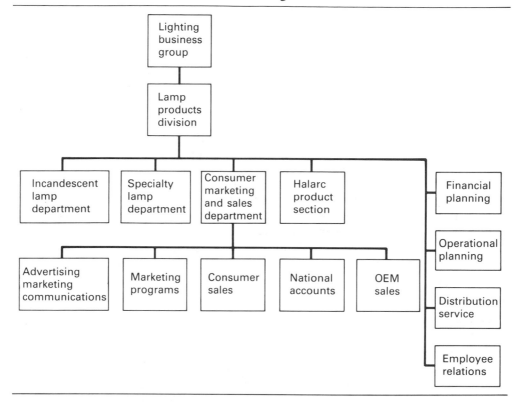

partments shared profit-and-loss responsibility for consumer incandescent lighting. Pricing strategies were discussed by both departments and approved by the LPD general manager.

THE CONSUMER INCANDESCENT LIGHTING MARKET

Consumer incandescent lamps were invented by Thomas Edison in 1880. During the next 60 years, a series of technical improvements increased the light intensity or lumens delivered per watt. However, since 1940, no major breakthroughs occurred until 1982 when GE launched the Miser ® line of energy-efficient lamps.

In 1982, manufacturers sold 1.19 billion consumer incandescent lamps in the United States valued at $445 million. Market demand for light bulbs was directly related to the size of the private housing stock and the size of the average housing unit. Industry sales typically correlated with the number of household light-bulb sockets. During the 1970s and 1980s, sales were flat due to heightened consumer interest in energy conservation following the oil price increases of 1973 and 1979 and due to periodic decreases in housing starts. The average annual growth rate in consumer incandescent lamp unit sales was 0.4% between 1970 and 1980. Most recently, unit sales had declined 1% between 1980 and 1982. Exhibit 2 graphs industry dollar and unit sales, and GE dollar and unit market shares, since 1973. GE's dollar and unit market shares both rose 1% during 1982.

Consumer incandescent lamps were generally divided into five product categories: soft white, inside-frost, three-way, PAR and R, and decorative. Soft white bulbs had whitened glass that helped diffuse light and reduced harshness and glare. Inside-frost bulbs, which represented an older technology than soft white, contained an inside frosting and did not diffuse light as effectively as soft white, but were lower priced and less costly to manufacture. Three-way bulbs, in conjunction with three-way lamps, allowed the user to select three different levels of brightness—such as 50, 100, and 150 watt. PAR lamps (parabolic reflectors) were for outdoor spotlighting. Reflector lamps (R) were primarily used as indoor floodlights. Decorative bulbs, the fastest growing category, were used in chandeliers and in concealed or specialty lighting fixtures. Exhibit 3 shows each product category's share of 1982 dollar and unit sales.

DISTRIBUTION

Consumer incandescent lamps were sold through four principal channels: food stores, discount stores, hardware stores, and drug stores. A 1981 consumer survey showed that consumers were most likely to purchase incandescent bulbs in food stores, but there were different channel patronage patterns for heavy versus light users (see Table 1).

TABLE 1   Channel patronage patterns

Outlets for purchase of incandescent bulbs in past two years	Total households (100%) (%)	Low (29%) (%)	Medium (44%) (%)	High* (26%) (%)
Food store	70	69	72	69
Discount store	52	47	52	59
Hardware store	32	26	34	38
Drug store	20	19	20	24
Department store	17	16	16	21
Home improvement center	14	9	13	21
Electric supply company	14	8	11	27
Other	6	1	7	8

*26% of households purchased 50% of consumer incandescent lamps in 1981.

EXHIBIT 2 Consumer incandescent industry sales and GE market share trends*

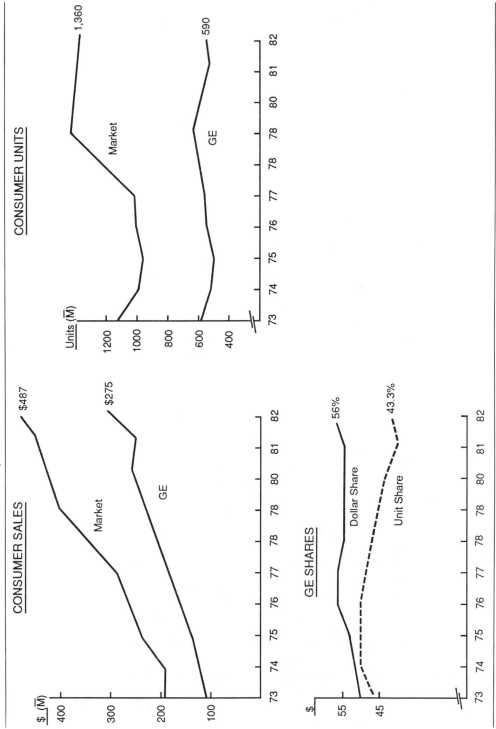

* These figures (in millions) are for all consumer sales: branded, private label, and generic.

EXHIBIT 3   Consumer incandescent dollar and unit sales and shares by product category: 1982*

	Product category's share of industry $ sales (%)	Product category's share of unit sales (%)	Product category's share of GE $ sales (%)
Soft-white	33%	38%	43%
Inside-frost	38	46	28
Three-way	9	5	13
PAR and R	13	2	10
Decorative	7	9	6

*These figures include branded, private-label, and generic consumer incandescent bulb sales, both for the industry and GE. Unit sales of nonbranded GE bulbs amounted to 20 million units in 1982.

Food stores were still the most important channel in 1982 though they had lost a point-of-share since 1980. An average food store carried 50 SKUs of light bulbs and turned its inventory six times a year. Most food stores carried a single branded line of bulbs, but many had recently added a private-label line. For many years light bulbs had been an important source of profit for food stores. Compared to their average gross margin of 22%, food stores earned a gross margin of 56% on light bulbs. A 1980 GE study indicated that light bulbs alone accounted for 11% of the profits of one major food store chain.

Discount stores and mass merchandisers increasingly used light bulbs as traffic builders, promoting them as often as six times a year. They typically carried as many as 100 SKUs including both a branded line and private-label line, but they often emphasized the latter. As many as 75% of the bulbs sold by some major discount chains were private label. Inventory turned six times each year. More bulbs were bought per purchase occasion in discount stores than in food stores. Discount store gross margins on light bulbs averaged 41% compared to the channel's overall average gross margin of 35%.

Hardware stores carried a broad line of lamp SKUs. They were more likely to carry new items and specialty bulbs. To hold their share of sales, hardware stores increasingly promoted inside-frost bulbs. Their gross margin on sales of lamps averaged 45% compared to an overall average gross margin of 21%. The corresponding figures for drug stores, which typically carried one branded line of bulbs, were 45% and 28%. Exhibit 4 breaks down the 1982 sales of consumer incandescent lamps by class of trade.

Within LPD's Consumer Marketing and Sales Department, sales to the major national discount store chains, hardware co-ops, and national drug chains were handled by a national accounts group. A separate field sales force dealt with the regional food, drug, and hardware accounts.

EXHIBIT 4   Channel growth trends and manufacturer unit market share by channel: 1982

	Food	Discount	Hardware and all other	Drug	Total
Channel unit share	45%	25%	23%	7%	100%
Change in channel unit share (1980–1981)*	(1)	—	1	—	—
Industry annual unit growth rate (1980–1982)	(3)	(1)	5	(2)	(1)
GE annual unit growth rate (1980–1982)	(6)	4	(1)	7	(3)

* ( ) Signifies negative growth rates.

GE's COMPETITIVE POSITION

General Electric's two main competitors in the consumer lighting business in 1982 were Westinghouse and Sylvania. Both had several decades of experience in the market and, like GE, had invested heavily in automated assembly processes for consumer incandescent lamps. Their unit costs of production were believed to be comparable. The fourth national brand was Norelco, manufactured by the U.S. subsidiary of Philips, the $16 billion Dutch electrical equipment manufacturer that dominated the consumer incandescent lamp market in Europe.

All of the major manufacturers not only sold their own brands but also contracted for private-label business. GE, the last to begin private-label manufacture, generated $4.0 million in consumer incandescent private-label lamp sales in 1981. Private-label unit market share was 15% in 1981 and 17% in 1982. Many of the imported lamps, which accounted for 10% of units sold in 1982, were for private label. The largest imported brand, Action, was made in Hungary and distributed in the United States by Action Industries. It was often used by hardware stores as an "in and out promotional item."[1]

The competitive structure of the consumer incandescent market in 1982 had evolved over the previous decade. At the end of 1973, GE held a 46.5% unit share of the consumer incandescent market and sold its bulbs at a 4% price premium over domestic competition and a 53% premium over imports, which then accounted for only 3% of the U.S. market.

General Electric bulbs were distributed to retailers on consignment. In other words, GE retained ownership until they were sold. Until 1973, GE operated on the "agency" system, a form of fair trading established during the 1930s. Consignment continued after 1973 but the resale price of GE bulbs was no longer maintained.

---

[1]The brand was not maintained by an account in continuous distribution but was stocked temporarily on special display when an especially attractive promotional deal could be arranged.

Between 1974 and 1977, GE's price premium over domestic competition increased to 12% and its premium over imports to 63%, in a large part owing to product mix changes. Moreover, a number of industry experts felt that imports of light bulbs from Eastern bloc countries were being "dumped" into the U.S. market at prices below cost. However, GE's unit share remained stable and GE maintained its position as the single supplier of light bulbs in 78% of its accounts. The GE sales force concentrated on selling the trade a profitability story. Imports during these three years captured 5% of the market, primarily in mass merchandise discount stores. Indeed, during this period, both the discount stores and the price brands secured their footholds. As one LPD executive explained:

> We were not encouraging the trade to put any special merchandising effort behind bulbs, although the category had a lot of potential as a traffic builder, a point that the discount stores recognized. Using private labels and generics, the discount stores began promoting light bulbs aggressively as traffic builders. Those that carried branded light bulbs often did so just as a comparison to drive their private-label sales.[2] As a result, the discount stores captured an increasing share of light bulb volume at the expense of the food and hardware channels where we were strong.
>
> Pretty soon, the food and hardware channels that had traditionally valued light bulbs for their good margins rather than as traffic builders started carrying private label and generic bulbs to stay competitive with the discount stores. The food and drug chains couldn't stand the embarrassment of promoting light bulbs at higher prices than discount stores in the free-standing inserts of the Sunday newspapers. At the same time, our branded competitors, faced with volume and share losses to private labels and generics, started pressing food stores for feature advertising support and offered deeper allowances to the trade to maintain their distribution. The price premium of GE bulbs over its branded competitors increased.

Between 1977 and 1979, the GE price premium grew to 19% over domestic competition. More discount chains began to market their own private-label bulbs. The import share of the market climbed to 8%. Norelco aggressively pursued food store distribution, offering substantial promotion allowances and arguing that food stores were collectively losing share to discount stores because of higher prices on GE bulbs. Westinghouse also was attempting to gain share by offering steeper discounts and competitive buy-outs to the trade. To new accounts, Westinghouse offered payments for the existing inventory that would be displaced, free display racks, minimal order size requirements, a progressive annual volume rebate program, and deeper than normal off-invoice promotional allowances on its inside-frost bulbs. Westinghouse's apparent strategy was to use an attractive price on inside-frost bulbs to gain access to an account and to earn its margin on its other consumer incandescent lines. During 1979, the trade's acquisition cost, net of trade promotion, for a Westinghouse inside-frost bulb was 25 cents a unit compared to 32 cents for a GE bulb. Many food chains appeared to pass through the Norelco and Westinghouse allowances to the

---

[2]A simultaneous promotion of both a branded and a private-label line with a "compare and save" message over the private-label display was known as a promotion split.

consumer in the form of lower retail prices, at the same time maintaining their unit profit margins on these lines.

Between 1975 and 1979, LPD recovered inflation with consumer incandescent price increases. LBG's return on investment peaked at an impressive 25% in 1979. However, two problems arose. First, as shown in Exhibit 5, GE's market share fell as its price premium over competition increased. Second, not all of GE's price increases were realized as LPD found it necessary to deal back some of the increases in additional trade promotion allowances. As one LPD executive explained:

> As discount store competition eroded the food chains' share of sales, they focused more on their acquisition costs. We had to devise a strategy that would let us maintain our share in our traditional channels but get a piece of the volume going through discount stores. Our first reaction was to secure distribution and offer our customers promotional packages that enabled them to lower their acquisition costs on both GE soft white and inside-frost bulbs. The problem was that many of our food accounts did not pass these discounts through to the consumer. The food stores' prices on GE light bulbs remained as high as ever and our market share continued to erode. At the same time, consumer price sensitivity was increased. I remember a March 1981 survey showing 35% of consumers bought light bulbs on sale. That figure was 6% in 1979.

The pattern continued into 1981. GE's dollar sales and unit volume in consumer incandescent lamps declined. For the first time, LPD experienced a net distribution loss of $1.5 million worth of business. In addition, the sales mix deteriorated. Inside-frost sales increased at the expense of higher margin soft-white sales when LPD tried to respond to the price premium by running a strong price promotion on inside-frost bulbs.

MARKET SEGMENTATION

The average consumer bought light bulbs five times each year. Some consumers bought them as needed, others kept an inventory on hand in their homes. Sixty percent of bulbs were bought for general room lighting. Other uses were reading and writing (9%), work aid (6%), decoration (7%), personal care (7%), security (5%), and outdoor lighting (4%).

As competitive pressures increased during the 1970s, LPD executives increasingly explored the segmentation of the consumer incandescent market. Their objective was to identify segments that might be interested in distinct product benefits and be willing to pay a price premium for them. To this end, five proprietary studies were conducted, four of them during 1980 and 1981.

☐   A 1974 Hale study clustered respondents according to the importance they attached to different lighting benefits. However, no single advertisable benefit stood out among those appealing to consumers in each of the five segments. In addition, GE's market share was similar across the segments (Exhibit 6).

EXHIBIT 5   Relationship between GE unit share and price premium, 1960–1981

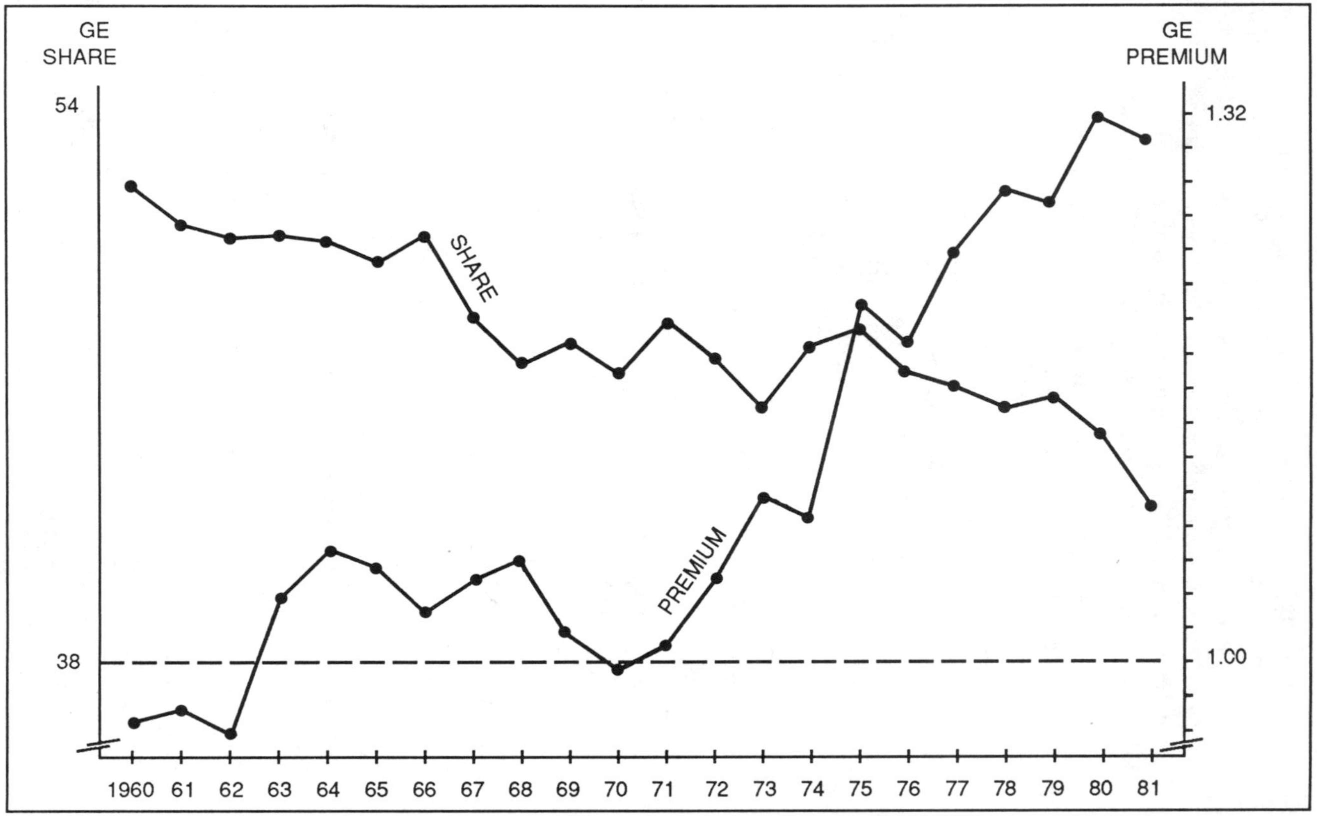

EXHIBIT 6   1974 Hale consumer attitude segmentation study

☐ Objective: Identify consumer attitude segments and the benefits motivating each.
☐ Methodology: 1,016 self-administered questionnaires to households representing all income levels.

Segment	Highest ranking interests	Percent of total market*	GE share of segment
1. Vision-value buyers	☐ Reasonable price ☐ Long lasting ☐ Good value ☐ Easy to read by ☐ Eliminates eye strain	18%	50%
2. Quality-product value buyers	☐ Economical to burn ☐ Reasonable price ☐ Long lasting	12	58
3. Quality-vision buyers	☐ Eliminates eye strain ☐ Reasonable price ☐ Long lasting	21	58
4. Practical (price) buyers	☐ Ready availability ☐ Glare-free light ☐ Easy to read by ☐ Good value	21	65
5. Aesthetic buyers	☐ Wide selection ☐ Attractive bulbs/good packaging ☐ Well-known manufacturer ☐ Guaranteed/pretested	28	58

Conclusions
☐ Could not identify segments where GE share was significantly higher or lower.
☐ Analysis of key interests of segments could not isolate advertisable consumer benefit.

Source: Company records

*Percent of light bulbs purchased by consumers falling into each segment rather than percent of consumers.

☐   A 1980 Yankelovich, Skelly, and White (YSW) study identified six segments based on consumer attitudes rather than a rank ordering of lighting benefits (Exhibit 7).

☐   A 1980 study identified six segments based on consumer rankings of different lighting benefits. GE's market share again varied only modestly from one segment to another (Exhibit 8).

☐   A 1980 Opinion Research Corporation study aimed to identify the relative importance of energy efficiency, price, package shape, bulb type, and light quality. A segment of consumers especially interested in energy efficiency was identified. GE's share of this segment was relatively low (Exhibit 9).

EXHIBIT 7 Yankelovich, Skelly and White, Inc. attitude segment study, 1980

☐ Objective: Isolate benefit segments and describe the attitudes and motivations of each.

☐ Methodology: 770 in-home personal interviews with consumers in households with annual income of $15,000 and above.

Segment	Description of segment motivations	Percent of total market
1. Cost conscious	☐ Lowest level of interest in light bulbs ☐ No reason to spend more than minimum ☐ No added value can be communicated ☐ Decide on price	12.3%
2. Convenience oriented	☐ Wants to save time and effort in changing or buying bulbs and will pay extra to achieve this ☐ Share some characteristics of cost conscious segment	12.3
3. Technology	☐ High motivation level ☐ Always searching for a better way to do things ☐ Early adopters . . . new means better ☐ But "new" quickly becomes "not new"	5.0
4. Energy conscious	☐ Highest motivation level ☐ Need is to save energy ☐ Socially responsible ☐ Very important to buy the very best bulb ☐ Will respond to new products	17.7
5. Undecided buyers	☐ Low level of motivation ☐ Want to reduce risk, avoid mistakes ☐ Tend to buy leading established brands ☐ Followers, not innovators	20.2
6. Home enhancers	☐ Seek better light to improve personal/home environment ☐ Extrinsic reasons for choice — other directed behavior ☐ Choose "quality" product to match peer group standards ☐ Brand loyal	32.5

Source: Company records

Note: GE share by segment not available in this study.

☐ A second YSW study in 1981 identified three segments based on level of involvement in lighting. Exhibits 10–12 profile these three segments.

LPD executives were especially interested in YSW's two benefit segments. They believed that GE soft white could be positioned to appeal to the quality-of-light segment while GE's new Miser line of energy-efficient bulbs, due to be launched in 1982, could be targeted at the utility/energy segment.

EXHIBIT 8   1980 consumer attitude segmentation study

☐ Objective: Develop market segments based on consumers' ranking of different light bulb benefits/
interests.

☐ Methodology: 1,387 self-administered mail questionnaires to consumers of all income levels.

Segment	Highest ranking interests	Percent of total market	GE share of segment
1. Vision/construction of light bulb	☐ Bulb is guaranteed ☐ Highest overall quality ☐ Bulb is attractive ☐ Bulb is pretested ☐ Bulb doesn't overheat	12%	45.5%
2. Value/vision	☐ Energy saved pays for bulb ☐ Efficient like fluorescent ☐ Economical ☐ Natural looking light ☐ Lasts as long as supposed to ☐ Good value for money	15	42.0
3. Positive attitudes	☐ No harsh shadows ☐ Helps eliminate eye strain ☐ Glare-free light ☐ Pleasing lighted appearance ☐ Easy to read by ☐ Makes things look nice ☐ Doesn't grow dim with age ☐ Natural looking light	16	54.5
4. Reputable manufacturer	☐ Readily available ☐ Well-known manufacturer ☐ Wide selection ☐ Screws easily in and out ☐ Is pretested ☐ Makes things look nice ☐ Pleasing lighted appearances	18	50.2
5. Value/reliability	☐ Reasonably priced ☐ Good value for money ☐ Lasts as long as supposed to ☐ Base doesn't twist off ☐ Durable, not easily broken ☐ Screws easily in and out ☐ Economical	19	54.8
6. No interest in lighting	☐ Light level adjustable ☐ Durable, not easily broken ☐ Bulb is attractive	20	52.5

Conclusions

☐ Interpretation hampered because the items ranked included usage needs, product attributes, and
general attitudes.

☐ A key advertisable consumer benefit for each segment was hard to identify.

Source: Company records

EXHIBIT 9 **1981 Opinion Research Corporation study**

☐ Objective: Determine the key additional benefit(s) by segment to support the basic long-life position of a new line of long-lasting GE bulbs.

☐ Methodology: 502 mall interviews with consumers of all income levels.

Segment	Highest ranking interests	Percent of total market	GE share of segment
1. Energy conscious	☐ Energy saving	16%	48.3%
2. Aesthetic	☐ Price ☐ Package quantity	30	67.0
3. Convenience	☐ Package quantity ☐ Bulb shape/type ☐ Price	21	63.4
4. Equal sensitivity	☐ Equal sensitivity for price light quality life ☐ *Not* energy conscious	33	55.5

Conclusion

☐ Segments were identified among which GE's share does differ significantly.

Source: Company records

THE 1981 TEST MARKET

Based in part on the results of the market segmentation studies, LPD marketing executives decided to test the impact of an advertising and promotion program designed to pull volume through the retail channel. Believing that LPD should develop more tailored programs for different products in the line, they fixed on quality of light as the differentiating benefit to build preference for GE soft-white bulbs. To address consumers interested in eye comfort and decor enhancement, a television advertisement was developed showing a painter fashioning a family portrait with the aid of GE soft-white bulbs (see Exhibit 13).

Between October and December 1981, LPD conducted a field experiment. In four control markets, LPD continued its two current merchandising programs. These were a one-dollar on-pack rebate offer to consumers who submitted purchase proofs for three packs of four bulbs and a cooperative advertising allowance of up to 6% of an account's purchases with the entire cost of advertisements paid for by LPD. In the four test markets (which accounted for 10% of U.S. consumer light bulb sales), 160 GRPs of advertising were aired per week at a national expenditure rate of $8 million, equivalent to the estimated cost of the rebate program. In addition, the trade received a three cents per unit off-invoice allowance on soft-white bulbs, plus an additional four or five cents bill-back allowance if one or two feature advertisements were run.

EXHIBIT 10   Yankelovich, Skelly and White consumer involvement segments*

Involved (35% of market)	Uninvolved (10%)	Latent (55%)
Seeking special lighting benefits atmosphere aesthetics modern, unique	Low attention to special benefits	Low attention to special benefits
Highest interest in function	Lowest interest in function	High interest in function
Into lighting	*Not* into lighting	Into lighting
Needs/wants vary most on room-by-room basis	Least variation by room	Some variation by room
Price sensitive	Less price sensitive	Price sensitive
More problems in achieving end results	Fewer end-result problems	Fewer end-result problems
Satisfied with lighting effects in major living areas	Not necessarily satisfied	Satisfied with lighting in specific rooms
Concern with illumination effectiveness avoiding glare interest in color	Less concern with illumination	Concern with illumination effectiveness avoiding harshness
Greatest attention to nearly all bulb attributes	Lower concern with bulb attributes	High concern with bulb attributes
Highest use of lamps/sockets/bulbs	Moderate use	Lowest use
More women	More men	More women
All ages—especially 30–64	Younger	Older
Average education	Most educated	Least educated
Most homeowners (largest homes)	Fewer homeowners (medium homes)	Fewer homeowners (smallest homes)

Source: Company records

*These segments were based on respondents importance and dissatisfaction rankings.

The test program limited trade allowances to one order per feature advertisement, whereas the existing cooperative advertising program allowed the trade to accrue allowances on all its purchases. One LPD marketing executive explained the rationale for the so-called "three-four-five" program:

> Because consumers buy bulbs in food and drug channels for convenience, our consumer rebate offer only had impact in discount stores where consumers are more likely to purchase bulbs in volume. On the other hand, consumer advertising was thought likely to benefit sales in all channels.
>
> The change in the allowance structure was designed to increase the feature advertising support given by the trade and turn the trade into a proactive marketing partner. The gap

EXHIBIT 11   YSW study: Consumer choice of outlet for lighting products

Rated "Major Consideration" in choice of outlet for lighting products	Total purchasers (%)	Segments		
		Involved (%)	Uninvolved (%)	Latent (%)
Convenience				
Convenient location	56	55	48	58
Shop at for *other* items	41	44	39	38
Light bulbs easy to locate	33	34	19	36
Outlet economy				
Lower prices regularly	51	50	39	55
Frequent sales/bargains	48	50	34	50
Full-line outlet				
Offers variety in bulbs— selection to choose from	33	40	19	30
Offers preferred brands	29	33	12	29
Offers best quality lighting	29	33	17	27
Offers "specialty" lighting	26	32	19	23
Offers full range of lighting products	26	30	11	25

Source: Company records

between an account's promotion acquisition cost and LPD's regular price remained at about eight cents per soft-white bulb, but now five cents of the discount was contingent on feature advertising support.

The highlights of the test results are summarized in Exhibit 14. GE gained share, increased its average selling price per bulb, and narrowed the price premium over competition. In addition to sales and share data, LPD executives had the survey results from two waves of interviews conducted before and after the experiment in both test and control markets.

Both surveys included comparative questions on perceived value for money of soft-white bulb brands at fixed price points for each brand and type. The GE soft-white brand price was given as either 69 cents, 79 cents, 89 cents, or 99 cents on each questionnaire on a four-way split sample basis. All competitive soft-white bulbs were priced at 79 cents. Respondents were asked to indicate their perception of value for money (on a four-point scale) for the brands listed at the prices shown.

As the price of the GE soft white increased from cell to cell, the proportion of consumers indicating that GE soft white was a "very good value" (the top of the scale) went down and the proportion indicating the same for other soft-white bulbs went up.

However, the rate of loss of relative demand for GE was not matched by gains in demand by competitive brands at higher GE price points. Before exposure to the advertising (Pre), every ten-cent increase in the GE soft-white price led to a loss of 8%

EXHIBIT 12   YSW study: Elements of purchase that were planned and unplanned on last light bulb purchase occasion

	Total purchasers (%)	Segments		
		Involved (%)	Uninvolved (%)	Latent (%)
Wattage				
Planned	84	85	86	84
Unplanned	15	13	18	15
Type of bulb				
Planned	83	83	80	83
Unplanned	16	16	19	16
Outlet				
Planned	83	83	85	83
Unplanned	16	15	15	15
Bulb quantity				
Planned	71	74	67	67
Unplanned	27	23	32	30
Brand purchase				
Planned	49	55	40	48
Unplanned	48	43	57	49

YSW study: Light bulb brand and type preferences by segment

	Involved	Uninvolved	Latent
Segment			
Believe GE is "best for regular bulbs"	56	47	46
Believe GE is "best for soft-white bulbs"	46	37	37
Believe GE is "best for long life"	44	33	26
Bought a soft-white bulb on last purchase occasion	53	55	41
Bought a GE bulb on last purchase occasion	57	50	43

Source: Company records

of the respondent base, but a gain of only 7% for each competitive soft-white brand. After exposure to the advertising campaign (Post), competitive gains in demand were only 2–3% per ten-cent increment. And at parity pricing the perceived "very good value" rating of GE soft-white-bulbs increased eight percentage points (48–56%) while competitive brands increased three to four percentage points (see Table 2).

From these and other test data, many LPD marketing executives believed that the power of a national consumer advertising campaign had been proven. Others were more skeptical. According to one LPD sales manager:

> In my opinion, 90% of the share gain was due to the feature advertising prices and 10% due to the national advertising. The quality and share of GE's feature advertisements

EXHIBIT 13   Soft white television commercial storyboard

This is the soft pure light of the GE Soft White bulb.

It creates a soft warm glow

that's beautiful to see by

and bright enough to work by,

with less glare and no harsh shadows.

Because its high-diffusion coating makes light that's soft, warm, glowing.

So you can see the world

the way you want to see it.

The Soft White by GE.

It puts your life in a better light.

GE

We bring good things to life.

EXHIBIT 14   Selected results of 1981 test market

☐ In test markets, GE soft white's unit market share increased during the experiment by 8 more points than it did in control markets. The point spread ranged from plus 23 points in drug channels to plus 1 point in food channels.

☐ In test markets, the unit market share of other GE bulbs increased during the experiment by 2 more points than it did in control markets. The net market share gain for all GE bulbs in test markets was plus 4 points, representing about 50 million annual unit sales.

☐ Partly as a result of shifting some purchasers to the higher unit margin soft-white bulb from inside frost, the average manufacturer selling price of GE bulbs purchased in the test markets was 6 cents higher than in control markets.

☐ In test markets, 36% of respondents reported seeing the GE soft white advertising, and 60% of them were able to recall key points of the advertising unaided.

☐ Of those consumers who saw the GE soft white advertising:
 — 68% agreed that light bulbs are very or somewhat different from each other (48% control markets).
 — 73% agreed that GE soft white is different from other soft white brands (68% control markets). Those who valued lighting for reading and for making a room more attractive were more likely to agree that GE soft white is different.
 — 79% named GE as their favorite brand of light bulb (71% control markets).
 — 15% stated that they would go to another store if GE soft-white bulbs were not available in their usual store (12% in control markets). The corresponding figures for GE inside-frost bulbs were 14% and 9%.

☐ 72% of consumers choose a type of bulb (e.g., inside frost, soft white) first before deciding among brand alternatives within a type.

☐ 42% of respondents who reported buying GE soft white when they last purchased were not certain of the price they paid. Corresponding figures for Sylvania and Westinghouse were 31% and 30%.

TABLE 2   Perceived value of soft-white bulb brands at fixed price points

GE Soft White test prices		% "Very Good Value"					
		GE		Sylvania		Westinghouse	
		Pre	Post	Pre	Post	Pre	Post
@69¢		61%	65%	21%	28%	25%	27%
@79¢	Competitive price point	48	56	34	37	33	37
@89¢		41	42	38	36	39	34
@99¢		38	34	42	38	45	36
Slope		−.8	−1.1	.7	.3	.7	.2

did improve in the food and drug channels, but not in the discount chains. These price features did close the gap between our soft white and the competition. The trade recovered the lost margin resulting from the more frequent features by increasing prices on nonpromoted GE and competitive bulbs.

THE 1982 MARKETING PROGRAM

LPD executives set out in 1982 to revitalize the consumer incandescent lighting business. Their program involved a reallocation of marketing expenditures, a new product launch, and the pursuit of new distribution opportunities.

New marketing mix.   In 1981, LPD had spent 10% of its marketing funds on advertising, 9% on consumer rebates, 63% on off-invoice allowances, 5% on bill-back allowances for feature advertisements, and 13% on merchandising aids. Based on the test results, funds were shifted from off-invoice allowances and consumer rebates into national advertising, consumer coupons, and bill-back allowances. In particular:

☐   National advertising, principally for GE soft-white bulbs, was increased by 40%. Some executives believed that it should have been more than doubled. However, GE's share of total category advertising was over 90% in 1982.

☐   The three-four-five program was implemented on GE soft-white and three-way bulbs, but not on inside frost. To qualify for bill-back allowances, the trade had to run feature advertisements of specified size during specified time periods which coincided with LPD's flights of national advertising.

☐   GE inside frost was offered at a special price once each quarter. The trade could place one order during each promotion event.

☐   The remaining smaller volume consumer incandescent products were grouped together each quarter in a dealer's choice promotion. A 10% bill-back allowance could be earned on one order of any item after a feature advertisement was run.

☐   Consumer rebates were curtailed. Coupons (usually 25-cent values) were used as an alternative consumer promotion on soft-white and three-way bulbs.

New products.   LPD planned to take its new Miser energy-efficient bulbs national by the end of 1982. Miser bulbs delivered 5% more lumens per watt than ordinary bulbs. Sixty percent of in-home use testers had rated Miser bulbs better than those they replaced. The Miser product group expected to sell 20 million Miser bulbs by the end of 1982. A Miser product line manager commented:

> There are three advantages to new products. First, if they change consumer preferences and expectations, they can put pressure on our competitors. Second, new products broaden our line, making it easier for us to fill all the slots on a trade account's promotion calendar. Third, new products give us something worth advertising. In my view, soft-white bulbs are old hat. Most of our national advertising should be put behind the Miser line.

New Distribution

LPD executives had initiated private-label sales in 1981 and had generated $4 million worth of business. In 1982, they decided to pursue more private-label business in order to both maintain their position in existing accounts and open up new accounts. The LPD national accounts manager explained the approach:

> Large trade accounts could acquire private-label bulbs at about half the price of GE bulbs. They could sell private-label bulbs at retail prices well below GE and make more money per unit. Private-label volume grew 30% in 1981. Given we were using only about 65% of our capacity for consumer incandescent bulbs, we decided in 1981 to go into private label. In order not to further commoditize the category, we decided to do this only under certain conditions. First, the customer had to be a GE account and second, had to already stock or be committed to stocking private label. Finally, we decided to supply only inside frost and not soft white on a private-label basis.
>
> Early in 1982, our national accounts group solicited several discount chains, particularly those that were less price oriented. First, we'd try to persuade the account to test substituting the GE line for private label in some of its stores. Failing this, we would make both branded and private-label bulbs for them. Even chains that took on both typically moved as much volume as before without trading all of its consumers down to private label. Profits have improved for us and for the chain, so much so that in one or two cases, we've been able to persuade trade accounts that used to carry only private label to subsequently delete the GE-made private-label product and sell only GE brand bulbs. In addition, by servicing both an account's private label and its brand name requirements, we thought we could better help manage the account's promotion calendar. Overall, what we've discovered is that by being involved in the private-label end of the business, we've gained a more complete market perspective and we're better able to deal with the growth of private label.

1982 Results

The performance of GE's consumer incandescent lighting business in 1982 suggested that some of the initiatives that had been taken were working:

- [ ] GE consumer incandescent bulb revenues increased from $205 million in 1981 to $227 million in 1982 and operating profits increased 24%.

- [ ] GE's unit share of the consumer incandescent bulb market increased from 43.0% in 1981 to 44.5% in 1982 while its share of branded light bulbs rose from 45% to 47%. Sales of GE brand lamps increased from 488 million to 508 million.

- [ ] GE's average factory price per branded lamp rose from 41 cents in 1981 to 44 cents in 1982 yet GE was able to maintain its price premium at 30%, the 1981 level.

- [ ] In 1982, trade feature advertisements for GE soft-white and/or Miser bulbs increased over 1981 by 60% in food stores, 47% in drug stores, and 19% in discount stores.

☐   GE sold $6.8 million worth of private-label consumer incandescent bulbs in 1982, 10% of all private-label units sold, and a 70% increase over GE's 1981 private-label sales.

☐   GE secured $10 million worth of consumer incandescent bulb sales to new accounts.

PLANNING FOR 1983

As Frago reviewed the 1982 results and his department's marketing plans for 1983, he was primarily concerned about which overall strategy his business should pursue. He debated the relative merits of the following: first, a plan to increase private label penetration, increase capacity utilization, reduce costs, and then reduce the price premium; second, a plan to secure increased distribution in emerging channels by increasing "push-oriented" off-invoice allowances; and third, a plan to reinstitute consumer advertising and merchandising performance allowances that had been cut back in mid-1982.

Price premium.   Several LPD executives believed that GE's share of the consumer incandescent market would never increase significantly until GE's price premium was reduced. According to one:

> The way to correct the price is to increase promotion allowances, take a list price cut or, at least to take price increases less than the inflation rate. If we become more price competitive, we'll gain distribution, sell more volume, and so maintain or even increase our total margin dollars. We could also improve our margins by investing in productivity improvements to increase our machine speeds and lower unit costs.

Frago believed that the price premium should be maintained at 30% but he asked for estimates of pretax income from the consumer incandescent business under the following three scenarios:

	Raise premium Scenario 1	Hold premium Scenario 2	Lower premium Scenario 3
GE price premium in year 7	43%	30%	25%
GE unit share in year 7	32%	45%	52%

The scenario analysis assumed a flat market, fixed marketing and sales expenses, steady changes in the price premium and unit share over the seven-year period, and an additional 0.5% annual productivity gain on increasing volume. The results of the scenario analysis, presented in Exhibit 15, seemed to support Frago's conclusion.

Promotion allowances.   Few doubted that bill-back allowances had been effective in encouraging the trade to merchandise GE bulbs more aggressively to

EXHIBIT 15   Pro forma projections: Three scenarios annual pretax income over seven years

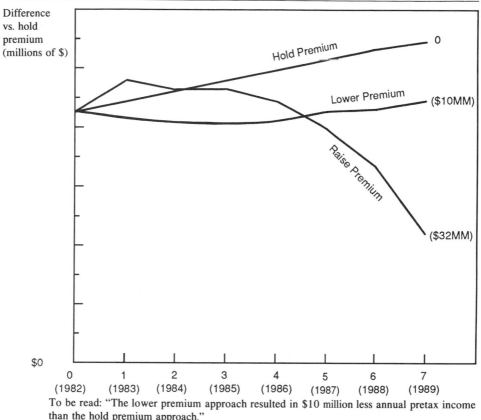

To be read: "The lower premium approach resulted in $10 million less annual pretax income than the hold premium approach."

the consumer. However, some problems were evident. According to one LPD sales manager:

> Checking performance on these allowances is an administrative nightmare and can lead to disputes with some of our most important accounts. We're rapidly overcomplicating our allowance structure. Our salespeople are too busy explaining conditions on our allowances to do any real selling. We should give the trade these allowances up front on the basis of an affidavit or letter of intent that they'll run the feature ads.

National advertising.   Several LPD marketing executives were arguing to reinstitute national advertising in 1983 to support GE's soft-white and Miser lines. The incremental funds were to come out of the budget for off-invoice allowances. The LPD sales force opposed this proposed shift of expenditures. Many LPD salespeople continued to be skeptical about the ability of national advertising to build the business.

The following exchange took place between an LPD regional sales manager and a product marketing manager:

Sales manager: A light bulb is a light bulb. There's no brand differentiation. When consumers want to improve their lighting, they think of adding a lamp or a fixture rather than changing the bulb they use. What's more, demand for light bulbs is not price-elastic. Consumers don't burn them up any faster if you give them away. In short, this is a push business. Your market share depends on your share of distribution.

Product manager: We should be selling light, not light bulbs. We have a story to tell the consumer. Soft white stands for quality light. Miser stands for energy efficiency. There's so little light bulb advertising that a strong LPD national advertising campaign will not go unnoticed. Our share of voice will be high, so I'd expect our advertising to have impact. In addition, think what it will mean to sales force morale to be able to present a really strong national advertising campaign to the trade.

Sales manager: I don't agree. Heavy national advertising will make us an even more attractive traffic builder to the trade. They'll give us more advertising features and lower their retail prices further. They'll make even less money on GE bulbs than they're making now, so they'll just continue using us as a traffic builder and then emphasize private-label bulbs in their store displays because they'll make more unit margin on those than they will on GE bulbs.

Product manager: But if we run a strong benefit-oriented national advertising program, we'll build our consumer franchise. More consumers will insist on the GE brand and be willing to pay a price premium over private label if we educate them in advertising as to why they should pay more. Our realized unit margins will improve. Yes, feature advertisements at discount prices can cause further commoditization, but only on brands which are not strongly advertised.

COFFEE BRANDS: DIRECT PRODUCT PROFIT/COST EXERCISE

JOHN A. QUELCH
MELANIE D. SPENCER
BRIAN COSACCHI

Traditionally, supermarkets and other consumer goods retailers used an item's gross margin and turnover rate as the basis for merchandising decisions. Retailers calculated the gross margin simply by subtracting the cost of the product from its selling price. The gross margin percentage (gross margin as a percentage of selling price) was used as a relative measurement of profitability to compare product categories, brands within each category, and the sizes of each brand. While the gross margin percentage was widely used as a decision-making tool by retailers, it was not a true reflection of a product's profit contribution because it did not consider the costs incurred by the retailer in getting the product from the manufacturer to the consumer. For example, one product might be far more expensive for the retailer to handle and inventory than another, yet both might have the same gross margin percentages.

The concept of Direct Product Profit (DPP) was developed to measure product profitability more accurately. DPP was defined as the net profit contribution of a product after all trade allowances were added to gross margin and after all handling, shipping, warehousing, and other costs attributable to the product were deducted. The DPP formula assigned retailer handling and distribution costs to each individual stockkeeping unit (SKU), as opposed to lumping such costs into "overhead," thereby allowing retailers to account for variations in item costs when making merchandising decisions. Nevertheless, when the concept was conceived in the late 1960s, it had little practical application; the cost measurements required for DPP analysis were too difficult to obtain and too expensive to manipulate at that time.

By 1986, industry analysts believed that the DPP concept and its use would grow in importance as retailers refined accounting practices and improved management information systems. UPC scanning[1] and the increasing cost effectiveness of computer applications involving large quantities of data were also expected to increase the use of DPP. Finally, in an industry such as grocery retailing characterized by thin before-tax profit margins of around 2%, the effective application of DPP was seen as providing a possible competitive edge.

CALCULATING DIRECT PRODUCT PROFIT

The Direct Product Profit formula had two major components, Direct Product Costs (DPCs) and Adjusted Gross Revenue. Direct Product Costs were defined as costs incurred by the retailer in moving each unit of a product from the manufacturer's shipping dock to the point at which it was purchased by a consumer. Exhibit 1 defines a variety of DPCs.

Adjusted Gross Revenue was defined as all revenue attributable to each unit of a product, including trade deals and allowances, cash discounts, backhaul monies, and forward-buy profits. Trade deals and allowances were monies associated with the temporary promotion of a product to stimulate inventory loading and additional retail merchandising support to sell the extra inventory through to the consumer. Cash discounts included discounts from the manufacturer for prompt payment of invoices. Backhaul monies were manufacturer allowances that compensated a retailer using a truck that was returning empty from a store to the retailer's warehouse to pick up product at the manufacturer's factory or warehouse, thus saving the manufacturer transportation costs. When a retailer purchased product on promotion for normal inventory rather than, or in addition to, the volume of product purchased for sale to the consumer at a lower-than-normal retail price, forward-buy profits were realized. These profits represented the difference between the manufacturer's regular price and the promotional price for the stock that the retailer sold at regular price after the promotion was over.

The DPP formula reflecting these definitions is shown in Exhibit 2. This equation yielded a DPP value per stockkeeping unit. Other useful measures of DPP could be obtained, such as DPP per case or DPP per week, by performing additional calculations. The actual DPP calculation could vary slightly depending on a manager's assumptions. Occupancy costs, for example, were sometimes excluded from the equation by users who believed that such costs could not be attributed to each unit of product and would have been incurred anyway.

RETAIL APPLICATIONS

DPP had two major applications for retail management: first, as a method to measure and reduce handling/operational costs and second, as a tool to achieve better

---

[1]Computerized scanning systems at retail checkouts could "read" bar codes (known as universal product codes, or UPCs) on product labels or packages and automatically ring up the correct price as well as record the transaction. In 1986, supermarkets accounting for 40% of U.S. grocery volume were equipped with UPC scanning systems.

EXHIBIT 1 **Factors in the calculation of Direct Product Profit (DPP)**

Factor	Explanations
Sales	Reconstructed from warehouse withdrawals or scanning data Adjusted for retail inventory changes Adjusted for retail promotions
Cost	Cost from invoice including off-invoice allowances*
Merchandising allowances	All non–off-invoice allowances*
Payment terms	Discount for early payment plus interest for days
Distribution allowance	Tax stamping allowance† Backhaul allowance per case cube Freight allowance
Warehouse direct labor (in- and out-labor)‡	Time standard model at hourly rate per pallet, case, cube, pound§
Warehouse operating labor	Supervision assigned by direct labor (in- and out-labor)‡ Operating expense assigned by space (warehouse space)
Warehouse investment cost (warehouse space)‡	Assigned by space
Transportation expense (transportation)‡	Calculated for cube volume
Warehouse inventory cost (inventory, cell = I39)‡	Based on buying model and current interest rates‖
Retail stocking labor (pricing and other labor)‡	Time standard model at hourly rate per case, cube, pound, package
Retail checkout labor (checking and bagging)‡	Time standard model at hourly rate per cube, package
Retail operating expense	Supervision assigned by direct labor (other labor)‡ Operating expense assigned by space (warehouse space)
Retail investment cost (selling space)‡	Assigned by space
Retail inventory cost (inventory, cell = I44)‡	Dollars of inventory at retailer's cost × current interest rate

*Off-invoice allowances were temporary price reductions offered by manufacturers to the trade that were deducted from the manufacturers' invoices.

† A tax-stamping allowance might be paid by a cigarette manufacturer to a trade account that affixed a tax stamp to each package at its warehouse.

‡ Descriptions in parentheses show Direct Product Cost components as they appear in the Direct Product Profit (DPP) model at the end of the text of this case.

§ A time standard model calculated the labor cost associated with moving a unit of product in and out of the warehouse based on the product's shape and weight.

‖ This model calculated the cost of financing the inventory in the warehouse, based on current interest rates.

merchandising decisions. Because real costs had to be assigned to each SKU in DPP analysis, management had to closely monitor these costs. If total operational costs were found to be increasing, retailers could determine which SKUs were contributing disproportionately to the increases. Once high-cost product lines were identified,

EXHIBIT 2 Overview of DPC/DPP calculations

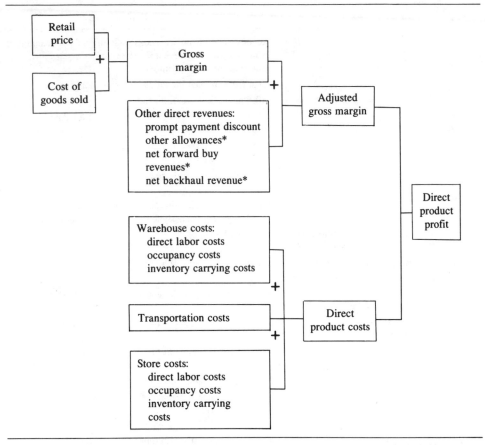

*If earning these revenues involves extra costs, the corresponding expenses should be included in the DPC calculation.

programs could be developed to improve existing handling practices in each cost area.

In the case of products with a high bulk-to-value ratio, package size and shape had an especially significant impact on the product's DPCs; thus, the profit contribution of the product as measured by DPP. Possible methods of reducing specific costs by using the information provided by the DPP formula included:

Warehouse: Develop a separate, specialized warehouse area for handling high-cube products.[2]

Receiving: Improve equipment efficiency and develop methods of unloading large numbers of cases at once.

[2]High-cube products were bulky items such as kitchen towels and ready-to-eat breakfast cereals.

Put away: Determine ways to increase the number of cases moved on each pallet.[3]

Replenish: Minimize the number of required pallet moves; for example, have large floor storage areas near the pick slots.[4]

Transportation: Ship high-cube products to the stores on slip sheets or dead-pile, thereby trading off equipment or labor costs at the store for transportation savings.[5]

Store: Develop methods of minimizing travel and storage time in the stocking process. Determine optimal packaging designs to reduce item stocking time.

By using DPP analysis, retailers could also tailor merchandising decisions to maximize sales of the high DPP items in general and/or in a particular product category. Merchandising and promotional considerations that could be affected by retailer DPP analyses included: pricing, product assortment and variety, new product listing decisions,[6] advertising and promotion, space allocation, and shelf and section location. Application priorities would likely vary according to each chain's overall merchandising philosophy (full service, discount price, one-stop shopping, etc.) and the competitive environment.

In 1986, use of DPP by grocery retailers varied widely. The more advanced chains used it to evaluate the relative profitability of different product categories through gross margins adjusted for DPCs and, in so doing, to optimize shelf space allocation.

MANUFACTURER IMPLICATIONS

For manufacturers, the use of DPP by retailers had significant implications. They would have to consider each trade account's DPCs in setting their policies on pricing, retail margins, and promotional allowances. In addition, they would have to work to reduce the DPCs on their products. For example, packaging changes that increased a product's "stackability" might significantly lower the cost of stocking shelves and therefore increase the product's unit DPP. This increase might be reflected in the product's retail price, the number of stores in which the product was distributed, shelf space/location, and promotional support. Manufacturers that made an effort to

---

[3]A pallet was a wooden base measuring 48″ × 40″ and 6″ high on which merchandise could be stacked for warehousing and transportation. The pallet size was standardized to facilitate movement by fork-lift trucks.

[4]A pick slot was a warehouse space in which a product was stored and from which stock was drawn.

[5]A slip sheet was a more efficient form of pallet. It measured 51″ × 43″ when its four 3″-high sides were folded down, and was only ½″ thick at its base. Deadpile merchandise was not stored on a pallet or slip sheet; therefore it had to be loaded and unloaded by hand.

[6]Listing occurred when a retail buying committee decided to stock a new product.

understand DPP from the perspective of the retailer and educated their sales forces about DPP were thought likely to gain a competitive advantage.

THE DIRECT PRODUCT PROFIT COMPUTER MODEL

A Direct Product Profit computer model for seven disguised coffee brands was developed for use with this case to provide an opportunity to practice working with DPP and DPC. The model is on diskette and is intended for use with the Lotus 1-2-3 version 1A software package on an IBM or IBM-compatible Personal Computer.

The model is based on the coffee product category and includes DPP and DPC factors used by the retail trade in 1986. The exercise does not cover all DPC factors and data. For example, advertising costs and revenues and forward-buying profits are not included, and unit costs are averaged over all the SKUs of each brand. The variety of DPCs contained in the model does, however, provide opportunities for realistic exploration of the impact of three hypothetical promotional scenarios presented at the end of this case.

The DPP model includes six sections. Sections I–III include basic information on the seven coffee brands and the DPC values associated with each. Section IV provides an area for input of variables for a hypothetical promotional scenario. Section V provides information on the effect of the hypothetical promotion on DPP. Section VI provides comparative DPP information on the seven brands and the three hypothetical promotions presented in the exercises at the end of the case. If the hypothetical promotion affects DPCs, changes to DPCs must be entered into the appropriate area of Section III.

Several cells in the model are protected; the values within the cells cannot be changed by entering new values into the model. Some protected cells contain formulas, however, and the values within these cells may change when other cells in the worksheet are modified. Unprotected cells, on the other hand, can be modified to reflect the assumptions of hypothetical scenarios simply by entering new values into the cells. In the model, unprotected cells appear in bolder type on the screen than do protected cells. Unprotected cells in each section are noted and described in the instructions that follow. *Do not insert new rows into the model; this will impair its function.*

INSTRUCTIONS FOR LOADING THE DPP MODEL

- ☐   Load Lotus 1-2-3 Spreadsheet in Drive A and
- ☐   Place DPP Model diskette in Drive B.
- ☐   Retrieve the file DPPFILE by typing: /FR DPPFILE and pressing the "enter" key.

DESCRIPTIONS OF SECTIONS OF THE DPP MODEL

Section I

Section I provides the following information for nonpromoted weeks for each of the seven coffee brands covered in the model: the number of stockkeeping units (SKUs) carried; cubic feet of shelf space; retail price; unit cost; gross margin percentage; weekly unit volume; weekly cost to retailer of all units sold; weekly retail dollar sales; direct product profit per unit, per cubic foot, and per week; and gross margin per unit, per cubic foot, and per week. It also shows the appropriate totals and averages for the coffee category. This section of the model is located in cells A1–X14 and AA1–AF13. When the model is loaded, the screens from Section I will appear as they are shown in Exhibit 3.

The information contained in Section I is the most basic data on the seven coffee brands, showing the characteristics of each brand under normal nonpromoted circumstances. Several cells in Section I are unprotected to allow flexibility in using the model; however these unprotected cells need not and should not be changed to complete the exercises at the end of this case. They already contain the necessary data for the exercises.

Unprotected cells	Information in cells
C6–C12	Number of SKUs
E6–E12	Cubic feet of shelf space
G6–G12	Retail price
I6–I12	Unit cost
M6–M12	Weekly unit sales
J1	Case pack (number of items per case)

If, in working with the model, changes are made to the unprotected cells, the other data in Section I can be calculated by pressing F9.

Section II

Section II shows a variety of Standard Direct Product Cost factors for each brand. Exhibit 4 shows Section II screens as they appear when the model is loaded. These DPC factors are presented in two sections, Warehousing DPCs and Store DPCs. Warehousing DPCs include costs incurred by the retailer before the brand reaches the store, such as: in-labor (labor used moving product from the truck to the appropriate place in the warehouse), out-labor (labor used selecting and moving product from warehouse to truck), warehouse space (allocation of warehouse costs to the warehouse space used by the product), invoice (cost of checking invoice), transportation, and inventory holding cost. Store DPCs include: pricing labor (labor to place prices on products), checking and bagging labor, other labor (primarily labor to stock shelves), selling space (allocation of store costs to the selling space

EXHIBIT 3 Section I screens

```
                                                                                READY

                 A                B        C         D      E     F      G       H
1                                 *                  DIRECT PRODU CT PROFIT--COFFEE
2  ****************************** ************************** ********************
3                                                    * CU.FT.   * RETAIL          *
4   CANNED COFFEE                 *  # SKU           * SHELF    * PRICE           *
5   ***************************** **************** ********** ******************
6   GOLD BLEND                    *               16 *    25.71 *           $2.92 *
7   MOUNTAIN TOP                  *                4 *     4.92 *           $2.36 *
8   MORNING GLORY                 *                9 *    10.45 *           $2.66 *
9   CABANA                        *                6 *     6.17 *           $2.42 *
10  LATIN PRIDE                   *               11 *     14.9 *           $2.64 *
11  PRIVATE LABEL                 *                6 *     8.75 *           $2.66 *
12  RICARDO                       *                4 *     10.1 *           $2.81 *
13  ***************************** **************** ********** ******************
14  TOTAL COFFEE                  *               56 *       81 *           $2.67 *
15  -----------------------------* ----------------* ---------* -----------------*

       I       J     K     L     M     N      O      P      Q     R S    T
1              24
2   ***********************************************************************
3   UNIT       * MARGIN  * WEEKLY   * WEEKLY COST * WEEKLY SALES* *  PER
4   COST       *         * UNITS    *             *             * *  UNIT
5   ***********  ******** ********** ************* ************* **********
6       $2.66 *    8.90%*       651 *   $1,731.66 *   $1,900.92 * *   $0.19
```

	U	V	W	X	Y	Z	AA	AB	AC	AD	AE	AF
7	**$2.06** *	12.71%*	417 *	859.02 *	984.12 *	*	$0.25					
8	**$2.41** *	9.40%*	280 *	674.80 *	744.80 *	*	$0.18					
9	**$2.06** *	14.88%*	144 *	$296.64 *	348.48 *	*	$0.29					
10	**$2.44** *	7.58%*	192 *	468.48 *	506.88 *	*	$0.10					
11	**$2.47** *	7.14%*	167 *	412.49 *	444.22 *	*	$0.12					
12	**$2.54** *	9.61%*	81 *	205.74 *	227.61 *	*	$0.16					
13	**********	**************	**********	************	************	**********	**********					
14	$2.41 *	9.85%*	1932 *	$4,648.83 *	$5,157.03 *	*	$0.18					
15	------- *	------ *	----- *	------ *	----- *							

	U	V	W	X	Y	Z	AA	AB	AC	AD	AE	AF
1	DIRECT PRODUCT PROFIT						GROSS MARGIN					
2	********************************						******************************					
3	* PER *	PER *					* PER *	PER *	PER			
4	* CU.FT. *	WEEK *					* UNIT *	CU.FT. *	WEEK			
5	*************						*************					
6	* $4.82 *	$124.02 *					* $0.26 *	$6.58 *	$169.26			
7	* $20.83 *	$102.50 *					* $0.30 *	$25.43 *	$125.10			
8	* $4.70 *	$49.14 *					* $0.25 *	$6.70 *	$70.00			
9	* $6.75 *	$41.63 *					* $0.36 *	$8.40 *	$51.84			
10	* $1.32 *	$19.68 *					* $0.20 *	$2.58 *	$38.40			
11	* $2.26 *	$19.76 *					* $0.19 *	$3.63 *	$31.73			
12	* $1.24 *	$12.57 *					* $0.27 *	$2.17 *	$21.87			
13	* **********	**********					* **********	**********	**********			
14	* $4.39 *	$355.54 *										
15	* ------ *	------ *										

Note: Boldface numbers designate unprotected cells.

EXHIBIT 4 Section II screens

	A	B	C	D	E	F	G	H
16	--------	*	--------	*	--------	*	--------	*
17	DIRECT PRODUCT COSTS	*		*	WAREHOUSING DPC			*
18	************************		IN		OUT		WHSE	
19	CANNED COFFEE	*	LABOR	*	LABOR	*	SPACE	*
20	************************		************		************		************	
21	GOLD BLEND	*	$0.0063	*	$0.0166	*	$0.0046	*
22	MOUNTAIN TOP	*	$0.0046	*	$0.0152	*	$0.0042	*
23	MORNING GLORY	*	$0.0079	*	$0.0165	*	$0.0038	*
24	CABANA	*	$0.0047	*	$0.0165	*	$0.0037	*
25	LATIN PRIDE	*	$0.0075	*	$0.0214	*	$0.0056	*
26	PRIVATE LABEL	*	$0.0055	*	$0.0171	*	$0.0049	*
27	RICARDO	*	$0.0106	*	$0.0274	*	$0.0067	*
28	************************		************		************		************	
29	TOTAL COFFEE	*	$0.0067	*	$0.0187	*	$0.0048	*
30	************************		************		************		************	

	I	J	K	L	M	N	O	P	Q	R	S	T
16	--------	*	--------	*	--------	*	--------	*				
17		*		*		*	PRICING	*	STORE		DPC	
18	INVOICE	*	TRANS	*	INVNTRY	*	LABOR	*	CHK & BAG	*	*OTHER	
19		*		*		*		*		*	*LABOR	
20	************		************		************		************		************		************	
21	$0.0005	*	$0.0063	*	$0.0013	**	$0.0016	*	$0.0086	* *	$0.0159	
22	$0.0006	*	$0.0062	*	$0.0004	**	$0.0016	*	$0.0084	* *	$0.0146	

150

```
     U           V          W          X          Y          Z          AA          AB          AC          AD    AE    AF
23              $0.0007 *  $0.0061 *  $0.0025 **             $0.0016 *              $0.0082 *  *  $0.0190
24              $0.0007 *  $0.0047 *  $0.0005 **             $0.0017 *              $0.0083 *  *  $0.0206
25              $0.0008 *  $0.0071 *  $0.0033 **             $0.0017 *              $0.0082 *  *  $0.0236
26              $0.0006 *  $0.0063 *  $0.0010 **             $0.0017 *              $0.0085 *  *  $0.0168
27              $0.0010 *  $0.0095 *  $0.0005 **             $0.0017 *              $0.0084 *  *  $0.0286
28          *********                            *********************************************  ***********
29              $0.0007 *  $0.0066 *  $0.0014 **             $0.0017 *              $0.0084 *  *  $0.0199
30          *********                            *********************************************  ***********
```

```
     U    V          W         X           Y       Z        AA       AB       AC       AD   AE   AF
16   *    --------*  --------*            *
17   *            *          *            *              DIRECT PRODUCT PROFIT TOTALS
18   *  SELLING *  INVTRY *  TOTAL    *  TOTAL    *  TOTAL    *
19   *  SPACE   *          *  WAREHOUSE *  STORE    *  DPC      *
20   *  *********  *********  *********  *********  *********  ***********
21   *  $0.0113 *  ($0.0035)*  $0.0356 *  $0.0339 *  $0.0695 *
22   *  $0.0031 *  ($0.0047)*  $0.0312 *  $0.0230 *  $0.0542 *
23   *  $0.0100 *  ($0.0018)*  $0.0375 *  $0.0370 *  $0.0745 *
24   *  $0.0123 *  ($0.0028)*  $0.0308 *  $0.0401 *  $0.0709 *
25   *  $0.0185 *  ($0.0002)*  $0.0457 *  $0.0518 *  $0.0975 *
26   *  $0.0127 *  ($0.0034)*  $0.0354 *  $0.0363 *  $0.0717 *
27   *  $0.0208 *  ($0.0004)*  $0.0557 *  $0.0591 *  $0.1148 *
28   *  *********  *********  *********  *********  *********  ***********
29   *  $0.0127 *  ($0.0024)*  $0.0388 *  $0.0402 *  $0.0790 *
30   *  *********  *********  *********  *********  *********  ***********
```

used by the product), inventory holding cost, and totals. Section II is located in cells A16–AE30. All of the data in this section have been protected. Entries of new values cannot be made. Changes to DPCs that would result from implementing the hypothetical promotion scenarios in the exercises at the end of this case should be made in Section III.

Section III

Section III provides product and cost data on a specific coffee brand. Section III screens are shown in Exhibit 5. The location of the section is in cells A31–E43 and G31–J46. The name of the specific coffee brand appears in cell C34. The coffee brand data appearing in Section III can be changed by holding down the "ALT" key and pressing the letter "M." A menu will appear in the upper left of the screen containing abbreviated brand names. Select a brand by moving the cursor using the right arrow, then press "Enter." All data in Columns C and I will change to reflect your selection (except C42 and I45).

Unprotected cells	Information in cells
C34–C41	Presents cost, price, DPP, and DPC data per unit and DPP data per cubic foot for normal nonpromoted weeks. *These cells are unprotected but data should not be entered here. The model will enter data for each brand when "ALT" and "M" are pressed and a brand selection is made.*
I34–44	Standard Direct Product Costs, as defined in Section II, which can be modified to reflect the influence of hypothetical promotional scenarios.

To change the brand data, hold down the "ALT" key and press the letter "M." A menu will appear in the upper left of the screen.

To calculate Cell C42, Cell I45, and Cells E35–42 press "F9."

"What Ifing" can be practiced with any DPC in Column I. (Results of changes will be seen in Section V.)

Caution: Information in Cells C34–41 and I34–44 is not protected. Care should be taken not to enter data inadvertently here.

Comment: If after bringing up the Special Brand Menu (Alt M) you wish to "Escape" without making a selection, press "CTRL" and "Break" at the same time.

Section IV

Major assumptions of hypothetical promotional offers should be entered in Section IV. This section is located in cells A43–E50. Exhibit 6 shows the screen for Section

EXHIBIT 5 Section III screen

```
           A                          B         C         D        E       F
31  ********************************************************************
32  PROMOTION                    PRESS ALT M FOR MACRO                     *
33  ********************************************************************
34  PRODUCT                     *      GOLDEN BLEND**                      *
35  NORMAL RETAIL/UNIT & /CASE  *           $2.92 **         $70.08        *
36  NORMAL % MARGIN             *           8.90%**          8.90%*
37  NORMAL DPP/UNIT & /CASE      *         $0.1905 **         $4.57        *
38  NORMAL COST/UNIT & /CASE     *          $2.66 **         $63.64        *
39  NORM WK_Y SALES-UNITS,CASES  *            651 **            35         *
40  NORMAL DPC/UNIT & /CASE      *         $0.0695 **         $1.67        *
41  NORMAL DPP/CU FT & PER WEEK  *          $4.82 ***       $124.02        *
42  NORMAL MARGIN/UNIT & /CASE   *          $0.26 **          $6.24        *
43  ********************************************************************


           F          G         H      I      J
31  ***************************************
32  **DIRECT PRODUCT COST CHANGES
33  ***************************************
34  **IN LABOR      **   $0.0063 **
35  **OUT LABOR     **   $0.0166 **
36  **WHSE SPACE    **   $0.0046 **
37  **INVOICE       **   $0.0005 **
38  **TRANSPORT     **   $0.0063 **
39  **INVENTORY     **   $0.0013 **
40  **PRICING       **   $0.0016 **
41  **CHK & BAG     **   $0.0086 **
42  **OTHER LABOR   **   $0.0159 **
43  **SELL SPACE    **   $0.0113 **
44  **INVENTORY     **  ($0.0035)**
45  **TOT. DPC      **   $0.0695 **
46  ***************************************
```

Note: Boldface numbers designate unprotected cells.

153

IV. Four pieces of information should be entered into the unprotected cells of this section: the type of offer (not necessary to the function of the model), the specific case allowance in dollars per case, the projected retail price during the feature period, and the anticipated increase in volume during the feature period shown by entering a number times normal volume (e.g., if volume were expected to increase 50%, the number entered would be 1.5). Cells E46–49 will calculate the assumptions on a per case basis.

Unprotected cells	Information to be entered
B44	Type of offer (maximum of 25 letters)
E45	Specific case allowance in dollars per case
C47	Projected retail price during the feature period
B49	Number times normal volume anticipated during the feature period

All other data in Section IV will be calculated after pressing "F9."

Section V

Section V provides an area to enter additional assumptions associated with each hypothetical promotion. These assumptions include, for example, the number of weeks the manufacturer offers a brand or trade deal prior to it being featured by the retailer. The DPP results for all data entered in other sections are also calculated in this section. Exhibit 6 also shows the Section V screen. It is located in cells A51–C65 and E52. The information that needs to be entered into the unprotected cells in this section is somewhat complicated. Each of the unprotected cells is described in the table below. An example follows these descriptions.

Unprotected cells	Information to be entered
C56	Enter number of weeks, if any, at pre-feature DPP before the brand is featured but while the promotional deal is in effect—for example, the two weeks preceding the brand feature but included in the period of the promotional offer.
C59	Following a brand feature, there is usually a decrease in brand volume that is proportionate to the magnitude of the feature. This cell accounts for the week(s) at that post-feature volume while the brand remains on deal to the retailer. Enter the percentage of normal volume (e.g., 0.5) for the week(s).
C61	Enter number of weeks, excluding the feature week(s), at post-feature volume—for example, the one week following the brand feature but included in the period of the promotional offer.

Example.   A manufacturer places a brand on deal for four weeks. For the first two weeks of the promotional period, the brand continues to be sold at its normal retail price (i.e., the brand is not yet featured). In cell C56, the number "2" should be entered to represent the two weeks. The brand is featured for one week. During the fourth week while the brand can still be bought on deal from the manufacturer, retail brand volume drops to 60% of pre-feature volume. The number "0.6" should be entered in cell C59 to account for this post-feature volume. To represent the one week of post-feature volume after the feature week, the number "1" should be entered into cell C61.

Definitions of calculated values:

C52—revised DPC, as determined by changes in Section III, Column I (Cell
    E52 = revised DPC per case).

C53—promotion week DPP/Loss—normal margin minus revised DPC times
    volume for the week(s) while the brand is featured.

C54–C63—other pre-feature/reduced volume weeks.

C55—pre-feature DPP plus any trade deal times pre-feature volume.

C58—total DPP at pre-feature week volume plus deal.

C60—post-feature DPP per week.

C63—total post-feature DPP.

C64—total DPP for all weeks.

Section VI

Section VI presents a table showing DPPs per unit, per cubic foot, and per week for the seven coffee brands. This section also provides a seven-brand average DPP and space for DPP information associated with the deals presented in the exercises at the end of the case. Section VI is located in cells A81–H100. The screen for Section VI is also shown in Exhibit 6. Once each DPP analysis in the exercises at the end of the case is performed and the "F9" key is pressed, the resulting DPP per unit, per cubic foot, and per week will appear in cells C100, E100, and G100, respectively. These numbers can then be entered into the appropriate cells for each exercise as follows:

Exercise 1:	C95	DPP per unit for Exercise 1
	E95	DPP per cubic foot for Exercise 1
	G95	DPP per week for Exercise 1
Exercise 2:	C96	DPP per unit for Exercise 2
	E96	DPP per cubic foot for Exercise 2
	G96	DPP per week for Exercise 2
Exercise 3:	C97	DPP per unit for Exercise 2
	E97	DPP per cubic foot for Exercise 2
	G97	DPP per week for Exercise 2

EXHIBIT 6 Section IV screen

	A	B	C	D	E	F	G	H
43	******************	************************SELL SPACE **						
44	TYPE OFFER	REDUCED PRICE FEATURE				**INVENTORY **		
45	CASE RATE	*		$0.00	**TOT. DPC **			
46	COST UNIT/CASE	*	$2.66	$63.84	******************			
47	RETAIL PRICE	*	$2.92	$70.08	**			
48	MARG. @ SUG.RET.	*	$0.26	$6.24	**			
49	PROMO VOL(X NORM)	1	651	27	**			
50	**							

Section V screen

	A	B	C	D	E	F	G	H
51	***							
52	REVISED DPC	*	$0.0695	**	$1.6680	**		
53	PROMO WK DPP/LOSS	*	$124.02					
54	OTHER WKS DPP/LOSS	*	**************					
55	NORMAL+TRADE DEAL	*	$124.02					
56	TIMES WEEKS	*	2					
57	TOTAL DPP NORMAL	*	-------------					
58	NON FEATURE WEEKS	*	$248.03					
59	OTHER(%NORMAL)+DEAL	*	100.00%					
60	OTHER WEEKS DPP	*	$124.02					
61	TIMES WEEKS	*	1					
62	TOTAL DPP ALL	*	-------------					
63	OTHER WEEKS	*	$124.02					

	A	B	C	D	E	F	G	H
64	TOTAL DPP ALL WEEKS	*			$496.06			
65	************************************							

Section VI screen

	A	B	C	D	E	F	G	H
81	COMPARISON OF DEALS WITH CURRENT TERMS USING THREE DPP MEASURES:							
82		*		DIRECT PRODUCT PROFIT				
83	***							
84			PER	*	PER	*	PER	*
85	CANNED COFFEE	*	UNIT	*	CUBIC FT	*	WEEK	*
86	***							
87	GOLDBL	*	$0.19	*	$4.82	*	$124.02	*
88	MTNTOP	*	$0.25	*	$20.83	*	$102.50	*
89	MOGLO	*	$0.18	*	$4.70	*	$49.14	*
90	CABANA	*	$0.29	*	$6.75	*	$41.63	*
91	LATIN	*	$0.10	*	$1.32	*	$19.68	*
92	PVTLBL	*	$0.12	*	$2.26	*	$19.76	*
93	RICARDO	*	$0.16	*	$1.24	*	$12.57	*
94	7 BRND AV	*	$0.18	*	$5.99	*	$52.76	*
95	DEAL #1	*	**$0.00**	*	**$0.00**	*	**$0.00**	*
96	DEAL #2	*	**$0.00**	*	**$0.00**	*	**$0.00**	*
97	DEAL #3	*	**$0.00**	*	**$0.00**	*	**$0.00**	*
98	AV W/DEAL 1&2		$0.11	*	$4.34	*	$29.09	*
99								
100	PROPOSED DEAL	*	$0.19	*	$4.82	*	$124.02	*

Note: Boldface numbers designate unprotected cells.

157

When the information above is entered into the model, average DPPs for the seven coffee brands, including the deals in Exercises 1 and 2, can be calculated by pressing the "F9" key. These averages will appear in cells C98, E98, and G98.

EXERCISES

The exercises in this section were designed to provide practice in using the DPP model and to show how the attractiveness of different manufacturer promotions to the trade may vary according to how the terms of the promotion impact DPCs. Three different scenarios are presented with promotional and DPC assumptions explained. The DPC assumptions are meant to represent the probable cost changes associated with each scenario and may not be all inclusive. Each assumption should be entered into the model in the appropriate place and the DPP should be calculated by pressing "F9" once changes are made.

1. Off-invoice trade allowance of $3.00 per statistical case on Cabana brand.

   Assumptions:
   a. trade allowance is $3.00 (cell E45 = 3)
   b. DPC: pricing up 20% (cell I40 = 0.0020)
            other labor up 50% (cell I42 = 0.0309) to deal with out-of-stocks
   c. retail price change to $2.29 (cell C47 = 2.29)
   d. promotional volume times normal = 3 (cell B49 = 3)
   e. 2 weeks at pre-feature volume (normal retail price) (cell C56 = 2)
   f. 1 post-feature week (cell C61 = 1) at 60% (cell C59 = 0.60) pre-feature volume

2. Direct store-door delivery (as opposed to warehouse delivery) of prepacked, prepriced floor stands of Gold Blend brand.

   Assumptions:
   a. DPC: no in-labor cost (i.e., drops to 0) (cell I34)
            no out-labor cost (cell I35)
            no warehouse space cost (cell I36)
            no transportation cost (cell I38)
            no warehouse inventory cost (cell I39)
            no pricing cost (cell I40)
            selling space up 100% (cell I43)
   b. no promotional offer (cell C45)
   c. retail price change to $2.85 (cell C47)
   d. promotional volume times normal = 1.5 (cell B49)
   e. 2 weeks at pre-feature volume (cell C56)

      f. 1 week at post-feature volume (cell C61) at 70% of pre-feature volume (cell C59 = .70)

  3. A pallet-sized end-aisle display with prepriced product and a trade allowance of $4.00 per statistical case delivered cross-dock (i.e., displays not placed or stored in trade warehouse, but moved directly across the dock to be transported to the chain's stores) for Morning Glory brand.

Assumptions:

a. trade allowance is $4.00

b. DPC: in-labor down 25%
        out-labor down 25%
        no warehouse space cost
        no warehouse inventory cost (cell = I39)
        pricing cost down 20% (prepriced package results in much lower cost; however, prepriced stock must be placed on shelves)
        other labor down 10% (restocking of shelves lower than normal because of end-aisle display)
        selling space up 150% (space for end-aisle display)

c. retail price change to $2.19 (prepriced by manufacturer)

d. promotional volume times normal = 10

e. 2 pre-feature weeks at pre-feature volume

f. 1 post-feature week at 40% pre-feature volume

If you were a salesperson presenting these three programs to a major trade account with the DPCs and DPPs presented in the model, what arguments would you make in each case? How might you amend or improve upon the assumptions provided? What concerns would you or the trade account have in each case? How would those concerns change if the trade account used gross margin rather than DPP to evaluate each deal?

The model also contains several graphs that can be used to compare brands and the deals presented in the exercises above. These graphs can be accessed by typing:

/GNU (This stands for the Lotus commands Graph, Name, and Use.)

The graph names will appear at the top of the screen. To view a graph, select a name using the cursor and press "Enter." The graph will appear on the screen.

INVENTORY RISK AND SOFT GOODS MERCHANDISING

JOHN A. QUELCH

The buying and selling of soft goods such as apparel and footwear typically involve more risk than buying and selling dry groceries. Product formulations of dry grocery brands remain constant from one year to the next; most manufacturers of apparel, in contrast, launch two or more multiple-item product lines each year that ideally shape, or at least reflect, the latest style and color preferences of consumers. Often these product lines must be manufactured out of the country with correspondingly long production and delivery lead times; this means that in determining the merchandise mix to be produced, manufacturers have to rely as much on their judgment as on orders placed by customers. The considerable uncertainty in accurately forecasting consumer demand raises the risk of excess inventory in the distribution channel, with the corresponding potential for large markdowns to be absorbed if the merchandise is not sold through. It is also one reason why distributor margins on apparel are so much higher than on dry groceries. Because inventory risk is high, a major challenge to the apparel manufacturer is to achieve the sell-in of its merchandise to the retailer. Whereas the manufacturer of a dry grocery line with a strong brand franchise is often concerned with excessive forward buying by the trade, the apparel manufacturer more often than not faces the opposite problem.

Note that soft goods are not all equally fashion-sensitive. For example, as Table 1 indicates, men's socks are less fashion-sensitive than women's dresses. Their styles are not seasonal and their purchase, therefore, involves less inventory risk. Not surprisingly, promotion and merchandising programs used for low-ticket, nonfashion-sensitive items—L'eggs pantyhose, for example—tend to more closely replicate those used for packaged grocery products. In general, a higher percentage of women's than men's clothing is fashion-sensitive, subject to inventory risks and sold at markdown prices, though the gap may narrow as style and fashion are apparently becoming more important in men's clothing.

Based on "Note on Inventory Risk and Soft Goods Merchandising" by John A. Quelch. Copyright © 1987 by the President and Fellows of Harvard College; all rights reserved. Harvard Business School N-589-022.

TABLE 1   Classification of soft goods by price point
and fashion intensity

	Higher fashion	Lower fashion
Higher unit price	Designer dresses	Men's suits
Lower unit price	Sneakers	Men's socks

CONTROLLING INVENTORY RISK

As apparel manufacturers have gone offshore to manufacture their goods at lower cost, production lead times have increased, adding to the inventory exposure in the channel. Manufacturers and retailers use several approaches to reducing inventory risk.

Marketing Strategy

Some companies view themselves as fashion leaders and build a proportionately higher level of inventory risk into their cost structure. Others are fashion followers, attempting to "knock-off" the acknowledged leaders quickly; manufacturer and distributor margins in these cases are usually less generous. To reduce inventory risk, some manufacturers test market summer season apparel in Florida the previous winter.

Franchise Strength and Product Continuity

Obviously, there is less risk to the retailer in buying apparel from manufacturers with strong brand names and proven quality. Brands like Ralph Lauren emphasize classic styles that can hold retail value from one season to the next, and so reduce the level of obsolete inventories and consequent retail markdowns. Other successful brands like Liz Claiborne offer not two but six separate lines during the year; the retailer's inventory risk is reduced by not having to commit to as large a purchase order at any one time, and the retailer also benefits from the more frequent arrival of new merchandise, which stimulates consumer traffic.

Merchandising Programs

As part of their permanent pricing structure, many manufacturers offer retailers merchandising programs designed to encourage them to commit to more inventory. Early-buy allowances and dating programs, for example, aim to persuade retailers to both place their orders and take delivery of merchandise early; cancellation and order-adjustment penalties aim to ensure the integrity of these orders on the basis of which manufacturers set their production requirements. Inventory risk is also addressed by so-called "back-end" protection programs such as stock balancing and returns allowances. Stock balancing permits a retailer to exchange some of its merchandise for another product line or size from the same manufacturer, with the aim of making it less risky for the retailer to order earlier and in greater quantities. Excess inventory is usually reduced as a result, so retail markdowns are fewer and the manufacturer's brand image is maintained.

Not all soft goods manufacturers, particularly those selling seasonal fashion merchandise, will accept returns. They believe that a generous returns policy motivates buyers to take the ordering and merchandising process more casually.

Rather than subsidize returns, manufacturers prefer to encourage their retail customers to dispose of their excess inventories in an orderly fashion. Initially, retailers usually try to sell off excess merchandise during storewide sales. Most department and specialty stores follow a sequential process that offers progressively increasing discounts on sale merchandise. Unsold merchandise from these sales is sometimes consolidated in selected outlets located in lower-income markets for an extended sale. Remaining leftovers and remnants are jobbed out to off-price and close-out retailers.

Many retailers would prefer their suppliers to acknowledge that close-out retail sales on some of their products are inevitable and to do a better job of preplanning them as well as subsidizing the margin reductions. Manufacturers, however, see such preplanned programs as a self-fulfilling prophecy; retailers will not push at full price items they know will be closed out later.

Management Information Systems

Nowhere are risk reduction opportunities more evident than through the use of inventory control systems. For example, sales of each style of women's shoes sold through every Fisher-Camuto Corporation store are entered into the company computer at the end of the day. Computer-transmitted orders for replenishment stocks are sent overnight to Fisher-Camuto's factories in Brazil. This management information system results in fewer out-of-stocks and fewer excess inventories of slower-moving styles; hence, fewer markdowns. In addition, poorly performing styles can be quickly identified and marked down as necessary. Overall inventory investment can be reduced while customer service (measured in terms of in-stocks of items customers want) and inventory turnover rate can be increased.

FROM COOPERATION TO CONFUSION

There has typically been a greater spirit of partnership between apparel manufacturers and the trade than exists in dry grocery distribution channels. All parties recognize the inventory risk problem and attempt to minimize the costly markdowns that occur if the product is not sold through. Moreover, major retailers cannot afford to jeopardize the business health of their suppliers by overordering and not accepting ordered merchandise.

The apparel retailer's standard buying approach is to purchase the bulk of its merchandise in two buying cycles each year. Manufacturers present their merchandise, including new products, and their promotional programs. Store buyers then determine order quantities for each resource and negotiate prices, terms, and the timing and nature of merchandising support. Manufacturers will often customize promotion and merchandising programs that mesh with the themes that their major retail accounts want. They may subsidize direct-mail promotions to their retailers' customers. They may provide other value-added services such as training salespeople to ensure better sales push behind their merchandise. Large manufacturers have more resources and are thereby better able to supply such services and thus insulate themselves from lower-priced competitors.

However, the environment of apparel retailing is changing and, as a result, the spirit of partnership between manufacturers and retailers that has dealt with the inventory risk issue in the past, is under pressure. The following five changes are evident.

First, the increase in the segmentation and heterogeneity of consumers has prompted the emergence of new store formats—from higher-priced specialty chains like Laura Ashley, to off-price retailers like Syms that carry brand name merchandise at substantial discounts. The opening of such stores is adding to the problem of excess retail capacity relative to consumer spending and leading to aggressive year-round price competition.

Second, manufacturers are being tempted to distribute their products more intensively to maintain or boost sales. Because of more frequent demand-forecasting errors in the early 1980s, some manufacturers embraced off-price retailers as a means to dispose of production overruns. Many off-price retailers are attractive as customers because they do not look for cooperative advertising support, they pay more promptly than department stores because their inventory turns more rapidly, and they do not seek to ship merchandise to multiple distribution points. However, off-price retailing has exacerbated consumer price sensitivity, eroded high-price service-intensive channels, and has led to increases in private labeling, described later.

Third, manufacturers producing offshore are no longer able to guarantee swift availability of back-up inventories. This has encouraged inexperienced retail buyers to overbuy to be sure of stocking enough of the winning lines, thereby exacerbating end-of-season excess inventory. Moreover, any inventory carryovers reduce the open-to-buy allowances that buyers have for placing orders for new merchandise with each manufacturer.

Fourth, to retain market share against off-price retailers, department stores and other traditional apparel retailers can no longer afford to have only two "defensive" end-of-season clearance sales to rid themselves of broken assortments, mismatches, floor models, and discontinued lines. As Table 2 shows, they must now run promotional in-season sales of basic merchandise and offer sale merchandise on more shopping days than ever before. This further erodes the credibility of their normal shelf prices and adds to the percentage of total volume sold on sale.

TABLE 2   Types of merchandise associated with different types of sale

	Basics—Regular merchandise	Nonbasic merchandise
Defensive (end-of-season)	Excess inventories	Seconds Discontinued lines
Promotional (in-season)	National brand tie-ins	In-and-out items Make-ups

Fifth, as the peaks and valleys of retail sales become more pronounced, the apparel retailer's ability to make accurate inventory stock and ordering decisions is weakened, and the inventory risk due to demand uncertainty is increased.

To insulate themselves from price competition, traditional service-intensive apparel retailers are trying to stock merchandise that is not broadly available in competitive outlets. To do so, they are taking the following approaches in product assortment.

☐ Developing exclusive private-label lines that competitors do not carry. Neiman Marcus, with its strong store name, has an especially successful private-label program. Offshore apparel production means that retailers are at no disadvantage to brand-name manufacturers in negotiating with resources. Paradoxically, increased floor space devoted to private-label merchandise places national apparel brand manufacturers under pressure to provide even more promotional support and also makes demand forecasting for their merchandise harder. It also drives manufacturers to sell to off-price retailers to compensate for the lost volume due to top private-label sales, and so further fuels price competition in the industry.

☐ Concentrating on depth of assortment with a few resources rather than cherry-picking the lines of a larger number of resources; encouraging these selected resources to provide rebates for the number of stockkeeping units carried and to provide promotions on the slower-moving items.

☐ Purchasing some items from established resources on a make-up (specially designed for that store) basis and/or items from nonestablished resources on an in-out basis (specifically to be placed on sale). In-out items are useful for promotional purposes, but can jeopardize the consistency of the store's image and assortment. For the manufacturer, producing make-ups complicates production planning and adds costs.

Overall, the intensity of competition is eroding the traditional cooperation between apparel manufacturers and retailers. Fewer and fewer brands remain in exclusive or selective distribution. Retailers are increasingly demanding additional price promotions and merchandising support or temporary adjustments to discount schedules and terms of sale, over and above those negotiated at the start of each season. Ostensibly this is done to sell through inventory that is not moving as fast as projected; in truth, it also reflects a weakening ability to project inventory needs. Retail buyers are also reserving an increasing portion of the open-to-buy dollars they have available to place orders with manufacturers at the outset of each season for the purchase of close-out products in mid-season. In some cases, they are also asking manufacturers to specify their close-out items earlier in the season; manufacturers believe that doing so will detract from the retailer's selling efforts.

MANUFACTURING RESPONSES

Clearly, manufacturers of soft goods with strong brand reputations have more negotiating leverage with the trade than weaker franchise brands. They can maximize the productivity of their promotional expenditures by, for example:

☐ Allocating individual retailers a quantity of promotional merchandise proportional to their purchases of basic, full-price merchandise.

☐ Securing slots in the retailer's promotional calendar that are earlier (rather than later) in the season or at peak consumer buying periods, and given a continuing strong sales performance, securing the same slots for one year to the next on an anniversary basis.

The smartest manufacturers are also responding to the pressure for additional promotion and merchandising support by using other elements of the marketing mix to insulate themselves from it. For example:

☐ By concentrating on developing new and appealing product assortments, manufacturers try to ensure a measure of consumer excitement that will pull the product through the channel regardless of price and promotional support.

☐ By developing additional and innovative value-added services, perhaps custom-tailored to the needs of their major accounts, larger manufacturers can cement partnerships that are now in danger of eroding.

Manufacturers are also trying to tighten their control of distribution channels. Several brand-name apparel manufacturers such as Ralph Lauren have established or licensed specialty stores selling their brands exclusively. These stores can be relied on to stock a full assortment of merchandise properly displayed to reflect the lifestyle that the manufacturer is promoting.

While Ralph Lauren stores are found in upscale locations, Van Heusen, discovering that many department stores wished to stock only Arrow and private-label shirts, has established over 100 Van Heusen factory outlet stores nationwide. These stores are sited in low-rent locations beyond the trading areas of a manufacturer's regular retailers. They offer manufacturers better control over pricing and disposal of merchandise, but are not appropriate for items that are highly seasonal, like toys, or for a line that is too narrow for its product category to justify its own store. In addition, factory outlets can begin to cannibalize sales through regular channels and put pressure on retail prices if outlets become too well known, a trend that is fueled by the development of factory outlet malls.

To summarize, through forward integration in the distribution channel, through product and service innovation, and through enhancing the productivity of their promotion and merchandising expenditures, soft goods manufacturers are trying to retain a measure of channel control in the face of a changing retail environment that is accentuating the level of inventory risk.

HARTMANN LUGGAGE COMPANY: PRICE PROMOTION POLICY

JOHN A. QUELCH
PENNY PITTMAN MERLISS

In January 1981, Ira Katz, president of the Hartmann Luggage Company, was evaluating past price promotions and considering whether to continue offering them in the coming year. A consultants' study endorsed by the company's chief financial officer had concluded that one of Hartmann's price promotions, though it increased sales, had generated a contribution below what would have been obtained if the promotion had not been run. On the other hand, Thomas Schuster, Hartmann's recently appointed vice president for sales and marketing, questioned several key assumptions of this study. He believed price promotions could increase trade interest in Hartmann, attract new customers, and encourage current customers to add new pieces to their existing Hartmann collections.

Katz remained dubious, commenting to Schuster:

> I think price promotion hurts the Hartmann image. We can do other exciting things to get dealer support, increase sales, and still maintain suggested retail prices. Remember, we increased sales by 20% in the year just ended with only a minor promotion but significantly more advertising. However, I'm open to persuasion. Let's reassess all our past promotions and review the consultants' study. In addition, let's consider how price promotion policy will fit with our future marketing strategy and, in particular, with the product line additions we're considering for 1981–1982.

COMPANY BACKGROUND

The Hartmann Luggage Company was founded in Milwaukee in 1877 to manufacture trunks; it began producing luggage in 1930. Katz became president in 1957, not long after his father purchased the company; in 1960 he moved both the corporate offices and manufacturing plant to Lebanon, Tennessee.

From the outset Hartmann's products were among the most expensive in the industry, designed for customers who demanded the highest quality and durability in luggage. The company distributed its merchandise only through leading department stores and luggage specialty shops, and until 1955 it restricted distribution to one carefully selected dealer in each market area. Under Katz's leadership Hartmann widened its distribution, reduced its product line, and developed a comprehensive training program for retail salespeople.

During 1980 Hartmann's revenues totaled $33 million with pretax earnings of about 12%. Company sales grew at an average annual rate of 22% between 1974 and 1980, compared with 5% for the luggage industry as a whole. Katz wanted Hartmann to achieve an earnings growth rate of 25–30% annually, maintain a prestigious image, and increase its share of the high-quality luggage market.

The Product Line

Hartmann's manufacturing process was relatively labor intensive. Among the distinctive features common to all framed Hartmann luggage were wooden frames, built square to allow extra space in packing, and 24-carat gold-plated Touch-O-Matic locks, recessed behind distinctive flaps and designed for easy opening. Handles were hand-sewn double loops bolted through case frames. All framed case interiors were lined with fabric specially treated with Zepel stain repellent.

All luggage was sold under the Hartmann name. Katz had considered manufacturing private-label luggage, but believed it might jeopardize the firm's quality image without increasing consumer recognition of the Hartmann brand. The product line included four series of luggage in both framed and soft-sided pieces. Models and styles were similar from one series to another, but prices differed within models on the basis of variations in outside covering. Exhibit 1 shows comparative retail selling prices and pieces available for the four series, with a summary of trade orders.

The most expensive series was the 4700, illustrated in Figure 1, a collection of men's luggage made from industrial belting leather. Prices on this line had increased 100% since 1975 because of the rising cost of leather. The 4800 series, available in both men's and women's models, was manufactured in two colors of Ultrasuede, a fabric (made popular by the fashion designer Halston) that looked like expensive suede but could be wiped clean with soap and water. The 4400 series was made of a durable synthetic fiber that resembled tweed and was trimmed with belting leather. Finally, the 4200 series was manufactured in both vinyl and fabric with vinyl trim.

As soft-sided, flexible, lighter-weight luggage became more popular in the 1960s and 1970s, Hartmann had developed the Nouveau Hobo line. It was available in belting leather (4700) and Ultrasuede (4800), but sold most widely in a strong

EXHIBIT 1 Retail prices, pieces available, and unit orders by series, 1976–1980

	1980 Retail prices*	1980 Pieces available	Unit orders‡ 1976 Spring†	1976 Fall	1977 Spring	1977 Fall	1978 Spring	1978 Fall	1979 Spring	1979 Fall	1980 Spring	1980 Fall
Men's styles												
Belting leather (4700)	$415	10	5,940 (100)	5,914 (100)	7,012 (118)	6,670 (113)	8,258 (139)	8,300 (140)	9,044 (152)	6,116 (103)	4,720 (79)	6,968 (118)
Ultrasuede (4300)	315	10	6,796 (100)	4,758 (100)	3,580 (53)	2,950 (62)	3,622 (53)	4,832 (102)	6,678 (98)	4,086 (86)	3,384 (50)	3,956 (83)
Fabric (4400)	215	17	14,120 (100)	21,232 (100)	19,912 (141)	19,426 (91)	22,278 (158)	21,916 (103)	43,298 (307)	27,030 (128)	37,692 (267)	35,656 (168)
Fabric/vinyl (4200)	150	9	1,652 (100)	996 (100)	–	–	–	–	–	–	–	750 (45)
Vinyl (4200)	140	10	21,994 (100)	21,556 (100)	36,652 (167)	46,116 (214)	59,164 (269)	42,404 (198)	50,892 (231)	40,022 (186)	40,938 (186)	49,060 (228)
Women's styles												
Ultrasuede (4800)	$295	9	4,052 (100)	6,532 (100)	5,240 (129)	4,076 (62)	4,968 (123)	3,102 (47)	5,182 (129)	3,034 (46)	2,364 (58)	3,038 (47)
Fabric (4400)	185	12	12,338 (100)	6,974 (100)	16,696 (135)	21,114 (303)	22,110 (179)	22,782 (327)	31,374 (254)	20,952 (301)	34,616 (281)	27,518 (395)
Fabric/vinyl (4200)	130	8	8,254 (100)	6,742 (100)	10,822 (131)	12,853 (191)	26,266 (318)	12,652 (188)	13,828 (168)	6,902 (102)	5,190 (63)	10,566 (157)
Vinyl (4200)	120	8	19,364 (100)	23,608 (100)	22,904 (118)	23,750 (101)	28,414 (147)	18,356 (78)	22,692 (117)	14,100 (60)	17,780 (92)	29,130 (123)

Source: Company records

*Prices are for a man's and a woman's under-seat carry-on.

†Spring 1976 index = 100.

‡Unit orders of in-line merchandise only. For example, spring 1980 figures do not include orders of the specially manufactured promotion pieces similar to the 4400 series.

For That Extra Touch

When traveling for business or pleasure, why shouldn't you have the ultimate in luggage? Natural Belting Leather - by Hartmann.
This three-piece "carry-on" luggage group consists of · Hanger garment carrier, made of strong, durable nylon and belting leather; may be carried open or folded. Capacity - 3 suits, 6 shirts, etc.
The carry-on single suiter has ample space as an over-nighter. All Belting Leather.
The attache case, also in Belting Leather, is attractive, spacious, with desk and three-pocket file. Even the interior trim is Belting Leather.
One or all three make you feel like a Special Person.

hartmann luggage

- Handcrafted.
- Flexible frame.
- Soft expanding sides.
- Rugged hand sewn leather handle.
- Touch-O-Matic locks cover flaps for neatness and safety.
- Zepel stain repellent.
- Removable desk and file section (attache case only).

FIGURE 1 Hartmann's
most expensive luggage
(4700 series)

Source: Merchandising sheet

nylon fabric trimmed with belting leather (4400), shown in Figure 2. Nouveau Hobo bags were for the most part highly flexible carry-ons and totes, built on a patented "Featherflex" skeleton frame to keep their shape. In the spring season of 1980, about 13,000 Nouveau Hobo pieces were ordered.

Katz was considering several changes to Hartmann's product line in 1981. Sales of the Ultrasuede line were weakening, and he was considering replacing it. Hartmann could also introduce an additional line of designer luggage at a price point 10% to 15% below that of the 4200 line. The firm's advertising agency believed that this brightly colored casual luggage designed by Gloria Vanderbilt could be distributed through women's specialty stores as well as department and luggage stores; it recommended that Hartmann budget $725,000 in 1982 to introduce the new line. Agency executives argued that the line would enable Hartmann to broaden its customer base to include women aged 25 or older from households with $25,000 or more in annual income. Management characterized its present customers as aged 35 or older and living in households with at least $35,000 annual income.

Source: Merchandising sheet

FIGURE 2   Nouveau Hobo, Hartmann's flexible luggage (4400 series)

The Luggage Industry

The dollar value (at manufacturers' prices) of all luggage products sold in the United States in 1980 totaled $664 million.[1] Sales were forecast to increase 9% in 1981—to $724 million. Imports, whose dollar value had risen at a compound annual rate of 34% since 1974, accounted for 29% of 1980 sales. During the 1970s most imports had been low-quality, nonleather items, but by 1980 many retailers were praising the quality and construction of the leather and leather-trimmed luggage from Italy and South America.

Government statistics listed 293 luggage manufacturers in the United States; only 124 had more than 20 employees. Two firms dominated the luggage market:

[1]The U.S. Commerce Department's definition of luggage products included, in addition to suitcases and travel bags, briefcases, bags for sports and hobby equipment (golf, photography, shooting), physicians' bags, and salespeople's sample cases.

Samsonite Corp. (a subsidiary of Beatrice Foods, Inc.), with estimated 1979 sales of $140 million (including some folding furniture), and American Tourister (a subsidiary of Hillenbrand Industries, Inc.), with 1979 sales of about $85 million. Both brands were priced about 75% below Hartmann's 4700 line. According to Katz, Hartmann's most significant direct competitors were Lark (a subsidiary of General Mills, Inc.), and French—both of which produced fashionably designed, durable, and expensive luggage of high quality. Katz estimated Lark's 1979 sales at $20 million and French's at $6 million. Louis Vuitton, an imported line priced 25% above Hartmann's 4700 series, sold an estimated $8 million in 1979; Katz believed this brand competed primarily with Hartmann's Ultrasuede.

In 1963, only 36% of all manufacturers' unit shipments of luggage were soft-sided; by 1979 the share had risen to 71%. (Hartmann's framed luggage was considered hard-sided luggage.) Items such as totes and garment bags were increasingly viewed by the trade as likely impulse purchases, so they were often displayed by retailers outside the traditional luggage department.

A further trend was the increasing percentage of luggage purchases by women. As a result, manufacturers were thought to be paying more attention to fashion and style in product development. Although some luggage retailers were skeptical about the growth potential of designer-name luggage, they welcomed increased fashion orientation because it permitted more exciting merchandising at the point-of-sale.

The dollar sales of luggage through various distribution channels in 1980 were:

Specialty stores	16%
Department stores	30
General merchandise chains (e.g., Sears)	18
Catalog showrooms	21
Discount stores (e.g., K mart)	11
Mail order	5

Katz considered luggage a postponable purchase and noted that sales were highly seasonal. The industry's retail year was divided into spring (February–July) and fall (August–January) seasons. Retail sales of Hartmann luggage by month in 1979 reflected this industry pattern:

January	6.8%	July	7.0%
February	5.0	August	7.0
March	5.4	September	7.7
April	6.5	October	6.8
May	9.4	November	8.8
June	9.8	December	19.8

The Luggage Consumer

Publicly available research on the luggage consumer was sparse. The latest reported survey had been conducted by *Luggage and Travelware* magazine in 1977. Questionnaires mailed to recent luggage purchasers in ten states generated a 47% response. Key findings are summarized in Exhibit 2.

Like most other firms in the industry, Hartmann had conducted little market research. In 1976, a questionnaire mailed to a sample of 1,000 Hartmann owners drawn from warranty cards generated a 57% response. It revealed that over 70% of Hartmann owners were aged 26–55; 49% shopped for luggage in traditional department stores; 36% shopped in luggage specialty stores; and 31% had received their luggage as gifts. Durability and style were considered the most important features in selecting luggage. (Price was not an option on the questionnaire.) Katz believed that four years later the profile of the typical Hartmann owner had not changed.

In 1979 Hartmann conducted a telephone survey of consumers over 25 years old with household incomes greater than $25,000. When presented with a list of names of luggage manufacturers, 17% recognized the Hartmann brand name; the overall aided awareness level ranged from 28% for respondents with over $35,000 in household income to 9% for respondents with $25,000–35,000. Comparable awareness levels for American Tourister and Samsonite were over 90%. Only 5% of respondents recalled having seen any Hartmann advertising.

EXHIBIT 2   Selected findings of *Luggage and Travelware* market research, June 1977 study

---

☐ 51% of respondents owned three or four pieces of luggage and 27% owned five or more.

☐ 47% of respondents had purchased their luggage in a department store, 28% in a luggage store, and 9% at a discount or variety store; 7% had purchased some pieces at sporting goods stores or specialty clothing shops; 41% had received luggage as a gift.

☐ 53% of respondents preferred a standard hard-sided suitcase (or set of these) in packing for a trip; 34% preferred a garment bag, either alone or with another piece such as a tote; 7% preferred a duffel bag.

☐ 69% of respondents would be motivated to buy new luggage because their present pieces were the wrong size. The least important reasons for buying new luggage were "out-of-date appearance of present luggage" and "the pieces I own don't match."

☐ 31% of respondents cited price as the most important criterion in selecting luggage; 21% cited it as the least important criterion.

☐ 48% of respondents believed they would favor a brand of luggage they recognized or had seen advertised; 38% said they would not.

☐ 47% of respondents stated that in deciding where to shop for luggage, they would be drawn to stores with attractive displays; 45% favored a full-service store with an informed sales staff; 26% would "wait for a sale, then go there to buy"; 13% said they might respond to TV, radio, magazine, or newspaper advertising.

Note: A questionnaire was mailed to a random sample of approximately 1,000 consumers nationwide; 47% of the questionnaires were completed and returned.

Sales and Distribution

Hartmann's sales force consisted of 16 territory managers who reported to four regional vice presidents. The vice presidents reported to Schuster and spent two-thirds of their time selling to their own accounts. Territory managers averaged $35,000 in annual earnings, typically receiving 60% of their compensation as salary and 40% as a bonus on dollar sales in excess of individual quotas. They averaged $1.5 million in annual sales and visited their major accounts several times a month. The salespeople of many luggage manufacturers with broader distribution or smaller sales forces visited their accounts only twice a year and acted primarily as order takers.

Hartmann luggage was sold through 100 department stores and 485 specialty luggage stores throughout the United States, representing just over 1,600 separate outlets. Each class of trade accounted for 50% of Hartmann's dollar volume. These stores accounted for approximately 40% of the dollar value of all U.S. luggage sales.

In choosing retailers, the company looked first for a reputation for carrying fine merchandise. Katz preferred stores to carry at least one other high-quality brand, such as Lark or French, because such a selection facilitated trade-up selling (i.e., retail clerks encouraged customers who asked for relatively lower-priced merchandise to buy more expensive goods, stressing their product benefits and higher quality). The company expected its retailers to display all four series of Hartmann luggage and to stock a minimum inventory of $11,000 per outlet at suggested retail prices.

Retail Merchandising Program

New accounts with at least three branches were required to participate in Hartmann's retail merchandising program. As of January, 1981, 94 accounts representing 482 retail outlets and about 50% of Hartmann's sales dollars were involved in the program, which Katz believed was unique in the industry. He noted:

> Most stores frown on incentive programs, but we felt we had to reward the sales clerks for their efforts, and we thought we could make the program stick if we stressed that its purpose was to help the entire luggage department. We've always stressed trade-up selling, but we tell retail salespeople to focus on any trade-up line—Lark, French, or Hartmann. That way our program appears less obviously self-interested to the retailer. Frankly, I would welcome more competition at the higher-priced end of the market. Hartmann sales could grow more rapidly if aggressive competitors helped to make the consumer more conscious of the advantages of better-quality, higher-priced, more fashionable luggage.

A key feature of Hartmann's retail merchandising program was a weekly sales goal for Hartmann merchandise for each store, determined jointly by the Hartmann sales force and retail management. Assuming satisfactory performance, sales goals for each store were raised about 25% in dollars and about 15% in units each year. Branches reaching and exceeding goals were recognized with awards and trophies. In addition, a sales-incentive point system rewarded outstanding individual sales clerks with free Hartmann luggage. A clerk could earn enough points to receive a $300 suitcase by selling $30,000 worth of luggage at retail. Katz estimated the cost of the incentive program at about 0.25% of Hartmann's factory sales.

The second major feature of Hartmann's retail merchandising program was training retail salespeople. Through breakfast seminars, films, and promotional hand-books, the Hartmann sales force taught salespeople first to approach each customer with a detailed description of one of the store's top luggage lines, usually Hartmann's belting leather. This presentation emphasized the high-quality construction, patented locks, and unique handles common to every Hartmann product. If, after this demon-stration, the customer viewed the belting leather line as too expensive, the salesperson presented a similar Hartmann model in the second most expensive series, noting the similarities in design and quality of construction despite the different exterior. Katz described this approach as "selling up by stepping down."

The program was well received by retailers. During 1979, 25 new outlets had joined the program and none had withdrawn. To demonstrate the higher profitability of more expensive luggage to department and specialty store buyers, Hartmann developed a chart in August 1979 (see Exhibit 3). Net profits before taxes to the retailer on Hartmann luggage sales ranged from 21% on the 4200 line to 36% on the 4700 line, compared with 13% on Samsonite's Silhouette line, and an average 8% on all luggage. By May, 1980, Hartmann's suggested retail prices offered retailers a margin of 54%, compared with a 51% average margin for luggage sold in department and specialty stores, and a 46% average margin for the luggage industry as a whole.

Pricing

Katz stated that the goal of Hartmann's pricing policy "was to make each piece stand on its own two feet." Between 1976 and 1980 Hartmann had increased prices each year, partly in response to the rapidly rising cost of leather. The average annual increase, weighted by sales volumes for each product, ranged from 10% in 1976 to 13% in 1980.[2] Katz gave advanced notice of each increase to Hartmann's trade accounts through a personal letter. Schuster estimated the company's overall contribution margin at 44%. The average for the luggage industry as a whole was 25% to 30%.

Hartmann attached price tags to all its luggage before shipment. Before resale price maintenance ended in 1975, the company had insisted that all retailers sell its luggage at only the full recommended retail price.[3] Hartmann set its suggested retail prices in round numbers, such as $100, rather than at price points, such as $99.95, and its executives believed that few trade customers substituted new price tags. Some

[2]The Consumer Price Index rose 6.5% in 1977 over 1976, 7.7% in 1978, 11.3% in 1979, and 14.4% in 1980.

[3]Resale price maintenance (or fair trade) laws permitted manufacturers or distributors of trade-marked products to determine their resale prices. They had initially been advocated by small, independent retailers seeking protection from price-cutting by large chains. National resale price maintenance legis-lation regulating interstate commerce, passed in 1938, was terminated in 1975 by the Consumer Goods Pricing Act.

EXHIBIT 3 Luggage retailer cost structures for Hartmann and competitive products, August 1979

	Department Average $	%	Samsonite Silhouette $	%	Hartmann 4200 (vinyl) $	%	Hartmann 4400 (fabric & leather) $	%	Hartmann 4800 (ultrasuede) $	%	Hartmann 4700 (belting leather) $	%
Average retail price	76.00	100.0	86.70	100.0	115.31	100.0	183.46	100.0	287.88	100.0	386.11	100.0
Merchandise cost[a]	38.00	50.0	42.48	49.0	55.35	48.0	88.06	48.0	138.18	48.0	185.33	48.0
Retail reductions[b]	3.88	5.1	4.42	5.1	5.88	5.1	9.36	5.1	14.68	5.1	19.69	5.1
Selling cost[c]	6.31	8.3	6.75	7.8	7.94	6.9	10.76	5.9	15.10	5.2	19.17	5.0
Fixed cost[d]	21.74	28.6	21.74	25.1	21.74	18.9	21.74	11.8	21.74	7.6	21.74	5.6
Net profit before taxes	6.07	8.0	11.31	13.0	24.40	21.1	53.54	29.2	98.18	34.1	140.18	36.3
Profit % of Sales	8%		13%		21%		29%		34%		36%	

Source: Financial and operating results of department and specialty stores, National Retail Merchants Association, 1978.

[a] *Merchandise Cost:* Beginning cost inventory plus net purchases inward transportation minus ending cost inventory minus cash discounts earned on purchases plus net alterations and workroom costs.

[b] *Retail Reductions:* Include markdowns, employee discounts, and inventory shortages (the excess of book inventory over physical inventory).

[c] *Selling cost:* Includes direct and indirect compensation for salespeople, checkout, and stock replenishment personnel.

[d] *Fixed Cost:* Includes all other expenses.

176

high-quality retailers, however, periodically offered up to 25% off the price tags, either on all luggage items in their stores or on selected lines, to stimulate consumer purchases during slow selling periods. In addition, retailers occasionally negotiated price with customers: for example, a 10% discount might be offered on the purchase of five pieces of luggage. Hartmann's executives discouraged such negotiation, and it was believed to be least prevalent in the types of outlets that carried Hartmann luggage.

Advertising

Hartmann spent approximately 5% of sales on a national advertising program, cooperative advertising, trade advertising, merchandising sheets, and other selling aids. Media expenditures for the national advertising program during 1977-1980 were reported by the company as follows:

	Number of publications	Cost of media space
1977 Spring	6	$286,596
Fall	7	390,935
1978 Spring	6	416,095
Fall	6	487,280
1979 Spring	10	478,030
Fall	9	725,470
1980 Spring	10	708,840
Fall	6	941,160

Katz estimated that Lark spent about 3% of sales on advertising; French placed no national advertising. In the industry as a whole, Hartmann was the third-largest advertiser—behind Samsonite and American Tourister, both of which used television as well as print media and spent about 2.5% of sales on national advertising. A typical Samsonite magazine ad is reproduced in Figure 3.

Hartmann's advertising for 1980 appeared in executive *Newsweek,*[4] *Time, Business Week, Glamour, Vogue, The New Yorker, Town and Country, Travel and Leisure,* and the *New York Times Magazine.* Traditionally, advertising had focused on the differentiating features of Hartmann luggage, particularly the more casual lines (see Figure 4). During 1980, the company also placed a series of smaller advertisements in the *Wall Street Journal;* these stressed Hartmann's name and reputation rather than particular models of luggage.

Unlike Samsonite and American Tourister, Hartmann did not aggressively promote its cooperative advertising program to its retailers. The company required

---

[4]Executive *Newsweek* was sent to 550,000 subscribers selected from the magazine's total circulation of 2,950,000. Advertisers paid a premium to reach this group of professionals, managers, and executives earning over $20,000 annually. The editorial content of executive and standard editions was identical.

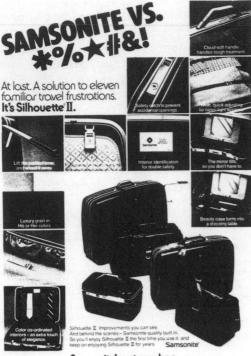

FIGURE 3
1980 Samsonite
magazine advertisement

FIGURE 4
1979 Hartmann
magazine advertisement

that all proposed co-op advertising be approved by Hartmann in advance and feature its name in the headline. Acceptable media were limited to individual retailer catalogs (such as Christmas catalogs), direct-mail promotions (including retailer statement stuffers), the national magazines in the company's current corporate campaign, and city magazines (such as *Boston* magazine) whose readership met Hartmann's upscale demographic criteria. Newspaper advertising which mentioned Hartmann did not qualify. Retailers could accumulate co-op allowances at the rate of 2.5% of their dollar purchases of full-priced in-line Hartmann luggage.[5] These funds could be used to cover 50% of the cost of eligible co-op advertisements. Allowance money could not be accumulated on purchases of promoted or discounted merchandise. The co-op advertising program cost Hartmann an estimated $130,000 for fiscal year 1981.

Because Hartmann funded no co-op advertising in newspapers, its price promotions were advertised only locally by larger retailers. Samsonite and American Tourister both permitted newspaper co-op advertising, so their price promotions were

---

[5]In-line merchandise was the most recent, prevailing product line, as distinct from items manufactured especially for promotions or discontinued items being sold off through promotions.

featured more extensively in local than in national media. By contrast, advertisements for Hartmann's price promotions in 1976, 1977, and 1979 were incorporated in the national advertising campaign. Some Hartmann executives believed the company should advertise its price promotions in newspapers or perhaps transfer the money spent on advertising the price promotions into a special co-op account against which retail accounts could draw if they wished to advertise them.

Price Promotion in the Luggage Industry

Price promotion strategies in the luggage industry varied widely. Dominant, popularly priced brands like Samsonite and American Tourister held several promotion events a year. Typically, a temporary price discount would be announced to the trade in advance, and an order placed during a specified period would be invoiced at a discount price. Usually only one order was allowed per promotion. Schuster believed many of these promotions were held to clear a manufacturer's surplus inventory rather than to increase long-term market share.

Price promotions were typically offered on some or all of the pieces at one price point in a manufacturer's standard product line. They rarely covered either all pieces at all price points or one piece across several price points. Schuster believed that, in general, more frequent promotions on narrower selections of luggage targeted at specific consumer segments would prove more profitable. Although some luggage manufacturers promoted either their lowest price points or their slower-selling pieces, Hartmann preferred the idea of promoting its most popular lines. "If and when we promote, we would emphasize a strength, not a weakness," Katz explained.

Among the more expensive brands, Lark ran no price promotions except occasional clearances of discontinued merchandise. French ran no national price promotions and never promoted in-line merchandise. However, French often bought closeout leather or fabrics at a discount and made up three- or four-piece sets of luggage in one of its standard designs. These were then offered to the trade at a price lower than that of similar in-line merchandise.

Most price promotions on luggage coincided with seasonal sales peaks, either before Christmas or during the late spring wedding and graduation period. Traditionally, Samsonite and American Tourister each ran a major promotion in May and June. Retail buyers, seeking to ensure a steady stream of promotion-generated traffic, preferred consecutive rather than concurrent promotions. Overlaps were becoming unavoidable, however, as the number of manufacturers running promotions, along with the frequency and average duration of the events, all increased. To appeal to retail buyers, some smaller manufacturers had begun to offer their promotions in February and March.

Hartmann's Gift-with-Purchase and Purchase-with-Purchase Promotions

In 1972 and between 1975 and 1977, Hartmann ran one promotion yearly that typically offered consumers either a gift or discounted merchandise with a specified purchase of in-line merchandise at the regular price. Discounts on in-line merchandise

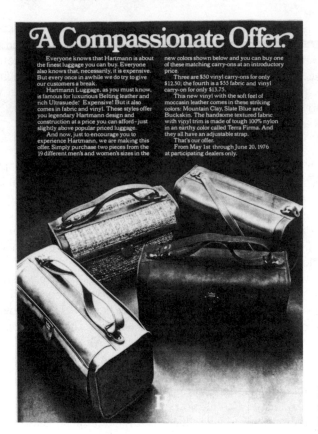

FIGURE 5   Magazine advertisement for 1976 promotion

were not offered during this period. In 1972 a gift-with-purchase (GWP) promotion offered a free "hanger" (garment bag) to customers purchasing three pieces from Hartmann's 4200 line. In 1976 one of four vinyl carry-ons, variously valued at $50 and $55, was offered between May 1 and June 20 at $12.50 or $13.75 to customers purchasing two matching pieces in the 4200 line. An advertisement for this promotion is reproduced in Figure 5. Approximately 9,800 of these purchase-with-purchase (PWP) carry-ons were sold. The focus of the 1977 promotion, which ran from May 2 to June 19, was also a PWP item, a "pancake" or flat-folding bag. Five insertions in national magazines, illustrated in Figure 6, advertised this promotion. The pancake, a $75 value, was offered for $18.95 to customers purchasing $200 worth of Hartmann luggage; about 13,000 pancakes were sold.

These gifts or discounted pieces were all specially manufactured for the promotions. Although some were similar in style to in-line merchandise, none matched exactly. Hartmann's efforts to sell these pieces later at full price were unsuccessful. "Any item that started out on promotion," one Hartmann executive noted, "was automatically killed when we tried to sustain it as a regular full-priced item in the line."

FIGURE 6   **Magazine advertisement for 1977 promotion**

Retailers grew increasingly unenthusiastic about GWP and PWP promotions. Because of lack of experience with such promotions, Hartmann did not know how many of each gift or discounted item to manufacture, and retailers did not know how many to order. The trade could place only one order for each promotion. At the end of the promotion period, retailers who had overordered were left with inventory that did not match the existing lines, and Hartmann refused to take back merchandise once it was shipped. Moreover, retailers complained that promotion merchandise occupied valuable floor and shelf space without adequate dollar returns. They argued that only price-off promotions on in-line merchandise could substantially increase store traffic and sales. Rather than absorb the cost of such price promotions themselves, they looked to manufacturers to cover the margin lost.

Hartmann's Price-Off Promotions

In 1978, Hartmann ran its first price-off promotion on in-line merchandise. The promotion was announced on January 1; the trade was permitted to place orders at promotion prices during the first quarter for delivery on March 25. From April 12 to

The Hartmann Carry-Ons.
For every piece you buy,
carry off a 20% discount.

From April 22 to May 6. 1979, you have a marvelous opportunity to get your hands on Hartmann Carry-Ons at a very considerable saving.

These are the celebrated Hartmann Carry-Ons that make it possible to check nothing, to take everything. A bag for under your seat. A bag for the compartment overhead. And a hanger to hang in the closet.

This functional trio—the Carry-Ons—are so light, so easy to carry on. But don't take their casual air casually. Every inch of every piece is Hartmann all the way. They're designed to fit every inch of allowable space the airlines offer you. And designed to let you take along enough for a weekend, or more than a week.

Hartmann offers you the Carry-Ons in four different materials:

1 Industrial Belting Leather 2 Halston designed Ultrasuede °3. A tough woven fabric with belting leather trim. 4 Nylon fabrics with vinyl trim. Or all vinyl.

Whichever material you choose, you aren't just choosing luggage. You're choosing Hartmann, an investment in luggage meticulously crafted to pay dividends far into the future.

Carrying the Carry-Ons—The

Over, The Under, and The Hanger—means you'll leave the plane with all your luggage. You may never again experience the thrill of landing in Los Angeles while your bags fly merrily on to Sacramento.

A last reminder. The Carry-Ons work equally as well when you carry them on to trains, busses, even stowed away in the trunks of cars.

The Hartmann Carry-Ons. At a 20% saving** you can't afford to leave without them.

THE CARRY-ONS BY
HARTMANN

FIGURE 7 Magazine advertisement for 1979 promotion

May 6, all 4200 pieces were sold at a 20% discount by participating retailers, who took a 48% margin on the promoted line instead of their normal 52%. The promotion was not featured in Hartmann's national advertising, but many participating stores ran local newspaper advertisements to announce it. A total of 75,788 units of 4200 luggage was sold to the trade during March–May, 1978, of which 75,174 were sold at promotion prices.

From April 22 to May 6, 1979, Hartmann offered an in-line, 20% price-off promotion featuring three popular carry-on pieces in all four luggage series. These items were selected because of the increasing popularity of carry-on luggage; management believed that this promotion would enhance Hartmann's fashionable, up-to-date image. Five insertions of the advertisement shown in Figure 7 in national magazines announced the promotion. Once again, participating retailers took a 48% margin. Although this promotion ended in early May, order backlogs resulted in deliveries of promoted merchandise as late as June. Katz noted that to avoid adding a second shift to the soft-sided production line, Hartmann had to begin producing inventory for a promotion at least six months in advance.

Orders for the three carry-on items fell significantly below 1978 levels following the promotion period. Hartmann's territory managers, however, assured Katz that dealers were simply selling off their delayed shipments. Schuster commented:

Assuming you don't restrict the quantity of promoted merchandise each dealer can buy, a 30% discount ensures that all promoted merchandise will be sold through to the end consumer. At only a 20% discount, you run the risk of just giving away margin. The trade loads up and the merchandise sits in inventory, stealing from future sales at full price.

Katz, however, opposed large discounts. He was disturbed by the trade's tendency to overbuy when Hartmann lowered its price during a promotion and then to sell promoted merchandise at full retail price after the promotion ended.

Hence, for its 1980 promotion (which ran during the first two weeks of June), Hartmann reverted to a promotion on specially manufactured pieces in nylon trimmed with leather, which sold at a 20% to 25% discount from similar models in the strong-selling 4400 series. To announce this promotion, Hartmann used merchandising sheets that described the items in the Hartmann product line (see Exhibit 4); these were distributed to retail accounts by Hartmann's salespeople

EXHIBIT 4   Merchandising sheet for 1980 promotion

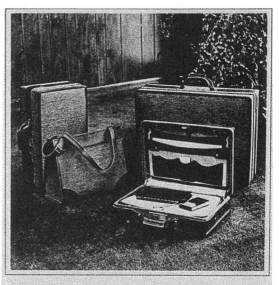

SUGGESTED PRICE LIST FOR HARTMANN FASHION INVESTMENT PROMOTION 4400 SERIES

WOMEN'S SIZES	SUGGESTED REGULAR RETAIL (4400)	PERCENTAGE DISCOUNT	SUGGESTED SALE RETAIL (4400)	PROMOTION WHOLESALE
747 UW The Under	165.00	20%	132.00	68.65
W24 Jr. Pullman	195.00	20%	156.00	81.15
W26 Pullman	217.00	25%	162.75	84.65
W29 Jumbo Pullman	240.00	25%	180.00	93.60
W17 Fashion Tote	138.00	25%	103.50	53.80
MEN'S SIZES				
A4 Deluxe Slender Dispatche	172.00	25%	129.00	67.10
A9 Deluxe Commute-tache	195.00	22%	152.00	79.10
747UM The Under	195.00	25%	146.25	76.05
M/S Men's Suiter	240.00	25%	180.00	93.60

Fashion Investment Promotion
by hartmann

25% to 20% OFF PROMOTION of Hartmann's Most Popular Price Point

4400 Special Promotion
(strong fashion fabric trimmed in full-grain leather)
STARTING JUNE 1st, 1980.

TABLE 1   Pricing data for Hartmann's 4200 line

Per unit	Nonpromoted	20% Promotion
Average retail selling price[a]	$100.00	$80.00
Average manufacturer's selling price[b]	48.00	41.60
Variable costs[c]	34.70	34.70
Average contribution[d]	13.30	6.90

[a] An average of the per-unit suggested retail selling price of each model in the 4200 line.

[b] Retailers shared cost of promotion with Hartmann by taking a 4% reduction in margin.

[c] Includes allocated general and administrative expenses and manufacturing overhead, 7% selling expenses, 5% advertising/promotion allocation, and direct labor and raw material costs.

[d] An average of the per-unit contributions of each model in the 4200 line. (This equals manufacturer's selling price minus all variable costs per unit, including share of general and administrative expenses as well as direct labor and raw material costs.)

or through the mail. Katz knew this would be less popular with retailers than a promotion on in-line merchandise; he viewed it as a step toward discontinuing promotions in 1981. About 14,400 of the 1980 promoted items were sold—only half of those forecast. Katz concluded that retailers would not oppose a decision to discontinue promotions.

CONSULTANTS' STUDY OF THE 1978 PROMOTION

Uncertainty about the profitability of Hartmann's promotions led the company to commission an investigation of the issue. Consultants assessed the profitability of Hartmann's first price-off promotion on in-line merchandise, run in 1978.

They first assembled pricing data for the 4200 line (see Table 1). On the basis of a computer-assisted time-series analysis of previous sales of the line, the consultants estimated that Hartmann's 4200 factory sales during the same period without promotion would have totaled 48,960 units, or 65% of the actual unit total. Using the formula shown in Table 2, they estimated that the 1978 promotion cost Hartmann $132,000 in lost contribution (excluding the contribution from 614 units in the 4200 line that sold at regular prices).

TABLE 2   Consultants' formula for estimating Hartmann's 1978 promotion cost

Incremental dollar gain (loss) from promotion	=	{ Promoted 4200 units	×	Promoted 4200 unit contribution }	−	{ Forecast 4200 units	×	Normal 4200 unit contribution }

The study also concluded that sales of the 4400 line had been cannibalized: 4400 unit sales for March–May, 1978 totaled 15,130—short of the forecast 17,070 units—for a contribution loss of $40,366. Had Hartmann not run the promotion, it could have maintained inventory at a normal level. Instead, the company fell behind schedule on production, and inventory levels dropped below normal. As a result, Hartmann saved $16,068 in inventory costs. No additional costs were incurred in financing receivables; Hartmann "factored" receivables as soon as they were billed, at a variable cost of 0.85% of invoiced sales (i.e., an independent factoring agent took title to Hartmann's receivables at a discount from the invoice value and assumed responsibility for their collection. In return, Hartmann received the invoice value less discount from the agent immediately upon billing).

The consultants concluded that Hartmann had suffered a net loss from the 1978 promotion. In their opinion the company could not expect to achieve rapid sales growth and high earnings growth simultaneously. They recommended that Hartmann discontinue its annual price promotions and concentrate on building brand awareness among target consumers by increasing advertising.

Debate Over the Study

After reviewing the sales history of the 4200 line (see Exhibit 5), Schuster questioned the conclusions of the study on two grounds. First, he believed that the forecast of nonpromoted volume based on the time-series analysis (48,960 units) had been too optimistic; 4200 sales had totaled only 31,742 in March–May, 1977. Noting furrther that 4200 sales in Januarry–February, 1978 had run 22% behind 1977 sales in that period, Schuster set his forecast for normal March–May sales 22% below the corresponding 1977 sales level and argued that the promotion had generated 49,760 incremental unit sales, not 26,214. Second, he believed that no additional fixed costs had been incurred from the promotion and that assigned overhead should not be

EXHIBIT 5   4200 Series trade orders, 1976-1978

	1976	1977	1978
January	4,536	18,616	10,706
February	4,012	8,166	10,124
March	5,606	11,168	19,334[a]
April	15,120	10,066	36,636[a]
May	14,768	10,508	19,818[a]
June	8,222	11,854	16,226
Total spring season	51,264	70,378	113,844
Total fall season	52,902	82,720	73,412
Year total	104,166	153,098	187,256
Year index	100	146	178

a. All except 614 units, shipped during March–May 1978, were sold at promotion prices.

included in the variable cost figure. His estimates of average unit variables costs were lower ($25.76)[6] and unit contribution higher than those of the consultants. Under his assumptions, a lower percentage increase in sales was required to compensate for the contribution loss of sales at the promoted price. Without considering cannibalization effects or savings on inventory carrying costs, Schuster concluded that the promotion had generated over $600,000 in incremental contribution.

Katz disagreed with Schuster's analysis for three reasons: (1) he viewed the consultants' assignment of fixed overhead before calculating unit contribution as more consistent with Hartmann's conservative accounting practices; (2) he believed that cannibalization effects and savings on inventory-carrying costs should not be ignored; and (3) he pointed out that, because the April–May 1978 promotion had been announced on January 1, Schuster should not have based his forecast of normal March–May 1978 sales of 4200 units on the fact that January–February 1978 sales at regular prices were 22% lower than in 1977. Indeed, Katz believed that a sales decrease of only 22% indicated the strength of 4200 sales at regular prices, considering that the trade had been able to place orders at promotion prices during January and February.

Although Katz respected Schuster's intelligence and strong background, he still wondered whether Hartmann's ability to achieve 1981 sales and earnings objectives would be helped or hindered by a price promotion. If a promotion was offered, he and Schuster would have to decide what merchandise should be featured, on what terms, when, and for how long.

[6]Includes direct labor and raw material costs only.

MURRAYHILL INC.

JOHN A. QUELCH
MELANIE D. SPENCER

C. Gifford Davis, president of Murrayhill Inc., a privately held manufacturer of high-quality men's shoes, carefully studied the sales forecasts for 1986. The problem the company now faced was very different from that of the previous decade. During the 1970s, Murrayhill's sales had dropped as the company's retail accounts were undergoing basic structural changes. Double-digit inflation had resulted in a move in the retail industry from full-priced outlets to discount stores, leading to less service for Murrayhill customers. Traditional Murrayhill retail accounts were faced with stiffer competition. Murrayhill's total reliance on nonproprietary retail distribution had resulted in excess capacity problems at the factory that had increased per item costs and lowered company profits. Direct-mail distribution through proprietary catalog sales and a broader-based product offering had solved the problem and had also enabled Murrayhill to exploit market niches that were less exposed to competition from imports or other U.S. manufacturers. In fact, the strengthening of the traditional retail business from 1983 to 1985 and the rapid growth of the direct-mail cataloging business presented Davis with another difficult problem: how to manage Murrayhill's growth with its only factory approaching full capacity.

Edward Wilson, executive vice president, reviewed Murrayhill's alternatives. Expanding capacity would be the most logical action, yet Wilson knew that skilled craftsmen were difficult to find and training "green" labor would be prohibitively expensive. Murrayhill could subcontract manufacturing or acquire a small U.S. manufacturer, but in either case, it would be two years before workers at another company could be trained in the complexities of welt shoe construction.[1] Other responses included raising prices further or restricting distribution, either through retail or direct channels, or both.

The irony of this situation was not lost on Christopher Hill, manager of Lynn Shoes, the Murrayhill direct-mail catalog operation. His objective with the catalog had been to fill excess plant capacity profitably. This objective had been

[1]Goodyear welt construction was a costly and time-consuming process by which a leather strip, or welt, was sewn to a channeled insole of a shoe to bond the shoe's upper and its sole. The welt gave lateral support around the forepart of the shoe and helped the shoe hold its shape. The result was a durable, heavy-grade shoe.

accomplished. However, the speed of Lynn Shoes' growth had been greater than anticipated. Now that excess capacity was no longer a problem, there was debate as to how aggressively the Lynn Shoes operation should be promoted and what percentages of the shoes made in Murrayhill's single factory should be made available to Lynn Shoes and to Murrayhill's nonproprietary retail outlets.[2]

COMPANY BACKGROUND

Thomas Murray and Mitchell Hill began manufacturing men's dress shoes in Lynn, Massachusetts in 1926. In 1930, they incorporated their business as Murrayhill, Inc. Throughout its history, the company maintained a reputation for exceptional quality and comfort. Integral to this reputation was the development of Murrayhill's special contour foot-beds in 1933. This concept was based on the belief that a sole molded in the shape of a footprint would be comfortable and would provide orthopedic benefits. In addition, Murrayhill employed a costly manufacturing process, the Goodyear welt construction, that securely bonded the shoe and sole to ensure exceptional durability.

Commitment to customer comfort and adherence to high-quality standards, both in raw materials and construction, built strong customer loyalty that sustained the demand for Murrayhill shoes through economic downturns. Murrayhill's commitment to quality also resulted in limitations. Because each pair of Murrayhill shoes still required over 100 separate hand operations and 20 formal inspections as of 1985, one pair of shoes took a full month to make. Manufacturing had kept pace with technological developments, but remained highly labor-intensive. In addition, many of the manufacturing processes required skilled and experienced craftsmen, who were increasingly hard to find in the 1980s.

Despite the market pressures placed on Murrayhill, the company remained profitable and had even diversified its distribution channels by establishing direct-mail cataloging in the late 1970s. In 1985, Murrayhill made an operating profit of 9% on sales of $27 million.

THE EVOLUTION OF THE SHOE INDUSTRY

From 1900 until the 1940s, there were approximately 400 shoe manufacturers operating in New England. By 1985, only 10% remained. Understanding this dramatic and rapid change requires an examination of the evolution of the American labor market.

In the early twentieth century, Boston served as a primary port of entry for European immigrants. As a result, labor in the Boston area was inexpensive, the work force was unskilled but eager to learn a trade, and productivity was high. New England became the predominant shoe manufacturing area in the United States.

---

[2]Nonproprietary retail stores were not owned by any manufacturer and carried multiple brands and product lines.

In the 1950s, unions demanded higher wages and benefits. Many industries responded by becoming more capital-intensive. However, the labor component of shoe manufacturing was essential to production. In search of lower labor costs, many shoe manufacturers moved operations southward, first to Pennsylvania, then to Arkansas. Several of those that could not afford to move went out of business.

These circumstances set the stage for the entry of imports. Once the supply of inexpensive labor in the United States was exhausted, the shoe industry progressed through Spain, Italy, Korea, Brazil, and Taiwan. By 1985, shoe manufacturing was well established in India, and industry experts expected the People's Republic of China to be the next major manufacturing center.

Murrayhill survived these changes and the growth of imports by producing a premium-quality product that was difficult to duplicate and appealed to a narrow market segment willing to pay high prices for Murrayhill quality. As fashion became a more important component of men's shoe purchasing behavior and casual styles became more popular, the company broadened its product line to include several fashionable and lightweight styles that retained the famous Murrayhill quality. Despite the degree of insulation provided by Murrayhill's market niche strategy, the company faced several strong domestic competitors and unrelenting price competition from imports.

In 1985, the men's premium shoe market was considered to include brands with a price range of $75 or higher. Murrayhill Inc., Johnston & Murphy, E.T. Wright & Company, Allen Edmonds, and Florsheim were the major domestic manufacturers producing premium shoes. The measurement of market share within the industry was difficult because so many of the manufacturers were private companies, like Murrayhill. In addition, these companies were not always in direct competition because of differences in distribution channels.

Allen Edmonds and E.T. Wright & Company were considered to be Murrayhill's closest domestic competitors with an estimated market share of 8% each, compared to Murrayhill's share of approximately 12%. Allen Edmonds' headquarters were in Wisconsin. The company relied primarily on nonproprietary retail outlets for its distribution. Advertising was a sizable expense for the company, with expenditures in the $1–$2 million range. Most of this money was spent promoting awareness of the brand name to consumers. Allen Edmonds also operated a small direct-mail catalog business. Edmonds' retail accounts handled the majority of the costs associated with the catalog operation. E.T. Wright & Company, headquartered in Massachusetts, operated an extensive direct-mail business and, like Murrayhill, relied on nonproprietary distribution. Johnston & Murphy, on the other hand, operated proprietary retail outlets and experimented in the mail-order business for both men's and ladies' premium shoes. Florsheim's product line covered several price points, including those in the premium market. Florsheim was, by far, the strongest competitor with an estimated market share of 18% and both nonproprietary and proprietary retail distribution channels. Hanover, a medium-price shoe manufacturer, was also noted for its direct distribution system. The company owned over 100 proprietary retail stores, operated a successful mail-order business, and produced private-label footwear for J.C. Penney and Sears, Roebuck department stores.

Imports accounted for a 50% share of sales of premium men's shoes, compared to a 77% share total men's shoe market. Bally represented the strongest competition. It was the leading imported brand in this market before 1975 and maintained a market share of close to 25% at that time. By 1985, other imported brands included Baker Benjes, Cole Hahn, Ferragamo, Bruno Magli, and Church's. The imported products differed from the domestic premium brands, however. Most of the imported shoes were lighter weight and designed to appeal to more fashion-conscious consumers.

THE RETAIL SHOE BUSINESS

Nonproprietary retail outlets were Murrayhill's principal distribution channel until 1979. The network consisted of approximately 450 retail outlets throughout the United States. Many of these locations also sold other brands of men's premium shoes. Murrayhill's shoes were sold wholesale to retailers at approximately 50% of the suggested retail price. Price increases were usually announced in February or August. The company did not offer its retail accounts quantity discounts.

Because highly skilled labor and specialized facilities were required to produce quality men's dress shoes, Murrayhill's entire product line had been produced at the company's manufacturing facility in Lynn, Massachusetts throughout most of the company's history. As consumer preferences changed and fashion became more important in men's shoes during the 1970s, Murrayhill began contracting with outside manufacturers to produce casual shoes that matched Murrayhill's quality and feature specifications, yet could extend the brand's franchise to a younger age group. Murrayhill's executives labeled these styles "outside" shoes, while those manufactured at the Lynn plant were called "inside" shoes. In 1985, the average price paid to Murrayhill by the retailer for a pair of inside shoes was $52 and, for a pair of outside shoes, $34. Variable manufacturing costs per pair of inside shoes were $40. The average cost of a pair of outside shoes to Murrayhill was $28.

Murraryhill sold approximately 160 inside shoe styles and 56 styles made by outside manufacturers. Since there were 80 sizes to each style, Murrayhill's total SKUs numbered around 17,280, requiring an inventory in stock of over 64,000 pairs. Both internal and external production schedules for each style were set in advance based on sales projections. Murrayhill rarely did "make-ups" (styles not included in Murrayhill's regular product line, manufactured to the specifications of a retailer) for a particular retail account.

Each of Murrayhill's 16 salespeople was assigned a geographic territory and was responsible for retailer sales and service within that area. Salespeople were also expected to perform "previews" at the beginning of the fall and spring seasons as a method of increasing both consumer and trade sales. Previews consisted of a sales presentation at a retail store where the Murrayhill salesperson would display and explain the company's entire line to store customers. A price promotion of $10 off any pair of Murrayhill shoes was offered by the retailer during the preview. The retailer was responsible for absorbing the cost of the promotion, and the cost of advertising placed to stimulate retail traffic during the preview was shared between Murrayhill and the retailer. The Murrayhill salesperson would spend time with the retailer's salespeople and customers describing the quality and comfort of Murrayhill shoes. Murrayhill management believed that consumers were likely to "trade up" to a higher-priced brand if they understood the features and benefits of premium shoes. They believed that retail salespeople often missed sales opportunities by assuming that casually dressed customers would not buy expensive, high-quality shoes. For this reason, one of Murrayhill's goals was to have retail salespeople try a pair of Murrayhill shoes on every customer. For some Murrayhill retail accounts, close to 30% of annual sales were made during the fall and spring previews.

Murrayhill management tracked the sales of each and every shoe style. If sales of a particular style began to slow, management might elect to replace only the middle sizes. This policy ensured that Murrayhill would end up with the most popular sizes of a style before the style was terminated or "closed out." Established retail accounts had the option of purchasing close-outs at a 30% discount from the regular wholesale price. A list of close-outs was sent to retail accounts twice each year. Retailers would often try to sell these styles at full retail price to increase their unit margins, then mark them down as necessary. Close-outs accounted for unit sales of 5500–6500 pairs of Murrayhill shoes per year.

Traditional retail outlets for Murrayhill shoes included department stores, clothing stores, family shoe stores, and men's shoe stores. The economic conditions of the 1970s, however, resulted in changes in Murrayhill's retail account mix. The channel mix and unit sales by type of retailer for 1978–79 and 1984–85 are shown in Exhibit 1. Between these two periods, sales through clothing stores and department stores showed dramatic decreases as Murrayhill lost several accounts and others reduced their orders. However, the percentage of sales through specialty shoe discount stores rose from 13.9% to 33.1% as this channel grew in importance. Murrayhill also became increasingly reliant on Hartwell, a large East Coast chain, for a sizable percentage of unit sales.

Partly in response to the loss of some accounts, Murrayhill established a program to attract additional retail accounts. Any new account that purchased at least 150 pairs of shoes was allowed to pay 20% in each of the five months following a 30-day period. A dedicated dealer could sell the 150 pairs before the first invoice payment was due. Forty new accounts were opened under this policy in 1984.

PROBLEMS WITH RETAIL DISTRIBUTION

Murrayhill's selective distribution system performed well during the early 1970s. With the 1973 recession, however, the retail trade began to undergo change. Consumers' limited purchasing power made them increasingly price-sensitive and value-conscious. Because of the downturn in sales during this period, retailers were under pressure to cut their inventory carrying expense. Orders of high inventory, low turnover items, including shoes, particularly top-of-the-line products, were reduced or eliminated. Since a wide range of shoe sizes had to be inventoried to ensure that a store could provide any customer with a proper fit, some stores responded by reduc-

EXHIBIT 1   Unit purchases of key retail accounts

September 1978–August 1979		September 1984–August 1985	
Account	Pairs	Account	Pairs
Hartwell's	39,685	Hartwell's	54,550
Discount stores		*Discount stores*	
Store 1	9,522	Store 2	23,429
Store 2	8,728	Store 3	9,928
Store 3	5,870	Store 34	7,584
Store 4	3,570	Store 1	6,325
Store 5	1,645	Store 4	5,115
Discount store total	29,335	Store 35	5,176
Family shoe stores		Store 36	3,792
Store 6	7,997	Store 5	2,722
Store 7	7,482	Store 37	2,363
Store 8	3,542	Store 38	1,915
Store 9	2,762	Discount store total	68,349
Store 10	2,581	*Family shoe stores*	
Store 11	2,414	Store 6	7,242
Store 12	2,216	Store 39	3,698
Store 13	2,200	Store 10	2,502
Store 14	2,190	Store 9	2,459
Store 15	1,726	Store 14	2,163
Store 16	1,691	Store 40	1,923
Family shoe total	36,801	Store 41	1,787
Clothing stores		Store 42	1,749
Store 17	12,512	Store 12	1,738
Store 18	8,566	Store 16	1,667
Store 19	6,339	Store 43	1,662
Store 20	3,347	Family shoe total	28,590
Store 21	1,770	*Clothing stores*	
Store 22	1,661	Store 20	4,789
Clothing store total	34,195	Store 44	3,424
Department stores		Clothing store total	8,213
Store 23	12,211	*Department stores*	
Store 24	4,933	Store 23	3,528
Store 25	3,480	Store 24	3,014
Store 26	2,976	Store 26	1,638
Store 27	2,934	Department store total	8,180
Department store total	26,534	*Men's shoe stores*	
Men's shoe stores		Store 29	11,110
Store 28	14,070	Store 28	10,254
Store 29	12,483	Store 30	6,202
Store 30	9,554	Store 31	3,424
Store 31	3,309	Store 33	3,013
Store 32	2,878	Store 32	2,418
Store 33	1,965	Store 45	1,907
Men's shoe store total	44,259	Men's shoe store total	38,328
Total	210,809	Total	206,210

ing the number of styles they carried. Murrayhill shoes and other premium brands such as Johnston & Murphy and E.T. Wright & Company achieved a retail turnover of only 1.7 times per year compared to an inventory turnover of three times per year for moderately priced brands.

Around 1975, traditional full-price retail outlets came under increasing pressure. Consumer purchasing trends, the effects of the recession, and inflation laid the groundwork for the emergence of off-price retailing. Off-price retailers typically sold shoes and other apparel below suggested retail prices. They were able to lower prices by eliminating expensive fixtures and displays, locating stores in areas with lower rents, and minimizing personnel. The result was a "warehouse" atmosphere, yet the savings on purchases overcame consumer resistance and the concept became increasingly popular. Many off-price retailers were unappealing to Murrayhill since they lacked the customer service that Murrayhill executives considered especially important to stimulate sales of higher-priced shoes. Some Murrayhill executives also believed that distribution of Murrayhill shoes to discounters might result in retail price erosion that would hurt relations with full-price outlets and perhaps put pressure on Murrayhill to lower wholesale prices. However, Murrayhill concluded from the growth of off-price retailing that it had to do business with these types of stores. The company selected only those off-price accounts that would carry substantial inventories and provide good in-store service.

Partly in response to population shifts and emerging competition from discounters, many department stores expanded their operations from the business districts of cities to the suburbs. Because the primary target for premium men's shoes, the businessman, remained in the business district, the better quality men's shoe business did not follow the department stores to their new locations. As a result, premium quality men's shoes became a less important component of department store sales.

The economic pressures placed on retailers during the late 1970s and the stiff competition from discounters caused Murrayhill's sales to suffer. Exhibit 2 shows sales trends through the 1970s. As consumer sales through traditional retail outlets

EXHIBIT 2   Sales in units and dollars for 1970–1980

Year	Pairs shipped	Dollar shipments	Average price
1970	444,747	$ 9,233,418	$20.76
1971	481,875	10,326,280	21.43
1972	556,590	12,430,848	22.33
1973	572,806	14,400,942	25.14
1974	485,194	13,255,635	27.32
1975	471,755	13,517,534	28.65
1976	516,760	16,035,339	31.03
1977	443,149	15,015,605	33.88
1978	436,288	16,315,626	37.40
1979	376,318	16,288,598	43.28
1980	353,795	16,097,558	45.49

declined, less well-capitalized retailers were forced to eliminate many low-turnover items, such as Murrayhill shoes. The company lost several accounts. Management became concerned about Murrayhill's exclusive reliance on nonproprietary retail distribution.

Competition from other manufacturers exacerbated problems with retail accounts. Some shoe companies introduced exchange privileges to stimulate retailers to place larger orders. Retailers were allowed to exchange styles that did not sell for new inventory, placing the burden of retail sales risk on manufacturers. Murrayhill refused to adopt an exchange privilege policy. While allowing exchanges might boost short-term sales, profitability would suffer because production schedules would be difficult to predict and returned shoes would probably have to be sold at a discount. Murrayhill executives also believed that such a policy would make retailers less concerned about the size and mix of the orders they placed. One manager remarked, "Personally, I think that the retailer must take some responsibility for sales. If we ship record numbers of shoes only to have them dribbling back later, we'll soon go out of business." A few retailers ceased placing orders with Murrayhill because of the company's position. Management felt that the policy resulted in a stronger distribution network, but sales lost during the 1970s resulted in underutilization of plant capacity. By 1978 the factory was operating at only 80% of capacity.

Murrayhill management considered several options to increase sales. One alternative was to open proprietary retail outlets where Murrayhill could maintain complete control over distribution. This choice was rejected because of the investment costs, Murrayhill's lack of retail experience, and the likelihood that the proprietary outlets would face the same problems that had troubled Murrayhill's retail accounts.

Manufacturing ladies' shoes was another alternative. Because women purchased a large portion of men's apparel, executives advocating this option believed that women were already familiar with the Murrayhill name. The quality and comfort associated with Murrayhill's men's footwear could be transferred easily to a ladies' product line. However, ladies' shoe styles were highly influenced by fashion and changed each season. Manufacturing economies were hard to realize. As soon as a shoe craftsman would learn how to handle one style efficiently, the style might be changed or deleted. In addition, personnel at Murrayhill had little experience either manufacturing or selling ladies' footwear. These problems led management to pursue other options.

DIRECT DISTRIBUTION

In the middle 1970s, C. Gifford Davis received a call from a direct marketer of ladies' shoes. He was interested in expanding his distribution to include men's shoes and proposed that Murrayhill include several styles in his catalog. Murrayhill had been receiving complaints from customers who could no longer find Murrayhill shoes in retail outlets. Davis concluded that adding a direct distribution system could help retain customers and use excess plant capacity with little risk to regular operations. Murrayhill accepted the proposal.

When the catalog was published a few months later, Murrayhill executives were disappointed. To increase his margins, the direct marketer had priced Murrayhill shoes far above what they sold for at retail. Styles in the catalog were poorly displayed and customers complained about the lack of service provided on orders. Davis held little hope for the success of the venture. Nevertheless, the catalog sold hundreds of pairs of Murrayhill shoes.

Management, therefore, continued to explore the possibilities of this form of distribution. With proper display and good service, Murrayhill executives believed that direct-mail catalog sales could alleviate the excess capacity problem. To gain control of the catalog operation, Murrayhill discontinued the initial catalog venture and hired two consultants to experiment with a proprietary direct-mail catalog. In January, 1977, Murrayhill ran its first advertisement in the *Wall Street Journal.* The copy described Murrayhill shoes and provided an inquiry form for consumers who were interested in receiving a catalog of Murrayhill men's shoes. The cost of the advertisement was approximately $2400. It generated 1120 inquiries and sales of 585 pairs shoes in the year after the advertisement was run.

During the early 1980s, direct sales through mail-order catalogs became an increasingly important method of distributing a wide variety of products, from specialty foods to camping equipment. As gas prices increased and two-career families had less time to devote to shopping in stores, purchases through catalogs became more popular as a convenient and cost-effective alternative for consumers. The success of the L.L. Bean catalog, which featured quality outdoor apparel and equipment, was credited by many industry analysts with developing the consumer's habit of purchasing by mail.

Sales of shoes through direct mail began in the nineteenth century. Sears, Roebuck & Co. and Spiegel both marketed shoes through their catalogs. In 1985, Spiegel still offered premium men's shoes in its catalogs, featuring brands such as Bally and Johnston & Murphy. Hanover, E.T. Wright, and Murrayhill were among the few manufacturers that operated successful proprietary catalogs. Estimates of premium men's shoes sold in 1985 through direct mail for seven leading companies are shown below:

Catalog company	Brands sold	Estimated units sold
Spiegel	J&M, Bally	150,000
Murrayhill	Murrayhill	110,000
E.T. Wright	Wright	40,000
Norm Thompson	Allen Edmonds, Bally, J&M	35,000
Hanover	Hanover, Bostonian	20,000
Luxury Leather	Nettleton	15,000
Brooks Brothers	Brooks own brand	15,000
Total		385,000

Some executives questioned whether Hanover was in direct competition with Murrayhill because its shoes were typically sold at somewhat lower price points. In addition to the seven companies listed, other direct-mail houses, such as L.L. Bean, sold lower-priced shoes through the mail.

THE DIRECT MAIL OPERATION

Murrayhill named its catalog operation Lynn Shoes. Murrayhill management was concerned about the possible reactions of their retail accounts to the new venture. For this reason, Murrayhill was not included in the catalog name although it was clear to the catalog reader that the shoes being offered were Murrayhill brand. Lynn Shoes "purchased" inside shoes at transfer prices equal to those paid by Murrayhill's retail customers.

Before 1982, Lynn Shoes used a simple approach to operating the catalog business. Advertisements were placed in magazines and newspapers, such as the *Wall Street Journal,* the *Smithsonian, Yankee,* and fraternal magazines that were likely to be read by potential Murrayhill customers. An inquiry from these advertisements would result in Murrayhill sending seven catalog mailings in the course of one year. The styles featured in the catalog varied by season. The items that were promoted were also different for each mailing. Almost all of the advertising budget was used to generate inquiry names for the catalog mailings. Half of the expenses of the catalog operation were for catalog production and mailings. The majority of the promotions featured reduced prices, but some also offered premiums, such as a shoe care kit, with a purchase.

The objective of regaining lost retail sales remained the primary focus of Lynn Shoes for close to three years. As the cataloging business evolved, however, Murrayhill executives found that the catalog was becoming particularly important to customers who needed uncommonly sized shoes, such as narrow or wide widths. Cost-control pressure on retailers had forced them to keep lower inventories that included primarily the more common sizes, making less popular sizes hard to find. Murrayhill expanded the focus of the catalog to include this market niche. By 1985, nearly one-half of catalog sales were in sizes not normally carried in retail stores and the availability of uncommon sizes became a prerequisite for any style to be included in the catalog.

Other changes in the product line offered by Lynn Shoes were the result of changes in company objectives. The more casual lifestyles adopted by consumers in the late 1970s resulted in the increased popularity of casual shoes, particularly among younger consumers. Murrayhill expanded its product line to include lightweight dress and casual shoe styles. One of the major objectives of catalog operations was to provide a source of supply to Murrayhill customers who could no longer locate a retailer who sold Murrayhill shoes. The Lynn Shoes' initial customer base consisted primarily of these individuals. Research had shown that the Lynn Shoes customer was an older, affluent man. As the catalog operation became increasingly successful, however, Murrayhill executives saw an opportunity to broaden the customer base of Lynn Shoes by including casual styles in the catalog. This move, initiated in 1982, dramatically changed the composition of Lynn Shoes' customer base. In 1985, almost

60% of Lynn Shoes' sales were from customers who had never purchased Murrayhill shoes before they made their first catalog purchase. Outside-produced casual styles constituted the fastest growing area of both Murrayhill's and Lynn Shoes' product lines.

The success of the catalog venture was far beyond expectations. After the first year, annual sales growth exceeded 25%. By 1982, the size of the catalog operation had grown to the point where a full-time manager was needed to handle the business. Davis hired Christopher Hill.

In 1984, Lynn Shoes expanded its sources of names for catalog mailings. Advertisements were continued in the publications read by Lynn Shoes' target audience, but direct mail lists of potential customers were also purchased. Only lists of consumers who had previously purchased through the mail were used by Lynn Shoes. With advertising space becoming increasingly expensive, these lists offered a cost-effective alternative for obtaining names of prospects. By 1985, Hill estimated that 85% of the $481,000 Lynn Shoes advertising budget paid for print space, and 15% was spent on purchasing lists of direct mail purchasers.[3]

In addition, Hill decided that the catalog mailings needed a more focused approach to soliciting business. In 1982, Murrayhill set up a system of sequential mailings, with one mailing every other month, that aimed to persuade prospects to buy from the catalog. Because the sequential mailings were initiated by a customer inquiry, which could occur at any time, Lynn Shoes could, in any given month, be mailing seven different catalogs to seven different groups of consumers. Each subsequent mailing offered the potential customer a more powerful price incentive to purchase Murrayhill shoes. Once a customer made a purchase, the sequence of promotional mailings would cease and the customer's name would be added to a list that received retention catalog mailings.

All seven promotional catalogs, except the last, were 40 pages long and included a brief history of shoemaking, a letter from the Lynn Shoes marketing manager, and the Murrayhill shoes unconditional guarantee of satisfaction. The center 32 pages of the catalog changed every six months, while the 8-page "wrapper" around the center of the catalog changed every 60 days. Generally, 80 styles of shoes were included in each catalog. These fell into three groups: 52 styles of "inside-made" shoes that were also available through retail, 12 styles of inside shoes made exclusively for the catalog, and 16 styles of casual shoes made by other manufacturers under contract to Murrayhill that could be purchased only through the catalog. Retail accounts were allowed to purchase styles exclusive to the catalog on special request but paid standard mark-ups, regardless of whether the style was promoted in the catalog. Catalog prices were slightly higher than suggested retail prices on shared styles to cover possible price increases during the run of a catalog. Shoes shared by the catalog and the wholesale business were never promoted in the catalog to ensure that the selling prices of retail accounts would not be undercut. All of the promotions offered in the catalog carried an expiration date in order to

---

[3]Murrayhill spent an additional $340,000 in 1985 on print advertisements for Murrayhill shoes that were not intended to generate inquiries for Lynn Shoes.

motivate purchase decisions that might otherwise be postponed. Exceptions to this policy might be made if a new customer ordered shortly after the expiration date. The promotional focus and the customer purchase rate for each of the catalogs are described below and summarized in Exhibit 3.

Mailing 1.   The first mailing attempted to stimulate sales through persuasion rather than price promotion. Two pairs of cashmere socks were offered to each customer for every two pairs of Murrayhill shoes purchased. A $2.00 handling fee was charged for the socks to partially offset the $10.00 total cost of the premium. Approximately 2.8% of consumers receiving catalogs purchased shoes. The average order size was 1.45 pairs.

Mailing 2.   Price promotions began with the second mailing. The catalog offered $15 off each pair of shoes purchased and an additional $15 off for every two pairs ordered. This promotional offer was surprisingly weak in impact, registering a closure rate of only 2.5% and an average order size of 1.45 pairs. On subsequent mailings, the $15 off promotion became a standard offer on any full-priced item displayed in each catalog.

Mailing 3.   The third mailing offered specific styles at reduced prices, displayed on the cover of the catalog. One of the basic, "traditional lace-up" inside-made dress styles not available to retailers was shown at 35% off the regular price. One other inside-made shoe was also promoted. Five outside-made casual styles, with factory costs of around $28, were offered at $55. When the sequential mailings were first developed, only the dress style was offered, and closure rates were about 3%. The addition of the casual styles to the promotion increased the closure rate to 6.2%.

Mailing 4.   The promotions in the fourth mailing were very similar to those in the third catalog. Six dress styles were featured at a discount. One inside-made dress shoe and outside-made casual were featured on the cover of the catalog. The standard $15 off on the purchase of any full-priced style was strengthened with the additional offer of a shoe shine kit for a $2 handling fee. The cost of the kit to Murrayhill was $4. For every two pairs of shoes that were purchased, a leather wallet would be provided free of charge. The cost to Lynn Shoes of each wallet was $8. The wallets were not considered to be a very effective sales incentive, with 25% of orders receiving the item. Around 4.3% of individuals receiving the fourth mailing ordered Murrayhill shoes.

Mailing 5.   Four dress styles were discounted on the cover of this mailing, priced from $149 to $99. Three casual styles were promoted on the inside of the catalog, with one featured at a very low price of $49. The highly discounted casual style did not appear on the cover, which Hill believed accounted for the relatively low 2.4% closure rate.

EXHIBIT 3 Summary of Lynn Shoes promotion offers and results

Mailing	1	2	3	4	5	6	7
Timing	On receipt	2 months	4 months	6 months	8 months	10 months	12 months
Number of sale styles	0	0	7	9	10	13	25
Regular price offer	0	$15 off each pair	$15 off each pair	Shoe shine kit and $15 off	Shoe shine kit and $15 off	Shoe shine kit and $15 off	1 pair at half price
Two pair offer	2 pair cashmere socks for $2 handling fee	$15 off order	2 pair cashmere socks for $2 handling fee	Free wallet each 2 pairs	$15 off order	$15 off order	None
Response	2.8	2.5	6.2	4.3	2.4	3.6	7.9
Average order	$154	$118	$110	$104	$113	$95	$58
Pair/order	1.4	1.45	1.55	1.56	1.54	1.35	1.11
$/pair	$110	$81	$71	$67	$73	$70	$52
Repeat factor (8 mo.)	33%	26%	23%	21%	18%	25%	11%
1985 Merchandise breakdown:							
Regular price inside-made	72%	68%	15%	12%	19%	12%	0%
Promotion price inside-made	0%	0%	30%	41%	59%	57%	58%
Total inside-made	72%	68%	45%	53%	78%	69%	58%
Regular price outside-made	28%	32%	5%	8%	8%	4%	0%
Promotional price outside-made	0%	0%	50%	39%	14%	27%	42%
Total outside	28%	32%	55%	47%	22%	31%	42%

Note: Data in this exhibit may not reconcile precisely with other case data due to differences in the number of catalogs distributed with each mailing.

Mailing 6.   The sixth mailing offered deeper price cuts on inside dress shoes, with four styles of $149 shoes at $89. Seven casual styles by outside manufacturers were promoted at $59. Closure rates for this mailing averaged slightly over 3.6%.

Mailing 7.   The seventh mailing did not include the 32-page center section and displayed only Lynn shoes. All of the shoes featured in the catalog were priced at "half price or less," with some casuals priced as low as $49. The closure rate for this catalog was 7.9%.

The overall response rate to solicitation mailings was 4.1%. The average pair of inside shoes sold through these mailings for $88 and the average pair of outside shoes for $60. On the earlier mailings, half of the responses were received by telephone and the other half by mail. With the later mailings, the ratio changed to 35% by telephone and 65% by mail. Of all items purchased, 80% were promoted shoes. Inside-made styles accounted for two-thirds of all shoes purchased at regular price. If a consumer who had inquired had not purchased by the seventh mailing, Lynn Shoes would send a "drop dead" letter informing customers that they would receive no further catalogs unless they returned an enclosed card. Close to 15% responded and, as a group, they displayed closure rates to the seven sequential mailings that were very similar to those of initial inquiries. Hill believed this high response rate was due to impulse purchasing and to some consumers simply waiting for shoes to wear out before purchasing a replacement pair.

In 1985, each catalog cost fifty cents to produce and mail. Premium costs totaled $230,000, $88,000 of which was offset by handling charges to consumers. Lynn Shoes also incurred variable processing costs of $1.50 per order and delivery costs of $1.75 per order. Customers were charged $3.50 to cover handling and delivery of each order.

The success of a mailing was not only judged by its initial response rate, but also by its repeat rate—the percentage of customers responding to any given mailing who also purchased Murrayhill shoes again. This repeat rate varied for each mailing from a high of 33% from respondents to the first catalog to a low of 11% from respondents to the last mailing. Christopher Hill explained Murrayhill's direct-mail catalog philosophy this way: "We sell such a high-quality, comfortable shoe that we have a very high customer retention rate. We can afford to run a break-even catalog operation to attract new customers because these customers are likely to continue to purchase Murrayhill shoes."

This philosophy was the basis for Lynn Shoes' retention mailing program. Once consumers had purchased from one of the sequential catalogs, they would be placed on the retention mailing list. Catalogs were mailed every 75 days with the objective of maximizing profit, rather than attracting new customers. Lynn Shoes mailed 700,000 retention catalogs and 1,020,000 solicitation catalogs in 1985. The retention catalogs were similar in appearance to the solicitation catalogs. Each had 40 pages with a 32-page core that remained the same and an 8-page "wrapper" that changed for each mailing. While the retention mailings included price promotions, discounts were not as deep and premiums always included the $2 handling charge. The merchandise offered in the catalogs was also seasonally adjusted, with one spring mailing devoted to white shoes. Lynn Shoes maintained a retention list of 156,300 customers in 1985. The typical response rate was 5.9%. The size of an order averaged 1.2 pairs and $111 compared to 1.45 pairs and $111 for a response to a solicitation mailing.

Hill conducted two pricing tests with the retention mailings. The first test attempted to determine the price sensitivity of Murrayhill customers by implementing a $10 price increase for each style in the retention catalog. Response from this mailing showed lower unit sales, but a higher dollar volume, indicating to Hill that such price increases might be a way of dealing with the capacity issue without lowering dollar sales. The second test was mailed to four randomly chosen groups of 10,000 customers from the retention list. The test catalog featured a hand-crafted imported shoe made of a specialty leather, lizard skin, that Murrayhill purchased for $89 per pair. The shoe included Murrayhill product features, such as the molded shoe sole. The four groups of customers were offered the shoe at price points shown below:

	Group 1	Group 2	Group 3	Group 4
Price	$210	$189	$179	$169
Units sold	58	212	220	383

Lynn Shoes had a consistently impressive record. Exhibit 4 shows key operating statistics for 1979 to 1985. In 1985, approximately 136,000 inquiries were handled by the catalog business, an increase of 16,000 inquiries over 1984. Lynn Shoes filled 83,050 orders accounting for 110,000 pairs of shoes in 1985, with 20% of respondents ordering more than one pair. Response from retention mailings accounted for 50,000 of these pairs. Lynn Shoes accounted for 35% of Murrayhill's total dollar sales and 17% of the pairs produced in the factory. Exhibit 5 compares sales for Lynn Shoes and Murrayhill's wholesale business from 1981 to 1985. The earlier program had solved Murrayhill's problem of excess capacity and had opened up new markets for Murrayhill shoes.

THE PROBLEM

In 1985, full production at the plant was 1,600 pairs per day or 400,000 pairs per year. With the capacity limitations of the factory, further growth in sales of inside-made shoes would place both manufacturing and customer service (i.e., speed of order fulfillment) under pressure. While purchasing additional capacity was an option, preliminary research on the availability of space, equipment, and labor resources had shown that this was not a viable solution in the short term. Some executives believed that, in the long run, Murrayhill could negotiate additional capacity through joint ventures with U.S. or foreign manufacturers. But, in the short run, Murrayhill executives had to consider other methods of managing the company's growth given the factory's capacity constraints. The two primary strategic alternatives

EXHIBIT 4 Key operating statistics for Lynn Shoes

	1979	1980	1981	1982	1983	1984	1985
New customers	6.4	16.0	17.6	19.2	25.6	25.6	45.9
List size	6.4	22.4	40.0	59.2	84.8	110.4	156.3
Orders	4.8	20.8	27.2	40.0	56.0	67.2	84.4
% repeat orders	14	18	24	32	36	42	46
Net sales	$445	$1,856	$2,864	$4,088	$5,570	$7,190	$9,120
Net pair inside	8.0	24.0	33.6	40.0	52.0	57.6	70.0
Net pair outside	0	0	0	8.0	14.4	28.8	40.0
Total	8.0	24.0	33.6	48.0	66.4	86.4	110.0
Gross margin (%)	37	47	49	47	47	53	48
Nonmerchandise expenses as % of sales							
Advertising/materials	33	23	27	31	19	19	18
All other expenses*	13	17	17	20	19	22	18
Total expenses	46	40	44	51	38	41	36
Contribution	−9	7	6	−5†	9	12	12

*Includes proportional allocations of Murrayhill overhead.

†In 1982, Murrayhill invested heavily in media advertising to acquire names of new prospects. Pay-off occurred in later years.

EXHIBIT 5 Comparison of wholesale and catalog operations

Year	Pairs shipped	Percent inside shoes	Percent outside shoes	Percent wholesale shoes	Percent Lynn Shoes	Shipments ($ million)	Percent wholesale shoes	Percent Lynn Shoes
1981	376,000	98%	2%	91%	9%	$18.0	86%	14%
1982	374,400	97	3	87	13	19.5	80	20
1983	401,600	95	5	83	17	21.4	76	24
1984	430,000	92	8	80	20	23.8	73	27
1985	456,000	89	11	76	24	27.1	65	35

were to slow the growth of Lynn Shoes, which had 156,300 customers by the end of 1985 and 197,000 customers expected by the end of 1986, or to reduce sales to retail accounts.

Slowing the growth of Lynn Shoes was controversial. The catalog offered Murrayhill one method of distribution over which the company had complete control. Despite assertions that the promotions in the catalog lowered unit contribution, tests conducted by Hill showed that increases in sales generated by the promotions more than made up for the cost of the discounts. The higher prices of the unpromoted items balanced the cost of promoted items such that Hill believed that direct sales were more profitable for the company than those through traditional channels. Nevertheless, of the four options being considered, three involved controlling the number of Lynn Shoes customers:

1. Lynn Shoes could reduce the number of initial inquiries by reducing advertising. The promotions offered in the seven catalogs would remain the same. Hill believed that this option offered the greatest flexibility. Any reduction in demand in Murrayhill's retail accounts could easily be made up by stepping up advertising. Hill also felt that the importance of promotions in attracting new business argued for their continuation.

2. Price could be raised and/or promotions eliminated, thereby increasing margins and discouraging sales. Advertising expenditures would remain the same. Several executives supported this option. They believed that excessive Lynn Shoes' price promotions could create an antagonistic relationship with some of Murrayhill's retail accounts and detracted from Murrayhill's reputation for quality. Price increases had also been used effectively in the past to curb demand and bolster profits. Nevertheless, pricing tests conducted by count on promoted styles resulted in little change in unit sales volumes. However, the proportion of higher-priced nonsale pairs sold to sales pairs sold increased.

3. The catalogs could include a reduced number of inside-made styles. However, if there was any reduction in sales of inside-made shoes to retailers, catalogs with fewer inside-made styles would not so easily make up the difference. Therefore, the catalog operation would become less effective as an alternative channel for Murrayhill.

4. Murrayhill could allow Lynn Shoes to grow at the expense of the wholesale business. One manager suggested that by no longer opening new accounts, eliminating marginal accounts, and increasing stocking requirements, Murrayhill could free up additional pairage to allow for the growth of the direct-mail operation.

Reducing sales to retail accounts was not a popular option. Most managers believed that curtailing the new account program could ease capacity pressure slightly without disrupting relations with established retail accounts. However, such measures as placing existing retailers on allocation met strong resistance from Murrayhill executives. They argued that wholesaling to retail outlets was the business that Murrayhill knew best and that most shoe purchases by consumers would continue to be made in stores. Edward Wilson was also concerned about the larger ramifications of such a sales reduction: "Retail distribution is vital to brand awareness for shoe manufacturers. Without the retailer, the consumers' view of Murrayhill shoes would be little more than a picture on a page."

By the end of 1985, the capacity problem at Murrayhill had developed into a critical issue. Orders were increasingly backlogged and Murrayhill's retail accounts were beginning to complain about delays in filling their orders. In light of industry and environmental trends, Murrayhill executives were uncertain how to balance the wholesale and direct-mail business and whether to emphasize one over the other. Davis realized that a plan of action to manage Murrayhill's growth would have to be implemented early in 1986.

CONSUMER PROMOTIONS IN SERVICE MARKETING

CHRISTOPHER H. LOVELOCK
JOHN A. QUELCH

Recent competitive activity in the airline, banking, lodging, and car rental industries highlights the increasing use by service marketers of temporary promotions directed at consumers. Consider the following efforts undertaken in 1982.

☐ Trying to loosen American Express's solid grip on the travelers check market, Chase Manhattan Bank offers discount coupon books to customers who purchase Visa-Chase travelers checks from Chase and other financial institutions. The program, scheduled to last a year, entitles purchasers to receive discounts from firms such as Hertz, Westin Hotels, U.S. Auto Club (motoring division), Fuji Photo Film, and Pentax Cameras.

☐ With hotel occupancy sharply down in New York City, the Milford Plaza puts together two promotional packages designed to appeal to nonbusiness travelers. The "Affordable New York Package" offers a welcome cocktail, gourmet dinner, and continental breakfast for $43 per person double occupancy (versus a standard price of $61–81 for a double room). Their "Broadway Sleeper Package" offers guests a $10 credit toward the cost of a room on presentation of a theater ticket or stub for that night, with another $5 off for a second ticket.

☐ Trying to get children between the ages of 10 and 16 to open savings accounts, Britain's Barclays Bank joins with Kellogg's in a three-month promotion. Participants may collect up to ten 50-pence. (80-cent) coupons printed on cereal packets and redeem these for a deposit in a special bank account opened in their name.

☐ Echoing the "twofers" commonly offered by theaters to boost attendance at plays on slack nights, Republic Airlines announces a two-for-the-price-of-one fare offer during the traditionally sluggish spring travel period. In a separate promotion scheduled to last through the summer, an adult paying full fare can take a child free on Republic by collecting five box tops from Ralston Purina cereal packages.

☐ To promote use of its services at airports, where it lacks the advantage of rental car facilities in or near the terminals, Thrifty Rent-A-Car offers a free Timex watch or travel alarm with each three-day rental; one-day renters can collect coupons toward these gifts.

FACTORS STIMULATING PROMOTIONS

Although short-term promotions are not new to the service sector, they have never before been used so widely. This trend can be seen as part of a general increase affecting packaged goods and durables, which reflects the difficulties in holding list prices at a time of both inflation and recession. But there are some factors that are specific to one or more service industries. Retail banking, for instance, has become increasingly competitive as the distinctions between commercial banks and savings and loans have blurred. Yet the different types of banking products are basically commodities. Offering promotions, especially gifts, provides not only a temporary competitive edge, but also a way of distinguishing one's products from the competition. Declining demand due to recession poses a particularly severe problem for service industries with high fixed costs, such as hotels and motels. One strategy is to avoid lowering the standard price too much and, instead, to run promotions (which may have a significant monetary value) in an attempt to stimulate demand without using price directly as a weapon; once the economy picks up, the number of promotions can be reduced or eliminated. Another contributing factor, especially in the airline business, is that companies in newly deregulated industries have no experience in how to send pricing signals clearly; the net result is an outbreak of promotion wars.

Whatever the factors underlying increased use of promotions, this growing trend raises some important questions for service marketers, who have traditionally lacked the experience and sophistication of their counterparts in packaged-goods firms. What, for instance, are the implications of the differences between goods and services for managing promotional activities in the service sector? What role should short-term promotion play in service marketing? What types of promotions are available to service marketers and what criteria should be employed in selecting and designing a specific promotional program?

In this article, we'll offer some guidelines to service marketers on several key aspects of promotion management. But we'll also urge caution regarding the burgeoning use of promotion in service businesses.

SERVICES VS. PACKAGED GOODS: IMPLICATIONS FOR STRATEGY

Three important differences distinguish consumer services from consumer packaged goods:

- ☐ "Finished" services cannot be inventoried, so unused productive capacity is perishable.

- ☐ Except for repair and maintenance, there are normally no physical distribution channels for services.

- ☐ Customer contact personnel often assume great importance in service delivery and may be considered an integral part of the product experience by consumers.

Absence of Inventories

Since finished services cannot be inventoried, a major objective of service marketers is to find ways of shaping demand to match the capacity available at any given time. Obvious strategies include seeking to reduce usage during peak demand periods and trying to stimulate it during off-peak periods. The latter strategy assumes added importance in situations where low patronage detracts from the marketer's image and the customer's satisfaction (as in a half-empty theater). Since time utilities vary among consumers, many services have been able to employ price discrimination to achieve their goal of smoothing demand over time—whether by day, week, or season. Given the scope for price discrimination, there is great opportunity for service marketers to design and deliver promotions that communicate an otherwise mundane and commonplace price reduction in an exciting and attention-getting manner. The opportunity is greatest for services with high fixed and low variable costs—those where a large gap exists between normal selling price and variable costs—permitting substantial price promotions to be offered to fill otherwise unused capacity. An important constraint, however, is the ability of service organizations to communicate an elaborate and frequently changing pricing schedule to their target customers and intermediaries (such as travel agents).

Packaged-goods promotions, by contrast, rarely seek to smooth demand. There are two main reasons for this. First, smoothing demand is relatively less important for most packaged goods, since it is easier to manage manufacturing capacity in the short run than it is to increase or decrease capacity for such high fixed-cost services as hotels and airlines. Second, because goods can be inventoried, a temporary promotion may prompt both the trade and consumers to stock up in excess of normal inventory requirements, resulting in a fall off in sales when the promotion is over. Thus, either an artificial seasonality of demand is induced, adding to production and distribution costs, or an already seasonal demand pattern is exaggerated as manufacturers compete for sell-ins to the trade prior to the peak selling season.

Packaged-goods marketers often run promotions to encourage multiple purchases and pantry loading in order to preclude purchases of competitive brands, accelerate product usage, and boost cash flow. Inventories are thereby shifted to consumers, who have lower holding costs than manufacturers and retailers.

Despite the absence of inventories, service marketers can effectively load consumers by offering "membership" relationships that entitle the customer to benefits over an extended period. For example, theaters offer season subscriptions, which some consumers are willing to purchase in advance, even though consumption of the service cannot be accelerated. These consumers trade off the financing costs of advance purchase against the convenience of making a single purchase to assure a known seating location for the entire season.

Other membership relationships, while not requiring advance purchases, reward consumers for their loyalty in selecting a particular service supplier. Just as retail establishments have traditionally offered trading stamps to promote customer loyalty, so the major airlines now offer rate reductions for various levels of accumulated flight mileage. Such programs may stimulate additional and/or accelerated use of the service as well as encourage customer loyalty to a specific airline.

Relative to packaged-goods promotions, however, service promotions seem less likely to guarantee expanded purchases of a particular brand. As a result, service marketers may be tempted to run more frequent promotions than packaged-goods marketers, who are sensitive to the risk that their own or competitive promotions may load trade intermediaries and consumers with sufficient quantities of the product to discourage further sales in the immediate future.

Since services cannot be inventoried, can service promotions be implemented more rapidly than packaged-goods promotions? Packaged-goods manufacturers have to ensure that additional merchandise can be shipped to the trade to meet the additional demand that they hope the promotion will stimulate. In addition, many packaged-goods promotions require product label changes to announce the offer or packaging changes to accommodate, for example, an on-pack premium or coupon. Services are not subject to similar lead time constraints unless the promotion is offered on physical goods that are an integral part of the service firm's product. For example, if a fast food chain offers a premium in return for the purchase of certain food items, management must ensure that an adequate supply of both the premium and the specified menu items are available at all participating restaurants.

In one respect, service promotions may be harder to implement than packaged-goods promotions, because it is more time consuming and expensive to communicate their existence to consumers. Most consumers of packaged goods visit a supermarket at least once a week, enabling grocery products manufacturers to reach their audience at the point-of-sale, independent of whether these consumers have previously been exposed to media advertisements for the promotion in question. With the exception of on-premise outdoor advertising or promotions of service boutiques within department stores, marketers cannot achieve similar "free" exposure to large numbers of nonusers. A higher level of advertising effort may therefore be necessary to communicate the existence of the service promotion.

Reduced Role of Intermediaries

Another major difference between services and packaged goods is that most services are not sold through channel intermediaries. What implications does this have for the planning and implementation of service promotions? Most packaged-goods marketers need to be concerned with resource allocation among advertising, consumer promotion, and trade promotion, but service marketers selling directly do not need to consider that last item. In the absence of trade promotion, service marketers can exert more control over effective expenditures of their promotion dollars than can packaged-goods marketers. They are spared the problem of having trade intermediaries pocket promotion allowances without providing commensurate merchandising support.

However, some service marketers do need to provide incentives to intermediaries. Firms in the travel and insurance industries, which make extensive use of independent agents and brokers, must compete with other "brands" for mental inventory, physical display space, and push from the intermediary. And even when competitive supplies do not have to be countered—as in the case of franchise organizations—franchisees may have to be motivated to implement and aggressively push a supplier-initiated promotion.

Service marketers who sell direct and implement high-volume promotions are sometimes confronted by ad hoc channel intermediaries. For instance, recent airline coupon promotions incurred much higher redemption rates (and therefore costs) than were forecast due to the emergence of both individual and entrepreneurial coupon resale efforts.

Importance of Contact Personnel

When intermediaries are absent, sales incentive programs for the service marketer's customer contact personnel assume greater importance. In packaged-goods marketing, individual retail personnel play a negligible role in the success of any transaction. The reverse is true in service marketing, where an acceptable interaction between customer and contact personnel is often critical to customer satisfaction. As a result, to ensure quality control in the service "facility," incentive programs directed at contact personnel are more widely used by service marketers than by packaged-goods marketers.

The importance of contact personnel in service selling can give the service marketer an advantage in implementing promotional efforts. Such promotions as the premiums offered by fast food chains can be personally delivered to the consumer at the time of sale. Central to successful implementation is ensuring a smooth and friendly interaction between consumer and contact personnel without compromising the speed and efficiency of delivering the basic service.

WHEN TO USE PROMOTIONS

When should service marketers consider the use of temporary consumer promotions? Table 1 summarizes a wide array of possible objectives relating to consumers, intermediaries, and competitors. As previously indicated, demand management, particularly the smoothing of demand, figures more frequently among the objectives of the service marketer than those of the packaged-goods marketer.

Which services lend themselves most readily to promotions? Here, similar criteria apply to services as to goods. High-risk, infrequently purchased services with which the consumer is not familiar and that are perceived to be differentiated on nonprice attributes lend themselves less to promotion—particularly if promotional efforts might jeopardize a carefully cultivated image of quality. For these reasons, promotions are rarely offered on professional or funeral home services. At the same time, industries such as the airlines are plagued by promotions. Why?

☐   Airline profitability is highly sensitive to volume and capacity utilization. A wide gap between normal selling price and variable cost offers scope for generous promotions.

TABLE 1   Possible objectives of consumer promotions for services

1. Objectives targeted at consumers
   - ☐ Increase awareness of the service.
   - ☐ Encourage trial of a new service.
   - ☐ Encourage trial of an existing service by current nonusers.
   - ☐ Persuade existing consumers to:
     —continue to purchase the service and not to switch.
     —increase their purchase frequency of the service.
     —regularly purchase their average quantity of the service.
     —commit to purchasing the service for an extended time period (thus taking the consumer out of the marketplace).
   - ☐ Smooth the pattern of consumer demand.
   - ☐ Communicate the distinctive benefits of the service.
   - ☐ Reinforce advertising for the service and increase audience attention to it.
   - ☐ Obtain market research information about the service.
   - ☐ Promote the service as part of a broader product line (or link it to sales of a complementary service marketed by another organization).
2. Objectives targeted at intermediaries
   - ☐ Persuade intermediaries to deliver a new or relaunched service.
   - ☐ Persuade existing intermediaries to provide additional push for the service, including point-of-sale merchandising.
   - ☐ Insulate the trade from consumer price negotiation at the point-of-purchase.
   - ☐ Insulate the trade from any temporary sales reduction that might result from a price increase.
3. Objectives targeted at competition
   - ☐ Move offensively or defensively on a temporary basis against one or more competitors of the service.

☐ Following deregulation of the U.S. airline industry, the level of new product activity (new airlines on new routes) has become intense. Promotions are necessary to induce trial of these new services as well as to build demand under recession-induced conditions of considerable excess capacity.

☐ Most consumers make their flight decisions on the basis of schedules and price, so brand loyalty is only a secondary consideration. Research suggests that many travelers perceive few significant differences among the major carriers.

☐ Many air travelers are highly price sensitive; these travelers are willing to undertake an extensive search to locate the lowest price. Their task is facilitated by the presence of specialist intermediaries—travel agents—who can provide up-to-date information by means of their computer terminals or through phone calls.

☐ Temporary promotions can stimulate interest in the purchase of discretionary services that might otherwise be postponable. These offer an opportunity to advance the timing of demand.

☐ Competitive market shares are both close and volatile on the limited number of major routes that represent the "bread and butter" of the industry.

ALTERNATIVE PROMOTION TECHNIQUES

Six promotional techniques are available to service marketers to add interest and excitement to straight price cuts. An example of each approach—samples, price/quality promotions, coupons, refunds, premiums, and price promotions—is presented in Table 2.

Although all six techniques can be used in both the service and manufacturing sectors, there may be some differences in emphasis for certain approaches between service and packaged-goods marketers:

TABLE 2   Examples of six types of consumer promotions for services

---

Sampling. A credit card company offers a free one-month trial to consumers interested in its newly introduced credit card protection program.

Price/quantity promotions. American Airlines Airpass offers consumers 5- to 15-year passes priced from $19,500 to $58,900.

Coupons. Cunard offers a $280 discount coupon in newspaper advertisements toward the cost of a stateroom on a Caribbean cruise.

Refunds and future discounts. TWA's Frequent Flight Bonus program offers a graduated scale of future in-flight discounts for various levels of accumulated mileage on TWA flights.

Premiums. A bank offers a graduated scale of premiums, ranging from kitchenware to clock radios, in return for varying levels of initial deposits.

Prize promotions. Listeners to a radio station have 15 minutes to claim instant cash prizes based on drawings of their sweepstakes entries.

☐ **Sampling** is used less frequently for services. Most services sell at prices that make free trial offers seem uneconomical to the organization (even though the incremental costs of serving an additional customer are often quite low). However, services such as bars and fast foods that deliver divisible, low-cost physical products to consumers can use sampling effectively.

☐ **Premiums** are frequently used to give an element of tangibility to otherwise intangible services and to distinguish the images of the service organizations that market them. For instance, the banking and insurance industries, whose services are not easily differentiable, were the sixth and ninth largest industry users of consumer premiums in the United States in 1980.

☐ **Prize promotions** can be used effectively to add involvement and excitement to the service experience when consumers represent a captive audience. Thus, airline passengers may welcome participation in in-flight games and contests to relieve the boredom of air travel. In selecting which promotional techniques to use, service marketers should review the criteria listed in Table 3. We believe

---

TABLE 3 Criteria for selecting a consumer promotion for a service

1. Objectives

☐ Is the promotion consistent with overall brand marketing objectives in general and with the overall objectives of consumer promotions for the service?

☐ Is the promotion versatile, capable of effectively reaching several groups (such as both new and existing users), and fulfilling several objectives (such as stimulating switching and multiple purchases) simultaneously?

☐ Does the promotion have appeal to consumers, to intermediaries, and to contact personnel?

☐ Can the promotion function efficiently as a national promotion and/or as a local promotion in select market areas? For example, coupon drops can be arranged in an individual market area, but sweepstakes or contests must generally be national.

2. The service

☐ Is the service a planned or an impulse purchase? If the latter, does the promotion make an impact at the point-of-service delivery?

☐ Is the product frequently or infrequently purchased? If the promotion offer requires multiple purchases, slippage will be greater to the extent that the product is less frequently purchased.

☐ Are the characteristics of the product appropriate for this promotional approach? For example indivisible services cannot be economically sampled.

3. The consumer

☐ Are target consumers accustomed to this promotional technique for this service? If not, might they perceive it as inappropriate?

☐ Does the promotion reduce perceived purchase risk?

☐ Are the terms of the promotion simple and easy to understand?

☐ Does the promotion offer an immediate or delayed reward to the consumer?

☐ How much consumer effort is required to take advantage of the promotional offer?

☐ Are the terms of the promotion flexible, offering options to the consumer?

4. The intermediaries

☐ How much incremental effort is required of intermediaries to successfully implement the promotion?

☐ Does the promotion offer a direct sales benefit to intermediaries? Some refund offers, for example, either require proof of purchase for a second related item or offer a refund in the form of a certificate toward the purchase of a second related item.

☐ How much flexibility does the promotion offer intermediaries in terms of timing and execution?

☐ Does the promotion permit intermediaries to appear to be the source of the offer?

☐ Does the promotion lend itself to creative and exciting point-of-sale displays?

5. Competition

☐ Are competitive products currently using this promotion technique?

☐ How rapidly can a competitor respond with a similar or superior promotion?

6. Cost effectiveness

☐ What is the maximum expected liability for the promotion?

☐ Can the terms of the promotional offer be designed to minimize liability? For example, the number of purchase proofs required for a refund offer can be increased such that slippage increases and actual costs decrease.

☐ How well can costs for the promotion be forecast? Is it vulnerable to the activities of ad hoc intermediaries (such as coupon brokers) such that forecast costs may be greatly exceeded?

☐ Will the promotion tie up manufacturer capital, for example in an inventory of premium merchandise?

☐ Are the expenses for the promotion incurred on a pay-as-you-go (couponing) or investment (sweepstakes) basis?

☐ Is this promotion vulnerable to waste and abuse through such activities as pilferage and misredemption?

☐ Can the promotion be designed to minimize the number of consumers who can take advantage of the offer more than once?

7. Integration

☐ Can the promotion be integrated easily with other elements of the communications mix, including advertising, personal selling, and point-of-sale displays?

☐ Can the promotion reinforce the service advertising theme and contribute to franchise building?

☐ Can the promotion be integrated with other promotional activities to create a dramatic event? For example, a sweepstakes is often used as an overlay to a refund and/or coupon offer.

☐ Can the promotion be used easily in line promotions involving several services as well as in single service promotions?

☐ Is the promotion part of a successful marketing tradition for this service category?

8. Implementation

☐ How much incremental effort is required of management and the salesforce to successfully implement the promotion?

☐ Does the salesforce expect the promotion to facilitate its selling task?

☐ To what extent are the services of outside agencies required to implement the promotion?

☐ Does management control the costs and timing of delivering the offer?

☐ Does management have prior experience with this type of promotion?

☐ How much lead time is required for implementation?

9. Measurement

☐ What measures are available to gauge response to the promotion and how valuable are they? For example, does the number of entries in a sweepstakes indicate the relative degree of positive impact on the sponsoring brand?

☐ Can the impact be inexpensively measured and compared to the impact of other promotions both of the same and of different types?

☐ Is response concentrated in a short time period after the promotion is launched or are there significant lag effects that may reduce the accuracy and increase the expense of measurement?

10. Legal

☐ Are there legal constraints on the design and use of this type of promotion?

☐ Can this type of promotion be implemented nationally or are there local laws which require adaptation of the offer in each state?

that many service promotions fail to meet these criteria and thus represent a suboptimal use of the marketer's resources.

DESIGNING A SPECIFIC PROMOTION

Once a technique has been selected, six elements must be considered in the design of a specific execution: product scope, market scope, value, timing, identification of beneficiary, and proofing against the competition.

Product Scope

Which specific services or facilitating goods will be promoted? If the objective of the promotion is defensive, the answer may be those services under competitive pressure. If the purpose is to attract new customers, a low-risk, inexpensive service may be promoted to "hook" customers who then become candidates for cross-selling of other services. Or, if the objective is to preempt competition, a promotion may be offered on a product (such as a six-month savings certificate) that locks the customer into a relationship with the service marketer for an extended period of time.

The broader the service product line, the more challenging the decision on which services to promote. An airline can promote little else but a seat on the plane unless it joins the hotels and rental car firms to promote a complete travel package. By contrast, a restaurant can offer any of several promotions on different menus, parts of the meal, or other aspects of the dining experience.

Market Scope

Will the promotion be generally available or offered only in selected markets? Given the opportunities for price discrimination, service marketers have more room for flexibility in this area than packaged-goods marketers. While a hotel chain may wish to run periodic national promotions to develop a consistent marketing image, it may also see a need for price promotions of varying levels in individual markets, depending on comparative market shares and occupancy rates. In addition, service marketers can, if they wish, limit a promotion to a particular demographic group—an approach which is almost always infeasible for the packaged-goods marketer. Transportation services often run special promotions for students and children, and some utilities charge reduced rates to senior citizens. However, local or state legislation sometimes constrains a service firm's ability to restrict a promotion to specific groups.

Value

Some promotions—particularly price/quantity promotions—offer consumers an immediate cash value directly associated with the promoted service. These promotions offer the same (or more) for a lower price. Other promotions, such as sweepstakes and premiums, offer consumers a delayed value that usually is not directly related to the price of the promoted service. These latter promotions offer "more for the same price." Clearly, the service marketer must take into account consumer preferences, likely costs, and promotion objectives in deciding on the form and level of value to be offered. When consumers' product usage levels vary widely, promotions can be designed to incorporate multiple options whereby different values are offered for different levels of consumption, as in the case of airline mileage promotions.

Any promotion offer incorporates an explicit discount rate from the "normal" price. Service marketers should recognize that consumer response functions are likely to vary by type of promotion and are unlikely to be linear; in other words, a 10% discount will not necessarily generate twice the incremental sales of a 5% discount.

In setting a discount rate, the service marketer should consider how the promoted service will be positioned competitively at the discounted price. Market share leaders usually do not need to offer as deep discounts as followers to achieve the same level of response. If a leader offers discounts below the category norm, this many compromise the strength of the brand franchise and contribute to discount rate escalation and price sensitivity within the category. In addition, a deep discount may attract many one-time customers who are extremely unlikely to repurchase the service at its normal price.

Timing

Service marketers developing promotions face three issues of concern: when, how long, and how often? As previously discussed most service promotions aim to smooth demand; hence, they are typically timed to counter, rather than exaggerate, a seasonal sales pattern. The length of any promotion should be a function of the target consumer's product purchase cycle and the value of the offer—the longer the interpurchase interval, the greater the need for a longer offer to ensure that all target consumers can be exposed. Similarly, the frequency of promotions should take account of competitive pressures and the typical consumer purchase cycle; service marketers should avoid the notion that promotions will be offered automatically in every season of the year.

Identification of Beneficiary

Since promotions are designed to influence or reinforce consumer behavior, it is very important to target the right individuals. For example, a service business may wish to reach only a specific segment of its existing customer base. To promote use of automatic teller machines (ATMs), BayBanks, a Boston-based banking organization, offered a voucher for a free ice cream at an adjacent store to those retail customers who participated in a demonstration of how to use an ATM. Two years later, by which time a substantial proportion of all retail customers had obtained cards to operate the machines, BayBanks sought to encourage expanded use of its ATMs by inviting all retail customers to participate in a sweepstakes each time they used an ATM, offering as first prize a trip to Hawaii.

Sometimes, users of a service do not have to pay for it themselves. This is particularly true of hotel and transportation services used by business travelers. Promotions offering discounts to individuals who are not on a fixed daily allowance are likely to have limited appeal since it is the employer who pockets the savings. Recently, airlines tried to finesse this situation by offering travelers coupons for discounts on future flights, hoping business travelers would be able to use the coupons for personal travel. But many firms insisted their employees turn in the coupons so the company could use them. Mileage bonuses credited to the traveler provide a way around this problem but, like coupons, suffer from the disadvantage that all airlines can easily copy the innovation.

A more creative approach is represented by joint promotions between a transportation firm and a brand-name gift manufacturer, as exemplified by the Thrifty Rent-A-Car tie-in with Timex watches. More sophisticated yet is Pan American Airlines' "Experience with Style" joint promotion with Sheraton Hotels. Travelers flying first or clipper class on PanAm and paying the regular or corporate rate of any of 41 Sheraton hotels in 14 countries will receive gift certificates worth $10 for each night a room is occupied. These can be redeemed for merchandise at such leading stores as Bonwit Teller, Dunhill's of London, and Saks Fifth Avenue. A promotion such as this offers significant value to the traveler—who generally makes the decisions on which airlines and hotels to patronize—but involves no discounting to the company paying the travel bills. The actual cost of the promotion is shared among the major participants, while the nature of the offer makes it noteworthy in its own right. Moreover, the images of the two major participants may benefit from association with the names of well-known and well-regarded retailers.

Competition-Proofing

The final element is to design promotions that provide a distinctive and continuing competitive advantage. Many service firms have developed a promotion only to find their competitors quickly copying it. For instance, airlines have run coupon wars, competing banks have engaged in gift wars, and all major airlines now offer mileage bonus programs for frequent fliers. It is most distressing for a manager who has developed and publicized a promotion to have it "kidnapped" by a competitor. For example, in late spring of 1982, Holiday Inn began offering bonus coupons, good for reduced rates at its hotels and motels. Within a relatively short period, Howard Johnson's was running a TV campaign in which it offered not only to accept Holiday Inn coupons at its own inns, but also to give guests a voucher good for a discount on their next visit to Howard Johnson's.

Most promotions are easily imitated and there is virtually nothing a firm can do to prevent a competitor from advertising its willingness to honor discount vouchers issued elsewhere. Two forms of competition-proofing are, first, to develop a promotion that will be too complex to imitate quickly (thus assuring the innovator a lengthy start), and second, to arrange with one or more well-known firms an exclusive joint promotion that cannot be directly duplicated. The PanAm-Sheraton retail gift voucher program described earlier meets both these criteria.

EFFECTIVE PROMOTION MANAGEMENT

Use of promotions by service marketers is burgeoning, but this important tool is easily misused. To avoid wasting money and efforts, we offer the following suggestions.

Plan a promotion strategy.   Rather than launching promotions indiscriminately as tactical responses to competitive actions, plan a promotion strategy on an annual basis. Develop a promotion calendar showing which services will be promoted, when they will be promoted, in which markets, with what objectives, and using which techniques. Such a planning process will ensure variety, internal consistency, and synergy in promotion efforts. The establishment of an in-house promotion department is essential to providing the necessary continuity in the planning process.

Limit promotion objectives.   Service marketers should not exaggerate the results that promotions can reasonably be expected to produce. They should also not attempt to achieve too many objectives through a single effort. Any given promotion should focus selectively on one or two objectives for which promotional expenditures can be expected to have maximum impact.

Consider promotion tie-ins.   Many services, particularly in the travel industry, are sold to consumers in packages or bundles. Service marketers can often effectively extend their promotion resources and develop higher-impact promotion events by simultaneously promoting several of their own services, or joining forces with each other. Thus, an airline and a hotel chain may advertise a joint sweepstakes, with holiday packages involving the marketers' services as prizes; each partner benefits from the implied endorsement of the other. Tie-ins with packaged goods firms offer a way of reaching new users through exposure to information on familiar brand packages; again there is a sharing of resources and implied endorsement.

Consider promotion overlays.   In order to break through the increasing level of promotion "clutter" in the marketplace, it is often appropriate to use several promotion techniques at once to create a blockbuster event. For example, a coupon may be offered with a sweepstakes and refund overlay.

Motivate the entire marketing system.   The most effective promotions are those which aim to simultaneously create a "push" and "pull" effect by motivating all parties in the selling process—consumers, contact personnel, and if necessary, sales intermediaries. For example, a sweepstakes might be promoted to consumers and sales contests with similar themes and prize structures offered to the other two groups.

Balance creativity with simplicity.   The design of consumer promotions offers great scope for creativity, and much is necessary to ensure that a promotion is sufficiently differentiated to stand out from the crowd. However, creativity should not be permitted to lead to over-complexity in promotion design; care of consumer understanding is essential to success. An example of an overly complicated promotion comes from the United Kindom. British Rail recently ran a promotion offering a monthly pass that entitled the bearer to free train travel if accompanied by another passenger paying full fare. To qualify, it was necessary to collect box tops or package labels from no less than nine common supermarket brands.

Evaluate promotion effectiveness.   Service marketers should measure the incremental contribution impact of each promotion, estimating in the process what sales would have been in the absence of promotion and the extent to which the promotion caused sales volume to be "stolen" from future business. Fortunately, evaluation of service promotions is not complicated by the packaged-goods firm's need to measure warehouse and retail-inventory levels.

Well-planned and well-executed promotions represent an important tactical weapon to service marketers in their search for profitability and competitive advantage. However, we would like to conclude by warning against the natural temptation to misuse a newly discovered weapon, lest this devalue its effectiveness through overuse or distract management attention from other marketing tools more appropriate to a specific situation. This leads us to offer the following cautions.

☐   Although promotions can stimulate consumer excitement, they can also increase consumer price sensitivity, so that many consumers eventually become unwilling to buy the service unless it is available at a promoted price. If a high percentage of sales are made on promotion, "normal" prices become artificially inflated and increasingly meaningless.

☐   Too much management effort and dollar resources devoted to promotion activity may detract from creativity in nonprice differentiation and franchise-building investments on which the long-term health of most service businesses usually depends.

☐   When promotions can be imitated easily by competitors, there is the risk of a zero sum game developing in which all parties lose, particularly when promotion activity cannot stimulate additional primary demand.

UNITED AIRLINES: PRICE PROMOTION POLICY

JOHN A. QUELCH
MELANIE D. SPENCER

"There are three ways to increase market share . . . price, price, and price," stated James Jackson, director of pricing for United Airlines, opening the marketing strategy session. The date was June 13, 1985, and the end of the month-long United pilots' strike appeared imminent, leaving marketing managers limited time to decide the best method for recovering traffic lost during the strike. There were differing opinions among members of the marketing staff as to what the strategy should be. One group of managers argued against any promotional activity by United on the grounds that it was sure to be matched by other carriers, leading to a new round of price and promotion fare wars. Another group was concerned that many of United's frequent flyers enrolled in its Mileage Plus Program had been forced to try American Airlines and other carriers during the strike.

The pilots' strike had forced United to cancel most flights to the majority of its flight destinations and to reduce substantially the number of aircraft servicing the others. Consequently, revenues had decreased dramatically and United's profitable business travelers had been forced to patronize other carriers. United, the largest airline in the free world, both in terms of revenues and reveue passenger miles (the sum of all miles flown on a carrier by its paying passengers), expected eventually to recover the traffic lost during the strike. However, there was concern about how long the traffic mix would remain diluted, meaning that a higher-than-normal number of passengers would be flying on discounted fares. The strike had also resulted in adverse publicity and some confusion about the airline's schedule.

COMPANY BACKGROUND

On April 6, 1926, the first private-contract air mail delivery took off for Elko, Nevada, giving birth to commercial air transportation and United Airlines, the oldest airline in the United States. Varney Air Lines was the name of the company that ran that first flight. Varney soon merged with Boeing Air Transport, part of a combination company that encompassed Boeing Airplane Company and Pratt & Whitney. United Airlines was created to manage the airline division of the corporation. In 1934, United became a separate entity when the larger company dissolved. Capital Airlines was acquired in 1961, substantially increasing United's service area and making it the world's largest privately owned carrier. In 1969, the airline was absorbed into a holding company, UAL, Inc., whose assets also included Westin Hotels and other properties.

Throughout its history, United led the commercial airline industry in innovation. In its early years, United introduced in-flight service and dining. United was the first to initiate coast-to-coast flights, to install an automatic baggage-conveyor system, to equip its airplanes with radar, to develop a nationwide computerized reservation system for travel agents, and to fly to all 50 states. This record of innovation was partially responsible for United's strong position relative to other U.S. carriers. The company's efforts to build further its reputation for quality service had been aided during the 1980s by its successful "Fly the Friendly Skies" advertising campaign, supported in 1984 by the largest advertising budget of any airline. Exhibit 1 summarizes the 1984 advertising expenditures of the major carriers. United's projected advertising expenditures in 1985 were $74 million (television $49 million, radio $9 million, and print $16 million).

United's emphasis on advertising appeared to be effective. United dominated the marketplace in 1984 with an 18.2% share of passenger traffic (measured in revenue passenger miles). Its two closest rivals were American at 14% and Delta at 11%. Exhibit 2 shows United's revenue passenger miles (RPMs) and other operating statistics from January 1983, to May 1985.

Generally, profits in the airline industry were dependent on the health of the economy. With deregulation and the adverse economic conditions of the late 1970s and early 1980s, UAL, Inc., suffered heavy losses. Although the corporation made a comeback in 1983, much of its $142 million profit that year was due to tax benefits associated with losses in preceding years and the purchase of equipment. The return

EXHIBIT 1   Advertising expenditures and financial performance of major airlines (in $ millions)

	Advertising		1984 Sales	1984 Earnings
	1984	1983		
UAL, Inc.*	$137	$132	$6,968	$643
American	111	89	5,354	234
Delta	67	65	3,657	260
Trans World	66	59	3,657	30
Eastern	61	71	4,364	38

Source: *Advertising Age,* September 26, 1985.

*Includes Westin Hotel advertising expenditures and revenues.

EXHIBIT 2 Monthly statistics for United Airlines domestic operations

	Jan.	Feb.	Mar.	Apr.	May	June	July	Aug.	Sept.	Oct.	Nov.	Dec.	Total
Passengers (000s)													
1983	2,139	2,252	2,993	2,764	2,624	3,090	3,018	3,027	2,710	3,030	2,808	2,705	33,160
1984	2,460	2,396	3,113	2,833	3,091	3,233	3,285	3,395	2,902	3,168	2,880	3,044	35,800
1985	2,805	2,591	3,679	3,523	2,304								14,902
Revenues (000,000s)													
1983	$236	$224	$293	294	$295	$352	$361	$369	$334	$388	$361	$338	$3,845
1984	321	316	398	354	396	411	407	417	361	389	343	347	4,462
1985	330	297	384	363	273								1,647
RPMs (000,000s)													
1983	2,152	2,231	3,050	2,747	2,596	3,068	3,068	3,067	2,652	2,923	2,654	2,622	32,830
1984	2,368	2,251	2,903	2,669	2,892	3,088	3,167	3,260	2,749	2,944	2,617	2,807	33,715
1985	2,640	2,407	3,401	3,269	2,165								13,882
Yield													
1983	11%	10%	9%	10%	11%	11%	11%	12%	12%	13%	13%	13%	
1984	13	14	13	13	13	13	12	12	13	13	13	12	
1985	12	12	11	11	11								

Notes:

Passengers = total number of domestic passengers per month of year indicated.

Revenues = total revenues in millions of dollars per month of year indicated.

RPMs = sum of per-passenger miles flown for every revenue-paying passenger per month of year indicated.

Yield = revenues/RPMs by month of year indicated.

of economic growth in 1984 heralded substantial improvement in performance with record operating revenues of $7 billion and $282 million in net earnings, with the airline contributing $259 million.

The improvement in profitability was partially due to the reorganization of United's route system. The "hub and spoke" concept was developed to increase operating efficiency and to permit United to compete with low-cost carriers such as People Express and New York Air. Chicago, Denver, and San Francisco became United's hub cities around which United's route system was organized. Exhibit 3 shows a map of United's route system. These cities served as collection and

EXHIBIT 3   Cities served and new routes added in 1984

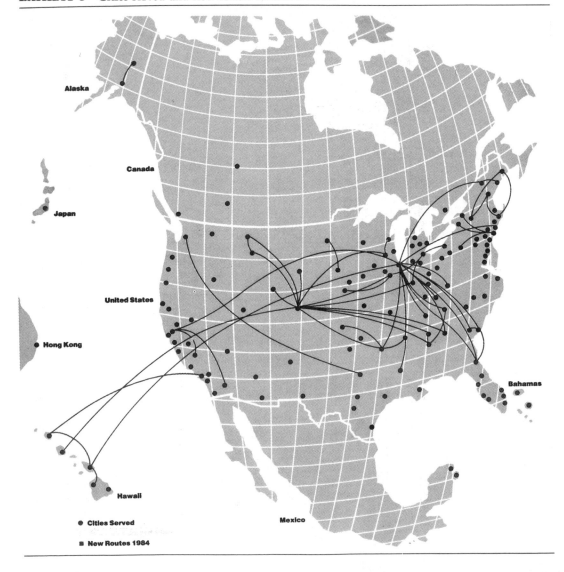

distribution points for passengers whose flights originated elsewhere. For example, a passenger flying from New York to Seattle and another flying from New York to Las Vegas would both fly first to Chicago where they would board connecting flights. Close to 90% of United's daily flights were routed through these hubs.

Other carriers also began to see improvement in profits. Many airlines channeled these funds into capital expenditures to add aircraft and flights. In the first several months of 1985, United's major rivals had expanded capacity at least 10%, while United's available seat miles had increased barely 1% in the same period. In May 1985, United had a fleet of approximately 320 planes.

The organization of the marketing function at United was based on this "hub and spoke" concept. As shown in Exhibit 4, marketing management was organized along geographic lines. Three market managers were each responsible for the volume, scheduling, profitability, pricing, advertising, and airport facilities of a hub city. Routes connecting two hub cities were allocated arbitrarily. Associate market managers, with responsibility for certain routes within a hub area, reported to each market manager. Market managers each led a team with associate managers and representatives from pricing, advertising, facilities, and scheduling departments. United tried to develop a career path that led a newly recruited MBA from an entry level position as a pricing analyst to market management.

DEREGULATION OF THE AIRLINE INDUSTRY

Prior to 1978, the commercial airline industry was regulated by the federal government through the Civil Aeronautics Board (CAB). The mission of the CAB was to ensure that passengers were serviced fairly and cost-effectively. This objective was accomplished through the CAB's control of airline fares, route systems, and company mergers. In the early 1970s, the CAB believed that air fares were rising too fast. Therefore, it launched the Domestic Passenger Fare Investigation in an attempt to relate air fares to industry costs. This study recommended that pricing for airline service be based on the mileage of each flight with a proportionate allocation of average fixed costs. The resulting fares for short-haul flights were viewed by some industry executives as excessive. Hence, the CAB attempted to subsidize short-haul fares by increasing prices for long-haul flights. The end result of CAB intervention, in the eyes of one observer, was "an industry with little competitive pressure and no incentive for keeping costs under control."

In 1978, the government proposed legislation to gradually lessen the control of the CAB over the airline industry. The changes were to culminate with the dissolution of the CAB in 1985. Reactions to the proposed deregulation were mixed. Executives of many major airlines were opposed. Thomas Taylor, a Trans World Airlines vice president, stated that deregulation ignored the need for a "sound air transport system" to ensure national security and defense.[1] Delta Air Lines even filed suit against the

---

[1]Albert R. Karr, "The Deregulator: CAB Chairman Kahn Leads Activists Spurring Competition," the *Wall Street Journal,* July 3, 1978.

EXHIBIT 4 United Airlines marketing organization chart

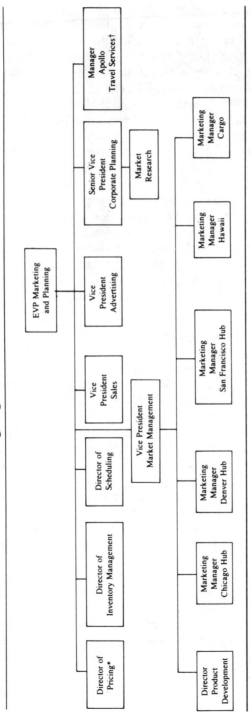

* Dotted line relationship existed between Pricing and Market Management.

† Apollo was United's computerized reservation system accessed by travel agents nationwide as well as United's own ticketing agents.

CAB for neglecting its responsibilities. Many legislators and consumer activists, on the other hand, saw deregulation as long overdue.

Surprisingly, a major force for deregulation was the CAB Chairman, Alfred Kahn. He believed that deregulation would benefit both the industry and the consumer by encouraging cost efficiency, more air travel, and lower fares. He countered criticism with humor. Departing from an awards ceremony, he remarked, "I have to go back and destroy the airline industry."[2] Many later contended that his actions accomplished just that.

Deregulation was finally approved in October, 1978. Initially, the legislation gave the airlines more latitude in determining fares and new routes. CAB approval was no longer needed to implement minor changes to the fare structure or to add a new route. The law also provided subsidies for commuter airlines servicing small towns. The industry, however, was slow to respond to the new opportunity for flexibility in pricing. Information on competitive fares was not readily available, and individual carriers had little data on which to base price changes. A computerized price list, updated daily, was developed by some carriers to remedy the situation. Pricing changes were sent to the Airline Tariff Publishing Company, which disseminated fares to all cariers for the purpose of updating their computer reservation systems. Each day, any carrier could access an industrywide price list. Pricing changes made on a given day would appear in the list on the following day, allowing for pricing responses within 24 hours. Price quickly became the focal point of competitive action.

Soon after deregulation began, unforeseen problems plagued the airline industry. The worldwide oil crisis dramatically increased fuel prices. Air travel plummeted with the onset of a severe recession. The concurrent deregulation of the banking industry combined with inflation and recession sent interest rates soaring. The air traffic controllers went on strike, substantially reducing the capacity of the nation's airports. As a consequence, many carriers, including United, suffered major financial losses in the years from 1979 to 1983.

Before deregulation, regional carriers had been permitted to serve only regional markets. They aided major carriers by feeding passengers to primary departure sites for longer flights on the larger airlines. In this way, the major carriers were saved the expense of maintaining extensive regional networks. After deregulation began, economic pressures led to intensified competition between carriers. Regional airlines began flying the more lucrative longer routes. Many major carriers operated nonstop flights on these routes. The smaller companies offered the same destinations but with one or more stops. These carriers could offer a lower fare on long-haul destinations because of their higher load factors resulting from many passengers flying portions of the overall route.[3] In this way, the smaller carrier could serve several destinations with a single flight, thereby lowering its relative fixed costs. Without these high fixed costs and the additional burdens of heavy debt and expensive labor agreements, regional

---

[2]Ibid.

[3]Load factor refers to the percentage of plane capacity filled.

carriers could compete aggressively on price in the long-haul markets. This situation placed more price pressure on the established carriers. Because of the squeeze on profits from lowered fares, major carriers cut schedules, eliminating many of their expensive, less heavily traveled, short-haul routes.

Entrepreneurs filled the market niches left by established carriers. The new companies they organized, such as People Express, Southwest Airlines, and New York Air, were free of heavy debt and high labor charges and their prices reflected these lower costs. In 1978, the United States had 36 domestic carriers; by 1985 the number had increased to more than 100. In an effort to retain passengers, major airlines reacted to competition from economy carriers by slashing prices, placing profits under additional pressure.

As deregulation progressed, the cost problems of the major airlines grew. Pricing pressures were continuing to lower revenues, yet cost-cutting measures were difficult to implement. The major carriers lost money while the new economy carriers generated substantial profits and, therefore, continued to engage in price competition. The result was the collapse of many weaker companies such as Continental Airlines and Braniff. Some of the companies attempted to reorganize, and in doing so, forced renegotiation of labor agreements. The shift of power in these companies from labor to management set a precedent industrywide. As labor contracts came up for renewal, companies that had been suffering losses decided to get tough with labor unions. They could no longer afford salaries and benefits established during regulation.

UNITED'S 1979 MACHINISTS' STRIKE

One of the first companies to feel the consequences of the labor/management struggle was United. On March 31, 1979, the International Association of Machinists began a 55-day strike at the airline after failing to reach a wage agreement. United had been under increasing pressure to lower costs as price competition increased. Labor was the single largest expense for carriers, accounting, on average, for 42% of costs. As one analyst stated, "Either an airline is going to control its costs, especially labor costs, or it's going to be difficult for it to compete."[4]

While United hoped the outcome of the strike would cut expenses and result in long-term revenue gains, the short-term revenue losses due to the strike were substantial. Estimates placed daily lost revenue at $9.5 million on 1978 average daily revenues of approximately $11 million. Restoring full operations once the strike was over would also take at least a week. In the meantime, passengers were switching to other carriers. The strike ended with the ratification of an agreement that set wage increases of 30% over three years.

United began limited service immediately after the strike ended. To regain traffic lost during the strike, United announced the offer of a 50% off coupon for any passenger traveling during the three weeks following the reinstatement of

---

[4]William M. Carley, "Squaring Off: United Airplanes Strike Reflects Industry Drive to Curb Labor Costs," the *Wall Street Journal*, May 11, 1979.

service. Coupons were distributed to passengers during their flights and could be redeemed against any one-way or round-trip ticket for a trip completed between July 1, 1979 and December 15, 1979. American immediately stated that it would honor United's coupons on the same terms. United's coupons therefore became transferable. A secondary market developed for the buying and selling of the coupons, counteracting some of the brand loyalty objectives of the promotion. United also initiated a $108 one-way fare between New York and Los Angeles, which American and TWA matched. This route represented roughly 2% of United's revenues prior to the promotion.

United's executives considered the coupon program a major success. Exhibit 5 shows the increase in load factors from the end of the strike to June 17, 1979 and the distribution by class of service of passengers using the coupons. In the industry a 65% load factor was considered normal except during the summer when load

EXHIBIT 5   Results of United Airlines 1979 coupon promotion

A. Passengers and load factors

Date	Passengers	Load factor
May 28	11,000	22%
May 29	27,000	36
May 30	40,000	46
May 31	51,000	42
June 1	65,000	45
June 2	50,000	37
June 3	74,000	47
June 4	91,000	48
June 5	88,000	45
June 6	96,000	57
June 7	109,000	68
June 8	110,000	69
June 9	96,000	59
June 10	115,000	65
June 11	126,000	72
June 12	121,000	69
June 13	128,000	71
June 14	140,000	79
June 15	142,000	80
June 16	128,000	75
June 17	141,000	80

B. Coupon redeemers by class of service

Class	July	August	September	October	November
First	19%	27%	30%	35%	42%
Coach	9	14	15	19	27
Economy*	5	7	7	10	16

*Economy = any discounted fare less than full fare coach.

factors averaged 70%. Of the 750,000 coupons issued, 70% were redeemed. People redeeming the coupons were more inclined to redeem them against first-class fares.

PRICING AND PROMOTIONS WITHIN THE AIRLINE INDUSTRY

In the consumer packaged-goods industry, coupon promotions similar to United's campaign were commonplace. Consumer packaged-goods companies, such as Procter & Gamble, used a variety of consumer promotions as short-term measures to increase sales or profitability. These strategies included cents-off packs, coupons, samples, refunds, premiums, and sweepstakes. The objective of the promotion would be the major factor in determining which type of strategy would be most effective. For example, if the intent of the campaign was to increase trials of the brand, a sample, which provided immediate value to the consumer without purchase risk, would be more appropriate than a refund, which provided delayed value.

Because of the intangible nature of products provided by the service sector, alternatives for consumer promotion were not as varied as in the consumer packaged-goods industry. Advertising was a challenge due to the perception that few distinguishing characteristics existed between the products of competitors. In addition, many service providers had historically operated under governmental regulation, which had rendered consumer promotion generally infeasible and unnecessary. Inexperience in planning promotions, the narrow scope of alternatives, and the ease with which pricing changes could be implemented limited the use of consumer promotions, other than straight price reductions, in the airline industry.

Two distinct market segments existed in the airline industry, the business traveler and the pleasure traveler. Exhibit 6 shows the distribution within fare type of United passengers by segment. The business traveler was considered United's "bread and butter," with an average per passenger fare of $128 during the first half of 1985. As one United executive remarked, "We can try to be everything to everybody, but the businessperson pays the bills." Demand from business travelers was relatively

EXHIBIT 6   United fare usage by trip purpose January–May 1985

Fare types	Business	Pleasure
First	4.2%	0.8%
Coach	29.6	3.3
Unrestricted discount	36.3	17.1
Super Saver	1.2	4.3
Easy Saver	9.8	18.1
Ultra Saver	10.4	37.6
Other	8.5	18.8
Total	100.0%	100.0%

stable and did not react as strongly to economic downturns as the pleasure market. An airline's schedule was the main factor influencing a business traveler's purchase decision. The business market was relatively price inelastic.

To build brand loyalty, American Airlines established the first "frequent-flyer" program in 1983. This promotion was primarily targeted at the business segment and permitted passengers to claim travel awards for accumulated travel mileage on American. The other major carriers implemented similar programs. Each airline hoped that its frequent-flyer program would induce a traveler to remain brand loyal in the face of slight inconveniences of schedule. However, most business travelers signed up for several programs, thereby limiting the effectiveness of the promotion for any one airline. The airlines then tried to make their programs more attractive by signing cooperative arrangements with regional and international carriers, permitting consumers to be credited with mileage for traveling on any one of a network of carriers. What began as a one-year promotion by American Airlines quickly became a permanent part of the industry structure. By 1985, United's "Mileage Plus" program had over two million members.

Pleasure travelers were typically more price sensitive and less brand loyal than business travelers. Price promotions were aimed principally at this segment and accounted for United's low $91 average pleasure passenger fare in the first half of 1985. Decreases in fares not only motivated brand-switching behavior, but also stimulated the overall demand for pleasure travel. Exhibit 7 shows the relative importance of factors affecting the purchase decisions of business versus pleasure travelers and of travelers selecting each of seven airlines.

After deregulation, consumer promotions based on fare reductions were prevalent. When an airline instituted such a promotion, it would invariably be matched

EXHIBIT 7 **Relative importance of factors determining airline choice**

Airline	Choice factor			
	Schedule convenience	Ticket price	Frequent flyer mileage program	Airline preference
Total	4.3	3.2	1.2	1.3
Business passengers	5.1	1.9	1.7	1.3
Pleasure passengers	3.5	4.6	0.6	1.3
American	4.1	2.9	1.5	1.5
Continental	4.0	4.3	0.9	0.8
Delta	4.1	2.5	1.5	1.9
Northwest	4.3	3.5	1.2	1.0
People Express	3.0	6.1	0.2	0.7
TWA	4.2	2.9	1.7	1.2
United	4.1	2.9	1.8	1.2

immediately by competitors, possibly resulting in a fare war. As one executive from a major carrier explained, "Either we don't match and we lose customers, or we match and then, because our costs are so high, we lose buckets of money."[5] The first industrywide consumer promotion used by the airlines was a discount fare, the Easy Saver, instituted in 1975. This fare, 30% off the regular coach fare, required passengers to purchase their tickets seven days in advance and to stay at their destination through one Sunday. The Easy Saver exhibited many characteristics that were typical of subsequent price promotions in the industry: discounts from coach fare, advance purchase requirements, and restrictions on the timing of the passenger's return. The restrictions, in large part, were imposed to prevent the business traveler from taking advantage of discount fares.

At the beginning of January, 1983, Pan Am anounced a new concept in discount fares, the deep discount. For $99 one way, a passenger could fly anywhere Pan Am flew as long as the travel was initiated before March 31, 1983. The restrictions on the fare were a seven-day advance purchase requirement, round-trip travel, and a seven-day minimum stay. TWA matched the fare systemwide, while United and American selectively met the discount in those markets where they competed with Pan Am, TWA, or other carriers that extended the fare to additional markets. United's routes from Chicago to the West Coast were especially affected.

Pan Am's pricing change had a dramatic impact on the airline industry. Customers who had been ticketed at higher fares reticketed. Passengers booked on long-haul flights were especially likely to take advantage of the discount, thereby reducing carriers' revenues. The discount from regular coach fares was between 60% and 75%. Traffic was extremely heavy during the promotion, with load factors approaching 80% on the affected routes. The principal users of the discount were pleasure travelers who were more likely to plan travel in advance. On some flights, business travelers were unable to obtain seats or, at best, only center seats because the windows and aisles had been reserved by the advance-purchase traveler. Revenues and yields suffered from a lower-than-normal percentage of seats being occupied by travelers at full coach fare. The 1983 annual report of UAL, Inc. noted: "Cutthroat pricing pushed average yield to the lowest level in three years."

In response to the adverse effect of Pan Am's promotion, American instituted a mileage-related pricing structure in the spring of 1983. American also expanded the seven-day advance purchase discount fare to all markets, but at 45% off the full coach price rather than the 60%–75% previously in effect. Many competitors followed American's lead with matching price increases. United, after initially matching American, used American's pricing structure as the basis for an alternative framework that incorporated variable costs in the calculation of each fare.[6] The resulting fares were $10–$20 above American's price levels. American and the other major carriers matched these increases.

[5]William M. Carley, "Rough Flying: Some Major Airlines Are Being Threatened by Low-Cost Carriers," the *Wall Street Journal*, October 12, 1983.

[6]Variable costs included ticketing, food, beverages, and cleaning the seating area. They averaged $15 per passenger per flight.

Beginning in 1984, American expanded its schedule and route system, adding several new planes. In order to generate traffic in its new markets and compete with the economy carriers, the company established a new non-promotional fare, the Ultra Saver. The new fare structure took effect in March, followed by a $20 across-the-board fare increase in May. While the Ultra Saver offered a deep discount of 70% off full coach fare, the ticket had to be purchased 30 days in advance and no more than 14 days after the reservation was made. In addition, there was a 25% price penalty if reservations were changed, locking consumers into their travel plans and making it difficult for other carriers to steal passengers, even with a promotion. United matched the new pricing in all markets, but disagreed with the strategy. Bernie Eilers, United's manager of system market pricing explained: "When we go in a new city, we start with our standard fare structure, not a promotion fare. We don't want to give customers a false perception of what prices will be. We try to deemphasize pricing as much as possible. You can lose so much money so fast."

American regulated the volume of passengers taking advantage of the new fare by establishing inventory controls, selling no more than 20% of seats on any flight at the Ultra Saver level. United did not set as stringent controls. Up to 45% of each United flight could be sold at Ultra Saver fares. Load factors for each of the airlines increased; however, at United, less inventory was available for business passengers, causing revenues per passenger to decrease. In light of the increasing dilution of traffic mix, United increased its Ultra Saver fares by $20 for weekend travel (Friday, Saturday, and Sunday). Because about half the Ultra Saver traffic consisted of pleasure travelers flying on weekends, the effective increase across the board was $10. American responded by including Mondays and Thursdays in its definition of a weekend, but, instead of increasing fares, lowered the midweek level by $10. United met this move in American's markets, but filed for further increases in non–American markets. Almost 45% of United's total RPMs were on routes also served by American. Exhibit 8 shows the percentage of United's RPMs that were competed for by each major carrier for the first half of 1985.

Promotional activity by the airlines created several fare levels. Exhibit 9 summarizes the various discount fares and the associated restrictions. The distribution of passengers, revenues, RPMs, and yields by fare type are shown in Exhibit 10. Because price promotions were matched by competitors, incremental revenues rarely offset the decreases in unit contribution resulting from the lower fares. This situation accounted for the see-saw strategies of various carriers. A price decrease would be implemented to increase volume. Competitors would follow suit. Volumes would increase slightly, but yields would decrease. A price increase would follow. The effects of the cycle of promotional pricing on industry yields are shown in Exhibit 11.

UNITED'S PILOTS' STRIKE

In early 1985, United Airlines made a further effort to curb labor costs by proposing a new wage structure for its pilots. Under the proposal, newly hired pilots would receive lower starting salaries than their predecessors. United also proposed that these

EXHIBIT 8   Percentage of United traffic in direct competition with major carriers for first half of 1985

Carrier	% of United's total RPMs
American	43.2%*
Continental	18.1
Pan Am	17.0
Northwest Orient	15.0
Frontier	14.2
Republic	7.9
Western	6.1
Delta	5.4
Eastern	5.2
PSA	4.8
Alaska	4.0
US Air	2.3
Southwest	1.1
Piedmont	0.6
Ozark	0.5
People Express	0.3

*To be read (for example): American was in direct competition with United for 43.2% of United's RPMs.

new pilots would not be able to reach higher salary levels as quickly as previously hired pilots. American Airlines had already implemented a similar cost-cutting wage structure. United's pilots responded by threatening to strike.

The threat of a strike adversely affected bookings on United. Travel agents began to reduce the number of reservations made with United for fear that they would be blamed if the pilots struck and their customers' travel plans were interrupted. Passengers who had ticketed in advance began to reticket on other airlines, even if

EXHIBIT 9   Ticket pricing structure by class: 1985

Class	Code	Restrictions	Maximum load*	Price
First	F	None	100%	Coach & premium†
Coach	Y	None	100	Full coach
Super Saver	B	None	80–90	70% of coach
Easy Saver	B	7-day advance	70	65% of coach
Ultra Saver	M	14-day advance	40	40–65% of coach
	Q	30-day advance	30	30–40% of coach

*Maximum load was an inventory control measurement indicating the maximum percentage of seats on a plane that United is willing to sell in a particular class.

†First class premium over coach was typically 60%.

EXHIBIT 10   Number of United domestic passengers by fare type (thousands)

Fare type	1983		1984		1985 (5 mos.)	
	#	%	#	%	#	%
First Class	879	2.7%	1,048	2.9%	399	2.5%
Coach	5,300	16.0	7,672	21.4	2,627	16.5
Discount coach	8,975	27.1	9,395	26.2	3,942	24.8
Easy Saver	3,196	9.6	5,921	16.5	1,862	11.7
Super Saver	6,599	19.9	5,087	14.2	598	3.8
Ultra Saver					4,013	25.2
Other	8,196	24.7	6,679	18.7	2,458	15.5
Total	33,145	100.0%	35,800	100.0%	15,899	100.0%

United domestic revenues by fare type ($ millions)

Fare type	1983		1984		1985 (5 mos.)	
	$	%	$	%	$	%
First Class	$269	7.0%	$325	7.3%	$125	7.2%
Coach	915	23.8	1,367	30.6	468	26.8
Discount coach	944	24.5	916	20.5	387	22.2
Easy Saver	366	9.5	646	14.5	187	10.7
Super Saver	619	16.1	532	11.9	58	3.3
Ultra Saver					249	14.2
Other	732	19.1	675	15.1	273	15.7
Total	$3,845	100.0%	$4,462	100.0%	$1,746	100.0%

United domestic RPMs by fare type (millions)

Fare type	1983		1984		1985 (5 mos.)	
	#	%	#	%	#	%
First Class	1,070	3.3%	1,158	3.4%	433	2.9%
Coach	4,277	13.0	6,061	18.0	2,010	13.5
Discount coach	8,678	26.4	7,269	21.6	3,121	21.0
Easy Saver	3,530	10.8	6,103	18.1	1,784	12.0
Super Saver	7,927	24.1	5,882	17.4	667	4.5
Ultra Saver					4,010	26.9
Other	7,348	22.4	7,242	21.5	2,866	19.2
Total	32,830	100.0%	33,715	100.0%	14,891	100.0%

United domestic yield by fare type

Fare type	1983	1984	1985 (5 mos.)
First Class	25%	28%	29%
Coach	20	22	23
Discount coach	11	12	11
Easy Saver	10	10	10
Super Saver	7	9	8
Ultra Saver			6
Other	9	11	
Total average	11%	13%	11%

EXHIBIT 11 Industry yield for major airlines

	1983					1984					1985	
	1st Qtr.	2nd Qtr.	3rd Qtr.	4th Qtr.	1983 Average	1st Qtr.	2nd Qtr.	3rd Qtr.	4th Qtr.	1984 Average	1st Qtr.	2nd Qtr.
American	9.9	10.8	11.9	13.0	11.4	12.5	11.8	11.2	11.7	11.8	11.6	11.5
Continental	10.3	11.1	11.9	8.9	10.7	10.7	10.2	9.7	9.6	9.7	9.6	9.3
Delta	11.4	12.7	14.7	15.5	13.5	15.5	15.3	15.2	15.8	15.4	15.1	14.4
Eastern	12.1	12.7	13.1	13.0	12.7	13.6	13.5	13.4	13.9	13.5	13.9	13.0
Northwest	10.2	10.3	10.0	10.5	10.0	10.3	10.0	9.7	10.0	10.0	9.6	9.7
Pan Am	10.3	10.4	10.0	10.4	9.8	10.4	10.3	10.3	10.7	10.3	9.4	9.5
Piedmont	15.0	15.5	16.3	16.6	15.8	16.3	17.1	17.9	17.9	17.6	16.6	15.6
Republic	12.9	13.0	15.8	16.5	14.4	16.5	16.5	16.6	16.8	16.6	16.1	14.9
TWA	9.7	10.7	10.4	11.3	10.5	12.1	11.2	10.4	10.9	11.0	9.9	9.8
United	9.4	10.3	11.0	11.9	10.5	12.0	11.6	11.3	11.2	11.6	10.6	10.0
US Air	18.1	17.3	18.8	19.5	18.1	19.3	18.8	18.2	18.5	18.6	17.3	16.5
Western	9.3	10.5	11.1	11.4	10.6	11.3	11.2	11.1	10.8	11.1	11.1	11.3

Note: Yield = Revenues/RPMs.

this meant paying higher fares because their available inventories of discounted seats had already been sold.

On May 18, 1985, unable to reach agreement, United pilots went on strike. While United's wage proposals did not affect the pay of pilots currently working for United, job security was a major issue. The pilots were concerned that pressures for United to reduce labor costs would result in United favoring the new pilots. The timing of the strike was no accident. To strengthen their case and encourage a quick and favorable settlement, the pilots chose to strike just before the start of the peak summer travel season, when damage to airline revenues would be highest.

The strike's effects were immediately evident. Average daily revenues dropped from $11.6 million to $3.8 million in May. Operations decreased to 14% of United's 1,550 daily scheduled flights. In an effort to minimize revenue loss, the flights that United maintained were those on its more profitable routes. Using management personnel, the Chicago hub maintained 30% of its normal daily schedule. However, routes to Hawaii and Florida were eliminated completely. Western Airlines added extra flights to build its business on the Hawaii route. By June, United's average daily revenues had decreased from a projected level of $13.3 million to $3.3 million.

United attempted to measure the effect of the strike on traveling behavior by sampling passengers on flights still in service. The findings indicated that business traffic (assumed to be all traffic except those traveling on Ultra Saver fares) had declined from 45% of total traffic before the strike to 24% of total traffic by June 1. Yields were adversely affected. Passengers holding the deeply discounted Ultra Saver fares stayed with United because of the advance purchase restrictions and therefore represented a higher-than-normal percentage of the remaining passengers. In addition, American refused to honor the Ultra Saver fares of displaced United passengers, except on a stand-by basis, while some other carriers accepted these passengers on a reservation basis.

United sought to combat the consequences of the strike by stepping up newspaper advertising in cities where it was still flying. The primary objective of the advertising was to make passengers aware of United's schedule and the fact that the carrier was still operating. Two examples of Chicago newspaper advertisements are shown in Exhibit 12. Regularly scheduled advertising was discontinued, except in markets where United continued service. However, United estimated advertising expenditures during the strike at $1.1 million per week, with approximately $.14 million of that representing incremental expense.

STRATEGIES FOR RECOVERY

As soon as the strike was announced, United's marketing and pricing executives began thinking through strategies to speed the airline's recovery once an agreement was reached. Although many ideas were generated, nothing was decided because of the uncertain length of the strike. After three weeks, when it appeared that a settlement was close at hand, John Zeeman, United's executive vice president of marketing and planning, called a meeting of his managers to discuss the alternatives.

EXHIBIT 12 United newspaper advertisements in Chicago

We're flying. 89 flights to 52 cities. Every day.

Count on it, Chicago. Here's our current schedule of nonstop and connecting flights from O'Hare.
And we're sticking to it. Every day. For reservations, call your Travel Agent. Or call United at 569-3000.

Atlanta
Leave	Return
11:55 a.m.	8:30 a.m.
4:55 p.m.	4:35 p.m.

Baltimore
Leave	Return
5:00 p.m.	7:30 a.m.

Boise
Leave	Return
3:45 p.m.	9:10 a.m.

Boston
Leave	Return
7:35 a.m.	7:45 a.m.
11:30 a.m.	10:35 a.m.
2:15 p.m.	1:30 p.m.
5:00 p.m.	4:00 p.m.

Buffalo/Niagara Falls
Leave	Return
1:55 p.m.	5:00 p.m.

Cincinnati
Leave	Return
2:37 p.m.	5:30 p.m.

Cleveland
Leave	Return
8:30 a.m.	8:37 a.m.
11:30 a.m.	11:40 a.m.
2:15 p.m.	2:30 p.m.
5:00 p.m.	5:15 p.m.

Columbus
Leave	Return
11:20 a.m.	5:20 p.m.

Dallas/Ft. Worth
Leave	Return
10:10 a.m.	8:25 a.m.
6:42 p.m.	2:10 p.m.

Dayton
Leave	Return
8:00 a.m.	10:41 a.m.
11:29 a.m.	5:00 p.m.

Denver
Leave	Return
10:10 a.m.	7:25 a.m.
1:00 p.m.	8:15 a.m.
3:45 p.m.	10:00 a.m.
5:30 p.m.	12:40 p.m.
6:30 p.m.	3:57 p.m.

Des Moines
Leave	Return
6:43 p.m.	9:15 a.m.

Detroit
Leave	Return
7:00 a.m.	11:50 a.m.
12:05 p.m.	3:00 p.m.
2:15 p.m.	5:38 p.m.

Grand Rapids
Leave	Return
2:15 p.m.	6:15 p.m.

Hartford/Springfield
Leave	Return
7:00 a.m.	10:45 a.m.
12:40 p.m.	4:20 p.m.

Honolulu
Leave	Return
10:10 a.m.	12:00 p.m.
Connect through LAX	
10:30 a.m.	4:30 p.m.
Nonstop service effective July 1	

Houston
Leave	Return
10:10 a.m.	8:00 a.m.
1:00 p.m.	1:27 p.m.
6:50 p.m.	4:45 p.m.

Indianapolis
Leave	Return
7:25 a.m.	11:00 a.m.

Las Vegas
Leave	Return
1:17 p.m.	10:35 a.m.
	12:16 p.m.*
*Connect via Denver	

Los Angeles
Leave	Return
10:10 a.m.	7:30 a.m.
1:00 p.m.	9:00 a.m.*
3:45 p.m.	10:20 a.m.
6:30 p.m.	1:10 p.m.
	11:55 p.m.
*Connect via Boise	

Minneapolis/St. Paul
Leave	Return
10:10 a.m.	12:10 p.m.

Newark
Leave	Return
7:00 a.m.	7:50 a.m.
11:30 a.m.	10:55 a.m.
2:20 p.m.	1:25 p.m.
5:00 p.m.	4:30 p.m.

New York (La Guardia)
Leave	Return
7:00 a.m.	8:00 a.m.
12:00 p.m.	11:00 a.m.
2:00 p.m.	1:00 p.m.
5:00 p.m.	4:00 p.m.
8:00 p.m.	7:00 p.m.

Norfolk/Portsmouth/Virginia Beach
Leave	Return
7:05 a.m.	10:45 a.m.
12:35 p.m.	4:30 p.m.

Oklahoma City
Leave	Return
1:00 p.m.	8:45 a.m.
7:00 p.m.	11:17 a.m.

Omaha
Leave	Return
9:55 a.m.	12:00 p.m.
1:00 p.m.	3:00 p.m.

Philadelphia/Wilmington
Leave	Return
7:00 a.m.	7:50 a.m.
11:30 a.m.	11:00 a.m.
3:15 p.m.	1:36 p.m.
5:00 p.m.	4:15 p.m.

Phoenix
Leave	Return
10:10 a.m.	7:45 a.m.
1:00 p.m.	1:50 p.m.

Pittsburgh
Leave	Return
11:30 a.m.	8:40 a.m.
2:15 p.m.	2:50 p.m.
5:15 p.m.	5:15 p.m.

Portland, OR
Leave	Return
10:10 a.m.	7:35 a.m.
1:00 p.m.	10:20 a.m.
7:15 p.m.	12:00 p.m.**
	10:30 p.m.*
*Direct via Seattle	
**Connect via Denver	

Raleigh/Durham
Leave	Return
4:59 p.m.	8:22 a.m.

Rochester
Leave	Return
1:55 p.m.	8:34 a.m.
5:40 p.m.	5:10 p.m.

St. Louis
Leave	Return
12:45 p.m.	2:35 p.m.

Salt Lake City
Leave	Return
10:10 a.m.	7:00 a.m.
6:30 p.m.*	1:50 p.m.*
*Connect via Denver	

San Diego
Leave	Return
12:45 p.m.	7:30 a.m.
6:55 p.m.	1:15 p.m.

San Francisco/Oakland/San José
Leave	Return
10:10 a.m.	12:01 a.m.
1:00 p.m.	6:45 a.m.*
3:45 p.m.	7:10 a.m.
6:30 p.m.*	10:00 a.m.
7:05 p.m.	11:45 a.m.*
	1:10 p.m.
*Connect via Denver	

Seattle/Tacoma
Leave	Return
10:15 a.m.	6:35 a.m.*
3:45 p.m.*	7:30 a.m.
6:30 p.m.	11:55 a.m.*
	1:25 p.m.
	11:45 p.m.
*Connect via Denver	

Tokyo
Leave	Return
10:15 a.m.	6:00 p.m.
Direct via SEA	

Toronto
Leave	Return
1:57 p.m.	8:40 a.m.
8:02 p.m.	5:10 p.m.

Tulsa
Leave	Return
6:30 p.m.	8:45 a.m.

Washington, D.C.
Leave	Return
6:45 a.m.	8:15 a.m.
11:30 a.m.	11:10 a.m.
2:00 p.m.	2:00 p.m.
5:20 p.m.	5:10 p.m.
7:30 p.m.	7:15 p.m.

fly the friendly skies.

United

EXHIBIT 12   (continued)

Flying is our job.
And we're staying on the job.

**From Chicago
we fly to all these cities.**

Our schedule is reduced temporarily, but we're still serving over 50 top cities.

We'll do everything we can to fly you to business, to vacation, or back home.

We're flying with skilled United pilots, with outstanding

- *Albany*
- *Atlanta*
- *Austin*
- *Baltimore*
- *Boise*
- *Boston*
- *Buffalo/Niagara Falls*
- *Cincinnati*
- *Cleveland*
- *Columbus*
- *Dallas/Ft.Worth*
- *Dayton*
- *Denver*
- *Des Moines*
- *Detroit*
- *Hartford/Springfield*
- *Honolulu*
- *Houston*
- *Indianapolis*
- *Las Vegas*
- *Los Angeles*
- *Minneapolis/St.Paul*
- *New York (La Guardia)*

- *Newark*
- *Norfolk/Portsmouth/ Virginia Beach*
- *Oklahoma City*
- *Omaha*
- *Orlando*
- *Philadelphia*
- *Phoenix*
- *Pittsburgh*
- *Portland, OR*
- *Raleigh/Durham*
- *Rochester*
- *Salt Lake City*
- *San Diego*
- *San Francisco*
- *Seattle/Tacoma*
- *Spokane*
- *St. Louis*
- *Syracuse*
- *Tampa/St. Petersburg*
- *Tokyo*
- *Toronto*
- *Washington, D.C.*

crews and the kind of service that has made us the friendly skies.

Call your Travel Agent for schedules and reservations. Or call United at 569-3000.

You're not just flying, you're flying the friendly skies.

Zeeman conducted strategy sessions informally, allowing managers to discuss the issues and soliciting opinions on various options. The immediacy of the problem, however, required quick decisions. Bernie Eilers focused the meeting: "Getting traffic back is the primary objective, but getting the right traffic back is just as important. American has taken many of our business passengers and they'll try to match anything we do."

James Jackson commented: "The business traveler is certainly important, but we must remember that the other carriers have the summer pleasure market locked up with advance purchase restrictions and cancellation penalties. That alone will have a severe impact on our load factors, regardless of what we do."

To put the problem in context, Eilers presented projections of load factors (see Exhibit 13) assuming United took no special actions to accelerate a recovery of its market share. Eilers expected load factors to climb to 67% by the end of August. Nevertheless, load factors for the month of July would average only 50%. The prestrike monthly forecast for 1985 and United's traffic mix before and during the strike, displayed in Exhibits 14 and 15, were also reviewed. Traffic-mix trends showed increasing dilution through the middle of the strike, but a slight recovery in Coach and Super Coach traffic as the strike drew to a close. Following this presentation, the executives began brainstorming a list of possible actions. Seven key alternatives and their costs are summarized below. Costs represent rough estimates based on traffic levels from March and April rather than the lower traffic levels that would occur immediately following the end of the strike.

Agency Commission Bonus

United could lower the number of bookings required of travel agents to qualify for performance bonuses and free passes or increase their booking commissions across the board. Assuming 75% of fares were booked by travel agents, the monthly cost of a 1% commission increase would be:

First Class	$225,000
Full Coach	750,000
Super Coach	750,000
Easy Saver	260,000
Ultra Saver	600,000
Other	415,000
Total	$3,000,000

Such a commission increase would encourage travel agents to favor United for booking customers' flights. Varying the commission by fare type could improve the traffic mix, as travel agents would then have an incentive to book specific fare types. This proposal could be easily matched by competitors, however, and could result in long-term increases in commission costs.

EXHIBIT 13   Projections of load factors assuming no promotion

Date		Passengers (000s)	Load factor
July	1–7	520	39.8%
	8–17	600	46.0
	18–24	720	55.1
	25–31	803	61.5
August	1–7	850	61.9%
	8–14	900	65.5
	15–21	926	67.4

EXHIBIT 14   Prestrike monthly forecast of industry and United performance

	Industry RPMs*	United RPMs	Industry revenues†	United revenues‡	United yield
January	16,772	2,772	$2,125	$332	12.18%
February	15,570	2,471	1,974	300	12.14
March	20,531	3,547	2,500	395	11.14
April	19,879	3,377	2,421	370	10.96
May	20,024	3,368	2,435	377	11.19
June	21,713	3,575	2,582	404	11.30
July	21,919	3,498	2,657	394	11.27
August	21,948	3,600	2,680	404	11.21
September	16,999	3,072	2,096	359	11.69
October	17,792	3,268	2,236	384	11.75
November	16,614	2,884	2,092	337	11.67
December	18,431	3,060	2,284	341	11.15
1985	228,192	38,442	$28,082	$4,396	11.44%

*RPMs = revenue passenger miles in millions.

†Revenues = millions of dollars.

‡RPMs and revenues of United for domestic operations only.

EXHIBIT 15   Traffix mix results during strike (%)

Ticket type	April 1985	May			May 26–June 1	June	
		5–11	17–18	19–25		2–8	9–15
First Class	2.0	3.1	0.5	1.2	0.9	1.1	2.5
Coach	20.2	16.5	6.5	6.8	5.0	5.8	11.3
Super Saver	18.7	23.5	7.9	7.9	8.0	10.0	15.4
Easy Saver	6.2	9.9	13.0	12.3	9.8	8.8	10.3
Ultra Saver	36.1	33.6	59.8	60.5	64.7	61.8	46.9
Other	16.8	13.4	12.3	11.3	11.6	12.5	13.6

Free First Class Upgrades

These could be offered to full-fare coach passengers and/or enrolled frequent flyers. The only additional expense would be the cost of meals and liquor for a relatively small percentage of passengers. Some managers argued that this promotion would attract additional full fare coach passengers, primarily business people, thereby reducing dilution. Trial of first class service could lead to regular usage by passengers not currently flying first class.

Mileage Plus Award Increase

If double mileage credit were offered to United's enrolled frequent flyers systemwide, the cost based on the average number of free trips awarded monthly at an average frequent-flyer fare of $140 would be $2.4 million per month. However this cost estimate did not take into account redemptions of accumulated mileage redeemed for trips that would not have been taken otherwise. This promotion would reward loyal customers and perhaps attract back some of those United business passengers believed to have switched to American during the strike. One manager suggested that a direct-mail piece (75 cents each) might be an effective way of communicating the details of such a promotion to Mileage Plus members. The mailer and the offer could be tailored to target different segments of passengers with different levels of accumulated mileage.

Free Liquor

For all passengers this would cost approximately $1.8 million per month. Such a promotion would appeal to only a limited segment of the market.

Waiver of Advance Purchase Restrictions

This promotion would effectively lower fares to business travelers. If advance purchase restrictions were waived on Ultra Saver, all business passengers staying over a Saturday (37% of business passengers) and all Easy Saver passengers would be able to qualify for this fare. The cost would be:

Business travelers	$47 million/month
Easy Savers	$10 million/month

If advance purchase restrictions were waived only on Easy Saver fares, the cost was estimated at $26 million per month. This type of promotion was seen as a way to attract business traffic back to United. For business travelers already flying with United, the effect of the promotion would be simply to lower their fares. Dilution of United's traffic mix was probable, but would be greater in the latter case. Such a promotion was unlikely to be matched by competitors because of high dilution costs.

Stand-by Fares

Such fares would help to fill capacity and attract passengers booked on later flights on other airlines. However, they would probably increase dilution by opening a new tier of lower prices and encouraging passengers who might have otherwise purchased tickets at a higher fare to use stand-by. In addition, stand-by fares could cause operational problems, including lower service quality and delayed departures.

Refund Offer

United could offer a partial refund to full-fare coach passengers. This would encourage the purchase of more high-yield, full-fare tickets. A refund claim form could be distributed to be mailed in by the consumer. A mail-in requirement would result in lower costs to United than a coupon because an estimated 30% of qualifying consumers would fail to claim the refund. The promotion cost would depend on the percentage of the fare refunded. The cost to competitors of matching this promotion would be relatively high due to their already high load factors. As United's load progressively increased following the end of the strike, the costs of this alternative would increase.

For a promotional strategy to be effective, most United managers believed that supporting advertising would also be necessary. Extra advertising could cost $5 to $10 million per month over and above the existing advertising budget.

While all concurred that any promotion would have to be designed so that competitors would have difficulty matching it, the managers could not agree on which alternative(s) to pursue. Many believed that several of the options should be incorporated into a single promotion or sequence of promotions. There was also disagreement on the appropriate target market and on the amount and nature of advertising that should be employed to announce any promotion. With the peak summer travel season close at hand, a quick decision was essential.

FOOD RANCH INC.

JOHN A. QUELCH

At the end of February, 1981, Jim Reed, director of grocery merchandising at Food Ranch Inc., had to finalize which grocery items to feature in his supermarket chain's newspaper advertisements during the week of March 15.

THE COMPETITIVE ENVIRONMENT

Food Ranch operated 14 stores in the Bradford market. Weekly sales volume per store averaged $130,000. During 1980, Food Ranch achieved a 23% gross margin (after deducting cost of goods from retail sales) and a 2.1% operating profit, close to the supermarket industry average. Food Ranch's 1980 gross margin on grocery items, which accounted for 50% of total sales, averaged 18%. Like other conventional supermarket chains, Food Ranch compensated for a below-average gross margin on grocery items with an above-average gross margin on meat, deli products, produce, health and beauty aids, and general merchandise.

Food Ranch's two principal competitors in the Bradford market were Longwood's (with 10 stores) and Parker's markets (with 11 stores). Like Food Ranch, neither of these two companies was affiliated with a national supermarket chain. Nevertheless, competition was intense because Food Ranch and Longwood's each held about 28% of grocery store sales in the Bradford market, while Parker's held 18%. Thirty-two percent of respondents to a 1980 survey of Bradford consumers cited Food Ranch as their preferred grocery store, 35% cited Longwood's, and 18% cited Parker's. Exhibit 1 summarizes the principal reasons offered by these respondents for their preferences; Exhibit 2 shows the demographic profiles of the customers who shopped most at each of the three chains.

All three competitors followed a similar merchandising approach. Every week, each chain would offer consumers reductions from regular shelf prices on a varying assortment of about 200 items. Many of these items would be stacked in large displays at the ends of the supermarket aisles during the week when they were promoted. In addition, about one-third of the items, including all those which received special in-store displays, would be featured in the double-page advertisements that each chain placed every week in the Sunday and Thursday issues of Bradford's two major newspapers.

242

EXHIBIT 1   Main reason for shopping at preferred grocery store

	Food Ranch	Longwood's	Parker's	All stores
Low prices	15%	23%	19%	28%
Advertised specials	10	16	6	10
Wide selection	19	19	13	15
Meats	5	3	17	6
Produce	5	2	1	2
Quality	11	9	10	8
Cleanliness	2	3	1	2
Friendliness	9	13	9	10
Relative works there	2	2	2	2
Familiar with store	2	1	1	1
Location	9	2	12	6
Close to home	1	1	1	1
Other	10	6	8	9

Source: Company records.

Note: To be read, for example: Fifteen percent of respondents who named Longwood's as their preferred grocery store cited "low prices" as the main reason for their preference.

In 1980, all three competitors spent about 1.3% of sales on advertising in newspapers and on television. Although television advertising occasionally highlighted the price specials offered during a particular week, its principal objectives were to remind consumers of the store name and store locations and to give them a reason to shop there. During 1980, Longwood's had appealed strongly to larger households by emphasizing the availability of family-sized servings, particularly in its meat and grocery departments. Parker's had attempted to increase store traffic by advertising the quality of its meat department, while Food Ranch had stressed the breadth of its product assortment in order to appeal to the one-stop shopper.

EXHIBIT 2   Customer characteristics by preferred store

	Food Ranch	Longwood's	Parker's	All stores
Median weekly purchases	$42.03	$45.67	$38.15	$42.87
Median age of adults	36	38	36	38
Percent college educated	47	46	35	44
Percent adults married	60	70	58	65
Median household income	$18,980	$20,100	$18,020	$19,560
Median household size	2.4	2.9	2.4	2.7
Percent owning home	64	75	64	72
Percent of households with children	39	50	39	47
Percent of working women	57	54	55	53

Source: Company records.

Note: To be read, for example: Respondents who stated that Food Ranch was their preferred grocery store purchased, on average, $42.03 of groceries each week.

NEWSPAPER ADVERTISING

Jim Reed explained the objectives of Food Ranch's newspaper advertising and how each advertisement was put together.

> We're trying to simultaneously retain the loyalty of our existing customers and persuade other customers who don't usually shop at Food Ranch to give us a try. Hopefully, they'll buy other items at full price along with the specials that brought them into the store, and maybe we'll be able to convert them to regular customers.
>
> To achieve these objectives, it's important that each advertisement have the broadest possible appeal. So we make sure that each department is represented in every advertisement. That's essential for employee morale and also emphasizes our breadth of assortment to the customer. However, the percentage of advertising space devoted to each department [see Exhibit 3] may not be proportionate to its percentage of sales. Right now, for example, we're trying to improve our quality image in meats, so that department is receiving a disproportionate share of advertising space.
>
> At this moment, I have to decide which grocery items to feature in our newspaper advertisements during the week of March 16. Like most chains, we only feature an item when we can buy it from the manufacturer on deal (that is, below normal list price), and we never sell at a price below our cost—although, to stay competitive with

EXHIBIT 3   Share of newspaper advertising space by department (1980 averages)

	Percent of total advertising space	Percent of departmental advertising space for:	
		Private label	Generic
Meat	20.2	—	—
Grocery	18.4	17.8	1.5
Institutional*	15.7	—	3.1
Produce	12.4	—	—
Frozen	7.6	—	—
Retail†	5.0	—	—
Dairy	4.5	45.5	2.1
Beverage	3.8	4.2	4.9
Deli	3.5	—	—
Household supplies	3.3	—	—
Bakery	3.1	5.9	2.3
Health and beauty aids	2.6	6.1	1.7

Source: Company records.

* Advertising space used to highlight the Food Ranch name, corporate logo, and slogan.

† Sales of merchandise displayed at the checkout registers including cigarettes.

Longwood's and Parker's, we often come close. Since in any week there are always more items on deal than we have feature advertising opportunities, we have to decide which ones to promote. Because we are short of warehouse space and because interest rates are so high, we do not generally buy merchandise on deal in excess of our normal requirements just to keep it in inventory. If we buy heavily on deal, it's because we intend to promote the product at a discount from its normal shelf price.

During any week, we aim to promote a balanced cross-section of grocery products. We consider when we and our major competitors last promoted each item. We also try to anticipate what items our competitors are likely to promote, since they, of course, are receiving exactly the same set of manufacturer deals as we are. I have a list here [see Exhibit 4] of the ten grocery items that we're prominently featuring in our newspaper advertisements during each of the three weeks before March 16.

We usually feature 20 items from the grocery department in our weekly newspaper advertisements. The amount of advertising space devoted to each item varies according to the depth of price cut we can offer, whether the deal permits us to hit an attractive retail price point (such as 99 cents), and the breadth of the item's appeal. The incremental sales that we can obtain also varies according to how prominently an item is featured in the body of the advertisement. We classify our grocery department features into the following four groups.

Size of feature advertisement*	Number of items each week	Typical reduction from normal shelf price	Number of normal week's sales during promoted week†
AA (largest)	4	20%	15
A	5	15%	8
B	4	10%	5
C (smallest)	7	0–5%	1

*This classification of feature advertisements was similar to that used by Majers Corporation, an advertising checking service. They classified advertisements into three groups weighted and defined as follows:

A ad (weight: 6) The most dominant product features in the retailer's ad.

B ad (weight: 3) Product features with secondary dominance in the retailer's ad.

C ad (weight: 1) Product features with least dominance in the retailer's ad (sometimes referred to as a line mention or obituary ad).

†These norms of incremental sales associated with different sizes of feature advertisements had been developed by Food Ranch from an analysis of the impact of feature advertisements during the previous three years.

I'm often asked why we bother to run C features. First, some consumers don't know the regular prices of most grocery items; in many cases, they'll buy in response to a feature advertisement even if the feature price is close to or the same as the normal price. Second, some manufacturers will pay us an allowance just to run an advertisement of any size for a particular product without requiring us to also reduce the normal shelf price.

EXHIBIT 4   Ten most prominently featured grocery items in Food Ranch supermarkets' newspaper advertisements

Week of 2/22	Week of 3/1	Week of 3/9
Heinz Ketchup	Chicken of the Sea Tuna	Velveeta Processed Cheese
Viva Kitchen Roll	Kraft Macaroni and Cheese	Skippy Peanut Butter
Cheer Laundry Detergent	Kraft Miracle Whip	Hellman's Mayonnaise
Totino's Pizza	Instant Nestea	Maxwell House Ground Coffee
Cheerios Cereal	Banquet Fried Chicken	Food Club Salmon
Mason's Root Beer	Food Club Tomato Soup	Pepsi-Cola
Food Club Fresh Eggs	Stouffer's Meat Pies	Mazola Oil
Ragu Spaghetti Sauce	Seven Seas Salad Dressing	Heinz Dill Pickles
Townhouse Crackers	Coca-Cola	Franco American Spaghetti
Betty Crocker Brownie Mix	Casino Mozzarella Cheese	Food Club Sour Cream

SELECTING GROCERY FEATURES FOR MARCH 16

At this point, Jim Reed reviewed a chart, which he regularly compiled, showing all of the grocery items that manufacturers offered on deal during the week of March 16. This chart is reproduced as Exhibit 5. The columns in the chart provide the following information:

1. The name of the promoted brand, the size promoted, the number of units per case, and the normal manufacturer price per case.
2. The item's share of its category sales in the Bradford market during 1980, based on warehouse withdrawal data supplied by Sales Area Marketing Inc. (SAMI).
3. The average number of cases of the item sold each week by all Food Ranch stores during 1980.
4. The per-case discount from manufacturer list price plus (where applicable) an additional per-case allowance that Food Ranch would receive if the item was featured in its newspaper advertising. On some items:
   a. Manufacturers offered several alternative allowances from among which the retailer could choose one depending upon the amount of merchandising support he was prepared to provide.
   b. Manufacturers provided an additional per-case allowance if a coupon (redeemable at the manufacturer's expense) was included in the retailer's advertisement.
   c. Manufacturers provided a flat sum (instead of or in addition to a per-case allowance) if an item or, more typically, a family of items was advertised.
5. The per-unit discount from manufacturer list price assuming that Food Ranch featured the item in its advertising.

EXHIBIT 5 Manufacturer deals available during week of March 16, 1981, in Bradford market

Brand/Size/Packages/Case Cost	Category market share	Weekly case movement	Deal per case	Deal per unit	Cost per unit on deal	Normal retail shelf price
Laundry detergent:						
Fresh Start/40 oz./6/$17.92	1.8	41	2.10 + 1.00	.52	2.47	3.85
Dynamo/64 oz./6/$18.05	1.0	40	3.00 + .50	.58	2.43	3.97
Tide/84 oz./8/$23.72	9.7	97	2.80 + .70	.44	2.57	3.63
Era/128 oz./3/$17.67	2.4	79	2.10 + .35	.82	5.07	6.91
Solo/128 oz./4/$23.55	1.2	40	2.80 + .35	.79	5.10	6.91
Bleach:						
Clorox Liquid Bleach 64 oz./8/$4.83	15.8	134	.32 + .20	.065	.54	.79
Purex Liquid Bleach/64 oz./8/$4.67	1.4	13	1.00	.125	.47	.79
Purex Liquid Bleach/128 oz./6/$5.00	6.2	8	.90 + .20	.18	.65	1.09
Fabric softener:						
Bounce/40 ct./12/$22.65	9.6	42	2.50 + .35	.28	1.60	2.55
Cling Free/36 ct./6/$10.18	2.4	26	1.80 + .85	.34	1.36	2.29
Purex Toss N Soft/40 ct./6/$8.96	2.1	31	1.50	.25	1.24	2.29
Sta Puf/64 oz./8/$6.57	1.6	18	.72	.09	.73	1.06
Sta Puf/96 oz./4/$10.87	1.5	15	1.60 + .25	.46	2.24	3.49
Dishwashing liquid:						
Dermassage/32 oz./9/$13.69	2.5	13	2.43 + .75	.35	1.18	1.89
Dawn/32 oz./12/$18.11	7.1	31	2.40 + .35	.23	1.28	1.86
Lux/22 oz./12/$10.29	1.4	7	.84	.07	.79	1.14
Joy/22 oz./16/$14.92	5.7	33	2.08 + .35	.15	.91	1.12
Ivory/22 oz./12/$15.71	8.2	40	2.40 + .35	.23	1.28	1.61
Palmolive/32 oz./9/$11.26	4.3	20	.50*	.06	1.20	1.54
Candy:						
M&M's/16 oz./24/$41.15	30.4	37	3.00 + 1.00 } 4.00	.17	1.55	2.55
Snickers/16 oz./24/$41.15	5.8	23	3.30	.14	1.58	2.49
Snickers/6 pk./24/$23.40	2.0	26	2.40	.10	.89	1.45
Milky Way Snack/16 oz./24/$41.15	2.3	13	3.30	.14	1.58	2.49
Butterfinger/16 oz./12/$18.96	1.4	15	.84	.07	1.51	2.29
Baby Ruth/16 oz./12/$18.96	1.1	9	.84	.07	1.51	2.29
Cake mix:						
Pillsbury Plus Cake Mix/18.5 oz./12/$9.92	13.9	154	1.08 + .92 } 2.00† / 1.08 + 2.04 CPN } 3.12	.17 / .26	.66 / .57	1.09

EXHIBIT 5 (continued)

Brand/Size/Packages/Case Cost	Category market share	Weekly case movement	Deal per case	Deal per unit	Cost per unit on deal	Normal retail shelf price
Betty Crocker Super Moist Cake Mix/18.5 oz./12/$9.92	20.7	120	1.08 + 2.04 CPN } 3.12	.39	.78	1.65
			1.08 + .92 } 2.00			
Pillsbury Brownie Mix/22 oz./12/$14.09	2.5	24	1.34 + 3.24 CPN } 4.68	.26	.92	1.74
			or 1.34 + 1.74 } 3.08			
Betty Crocker Super/22 oz./12/$15.29	2.3	28	.24 + 1.20 } 1.44	.12	1.15	1.55
Pillsbury Angel Food/16 oz./$13.95	.7	9	.48 + 2.31 } 2.79	.23	.93	1.55
Betty Crocker Angel Food/16 oz./12/$13.95	6.3	66	.24 + 1.56 } 1.80	.15	1.01	1.55
			or .99	.08	1.08	
Duncan Hines Angel Food/15 oz./12/$12.16	1.2	17	.85	.07	.94	1.55
Orange juice:						
Bright & Early/6 oz./48/$13.06	10.0	18	1.44	.03	.24	.40
Bright & Early/12 oz./24/$12.77	6.9	28	1.44	.06	.47	.79
Awake/12 oz./24/$13.98	11.6	26	1.20	.05	.53	.89
			or .24 + 2.40 CPN } 2.64	.11	.47	
Margarine:						
Blue Bonnet Margarine/2/8 oz. Tub/30/$19.63	2.5	30	3.30 + .90 } 4.20	.14	.64	.89
Dessert topping:						
B/E Cool Whip/8 oz./24/$16.46	36.4	52	1.20 + .24 } 1.44	.06	.63	.99
Dream Whip/5 oz./12/$13.19 or Retailer In-Ad CPN	60.6	21	1.68	.14	.96	1.53
			or 1.08 + 2.40 CPN } 3.48	.29	.81	1.53
Milkmate Choc Syrup/20 oz./12/$13.76	1.8	10	2.40 + .60 } 3.00	.25	.90	1.57
Hershey Choc Syrup/16 oz./24/$17.04	11.9	65	1.08	.05	.67	.87
Hershey Fudge Topping/16 oz./24/$27.36	9.4	8	2.40	.10	1.04	1.59
Magic Shell Choc/7.24 oz./12/$11.88	11.3	10	1.20	.10	.89	1.39
Cereal:						
Kellogg's Corn Flakes/18 oz./24/$23.60	.9	45	1.92	.08	.90	1.23
Alpha Bits/15 oz./24/$30.54	1.1	28	.24 + 3.60 CPN } 3.84	.16	1.11	1.69
			or .96	.04	1.23	1.69
Apple Jacks/11 oz./24/$30.00	.8	13	2.40	.10	1.15	1.65
CW Post/15 oz./12/$13.34	.4	22	1.20	.10	1.11	1.47
			or 1.80 CPN } 2.04	.17	.94	1.47
Total/12 oz./12/$13.98	1.1	75	.72 + 1.80 CPN } 2.52	.21	.96	1.54
Cheerios/15 oz./24/$29.54	2.8	96	.96	.04	1.19	1.54
			or 4.56 CPN	.19	1.04	1.54

Product						
Big G Wheaties/18 oz./24/$29.06	2.6	58	.48 + 3.76 } 4.24	.18	1.03	1.49
Diapers:						
Pampers/Toddler-12/18/$33.16	9.0	47	1.00	.06	1.79	2.19
Johnson/Toddler-12/12/$24.65	3.1	26	1.50 + .50 } 2.00	.17	1.89	2.45
Kleenex Huggies/Toddler-12/12/$31.41	4.9	27	1.20‡	.10	2.51	3.15
Kleenex Huggies/Newborn-24/12/$31.41	2.1	16	1.20‡	.10	2.51	3.15
Syrup:						
Golden Griddle/24 oz./12/$16.56	9.6	38	.36 + 2.40 CPN } 2.76	.20§	1.18	1.95
			or 2.76	.23	1.15	1.95
Aunt Jemima Lite/24 oz./12/$16.57	2.8	21	2.40	.20	1.18	1.95
Staley/36 oz./8/$14.22	3.1	12	2.00 + .40 } 2.40	.30	1.48	1.69
Mrs. Butterworth's/24 oz./12/$17.03	9.8	30	2.04 + .42 } 2.46	.21	1.21	1.99
Log Cabin/24 oz. + 4 oz. Bonus/12/$16.57	7.2	21	.72	.06	1.32	1.95
Soup:						
Campbell's Chicken Noodle/10¾ oz./48/$13.40	6.8	177	.84	.02	.26	.37
Tuna fish:						
Chicken of the Sea Tuna/6½ oz./48/$49	33.5	81	8.00 + 1.00 } 9.00	.19	.83	1.09
Chicken of the Sea Tuna/12½ oz./24/$46.05	3.6	17	4.50 + .75 } 5.25	.22	1.70	2.49
Star Kist/6½ oz./48/$51.00	29.2	78	9.00 + 1.00 } 10.00	.21	.85	1.09
Coffee:						
Butternut GRD Coffee/2 lb./12/$60.96	16.8	49	7.68	.64	4.44	5.55
Butternut GRD Coffee/3 lb./8/$60.72	8.7	33	3.60	.45	7.14	8.29
Folgers/2 lb./12/$60.96	17.5	72	3.00	.25	4.83	5.55
Folgers/3 lb./8/$60.72	11.7	45	3.20	.40	7.19	8.29
Maxwell House/2 lb./12/$61.28	4.4	24	6.00 + 6.48 } 12.48	1.04	4.07	5.23
Beverages:						
Hawaiian Punch/46 oz./12/8.94	6.5	57	.84	.07	.68	1.05
Hi-C/46 oz./12/$8.82	30.1	348	.60 + .48 } 1.08	.09	.65	.85
Paper products:						
Bounty Towels/Jumbo-1/30/$24.00	14.4	80	4.20	.14	.66	1.07
Viva/Jumbo-1/30/$24.10	9.5	58	3.60 + 1.00 } 4.60	.15	.65	1.05
Gala/Jumbo-1/30/$21.10	4.0	28	2.85 + 1.50 } 4.35‖	.15	.56	.95
Bolt/Jumbo-2rl./12/$18.62	13.6	45	4.25	.35	1.20	.89
Kleenex Tissues/200 ct./36/$25.95	22.6	58	5.60**	.16	.57	.97
Puffs/200 ct./36/$25.95	15.7	62	6.15	.17	.55	.97
Puffs/280 ct./24/$23.30	10.2	61	3.60	.15	.82	1.29
Scotties/200 ct./36/$25.85	10.5	46	5.40 + .25 } 5.65	.16	.56	.95
Charmin Bath/4 pk./24/$26.25	24.7	218	4.00	.17	.93	1.43
White Cloud/4 pk./24/$26.25	8.3	64	4.00	.17	.93	1.43
Soft N' Pretty/4 pk./24/$26.35	13.3	66	4.00 + 1.00 } 5.00	.21	.89	1.43
Northern Bath/4 pk./24/$26.25	2.22	86	4.50 + .50 } 5.00††	.21	.89	1.33

EXHIBIT 5 (continued)

Brand/Size/Packages/Case Cost	Category market share	Weekly case movement	Deal per case	Deal per unit	Cost per unit on deal	Normal retail shelf price
Canned vegetables:						
Green Giant Green Beans/16 oz./24/$9.55	9.8	32	.96	.04	.36	.52
GG Corn/17 oz./24/$9.41	10.4	28	.96	.04	.35	.52
GG Peas/17 oz./24/$9.70	9.0	18	.96	.04	.36	.51
Del Monte Corn/17 oz./24/$9.72	17.3	20	.84	.04	.37	.46
DM Peas/17 oz./24/$9.80	16.6	20	.84	.04	.37	.49
Stokley Cut Green Beans/16 oz./24/$8.52	.6	10	1.44	.06	.30	.49

*$500 additional merchandise fund.

†Plus special $2,000 allowance for ads of six separate products.

‡$400 for Family Feature all four sizes of Huggies.

§Calculations of coupon values do not include handling charges.

‖Special $100 ad allowance.

**Special $750 ad allowance.

††Special $1,000 ad allowance.

250

EXHIBIT 6 Grocery department newspaper advertising planning chart

Product	Ad type	Normal weeks volume	Promoted retail price	Unit markdown	Total markdown	Normal weekly margin	Promotion week margin
Fresh Start	AA	15	$2.49	$1.36	$5018	$212	$72
	AA	15					
	AA	15					
	AA	15					
	A	8					
	A	8					
	A	8					
	A	8					
	A	8					
	B	5					
	B	5					
	B	5					
	B	5					
	C	0					
	C	0					
	C	0					
	C	0					
	C	0					
	C	0					
	C	0					

6. The per-unit price of the item to Food Ranch after deduction of the per-unit discount from manufacturer list price.

7. Food Ranch's normal retail shelf price for the item.

Jim Reed next referred to a planning chart (see Exhibit 6) that he and his colleagues in other departments completed each week to summarize the financial implications of their decisions on which items to advertise and at what prices. As an illustration, he calculated the dollar margin that Food Ranch would make if it priced Fresh Start at $2.49 to the consumer and allocated an AA advertising feature to this item. He also calculated the total markdown from normal retail price that would be associated with selling 15 weeks' worth of normal volume at $2.49 per unit.

Reed had to deliver his completed planning chart to the vice president of merchandising, who would review it along with similar charts submitted by other departmental merchandising directors. In deciding on which items to promote and at what prices, Reed had to bear in mind two policies established by the vice president of merchandising for promotions of grocery items:

1. The total margin forecast for all promoted grocery items during the week of their promotion had to exceed the total margin that would have been obtained on sales of these items during a normal week.

2. The total markdown for all promoted grocery items had to average $50,000 each week during the first half of 1981.

GENERAL MOTORS ACCEPTANCE CORPORATION (A)

JOHN A. QUELCH

Gordon Roberts, executive vice president of General Motors Acceptance Corporation (GMAC), was reviewing the issues for discussion at a meeting scheduled three days later on July 19, 1981. At the meeting, GMAC and General Motors (GM) executives would have to decide whether to temporarily offer consumers a low interest rate on the financing of new GM cars. If they agreed to proceed, decisions would have to be made on the interest rate level, the scope and timing of the promotion, and advertising support. But the major issue promised to be how to allocate the cost savings to the consumer among the parties involved—GMAC, GM, and its dealers.

COMPANY BACKGROUND

General Motors was the largest automobile manufacturer in the world. With 1980 sales of $58 billion, GM ranked third after Exxon and Mobil on the *Fortune* 500. However, 1980 had been a disappointing year. GM had shipped only 4.1 million passenger cars through its Chevrolet, Pontiac, Oldsmobile, Buick, and Cadillac divisions, plus 0.94 million light trucks through its Chevrolet and GMC truck divisions. These unit shipments were 17% fewer than in 1979. GM posted a $763 million loss for 1980.

Nevertheless during 1980, GM had held its share of U.S. car and light truck sales at 42%. Imports had increased their penetration of units sold by only 2% to 26%. Looking forward to the launch in May, 1981 of the new J line of subcompacts (such as the Chevrolet Cavalier), designed to counter Japanese competition, GM executives entered the new year optimistically. As the 1980 GM annual report stated: "GM anticipates at least 13 million new vehicles delivered in the United States in 1981 compared to 11.5 million in 1980."

General Motors cars were distributed through 11,000 franchised dealerships in the United States. There were 23,000 new-car dealers throughout the United States in 1981. Some 1600 dealerships had ceased business during the year preceding June, 1981. An increasing number of GM dealers stocked more than one of the six GM makes and offered one or more non-GM makes as well.

GMAC AND AUTOMOBILE FINANCING

GMAC was established in 1919 as a wholly owned subsidiary of General Motors. By 1981, it had over 300 offices in the United States and 50 more overseas. GMAC's primary activities were wholesale and retail automobile financing. As such, GMAC provided substantial earnings to the parent corporation that were especially important during recession periods when sales of new vehicles were slow.

By any measure, GMAC was the largest automobile financing institution in the world. At the beginning of 1981, it held 1.6 times the dollar value of consumer automobile loans held by the 100 largest commercial bank automobile lenders in the United States. Automobile loans outstanding at the end of the following years (in billions of dollars) were:

	1978	1979	1980
GMAC	13.5	17.5	20.3
Ford Motor Credit Corp.	6.5	7.7	9.0
Chrysler Financial Corp.	1.7	1.5	1.7
Commercial banks	60.5	67.4	62.5
Credit unions and other	19.4	22.3	24.3
Total	101.6	116.4	116.8

Credit lines of $7.4 billion were available to GMAC at the start of 1981; borrowings against these were $1 billion. The financing subsidiaries of Ford and Chrysler had to borrow more from banks and were, therefore, typically unable to beat the financing rates GMAC offered to consumers.

Wholesale financing accounted for 25% of GMAC's loan portfolio as of December 31, 1980. GMAC financed 80% of all new cars acquired by GM dealers in 1980. These included non-GM cars sold through GM dealers, 10% of the total vehicles financed by GMAC. GMAC retained a security interest in each financed vehicle until the dealer sold it to a customer and paid off the principal and accrued interest.

Although GMAC's rates were adjusted every 15 days in response to changes in the prime rate, GMAC's rates were not nearly as volatile as the prime. In addition, each GM division subsidized its dealers for the first 90 days a vehicle was in inventory or until it was sold by paying the difference between a 4 % financing charge to the dealer and whatever the GMAC financing rate happened to be at any time. As a result, GM enabled the typical dealer to stabilize its inventory carrying costs and to stock more cars than might otherwise have been the case. The GM divisions were heavily involved in determining each dealer's inventory, based on previous years' sales, the market potential of the dealer's trading area, and the dealer's capitalization.

During 1980, the wholesale financed inventory turned approximately once every 76 days.

Retail financing contracts accounted for 60% of GMAC's loan portfolio in the United States. At the end of 1980, GMAC had over five million retail customers, between a quarter and a third of whom turned over each year. GMAC's penetration of new GM car purchases rose from 22.4% in January, 1980 to 26.9% in January, 1981 and 30.0% in June, 1981. In that month, GMAC also financed 27.2% of GM dealers' used-car sales. GMAC financed 14% fewer new cars and trucks and 15% more used at retail in 1980 than 1979. The average term of GMAC new car loans to consumers in 1980 was 42.7 months. In June, 1981, this figure had risen to 43.8 months. The average principal balance financed on new cars in that month was $7,593.[1]

GMAC purchased from GM dealers retail installment obligations contracted by customers who purchased GM vehicles. The gap between the interest rate the customer paid and the interest rate at which GMAC purchased the obligation from the dealer represented the dealer's profit. In July, 1981, these two rates were 17.22% and 15.35%. In that month, GMAC's marginal cost of funds was 14%.

After a dealer transferred a contract to GMAC, GMAC collected the payments from the consumer and repossessed the car if necessary. In 1980, collection and repossession expenses were only 0.03% of average receivables. Some contracts submitted by dealers might be rejected as too risky by GMAC's credit analysts, in which case the dealer might be advised to secure a larger down payment from the customer and resubmit the contract. A high percentage of GMAC's contracts were terminated early as a result of consumers selling their cars before the financing contract expired.

Exhibit 1 shows for the 14 months up to July, 1981, the prime rate, the average rate paid by consumers on GMAC new car financing contracts, the average discount rate paid by GM dealers to GMAC for these contracts, and the percentage of contracts submitted that were rejected by GMAC. Salespeople in the GMAC organization did not receive bonuses based on the quality and quantity of financing contracts placed by their dealers.

GMAC advertised to both consumers and dealers. In 1980, a budget of $2,750,000 was authorized to support GMAC billboard, radio, and print advertising. That budget was reduced by $1 million in May to improve profits. In December, $2 million was allocated to a radio advertising blitz that was supplemented in January, 1981 with an additional $650,000 in newspaper advertising, $300,000 of which was paid by GM. These advertisements (see Exhibit 2 for an example) emphasized the difference between GMAC's rate and the prime but did not mention a specific interest rate. GMAC's advertising budget for the rest of 1981 was $4 million, 85% of which was assigned to network television.

---

[1]The total transaction price net of the consumer's down payment.

EXHIBIT 1   Financing GMAC rates on new GM cars: June 1980–July 1981

	Average bank prime rate	Average GMAC customer rate	Average GMAC discount rate*	Rejections as % of contracts submitted
1980				
June	12.63%	15.46%	13.72%	22.5%
July	11.48	15.39	13.65	21.6
August	11.12	15.12	13.41	21.7
September	12.23	15.09	13.31	20.6
October	13.79	15.11	13.30	20.4
November	16.06	15.16	13.33	19.4
December	20.35	15.28	13.39	18.3
1981				
January	20.16%	15.41%	13.45%	16.5%
February	19.43	15.68	13.82	17.1
March	18.05	15.89	14.05	18.8
April	17.15	15.94	14.08	18.1
May	19.61	16.07	14.13	17.4
June	20.03	17.02	14.66	17.2
July (est.)	20.39	17.22	14.88	16.4

Source: Company records.

*A retail contract purchased by GMAC on a nonrecourse basis was discounted at a higher rate than was a comparable transaction purchased with recourse to the selling dealer. The difference was credited to the loss allowance. These average discount rates are net of the nonrecourse increments; reimbursement rates gave effect to such increments.

AUTOMOBILE FINANCING BY BANKS AND CREDIT UNIONS

During the first half of 1981, about 70% of all new car sales through dealers were financed, either by auto finance companies, commercial banks, or credit unions. The percentage of new GM cars financed by consumers matched the industry total.

Commercial banks were involved in automobile financing in three ways. They financed dealer inventories, wrote loans directly with consumers, and purchased contracts from dealers. Because commercial banks typically used short-term funds for automobile financing, any increase in the prime rate was quickly reflected in higher automobile loan rates from the commercial banks. In addition, funding a 48-month car loan at a fixed rate was seen as increasingly risky. Not only did many commercial banks increase their auto loan rates, increase their down payments, and decrease the repayment periods from 48 to 36 months during the first half of 1981, many also suspended auto financing entirely. In May, 1981, the average commercial bank auto loan interest rate among the limited number of banks still offering loans

EXHIBIT 2   1981 GMAC newspaper advertisement

HOW TO BEAT THE BANK PRIME RATE AND GET THAT NEW GM CAR OR TRUCK YOU WANT <u>NOW</u>.

GMAC is in business to help you buy that new GM car or truck you want—at rates that make good sense.

<u>In spite of the rise in the bank prime rate, the cost of financing your car or truck with GMAC hasn't rocketed up.</u>

In fact, auto financing rates haven't changed that much from three or four years ago.

Your GM Dealer who uses GMAC has money available right now—to help you get that new GM car or truck you've had your eye on.

Check out all the 1981 models at your Chevy, Pontiac, Olds, Buick, Cadillac or GMC Truck Dealer today.

GMAC
The financing people from General Motors

CHEVROLET · PONTIAC · OLDSMOBILE · BUICK · CADILLAC · GMC TRUCKS

was 16.04%. The auto finance companies took up the slack and GMAC increased its penetration.

Credit unions were increasingly involved in retail automobile financing for their members. Some 44% of their total loan portfolio consisted of automobile loans. They did no wholesale financing. They typically provided faster turnaround than commercial banks and often paid the dealer between $30 and $65 per signed new car contract to cover paperwork costs. Foreign auto manufacturers that did not have established financing companies in the United States increasingly permitted their dealers to negotiate subsidized retail auto financing rates through credit unions. Under these arrangements, the manufacturer and the dealer paid the credit union 75% to 100% of the difference between the subsidized and the market rates.

CONSUMER BEHAVIOR

In early 1981, there were some 85 million passenger cars on the road in the United States. The average American consumer was in love with his or her automobile and quite knowledgeable about cars. An Opinion Survey Center Inc. study in March, 1981 classified car buyers into seven psychographic segments.[2]

1.	Practical price and value	22%
2.	A car is a car	13
3.	Engineering/I know cars	16
4.	Car of my dreams	22
5.	The driver	11
6.	First on the block	9
7.	King size	7

According to the study, the first three segments included consumers who made logical, step-by-step buying decisions, but who were swayed by economic conditions. The others were "emotional" shoppers whose purchase behavior focused on styling (4), snob appeal (5), newness (6), or on trust and tradition (7).

The typical consumer attempted to negotiate price with the dealer. The bargain a consumer struck with a dealer depended on the trade-in price negotiated for a used car; the incremental dealer-installed options (such as rustproofing, stereo, security systems, and service contract) on which the dealer typically made a high margin; and the discount from the retail sticker price, largely a function of the dealer's inventory position and recent sales. Most dealers employed a financing salesperson who would arrange convenient financing for purchases through an automobile credit company, a local bank, or a local credit union.

By the middle of 1981, it was clear that uncertain economic conditions were leading many consumers to hold onto and repair their existing cars longer and to postpone replacement purchases. The used car market was also soft, indicating that consumers were not substituting replacement used cars for new cars.

[2]Al Fleming, "Psychographics: Poking Into Buyer Personalities," *Ward's Auto World,* April 1981, p. 63.

Consumers were reluctant to make major purchases. The Survey Research Center of the University of Michigan tracked consumer attitudes monthly and reported the following:

☐   In February, 1981, 69% of families with savings stated that now was *not* a good time to use savings to make major purchases, up from 54% in February, 1980.

☐   In February, 1981, 85% of families with access to credit stated that now was *not* a good time to use credit to make major purchases, up from 80% in February, 1980.

☐   In June, 1981, 35% of households indicated that they had postponed purchases during the previous six months due to high interest rates. The median highest interest rate that these households were willing to pay to make such purchases was 11.9%.

In addition, respondents were asked to cite reasons why they believed now was a good or bad time to buy an automobile. Monthly results from June, 1980 through June, 1981 are reported in Exhibit 3.

A survey of dealers explored the causes of buyer resistance to new-car purchases. As shown in Exhibit 4, financing (availability and/or rates) was the most frequently mentioned barrier to purchase. Qualifying buyers for loans was a major problem. According to one dealer: "We've written 70 deals in the past month but we could only close 33 of them." Overall, 22% of auto financing proposals were thought to have been rejected during the first half of 1981.

THE SITUATION IN JUNE, 1981

By the middle of the year, GM executives were concerned that the company's performance in 1981 might be even worse than in 1980. One divisional vice president summed up the situation as follows:

> We are looking at 1981 U.S. auto industry sales of 9.4 million units compared to 11 million units in 1980. GM shipments by the end of July this year will be 7% down on last year. In addition, there is a serious inventory log jam. GM passenger car inventories are at 97 days supply compared to a normal level of 60 days, and a 42 day supply for imported cars. Even though we're now financing dealer inventories for an average of 45 days rather than the normal 15, many dealers are only taking deliveries of new cars if they have been presold.[3] To add insult to injury, in June, for the first time, the average retail price of imported cars ($8,910) exceeded that of GM cars ($8,501). We have just canceled 5,500 units for which production material had been purchased from what remains of the 1981 model production schedule. More cancellations are likely.

Exhibit 5 presents monthly GM sales and inventory data from October, 1979 through July, 1981. Monthly breakdowns of car sales by body type for the first half

---

[3]GM used to pay for 15 days financing on every car delivered to a dealer regardless of when it was sold.

EXHIBIT 3 Consumer opinions about buying conditions for cars: June 1980–June 1981

	Good time	Uncertain	Bad time	Good Time to Buy: Reasons Why				Bad Time to Buy: Reasons Why				
				Low prices/ good buys	Prices won't come down	low interest rates	Good mileage	High prices	High interest rates	Lack of purchasing power	Gas price	Poor selection quality
June (1980)	37%*	14%	49%	27%†	9%	3%	5%	24%	22%	6%	9%	10%
July	36	14	50	25	13	4	3	27	11	9	6	13
August	42	12	46	24	12	4	7	27	11	9	5	13
September	42	14	44	20	19	4	9	31	10	6	5	11
October	45	16	39	17	17	3	12	23	14	8	4	13
November	41	15	44	17	16	3	7	28	17	7	4	10
December	33	8	59	13	12	4	5	31	29	9	5	12
January (1981)	36	13	51	18	13	5	4	33	28	7	4	9
February	39	11	50	22	12	3	4	31	27	7	8	9
March	39	11	50	30	10	2	6	34	21	10	6	9
April	42	9	49	25	19	3	4	31	22	8	5	8
May	44	7	49	23	15	4	5	33	17	6	3	10
June	33	10	57	14	12	2	5	34	28	6	2	9

Source: Survey of Consumer Attitudes, Survey Research Center, University of Michigan.

*Thirty-seven percent of all survey respondents in June, 1980 said now was a good time to buy a car.

†Twenty-seven percent of *all* respondents said now was a good time to buy because of low prices and good buys. Multiple responses were permitted.

EXHIBIT 4   Dealer perceptions of causes of
consumer resistance to buying new cars

	Domestic car dealers	Import car dealers
Car prices	15.6%	16.8%
Financing	23.7	23.6
Trade-ins	9.7	21.5
Down payments	5.8	6.2
Gas prices	19.5	3.1
Gas availability	4.8	2.1
Inflation	5.7	8.2
Economics, politics	15.2	18.5

Source: Al Fleming, "Psychographics: Poking into Buyer Personalities," *Ward's Auto World,* April 1981.

of 1981 are shown in Exhibit 6. Similar breakdowns for GM's five passenger car divisions are presented in Exhibit 7.

Given these data, GM executives were increasingly interested in exploring additional sales promotions beyond those already planned in order to boost short-term sales. While some argued for rebates or price roll-backs on selected models, attention focused on a low-interest financing promotion. Informal discussions between GM and GMAC executives resulted in a tentative proposal to offer consumers 13.8% financing on all new 1981 GM cars as well as 1982 J cars during the entire month of August. Cars qualifying for reduced rate financing would have to be delivered to consumers by September 23.

MANUFACTURER SALES PROMOTION

Before the early 1970s, sales promotion played a modest role in automobile marketing. Beyond occasional incentives to dealer salespeople and liquidation allowances to clear inventories at the end of each model year, there was little promotion activity. Consumer demand patterns were sufficiently predictable that minor adjustments to the production schedule could take care of any deviations from forecast.

The oil crisis of 1973 and the incursion of Japanese imports complicated the competitive environment and made consumer demand for automobiles less predictable. At the same time, new labor contracts made short-term adjustments to the production schedule more costly and difficult to execute. A decade before the advent of flexible manufacturing systems, it took a U.S. automobile manufacturer six months to prepare for adding a second shift and three months to adjust the supply of parts to increase plant output.

Under these circumstances, the U.S. manufacturers tended to err on the side of overproduction since excess inventory could always be moved through the use of temporary sales promotions. Underproduction, on the other hand, could only lead to lost sales.

By 1981, all three major U.S. automobile manufacturers were running frequent

EXHIBIT 5   General Motors sales and inventory data (thousands of units)

| | | | | | Days supply | |
| | Factory | Dealer | Net field | Gross | Net | Gross |
Date*	sales	salest	stock‡	stock	stock	stock
10/79	502	431	622	909	45	65
11/79	435	370	670	934	54	76
12/79	331	338	699	887	64	81
1/80	403	381	595	874	48	71
2/80	437	372	620	900	48	70
3/80	416	390	637	884	51	70
4/80	385	347	642	889	56	77
5/80	341	310	654	886	65	89
6/80	377	315	687	920	65	88
7/80	353	348	679	893	61	80
8/80	170	316	543	751	53	74
9/80	350	317	534	764	50	72
10/80	432	419	510	747	38	55
11/80	368	330	556	764	51	69
12/80	340	272	645	807	73	92
1/81	314	293	612	816	65	86
2/81	314	331	557	776	47	66
3/81	402	438	487	711	34	50
4/81	420	310	545	793	53	77
5/81	434	315	642	877	63	86
6/81	469	311	753	1004	73	97
7/81 (est.)	365	304	828	1040	84	106

Source: Company records.

* All figures are as of month-end and exlude fleet sales.

† By July, 1981, dealer used-car sales were expected to be 110.3% of those sold during the first seven months of 1980.

‡ Gross stock represents all cars that have been produced but have not yet been sold by dealers. Net field stock equals gross stock less factory float, company cars, cars in transit, cars in company warehouses, and dealer demonstrator vehicles. "Normal" auto industry supply levels are 60 days (gross stock) and 45 days (net stock).

promotions to stimulate showroom traffic and retail sales. Chrysler was especially aggressive, but Ford was the only manufacturer to have experimented with a low-interest financing program in the United States. Between December 5, 1980 and February 7, 1981, Ford offered 12% financing on purchases of new Granadas, Thunderbirds, and Mustangs. Consumer sales of these three models were as follows:

	Nov. 1980	Dec. 1980	Jan. 1981
Granadas	7,656	7,416 (99)	7,614 (107)
Thunderbirds	6,539	7,189 (45)	6,299 (51)
Mustangs	14,216	12,639 (67)	11,490 (57)

Note: Numbers in parentheses represent percentage comparisons to sales in the same month of the previous year.

EXHIBIT 6 General Motors car deliveries to consumers by body type: January–July 1981

	Subcompacts*	Compacts	Mid-size	Regular	High end	Total
January	43,178 (74)†	62,136 (74)	109,105 (86)	42,456 (65)	36,344 (79)	293,219 (77)
February	58,720 (93)	81,242 (99)	115,680 (99)	39,460 (58)	35,855 (86)	330,957 (89)
March	65,035 (87)	120,250 (131)	168,542 (132)	44,778 (76)	39,279 (105)	437,884 (112)
April	31,450 (67)	65,090 (77)	120,315 (98)	47,193 (105)	45,614 (134)	309,662 (89)
May	39,241 (83)	69,261 (89)	119,383 (112)	47,339 (107)	39,540 (115)	314,764 (102)
June	41,518 (87)	67,595 (91)	115,454 (103)	47,216 (100)	39,103 (117)	310,886 (99)
July (est.)	47,713 (90)	70,602 (87)	102,829 (83)	47,882 (94)	37,109 (96)	304,135 (87)
Percent financed by GMAC (Jan.–June)						
1981	37	26	25	29		28
1980	34	24	22	28		26

Source: Company records.

Note: During the first half of 1981, 46.9% of new GM car sales were of the higher priced lines—Buicks, Oldsmobiles, and Cadillacs—while the remainder were Pontiacs and Chevrolets. During the first half of 1980, the comparable figure was 42.6%.

*To illustrate GM's model classification system, in the Chevrolet division the Chevette and Monza models were subcompacts, the Citation and Camaro were compacts, the Malibu and Monte Carlo were mid-size, the Impala and Caprice were regular, and the Corvette was high end.

† Numbers in parentheses represent 1981 deliveries as a percentage of 1980 deliveries by month and body type.

EXHIBIT 7 General Motors car deliveries to consumers by division January–July 1981

	Chevrolet	Pontiac	Oldsmobile	Buick	Cadillac	Total
January	114,255 (70)*	43,020 (73)	67,902 (90)	51,448 (86)	16,594 (73)	293,219 (77)
February	139,323 (85)	46,845 (89)	68,140 (95)	59,505 (95)	17,144 (89)	330,957 (89)
March	187,782 (103)	59,547 (105)	93,330 (127)	79,427 (132)	17,798 (99)	437,884 (112)
April	107,696 (74)	41,454 (74)	72,610 (104)	66,706 (113)	21,200 (135)	309,666 (89)
May	109,752 (81)	51,427 (122)	76,239 (125)	59,182 (107)	18,164 (110)	314,764 (102)
June	113,320 (86)	45,136 (93)	75,709 (115)	58,352 (107)	18,369 (132)	310,886 (99)
July (est.)	120,600 (83)	48,704 (94)	65,040 (89)	51,590 (88)	18,201 (104)	304,135 (87)
Percent financed by GMAC (Jan.–June)						
1981	32	31	23	24	23	28
1980	29	29	21	22	21	26

Source: Company records.

*Numbers in parentheses represent 1981 deliveries as a percentage of 1980 deliveries by month and division.

Most manufacturer promotions offered consumer rebates on new-car purchases. These rebates were offered either as an absolute dollar amount ($300, for example) or as a flat percentage reduction off the retail sticker price. The rebate could be taken as a check from the manufacturer after delivery or applied to the consumer's down payment. Rebates were usually applicable to designated models ordered during the promotion period, even if delivery occurred after the end of the promotion. Most rebate programs set a limit of five cars per customer to prevent fleet buyers taking advantage of them.

The cost of each rebate was typically shared by the dealer and manufacturer. This was usually stated in advertising announcing the rebate to condition consumers to expect a lower dealer discount than they otherwise would have. Occasionally, the manufacturer would absorb the dealer portion of the shared rebate cost on cars delivered, rather than just ordered, during the rebate period.

During the first quarter of 1981, Chrysler ran a variable rebate promotion called the Interest Allowance Plan. The rebate was offered to consumers who financed their new-car purchases through Chrysler. The rebate varied according to the prime rate. On any day during the promotion, it was set at the number of percentage points by which the prime rate exceeded 12 %. This percentage was then deducted from the retail sticker price. Halfway through the promotion, the requirement that consumers finance their cars through Chrysler to qualify was dropped. Thereafter, dealers had to contribute $200 toward each rebate.

Three other types of consumer promotions were also tried in 1981. GM offered a tie-in promotion of two free round-trip tickets on Eastern Airlines with the purchase of any new Chevrolet. To build dealer traffic, Chrysler offered cash incentives of $25 to $50 for consumers who test drove specified models. Chrysler also offered a special value model preequipped with options at a lower sticker price than if the options were added separately. Chrysler gave dealers a $200 allowance on each Plymouth Horizon TC3 sold during the promotion period that did not have the special value package to ensure continuing sales of the basic model.

In addition to consumer promotions, automobile manufacturers also offered bonuses to dealers for achieving target sales levels on specified models during designated promotion periods. The unit bonus typically increased with the number of cars a dealer sold. Dealers usually allocated a portion of their bonus payments to their sales managers and floor salespeople. Sometimes manufacturers offered an incremental "fast start" bonus to motivate salespeople to achieve their targets early in the promotion period. Manufacturers occasionally paid the bonuses to their dealers in advance on the basis of estimated sales in order to assist dealers' cash flow.

Finally, close-out allowances were also offered by all the major U.S. manufacturers on cars that had not sold off dealers' lots by the end of the model year. GM expected to pay dealers an average of $500 for each 1981 car still in stock and unsold by September 23.

THE 13.8% RATE FINANCING PROPOSAL

Among both GM and GMAC executives, there was considerable debate about the merits of the 13.8% rate financing proposal and the specifics of program implementation. First, was the 13.8% rate sufficiently low to attract consumer attention, build dealer traffic, and sell more cars? Some executives agreed that a more attractive rate such as 12.9% would guarantee the program's success, especially if short-term interest rates unexpectedly declined.

Second, to which cars should the promotion apply? Some GM executives argued that it should be restricted to those 1981 models with the most sluggish sales and/or greatest inventory problems. Others, noting that inventory levels varied by model from one region to another, proposed that each dealer be allowed to offer the low interest rate on the models of its choice. A third group believed that this local option approach would preclude national advertising. They advocated a blockbuster promotion that would offer the low interest rate not only on all 1981 models but also on 1982 J cars already in dealer showrooms.[4]

Third, when should the promotion be run and for how long? Some argued that it should be delayed so as not to overlap with a July promotion on GM X cars. Others cited arguments for a promotion shorter than one month. First, if the promotion proved successful, it could be extremely expensive; a two-week promotion that could be extended would be a safer approach. Second, unless a low-interest promotion could be justified as strictly temporary, GM was legally bound to offer the same interest rate to purchasers of GM cars through other financial institutions. This requirement resulted from a 1952 consent decree in which GM had agreed not to give its captive finance company, GMAC, any advantage versus other organizations engaged in consumer financing.

PROMOTION COST ALLOCATION

A fourth issue was how the cost of the promotion should be shared. On a $7,500 contract financed over 45 months at 13.8% rather than 17%, the nominal dollar savings to the consumer would be $545.[5] How should these savings be allocated among GMAC, GM, and the dealer? Several GMAC executives argued against any financial involvement. As one explained:

> The purpose of this program is to sell GM cars, not to build GMAC's business. GM should absorb the whole cost or split it with the dealers. We at GMAC will provide the financing, but we want our normal profit margin. In fact, for three reasons, we may even need to impose a surcharge. First, the program may attract more marginally qualified applicants, pushing up our long-term delinquency and loss rates.[6] Second, if the program increases financing applications too rapidly, our operations may be strained. We may have to bring people in from the field to process the extra applications. Third, if the

---

[4]GM projected sales of 32,000 J cars during August 1981 without the 13.8% retail financing promotion.

[5]The total consumer payments at 17% would be $10,194 versus $9,649 at 13.8%, and $9,903 at 15.3%.

[6]The delinquency rate was 2.75% of accounts outstanding in 1980, and losses charged against income were 0.27% of receivables outstanding. Higher than expected losses were due, in part, to the low resale value on repossessed full-size cars following the 1979 gas shortage.

costs are shared, we'll have to rework our accounting procedures in order to bill each GM division to make sure we collect its share of the financing subsidy.

GM executives countered that GMAC would undoubtedly gain more business as a result of the promotion. Hence, a compromise proposal was developed for discussion at the July 19 meeting that would allocate the $545 consumer savings as follows:

GM support	$254
GMAC support	87
Dealer support	204

However, both GM and GMAC executives were uncertain whether dealers would support the program. Dealers could not be directly canvassed because, if word about the program leaked, consumers might delay purchases in anticipation and a competitor might preempt the promotion. Through the first half of 1981, GM dealers nationwide averaged $300 finance income on each new GMAC contract. Most dealers were thought unlikely to back the program if their profits on financing contracts, typically 30% to 35% of their total car sale profits, were eliminated. An initial proposal was for GMAC to give each dealer $100 for each new contract written under the 13.8% program. However, GMAC executives discovered that, in certain states, dealers were already competing on the basis of below-market interest rates. For example, throughout the first half of 1981, dealers in Iowa averaged only $25 profit per financing contract. The $100 proposal would, therefore, overcompensate them, and dealers in other states where the average profit had exceeded $300 would find the $100 less acceptable. The compromise proposal, therefore, changed the GMAC subsidy to each dealer from $100 per contract to 30% of the average dealer profit for financing the contracts written with GMAC during June, 1981.[7]

The level of dealer support for the program was expected to vary from state to state. In Arkansas, where the state law set an interest rate ceiling of 10%, the program could not be made available to dealers. In Texas, aggressive lobbying by dealers had recently led to a similar interest rate ceiling being rescinded. Texas dealers averaged $570 profit per financing contract in June, 1981 and were in no mood to accept a 70% reduction in this figure. One GMAC executive just back from Texas expressed doubt as to whether any dealer in Texas would participate in the program as proposed because it required that all GMAC contracts written during the promotion period had to be at the 13.8% rate. Dealers could opt not to participate in the program, but, if they did participate, the program currently prohibited them from offering the 13.8% rate on a selective basis to only those customers whom they thought required this extra incentive to make a purchase. Likewise, dealers in markets where financing rates were already a key element in interdealer competition could not selectively offer a rate below the 13.8% level, even if they were prepared to make up 100% of the difference themselves.

---

[7]Average dealer profit per financing contract in June, 1981 was $291.

Some dealers were known to be more interested in obtaining assistance from GMAC on wholesale financing of their inventories rather than a retail financing program designed to move them through to the public. Other dealers had their inventories under control, were not overstocked, and were likely to resent being pressured to participate in a program designed to help other less judicious dealers. Finally, dealers with a high proportion of their business in fleet sales were likely to be, at best, indifferent since the proposed program only applied to individual consumer purchases.

ADVERTISING

A further area of debate was whether the 13.8% program should be nationally advertised and if so, how aggressively and by whom. GM executives were willing to tag their national television commercials with information about the availability of the 13.8% program and a recommendation to consumers to check with participating local dealers for further information.[8] They were not, however, prepared to commit additional funds to advertising specifically dedicated to the 13.8% program.

Proponents of the promotion at GMAC had developed an advertising plan to support its introduction. In addition to the $4 million already budgeted for GMAC advertising in 1981, they proposed spending $5,370,000 during August, broken down as follows:

Network television	$1,800,000
Radio	700,000
Newspaper	2,570,000
Magazines	300,000

In addition, window posters, car toppers, and other merchandising aids would be provided by GMAC to GM dealers. No cooperative advertising program specific to the 13.8% promotion was proposed. However, ad mats announcing the promotion would be provided free to dealers for incorporation into their own newspaper advertisements if they wished.

Some GMAC executives viewed this proposed expenditure as excessive, particularly if GM was not prepared to subsidize part of the advertising cost. These executives also argued that the potential consumer savings associated with the 13.8% rate could not be advertised in national media because interest rates varied from state to state. The following data for June, 1981 for four states illustrate these differences:

	Average GMAC consumer rate (%)	Nominal dollar savings to consumer under 13.8% promotion
Nevada	19.0	$880
New Jersey	18.0	710
Pennsylvania	16.5	460
Oregon	14.3	90

[8]Under the terms of the 1952 consent decree, GM could not mention GMAC by name in its advertising.

Advocates of the promotion replied that the average consumer savings could be calculated for each state, rounded down to the nearest $25, and inserted into otherwise identical newspaper and radio advertisements on a state-by-state basis. Exhibits 8 and 9 present examples of newspaper advertisements proposed by GMAC's agency. One was a general announcement of the 13.8% rate, the other a specific announcement of the dollar savings available to Michigan consumers.[9]

CANADIAN EVIDENCE

GMAC and GM executives were aware of two low-interest financing promotions that had been offered to Canadian consumers during 1981:

☐ Between January 1 and April 30, GMAC Canada offered consumers a 14.2% financing rate on new cars. GMAC's standard rate on January 1 was 18.2%. The costs were shared by GM Canada (2 percentage points), GMAC Canada (1 point), and the dealer (1 point).

☐ Between June 16 and July 10, GMAC Canada offered a 17.75% financing rate on new cars compared to its published auto loan rate of 20.75%. The costs of this promotion were shared between GMAC Canada (40%) and the dealer (60%).

During 1980, GMAC Canada financed 20.7% of cars delivered by GM dealers. As shown in Exhibit 10, GMAC doubled its penetration rate during the first seven months of 1981. Some executives believed that GMAC in the United States would be able to do even better. First, GMAC Canada's asset base was more short term; its rates were therefore more sensitive to fluctuations in the prime rate. Second, the five largest Canadian banks advertised nationally available automobile loan rates that were highly competitive with the automobile financing companies.

ESTIMATING PROGRAM COSTS

In advance of the July 19 meeting, members of GM's Price Review Group had to finalize cost projections for the program. At a previous session, GM executives had projected an additional 40,000 new car sales during August if the 13.8% program were launched, resulting in total August sales of 350,000 units. Of the incremental sales, 25,000 would be from dealer stock and 15,000 would be plus sales from GM to its dealers. At the same meeting, GMAC executives had estimated that they would finance 77,500 new GM cars during August in the absence of the program and an additional 97,500 units (including all 40,000 incremental sales) if the program was launched. Other assumptions agreed to were as follows:

☐ GMAC's long-term cost of capital and its marginal cost of funds would be treated as 12% and 14% respectively.

[9]There was some concern over whether the absolute dollar savings represented by 13.8% financing should be presented on a net present value basis in any advertising.

EXHIBIT 8   Proposed newspaper advertisement for 13.8% program

GOOD NEWS FOR CAR BUYERS

GMAC LOWERS CAR FINANCING RATE TO

13.8%

ANNUAL PERCENTAGE RATE

ON AUGUST DELIVERIES OF CHEVROLETS · PONTIACS · OLDSMOBILES BUICKS · CADILLACS

This can result in a savings of hundreds of dollars to you.*

Here's the best news you've seen in months. GMAC and your participating GM dealer are now offering GMAC car financing at only 13.8%.

That's right! You can finance any new General Motors car delivered in August at just 13.8%. And this means big savings to you.

Your participating GM dealer is ready now to offer you this new 13.8% financing rate on all new GM cars, including the new Chevrolet Cavalier, Pontiac J2000 and Cimarron by Cadillac.

So see your GM dealer today and pick out that new Chevy, Pontiac, Oldsmobile, Buick or Cadillac that you've been waiting to buy.

GMAC
THE FINANCING PEOPLE FROM GENERAL MOTORS

*Actual savings will depend on the amount financed, the length of the contract and your State's automobile financing law.

EXHIBIT 9   Proposed Michigan newspaper advertisement for 13.8% program

GOOD NEWS FOR CAR BUYERS

GMAC LOWERS CAR FINANCING RATE TO

13.8%

ANNUAL PERCENTAGE RATE

ON AUGUST DELIVERIES OF CHEVROLETS · PONTIACS · OLDSMOBILES BUICKS · CADILLACS

This will result in an average saving of $425 in Michigan.*

Here's the best news you've seen in months. GMAC and your participating GM dealer are now offering GMAC car financing at only 13.8%.

That's right! You can finance any new General Motors car delivered in August at just 13.8%. And this means big savings to you.

Your participating GM dealer is ready now to offer you this new 13.8% financing rate on all new GM cars, including the new J-Cars.

So see your GM dealer today and pick out that new Chevy, Pontiac, Oldsmobile, Buick or Cadillac that you've been waiting to buy.

*Based on GMAC financing data for June 1981 and the Michigan statutory rate ceiling applicable to automobile financing. Actual savings will depend on the amount financed and the length of the contract.

GMAC
THE FINANCING PEOPLE FROM GENERAL MOTORS

**EXHIBIT 10   GM dealer deliveries
and percent financed by GMAC
Canada: January 1980-July 1981**

	GM dealer car deliveries	Percent financed
January 1980	30,689	21.9%
February	35,550	19.9
March	42,819	20.0
April	45,066	28.1
May	42,911	21.7
June	40,421	19.2
July	40,216	18.3
August	35,021	17.1
September	30,115	16.7
October	42,665	18.4
November	31,654	21.9
December	23,858	26.1
January 1981	27,173	35.7
February	27,994	45.2
March	40,081	44.1
April	45,280	44.8
May	34,829	47.0
June	36,272	29.5
July (est.)	27,154	42.1

Source: Company records.

☐ GM's average profit per car after variable cost would be treated as $2,000.

☐ GMAC would incur incremental administrative costs of $2 per month on each of the additional 97,500 contracts.

☐ By selling through 40,000 additional cars, GM would avoid obsolescence costs of $5 million on assemblies and components already purchased that could not be used to produce 1982 models.

CONCLUSION

At the July 19 meeting, Roberts, his GMAC colleagues, and GM executives would have to make a final decision on whether to go ahead with the promotion. If they decided in favor, details of the promotion's scope and timing would have to be finalized. In addition, a complete financial forecast and communications program would have to be developed.

The previous week, an internal memo had indicated that GM would be holding its annual price increases, to be announced in August, to below 5%. Ford and Chrysler were expected to do the same.

OPPORTUNITIES AND RISKS OF DURABLE-GOODS PROMOTION

JOHN A. QUELCH
SCOTT A. NESLIN
LOIS B. OLSON

The last decade has witnessed dramatic changes in consumer lifestyles, technology, and competition that force durable-goods manufacturers to reexamine their marketing strategies. Among the elements of marketing strategy, sales promotion has emerged with new prominence and potential. Durable-goods managers now find it necessary to understand sales promotion so that they can better manage that element of the marketing mix.

Durables manufacturers offer a broad variety of advertising and sales promotion programs, often more diverse than those offered by packaged-goods manufacturers. These programs can be grouped into four broad categories (see Table 1) on the basis of two criteria: whether they are directed at the trade (push) or the end consumer (pull), and whether the goal is to deliver an economic incentive or product information. Sales promotions such as rebates, trade discounts, premiums, and financing plans typically deliver an economic incentive. In 1985, the expenditure mix of two durables manufacturers we studied was as follows:

Type of expenditure	Major kitchen appliance manufacturer	Small household appliance manufacturer
Informational—Pull	32%	35%
Informational—Push	5	1
Economic—Pull	9	14
Economic—Push	53	49

TABLE 1 Advertising and promotion programs used by durable goods manufacturers

	Informational (Advertising)	Economic (Sales promotion)
Pull (End consumer)	☐ National advertising ☐ Key city advertising ☐ Local/cooperative advertising	Consumer promotions ☐ Rebates ☐ Price/quantity promotions ☐ Coupons ☐ Sweepstakes ☐ Accessories/premiums ☐ Testers/loaners ☐ Tie-in promotions ☐ Trade-in allowances ☐ Financing incentives ☐ Service contracts ☐ Finders' fees
Push (Trade)	☐ Trade advertising ☐ Trade shows ☐ Preview events ☐ Point-of-purchase materials	☐ Off-invoice purchase allowances ☐ Volume rebates, quantity discounts, contract prices ☐ Inventory financing, dating, floor plans, stock balancing ☐ Backhauling allowances ☐ Sales force incentives

These data are consistent with a PIMS-based study that found promotion, as a percentage of combined advertising and promotion expenditures, averaged 66% across 190 consumer durables businesses, versus 58% across 265 consumer nondurables businesses.[1] A 1985 study found that 76% of major applicance purchasers reported having bought on deal.[2] Clearly, sales promotion is an important part of the durables manufacturer's marketing mix. Moreover, in recent years, promotions—particularly short-term promotions directed at the consumer, as distinct from inventory financing and other merchandising programs that are part of the permanent pricing structure—have assumed an increasing percentage of the durables manufacturer's marketing budget, often at the expense of national advertising.[3]

However, though durables account for 37% of retail purchases, their sales promotion has rarely been addressed in the literature except tangentially in the con-

[1] J.A. Quelch, C.T. Marshall, and D.R. Chang, "Structural Determinants of Ratios of Promotion and Advertising to Sales" in *Research on Sales Promotion: Selected Papers*, ed. Katherine E. Jocz (Cambridge, MA: Marketing Science Institute, July 1984).

[2] W.L. Wilkie and P.R. Dickson, "Shopping for Appliances: Consumers' Strategies and Patterns of Information Search" (Cambridge, MA: Marketing Science Institute, November 1985).

[3] "Detroit Will Keep Rolling Out The Incentives," *Business Week*, 13 January 1986, p. 62.

text of information processing, price-quality relationships, and manufacturer-trade relations.[4] In this article, we first examine the reasons why promotion expenditures have increased and the concerns this increase is generating. Second, we review how durables manufacturers use promotions and the range of promotion options available to them. Third, we offer advice on how to design a specific promotion and on other ways to increase the productivity of promotion expenditures. Throughout, we draw contrasts between sales promotion for durables and for packaged goods.

This article represents a synthesis of existing academic research and material in business periodicals. In addition, we benefited greatly from 20 interviews with executives of six *Fortune* 500 durables-product manufacturing firms. The interviewees included line and staff marketing and product managers, as well as in-house promotion specialists. The firms were manufacturers of small appliances, large appliances, and automobiles.

SALES PROMOTIONS: INCREASING IMPORTANCE, GROWING CONCERN

Although short-term promotions are not new to consumer durables, they have never been used more widely. Nine factors explain the increasing use of promotions.

☐   The cost effectiveness of media advertising is declining because of audience fragmentation, advertising clutter, consumer "zapping" of commercials, and rate hikes that have outpaced inflation.[5] On the other hand, sales promotions such as a direct-mail rebate offer can be targeted at particular consumer segments, and can deliver information about the product's benefits.

☐   Just as the effectiveness of pull advertising is weakening, so is the quality of push communications by retail salespeople. Part-time salespeople often lack adequate product knowledge, and responsibility for negotiating the retail price cannot easily be delegated to them. Add this to the consumer trend toward more impulse buying, even of durables, and it becomes essential for the durables manufacturer to manage the point-of-purchase using consumer-directed promotions and educational displays.[6]

☐   The inflationary late 1970s provided a harsh initiation to the new generation of baby-boom consumers and shook the confidence of older consumers. The result was a dramatic increase in consumer price sensitivity. This sensitivity meshes well with the economic themes that characterize most sales promotions.

☐   The popularity of sales promotions for packaged goods educated consumers about the merits of "smart shopping" and produced a segment of habitual

---

[4]See, for example, R.A. Westbrook and C. Fornell, "Patterns of Information Source Usage among Durable Goods Buyers," *Journal of Marketing Research* 16 (1979): 303–12; and R.F. Lusch, "Sources of Power: Their Impact on Intrachannel Conflict," *Journal of Marketing Research* 13 (1976): 382–90.

[5]S. Flax, "Squeeze on the Networks," *Fortune,* 5 September 1983, pp. 84–94.

[6]J.A. Quelch and K. Cannon-Bonventre, "Better Marketing at the Point-of-Purchase," *Harvard Business Review* (November–December 1983): 162–69.

"deal-prone" consumers.[7] Consumers found it easy to transfer the skills and expectations developed in purchasing packaged goods to durable goods. The consumer also learned that promoted products are no longer necessarily of low quality.

☐ Consumers learned during the last decade that prices for new durable-goods categories, such as calculators and VCRs, decrease over time. As a result, manufacturers need sales promotions as an incentive for the consumer to buy such postponable durables *now.*

☐ Many durable-goods categories, such as major appliances, reached maturity during the last decade. Concurrently, net new household formations were only 1.6% per year in the 1980s, compared to 2.4% in the 1970s. Together, these two factors yield slow-growth markets. Promotions can be used to accelerate the timing of demand and build market share.[8]

☐ Prompted by Japanese price competition, many durables manufacturers are aiming for higher-volume production to achieve lower-cost products. The result is often capacity and production in excess of demand and the consequent need for promotions that stimulate sales volume.

☐ Durables manufacturers face distribution channels that are becoming more complicated, more diverse, and more likely to carry multiple brands—and that are consequently harder to manage. Excess retail floor space, plus an increasing emphasis on maximizing volume rather than unit margin, is stimulating retail price competition. As a result, durables retailers put more pressure on manufacturers for merchandising programs and promotions.[9]

☐ The professionalism of sales promotion planning and execution, both by in-house staff groups and outside agencies, increases as promotion becomes a more important element of the marketing mix. In addition, durables manufacturers are discovering new promotion techniques from migrating packaged-goods product managers.

Manufacturer Concerns

Increasing promotion expenditures concern durables manufacturers, just as they do packaged-goods manufacturers.[10] This is the case especially in categories like automobiles, where promotions have reached epidemic levels.[11] There are five main sources of concern.

[7]R.C. Blattberg et al., "Identifying the Deal Prone Segment," *Journal of Marketing Research* 15 (1978): 369–77.

[8]S.A. Neslin, C. Henderson, and J.A. Quelch, "Consumer Promotions and the Acceleration of Product Purchases," *Marketing Science* 4 (1985): 147–65.

[9]S.H. Sloan, "Retailing Seems to Be Increasingly Price Driven," *Chain Store Age Executive,* December 1984, p. 4.

[10]J.A. Quelch, "It's Time to Make Trade Promotion More Productive," *Harvard Business Review* (May–June 1983): 130–36.

[11]W.J. Hampton, "Detroit's Big Gamble," *Business Week,* 13 January 1986, pp. 30–31.

First, rising promotion expenditures decrease the dollars available for building a brand's franchise through advertising. By further increasing consumer price sensitivity, promotion also can weaken brand loyalty. Though the negative impact may be less when promotion becomes endemic in a category, it is still hard for a company to advertise a quality story about a new product line when most of its existing line is being sold on promotion.

Second, promotion expenditures can quickly grow out of control. An out-of-season promotion initiated to flush excess inventory of a weak item in a product line soon becomes an in-season promotion offered across the entire line. Dealers and consumers alike start to view promotions as entitlement programs, and the promotions quickly become an integral part of the pricing structure. Manufacturers can find themselves in a zero-sum game, trying to out-promote each other, being matched by the competition, and eventually eroding category profit margins.

Third, when promotions become frequent or predictable, consumers—sometimes acting on information from retail salespeople—may postpone purchases until the products they want are promoted.[12] Alternatively, if promotion causes consumers to buy earlier than they would have done otherwise, the manufacturer may simply have stolen from future sales without stimulating primary demand. This problem is more acute for the durables than the packaged-goods manufacturer, because the consumer's purchase timing decision for durables is more flexible.

The fourth area of concern is that many durables marketers offer multiple models within a single product category under the same brand umbrella. Promotions on individual models are hard to implement if they disrupt the logic of the line's pricing structure by cannibalizing other models and prompting consumers to trade down rather than up.

And finally, manufacturers must make equivalent promotion offers available to all trade accounts in any market area. Differences in discounts across accounts must be cost justified to be legally sustainable. For many manufacturers, this constraint is especially difficult because the channels they supply are so diverse. Retailers range from specialty independent dealers who value service and merchandising support to powerful mass merchandisers who want to achieve the lowest possible price by cutting the published price list. When working with these large mass merchandisers, manufacturers often have trouble achieving the promised level of merchandising support, as well as full pass-through of promotion dollars to the end consumer.

THE USES OF SALES PROMOTION

In light of all these problems, why are durables manufacturers running sales promotions? Table 2 summarizes the range of objectives a durables manufacturer might consider.[13] If we compared this list with one for a packaged-goods manufacturer, we would find several differences in emphasis.

[12]P. Doyle and J. Saunders, "The Lead Effect of Marketing Decisions," *Journal of Marketing Research* 22 (1985): 54–65.

[13]Table 2 is adapted from a table in P.W. Farris and J.A. Quelch, *Advertising and Promotion Management* (Radnor, PA: Chilton Book Company, 1983), p. 107.

TABLE 2   Possible promotion objectives for Durable Brand X

Consumer Objectives

1. To persuade consumers to:
   - ☐ Accelerate the timing of their initial or replacement purchase of Durable Brand X.
   - ☐ Select Durable Brand X for their initial purchase.
   - ☐ Stay loyal to or switch to Durable Brand X on their repeat/replacement purchases.
   - ☐ Purchase a more expensive, heavily featured model of Durable Brand X than they may have intended.
   - ☐ Purchase accessories in addition to the basic model.
   - ☐ Upgrade, add accessories to, or purchase consumables for the model of Durable Brand X they currently own.

2. To overcome objections to purchase that consumers may have based on:
   - ☐ Disposal of an existing durable.
   - ☐ Affordability of the purchase.
   - ☐ Service risk.

Trade Objectives

1. To persuade existing outlets to:
   - ☐ Maintain existing floor/shelf space for Durable Brand X.
   - ☐ Stock additional in-line models or out-of-line promotional versions of Durable Brand X.
   - ☐ Provide additional floor/shelf space for Durable Brand X.
   - ☐ Provide special displays and advertising features for Durable Brand X.
   - ☐ Increase inventories of Durable Brand X.

2. To persuade new outlets to stock Durable Brand X.
3. To insulate the trade from consumer-price negotiation at the point-of-purchase.
4. To insulate the trade from a temporary sales reduction that might be caused by an increase in the price of Durable Brand X.
5. To compensate the trade when the traditional retail margins in a category have been eroded by price competition.
6. To identify which items in the Durable Brand X product line a dealer should push during particular periods.
7. To motivate the sales force to devote more effort to a particular line or brand.

Competitor Objectives

1. To move offensively or defensively on a temporary basis against one or more competitors of Durable Brand X.
2. To temporarily narrow the price gap between Durable Brand X and lower-priced competitive brands.
3. To load the trade with inventory in advance of a competitive new product launch.

Company Objectives: Brand Development

1. To increase awareness of Durable Brand X.
2. To communicate the distinctive benefits of Durable Brand X.
3. To reinforce Durable Brand X advertising and increase advertising readership (when promotion is advertised).
4. To maintain awareness of Durable Brand X during an advertising hiatus (when promotion is not advertised).
5. To obtain market research information about Durable Brand X.
6. To present Durable Brand X as part of a line of products in a tie-in event.

TABLE 2 (continued)

7. To develop awareness and sales of a consumable upon which use of Durable Brand X depends and which is made by the same manufacturer.

Company Objectives: Demand Management

1. To motivate dealers to supply accurate forecasts of future sales for Durable Brand X by linking dealers' promotion incentives to their achievement of sell-through forecasts.
2. To smooth demand such that preplanned production levels can be maintained.
3. To flush dealer inventories at the end of a season or model year.
4. To reduce corporate vulnerability to the business cycle and the lower capacity utilization that can occur during a downturn.

□   Because durables turn more slowly than packaged goods, the role of promotion in helping to manage channel inventories is more important. For durable goods, promotions are often used to flush retail inventories at the end of a season, regardless of whether a model change has been instituted.

□   Compared to packaged goods, production of durables is more capital intensive and requires longer lead times. At the same time, consumer demand for durables is more sensitive to the business cycle. Several durables manufacturers use promotions to even out consumer demand, either with respect to seasons or business cycles.

□   Packaged-goods promotions often aim to either increase the package size or number of units purchased, or to accelerate purchase timing. While durables promotions can accelerate the timing of demand, the opportunity to persuade the consumer to purchase multiple units is rare. Like the packaged-goods manufacturer inducing the customer to buy a larger size, the durables manufacturer focuses on trading the consumer up to a model with more features.

□   Packaged-goods promotions often attempt to increase repeat purchases of the brand. For durable goods, the goal of eventually repurchasing the promoted product is also important, but there are other relevant aspects of repeat purchasing. These include the opportunity to sell consumables (such as film for cameras), accessories, and postpurchase services, as well as the potential for eventual purchase of another product under the same brand name. The strong brand names established in many durables categories fit well with this objective.

□   Unlike packaged-goods promotions, durables promotions emphasize generating store traffic. Most consumers visit a supermarket every week, but visits to durables dealers are not routine. Manufacturers, therefore, have to work with retailers to generate traffic in the first place, in addition to promoting their particular brands once consumers are in the store. To cement manufacturer-dealer relationships and achieve these objectives, many promotion programs are cooperatively funded.

□   Once a consumer is interested in acquiring a packaged good, the financial risk is minimal. The risk of acquiring a durable is much higher. Consequently durables sales promotion includes addressing specific concerns such as handling a trade-in, service risk, and financing. Tactics have been developed by durables manufacturers to overcome the consumer's sense of risk.

☐   Offering salespeople incentives to close sales is especially important in durables retailing, because of both the salesperson's importance in consumer decision making and the consumer's tendency to comparison shop and postpone purchases.

Consumer-directed Promotions

As noted earlier, promotions directed at the consumer appear to be increasing in importance more quickly than those directed at the trade. We therefore discuss consumer promotions in more depth.

Two promotion techniques that packaged-goods marketers use have also proven effective in durables promotion: accessories and rebates. The accessories that durables manufacturers and dealers offer free or at a reduced price—for example, a free bag attachment with a lawnmower—are analogous to the gift-with-purchase and purchase-with-purchase premiums offered by cosmetics companies. The appeal of an accessory promotion over a straight price cut is that the advertisable retail value of the accessory is much greater than the manufacturer's actual cost. Unless the economic value of the accessory is relatively large, however, accessory promotions do not usually persuade a consumer to trade up to a model with a higher basic price. "Free" accessories are more likely to be tie breakers among competitive models within the consumer's selected price range.

Rebates are a more powerful promotion device for durables than for packaged goods. Because durables are more expensive, the absolute dollar value of a rebate can be correspondingly higher but still low in percentage-of-sales terms. Consumers find the effort involved in claiming a $50 rebate worthwhile relative to the value received. On the other hand, making out a form for a one-dollar refund on a packaged good hardly seems worth the bother to the average consumer.

Rebates are especially cost effective in categories where a high percentage of consumer purchases are gifts, because the proportion of claims will be correspondingly lower. In addition, manufacturer rebates involve minimal misredemption and the durables dealer does not have to handle and process claims. However, dealers now resist rebates that require cost sharing between manufacturer and dealer. Many consumers do not understand that dealers pick up part of the cost of a manufacturer's rebate, even when a manufacturer includes such a statement in rebate advertising. These consumers, therefore, expect to receive as good a deal from the retailer as they would have had there been no rebate.

A second group of promotion techniques—including financing incentives, trade-in allowances, service contracts, and finders' fees—is especially applicable to higher-ticket items and is not evident in packaged-goods marketing.

The first, financing incentives, is the most important. In response to the high interest rates of the late 1970s, durables manufacturers began to subsidize the interest costs on loans, thus enabling consumers to acquire high-ticket items that they would otherwise have been unable to purchase. Financing incentives are especially applicable to products like air conditioners that may be needed urgently and for which the consumer has not been saving in advance; products like home furnishings that would not otherwise be purchased at a particular time of year because consumer spending priorities are directed elsewhere; and products such as rider mowers—but not walking mowers—that cost more than the typical consumer's monthly credit card limit.

Manufacturers often prefer financing incentives, which spread the promotion cost over the life of a loan, to up-front cash rebates. For some companies, financing promotions also offer a strategic advantage. The more cars General Motors can finance through its financing subsidiary, General Motors Acceptance Corporation, the more it can even out its cash inflows and so reduce vulnerability to the business cycle. GMAC earns high returns on its assets and, by virtue of its size, can borrow more cheaply than the financing arms of other auto companies. Therefore, it can either offer lower financing rates than the others or make more money at matching rates.

A legitimate concern regarding financing promotions is their potential for attracting marginally qualified applicants who, if accepted, may later default on their loans. If, however, the promotional financing rate is set at or below the interest consumers can obtain from deposits in money market funds, good-quality consumers who would otherwise have paid cash can be attracted into the financing program.

Three other promotion techniques heavily used by packaged-goods marketers—couponing, sampling, and price/quantity promotions—are much less prominent in the durables manufacturer's promotion mix.

There has never been a tradition of couponing for consumer durables, and with good reason. First, the misredemption risks for high-value coupons on durables would be substantial. Second, the coupon redemption process would be a logistical and cash flow burden on the small specialty retailers that have traditionally sold durable goods. Third, in the absence of significant couponing, no redemption services are organized to link up with the multiple channels that sell different durable goods. However, manufacturers of durables with cascaded demand potential now pack time-release coupons for consumables needed for use with a durable product. Polaroid customers receive a series of coupons for instant film, each with a different expiration date, when they buy instant cameras; the coupons add value and encourage use.

The nondivisibility and cost of most durables makes sampling in trial sizes impossible. However, precisely because durables are not packaged, some—such as automobiles and television sets—can be tested before purchase. Apple Computer recently offered consumers a twenty-four-hour "test drive" of its Macintosh model to permit all family members to try the product at home.

Although volume rebate programs targeted at the trade are widely used by durables manufacturers, "Buy two, get one free" offers targeted at consumers are applicable only to those durables typically bought in multiple units, such as tires and shock absorbers. Price/quantity promotions are not relevant for durable goods owned on a one-per-household basis.

Matching Promotions and Products

So far, we have not distinguished among different types of durables. But the relative importance of different promotion objectives and the suitability of different types of promotion do vary by product category. At one end of the spectrum are packaged durables, such as small, low-ticket household appliances, often purchased as gifts. They are not complex, do not need extensive retail sales support and are, therefore, intensively distributed. The small appliance manufacturer's top priority is to secure chainwide distribution from the largest mass merchandisers for as many items in the product line as possible.

At the other end of the price spectrum are automobiles sold through exclusive dealerships. The auto manufacturer's key promotion objective is to generate dealer traffic. An automobile purchase requires the consumer not merely to decide when, where, and what model to buy, but also a myriad of other issues regarding options, service contracts, and financing. The sale of an automobile leads to cascaded demand for consumables (gasoline), accessories, and post-purchase service. The number of decisions involved in the purchase process, plus the financial risk, necessitate extensive salesperson involvement.

Between these two extremes are large appliances (such as refrigerators) and system purchases (such as personal computers or stereo systems) that require the consumer to make decisions on a package of several integrated items. A custom-designed system including components from several manufacturers is clearly more complex than the prepackaged stereo system that includes four pieces by the same manufacturer. These types of durables are usually selectively distributed through multiple-brand outlets. In such cases, a manufacturer's promotion objectives are to maximize its share of dealer floor space and to highlight and thus add value to its brand at the point-of-sale.

The applicability of short-term sales promotions—particularly consumer promotions—varies by type of durable depending on whether it is (a) a low- or high-ticket product, (b) an item or system purchase, or (c) a product that, once sold, generates cascaded demand. Table 3 shows which of 11 types of consumer promotions—based on a combination of our management interviews and judgment—we believe to be most applicable to eight specific consumer durables.

SALES PROMOTION PLANNING

Promotion planning is a multistage process involving corporate strategy and budgeting as well as the selection of promotion tactics.[14] A framework for this process is shown in Figure 1. For too long, promotion was the element of the marketing mix in which senior management was least involved. Rising promotion expenditures, however, have begun to attract senior management's attention. Increasingly, top management is taking the lead in identifying the role of sales promotion in over-

---

[14]T.A. Petit and M.R. McEnally, "Putting Strategy into Promotion Mix Decisions," *Journal of Consumer Marketing* (Winter 1985): 41–47.

TABLE 3 Applicability of consumer promotions by type of consumer durable

Price	Lower ticket (disposables)				Higher ticket (serviceables)			
Product type	Item		System		Item		System	
Cascaded demand	No	Yes	No	Yes	No	Yes	No	Yes
Example	Iron	Instamatic camera	Tires	Skis	Refrigerator	Automobile	Home security system	Personal computer
Rebates	□	□	□	□	□	□	□	□
Price/quantity/promotions	□		□					
Coupons	□	□	□					
Sweepstakes		□						□
Accessories/premiums		□		□				□
Testers/loaners/sample						□		□
Tie-in promotions		□	□	□				□
Trade-in allowances				□	□	□		□
Financing incentives					□	□		□
Service contracts					□	□		
Finders' fees							□	

FIGURE 1   A Framework for Planning Durable-Goods Promotion

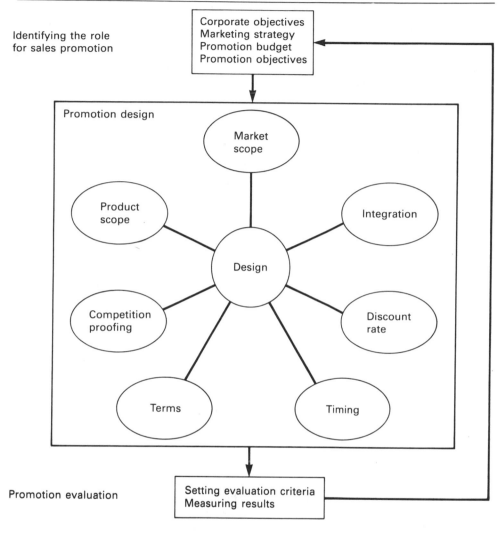

all marketing strategy. For example, in one company top executives stated that only promotions that genuinely increase demand, rather than merely pull it forward, are acceptable. At another company, senior managers are sanctioning increased promotion spending to boost market share as fast as possible.

Once the strategic role of promotion is determined, management will be in a position to set the appropriate level of the promotion budget in total and vis-à-vis the advertising budget. Often the driving force behind this allocation will be the marketing environment faced by the firm. One study found that the determinants of the promotion-to-sales ratio for durable marketers were positively related to the number of competitors in a market, the market share of a company's three largest competitors, the length of time between purchases, the level of new product activity, and the importance of the product to trade customers as a percentage of their total purchases.[15]

Once the overall promotion budget is set, it must be allocated in a balanced fashion among various promotion objectives (see Table 2). In most companies, this allocation reflects a bottom-up rather than top-down planning process. Individual product managers set their promotion objectives and develop a schedule of events for their products. Compromises among individual managers are then negotiated to ensure that the sales force does not have too many promotions to present to the trade in one quarter and not enough in another. The company's overall promotion plan is summarized in a promotion calendar showing which products will be promoted, when they will be promoted, in which markets, with what objectives, using which techniques, and on what terms. This planning process ensures variety, internal consistency, and synergy, and it reduces the chances of a single promotion event being assigned too many objectives.

Promotion Design

Most companies rely not on one but on several promotions during any planning cycle. Yet each event must be carefully designed, taking into account the objectives and budgets developed earlier. Figure 1 identifies seven elements of the design task.

Product scope.   Product scope refers to the range of sizes, models, and products to which a particular promotion offer should be extended. The complexity of the product-scope decision is directly related to the number of units under the brand umbrella. For example, the Hartmann Luggage Company manufactures a multitude of hard-sided and soft-sided luggage items. Most items are made in each of four fabrics (representing different price points) and in both men's and women's styles. Should Hartmann promote the entire line, the higher or the lower price points, the more or less popular items? Should all items in a single fabric line, or a single item across all four fabrics, be promoted at the same time? Or is the Hartmann brand name and quality image such that promotions on "in-line" merchandise should be avoided altogether and promotions run only on "out-of-line" merchandise specially made for that purpose?

This level of complexity is common among durables manufacturers, because they typically market many models of many product types under the same brand umbrella. By contrast, the product-scope issue for the Procter & Gamble brand manager is simply whether to offer a promotion on one, two, or three sizes of the brand.

In the case of high-ticket products, consumers who purchase less expensive models tend to be more price- and deal-sensitive. Thus, some product managers selectively promote the smaller models in their brand lines in the hope of attracting new category buyers whose loyalty can, they hope, be retained on subsequent replacement

---

[15]Quelch, Marshall, and Chang, op. cit.

purchases. Others selectively promote their weaker models to build dealer traffic in the expectation that some consumers will then trade up to more expensive models. Still others favor promoting higher-priced models since the advertising will give the brand as a whole a better image. In addition, promoting higher-priced models can persuade dealers to adjust their product mixes upward, so that they and the manufacturer achieve a higher average unit margin.

Different types of promotion are usually applicable to different models in a product line. For example, major appliance manufacturers find that rebates are more effective on higher- than lower-priced models. First, a larger rebate in absolute dollar terms can be offered. Second, the purchaser of a higher-priced model can afford to pay the full price and does not object to waiting for a rebate, whereas the purchaser of a lower-priced model usually prefers immediate cash savings.

Market scope.   Should the same promotion program be offered in all market areas? Not when a brand's market share, competitive activity, retail environment, consumer demand patterns, or responsiveness to particular promotion offers vary from one market area to another. Toro, for example, permits its dealers to customize their lawnmower promotion programs because of regional climate differences that affect the timing of consumer demand, variations in consumer model preferences by region, and the fragmentation of the distribution structure. A further argument for regional promotions is that a national promotion calendar can be quickly uncovered and selectively matched or beaten by competitors.[16]

Many companies develop promotion calendars that include a combination of national and regional promotions. Promotions often need to be tailored not only by geographic region, but also by consumer segment and channel type. The effectiveness of different promotion techniques can vary according to where consumers shop, whether they are comparison or one-shop shoppers, whether they make planned or impulse purchases, what information sources they consult before buying, and whether they are first-time or replacement buyers.

In addition, although any promotion must be offered to all trade accounts in a market area, differences among classes of trade and even among key accounts require durables marketers, especially those selling in multiple nonexclusive channels, to customize their promotion plans. Channels and accounts differ in their marketing strategies, inventory buying patterns, buyer evaluation criteria, and in how they decide which product lines need special merchandising support.

Integration.   To maximize effectiveness, promotions targeting the trade should be run concurrently with consumer promotions. Even greater impact is likely to result if advertising incorporates the consumer promotion (such as a financing or rebate offer) and if a special incentive program is offered to the sales force. When the product is at once pulled and pushed through the distribution channel, trade buyers tend to increase their purchases and to schedule special merchandising support. Indeed, support may be given in response to a less attractive trade incentive than would otherwise be needed if it coincides with an attractive consumer promotion.

[16]"Greater Profitability Found in Local Market Promotion," *Marketing News,* 21 June 1985, p. 22.

For example, manufacturers increasingly are offering consumers certificates toward the purchase of additional products at the dealership where the original purchase was made. Because the manufacturer rebate adds to the dealer's business, the latter has more incentive to support the promotion. Similarly, a manufacturer may simultaneously run a widely advertised cash rebate built around a seasonal theme relevant to store merchandisers, offer an off-invoice purchase allowance, and distribute specially designed displays and point-of-sale materials to attract consumer attention and stimulate retail support.

In addition to being integrated among themselves, promotions also need to be linked with advertising. Any communication included in the promotion should reinforce the messages delivered in the brand's advertising.[17]

Discount rate.   In setting the discount rate for a promotion, a manufacturer must consider the competitive set the promoted product will be compared to at the promoted price and the resulting impact on brand image. Market-share leaders can offer smaller discounts than followers and still achieve the same consumer response. Moreover, deep discounts are less often profitable for leaders, because they must secure enough incremental sales to cover the margin loss from consumers who would have purchased at full price had there been no promotion. Although the proportional required increase in sales is usually the same for large and small brands, the large-share brand needs higher absolute numbers. For example, a "twenty-share" brand will have more difficulty doubling sales than a "five-share" brand.

Some promotions, such as financing incentives, offer a delayed benefit to the consumer, whereas cash rebates offer an immediate benefit. Consumer response functions often vary by type of promotion and are not usually linear; a 20% reduction, for example, will not typically generate twice the additional sales of a 10% discount.

Consumer response to two promotion offers of the same value may also vary according to how they are packaged. A financing incentive, for example, can be offered in several ways. First, a lower interest rate can be offered. Second, the repayment period can be extended. Both of these approaches lower the monthly payment over the life of the loan. Research indicates that the monthly payment heavily affects consumer willingness to finance new durables purchases. A third option is for the manufacturer to absorb the first several months' payments. The durables manufacturer can elect to use whichever option best addresses the preferences of its target consumers.

Timing.   Timing issues include when to promote, how often to promote, and how long to promote. Promotions should be offered when trade inventories of the product category, brand, or specific models are either (a) below normal, the objective of the promotion then being to build inventories, or (b) above normal, the objective then being to flush them. Retaliatory promotions closely following a competitor's are often unprofitable because trade pipelines are still loaded with the inventory

---

[17]P.R. Varadarajan, "Joint Sales Promotion: An Emerging Marketing Tool," *Business Horizons,* September–October 1985, pp. 43–49.

of the competing brand. Similarly, if a manufacturer runs two promotions in rapid succession, the second will generally be unprofitable even if it offers a higher discount rate, because trade inventory increases in response to the first deal will not have been worked down.

The timing and frequency of promotions on durables sold through mass merchandisers are strongly influenced by both trade and product management planning cycles. First, most major chains have two open-to-buy periods per year for durables, when they determine the items they will stock, place their orders, and plan their merchandise calendars. Hence, product managers must inform major trade accounts of their promotion plans well in advance to stand a chance of getting on retail merchandise calendars. Second, to avoid confusion in the trade, the effective periods of different deals on the same product should not overlap. Third, since many product managers are evaluated against quarterly sales projections, they plan at least one promotion each quarter. Finally, as product managers take a more strategic approach to promotion management and as tie-in promotions involving multiple models, product lines, and brands grow in popularity, advance planning of the timing of promotions and early notification of the sales force become necessary.

Many durables are subject to seasonal consumer demand induced by climatic conditions, the timing of annual model changes, and peaks in gift purchases. Manufacturers must develop promotion objectives and programs for each season of the year. Table 4 summarizes the seasonal promotion objectives for Toro snowthrowers. Toro recently ran two highly successful preseason promotions. The first offered a $50 rebate on a trade-in model. Because the promotion was preseason, it gave a dealer the opportunity to recondition and resell the trade-in at a profit that same season. The second promotion, known as SnoRisk, addressed a major consumer objection to early buying by guaranteeing preseason purchasers rebates according to the degree to which snowfall in their areas fell short of the ten-year average.

Some managers believe that a durables manufacturer with excess capacity should always have a promotion on at least one model in a product line. There

TABLE 4 Toro snowthrower promotion objectives by season

Time	Promotion objective(s)
Off-season	☐ Maintain category interest ☐ Even out demand
Pre-season	☐ Persuade consumers to plan and purchase ahead of knowing level of snowfall ☐ Convert pre-season service customers to purchase new models
In-season	☐ Adjust promotion intensity according to snowfall ☐ Trade up buyer to higher priced models from price impression models
Post-season	☐ Flush excess dealer inventories

are two reasons for this. First, nonexclusive retail accounts will have more reason to push the manufacturer's line to the consumer. Second, consumers are so infrequently in the market for specifc durables that the manufacturer will risk forgoing the promotion-sensitive segment entirely whenever a promotion is not being offered. The packaged-goods product manager can always hope to attract such consumers on the next purchase occasion in a couple of weeks, whereas the durables product manager may have to wait years to get another crack at them. In addition, because the interpurchase interval and consumer search times for more complex durables are longer, there is a need for longer offers to ensure that the maximum number of customers is exposed.

Terms.   The terms of any promotion offer can greatly influence the financial exposure of the durables manufacturer. Small-appliance manufacturers, for example, offer rebates during peak gift-giving periods. If the requirements to claim the rebate include the purchase receipt, application form, *and* a decal from the package, it is less likely that either giver or recipient will have all the documentation. Because of high slippage rates, manufacturers can offer proportionately more attractive rebates at the point-of-sale.

Likewise, in designing their low-interest financing programs, the auto manufacturers usually state that qualifying vehicles must be delivered by a date shortly after the end of the promotion period. Given lead times on filling customer orders, the effect of this restriction is to limit the promotion to vehicles already on dealer lots and so flush their inventories.

Consumer promotions increasingly offer multiple options to cater to the promotion preferences of different consumer segments. Chrysler, for example, has offered consumers the choice of low-interest financing *or* a cash rebate. Trade promotions also now offer options that respond to the preferences of different classes of trade.

Competition proofing.   Promotions should provide a unique and enduring competitive advantage. Most promotions are easily imitated, but sometimes it is possible to develop a promotion that is too complex to imitate quickly but not so complicated that ease of consumer understanding is jeopardized. Toro's creative SnoRisk promotion could not be matched until the following year by Toro's competitors and, as a result, Toro's sales in the SnoRisk season were 30% ahead of projections.

A second approach to competition proofing is to arrange an exclusive tie-in promotion with another firm that cannot be directly copied. A third method is to emphasize a promotion vehicle for the delivery of which a manufacturer enjoys a sustained financial advantage, as, for example, GMAC does in the delivery of auto financing incentives.

Promotion Evaluation

Managers should consider promotion evaluation an integral part of the planning process. Evaluation criteria should be set in advance and preliminary calculations made during the design stage to determine whether the promotion could possibly achieve these criteria. After the promotion is executed, it should be evaluated according to these criteria; the knowledge gained from the experience will help more effective planning of future promotions.

As an example of deriving evaluation criteria, consider the following case. A major appliance manufacturer is considering a trade promotion for the fall season. The promotion will involve a discount to retailers plus cooperative advertising money. Let:

D = size of discount per unit, in \$;

M = gross manufacturer margin per unit, in \$;

C = amount spent on cooperative advertising;

X = normal number of units sold during the fall season; and

Y = number of units that will be sold if promotion is implemented.

Without promotion, manufacturer profits will equal XM. With the promotion, profits will be $Y(M - D) - C$. In order for the promotion to break even, or do better, we can set $Y(M - D) - C \geq XM$, and solve for Y/X, yielding:

$$\frac{Y}{X} \geq \left(1 + \frac{C}{XM}\right)\left(\frac{M}{M - D}\right)$$

The inequality shows the percentage increase in sales needed in order for the promotion to be profitable. For example, if normal fall sales were 5,000 units, each with a margin of \$200, and the manufacturer offered a \$60 discount to dealers and anticipated spending \$100,000 in cooperative advertising, we would require:

$$\frac{Y}{X} = \frac{Y}{5000} \geq \left(1 + \frac{100,000}{(5000)(200)}\right)\left(\frac{200}{200 - 60}\right) = 1.57$$

In order for the promotion to be profitable, we would now have to sell 7,857 units rather than 5,000, a 57% increase. If this seemed infeasible, the manufacturer could cut the discount rate or the cooperative advertising. If the decision is made to go forward with the promotion, an evaluation criterion (increase of 2,857 units) has been set up as a benchmark.

Running the actual evaluation involves careful monitoring of sales shipped on deal. It may also be necessary to use a statistical model to calculate incremental sales. Sometimes, sales and profit will not be the appropriate evaluation criteria. Other criteria, such as share of selling floor space or percentage of dealers carrying the full line, might be relevant.

FACING THE CHALLENGE

Sales promotions offer durable-goods manufacturers a versatile tool for achieving the many objectives listed in Table 2. However, as we noted at the outset, there are several legitimate concerns manufacturers have about using this tool. The challenge is to use promotions in a way that maximizes the benefits while mitigating the concerns. We conclude by suggesting ways that the two major problems noted earlier can be addressed.

The first is that sales promotions absorb dollars from franchise-building advertising. One way to address this issue is to apply strict payback criteria to promotions. In this way, the promotion "pays its own way." Senior management must offer product managers the carrot of flexibility in marketing budgets, subject to the stick of strict accountability for sales promotion productivity.

Another way to address the issue is to tie in promotions with advertising activity. For example, point-of-purchase material for a special display should emphasize the same themes and spokespeople found in advertising. There is some evidence that delivering promotions such as coupons and rebate offers in advertisements can make the advertising more effective.[18]

A second major concern is that promotion expenditures draw manufacturers into price wars that lower industry profits. Again, one key to addressing this issue is to plan and evaluate. The planning effort should include anticipating competitive response and competition-proofing promotions. Another key is understanding the role of promotions for the brand so that one can more accurately anticipate the consequences of any increase or decrease in promotion efforts. General Electric tried to withdraw rebates on irons and toaster ovens in 1983, putting the savings into price reductions and increased advertising. Towle cut promotion allowances and rolled back list prices proportionately on its silver flatware. Both manufacturers lost market share for two reasons. First, competitors did not follow; instead, they promoted more aggresively than ever. Second, on infrequently purchased items, consumers often use suggested retail prices as a quality indicator when comparing brands.

A second, more challenging, and longer-term way to avoid promotion wars is to develop new products that are truly differentiated and are therefore not seen by consumers as part of a commodity group. General Electric's electronic dishwashers and the Black and Decker Spacemaker line of under-the-cabinet kitchen appliances are good examples, providing unit margins far above those on comparable electromechanical and countertop models. The point here is that sales promotion has its proper role in the marketing mix, but sales promotion functions best as one aspect of a strong overall strategy.

In summary, there is no simple prescription for using durable-goods promotions effectively. However, we have gained perspective from the packaged-goods industry and can draw on that experience appropriately in managing durable goods. In addition, there are many characteristics, which we have noted, that are particular to durable goods; these dictate specific opportunities and challenges.

---

[18]R. Bowman, *Couponing and Rebates: Profit on the Dotted Line* (New York: Lebhar-Friedman Books, 1980).

BLACK & DECKER CORPORATION: HOUSEHOLD PRODUCTS GROUP (A)

JOHN A. QUELCH
CYNTHIA A. BATES

In April 1984, Black & Decker Corp. (B&D) acquired the Housewares Division of General Electric Co. (GE), combining the GE small-appliance product line with its own household product line to form the Household Products Group. The terms of the acquisition set the stage for a unique marketing challenge. B&D was permitted to manufacture and market appliances carrying the GE name, but only until April 1987. During the intervening three years, B&D, therefore, had to replace the GE name with its own brand name on all the acquired GE models.

Kenneth Homa, vice president of marketing, was responsible for planning the details of the brand transition. These included determining the sequence in which the GE product lines should be transitioned and the roles that advertising, promotion, and merchandising should play in supporting the brand transition. By December, 1984, product plans and marketing budgets for 1985 had been set, but Homa wanted to review again B&D's mix of promotion and merchandising programs to ensure that resources were being allocated appropriately and to determine if any improvements could be made. He, therefore, called a meeting on December 10 with Ed May, vice president of sales, and Dave Lessard, director of merchandising and advertising, to discuss these issues.

THE ACQUISITION

With 1983 sales of $1,167 million, B&D was the leading worldwide manufacturer of professional and consumer hand-held power tools. Over 100 products were produced in 21 factories around the world. By the late 1970s, B&D was confronting two major problems—a slower growth rate for the power tool market worldwide and increasing foreign competition. At the same time, the company realized that the American housewares market presented a significant opportunity. Capitalizing on its expertise in small motor production[1] and cordless appliance technology, B&D introduced in 1979 the Dustbuster® rechargeable hand-held vacuum cleaner. The Dustbuster Vac "moved B&D from the garage into the house" and 60% of Dustbuster purchases were made by women. The Dustbuster's success prompted the launch of two other rechargeable products, the Spotliter™ rechargeable flashlight and the Scrub Brusher™ cordless scrubber. In 1983, these three products generated revenues of over $100 million, almost one-third of B&D's U.S. consumer product sales. Pretax profit margins on these products were estimated at a healthy 10%. Sales of the three products were expected to increase by 30% annually between 1983 and 1985.

Consumer demand for these three innovative products led B&D executives to conclude that further penetration of the housewares market could generate substantial sales and profits for the company. B&D executives resolved to develop a family of products that could address consumer needs "everywhere in the house, not just in the basement or garage." However, a significant impediment to growth was B&D's limited access to housewares buyers of the major retail chains. B&D's three housewares products were sold along with B&D's power tools through hardware distributors to hardware buyers and were typically stocked in the hardware sections of retail stores. The acquisition of an existing competitor in the housewares market promised to address this problem.

With 1983 sales of $500 million, GE's Housewares Division was the largest competitor in the U.S. electric housewares or small appliance market.[2] GE sold almost 150 models of products in 14 categories covering food preparation, ovening, garment care, personal care, and home security.[3] In all the appliance categories in which it competed, except food processors, hair care products, and toasters, GE ranked first or second in market share. GE's success was largely a result of continuing attention to product innovation. For example, the GE product line included the recently introduced Spacemaker™ series of premium-priced under-the-cabinet kitchen appliances.[4] The Division's 150-person sales force called on housewares buyers in all channels of distribution. At the same time, the Housewares Division accounted for only 2% of GE's total sales and 7% of consumer product sales. Compared to other GE consumer goods businesses, such as major appliances, the Housewares Division's returns on sales and investment were relatively low. Small

---

[1]In 1983, B&D produced 20 million small motors, four times as many as its closest competitor.

[2]GE sales of small appliances outside the United States were limited. By contrast, 40% of B&D's total sales were made in Europe.

[3]The categories were food processors, portable mixers, electric knives, can openers, drip coffeemakers, toaster ovens, toasters, electric skillets, grills and griddles, irons, hair dryers, curling brushes/irons, scales, and security alarms.

[4]The first Spacemaker appliance was a microwave oven introduced in the second half of 1983 by GE's Major Appliance Business Group.

appliances were relatively simple to produce and significant scale economies could not be realized.

Discussions between GE and B&D culminated in an agreement, announced in February, 1984, whereby B&D would acquire the Housewares Division for $110 million in cash, a $32 million three-year note, and 6% of B&D stock. In return, B&D acquired seven plants in the United States, Mexico, Brazil, and Singapore, five distribution centers, sixteen service centers and the Housewares Division's sales and management team. GE retained rights to the accounts receivable at the time of the transfer. Finally, B&D negotiated the right to continue to use the GE name on appliances in the Housewares Division product line for three years from the signing of the acquisition papers in April, 1984.[5] At a stroke, the acquisition transformed B&D from a specialist housewares manufacturer into the dominant full-line player in the housewares market.

THE HOUSEWARES MARKET

Product Lines and Pricing

GE participated in five broad housewares categories with aggregate industry sales of $1.4 billion divided as follows:[6]

Food preparation	$275 million
Beverage makers	$325 million
Ovening	$250 million
Garment care	$200 million
Personal care	$350 million

The housewares market was mature and fragmented. Industry growth depended primarily on the rate of household formation and the pace of new product development. About one-tenth of all small appliances in use were replaced each year. The timing of replacement purchases could be accelerated if manufacturers could persuade consumers to trade-up to more highly featured, higher prices, higher margin models of a particular appliance.

Following the acquisition, B&D offered one of the broadest lines of any manufacturer, competing in 17 product categories. Market performance data for the principal product lines are summarized in Exhibit 1. In all these categories, B&D marketed multiple models that covered almost all price points and product feature configurations. For example, the B&D line included 18 different irons with suggested retail prices from $14.76 to $25.89. The range included promotional, step-up, and premium models. Sunbeam, B&D's closest competitor in this category, offered 12 models.

B&D's models were priced competitively within each price-feature segment but, overall, B&D's share tended to be stronger in the medium- and upper- rather

[5]B&D could not use the GE name on any new appliances introduced after the acquisition.
[6]Sales of rechargeable vacuums and lights, scales and alarms were not included in this figure.

EXHIBIT 1 Market performance summary for selected product lines

Product	Year	GE/B&D unit share (%)	Feature ad share (%)	Trendex average retail price ($)	GE/B&D share rank in 1984	Major competitors (share and rank)		
Food processors	1983	16%	9%	$55.00	3	Cuisinart	25%	(1)
	1984	13	7	72.00		Hamilton Beach	21	(2)
	1985 (est)	15	8	n.a.		Moulinex	11	(4)
						Sunbeam	7	(5)
Mixers	1983	31	22	16.00	2	Sunbeam	28	(1)
	1984	26	20	15.40		Hamilton Beach	21	(3)
	1985 (est)	35	16	n.a.				
Can openers	1983	28	25	17.65	1	Rival	30	(2)
	1984	34	23	20.52		Sunbeam	8	(3)
	1985 (est)	30	26	n.a.		Hamilton Beach	6	(4)
Toasters	1983	13	16	16.63	3	Toastmaster	32	(1)
	1984	12	10	21.01		Proctor Silex	30	(2)
	1985 (est)	11	10	n.a.				
Toaster ovens	1983	56	49	45.51	1	Toastmaster	25	(2)
	1984	52	39	47.85		Proctor Silex	8	(3)
	1985 (est)	50	40	n.a.		Norelco	4	(4)
Drip coffeemakers	1983	17	13	34.48	2	Mr. Coffee	19	(1)
	1984	18	15	37.63		Norelco	17	(3)
	1985 (est)	17	16	n.a.		Hamilton Beach	9	(4)
						Proctor Silex	8	(5)

Category	1983	1984	1985 (est)						Brand		
Electric knives	39	37	39	n.a.	n.a.	n.a.	13.54	17.28	17.65	2	Hamilton Beach 47 (1)
											Moulinex 8 (3)
Irons	52	46	45	39	29	29	20.44	21.83	n.a.	1	Proctor Silex 18 (2)
											Sunbeam 13 (3)
											Hamilton Beach 11 (4)
Hair care	8	6	5	8	4	3	17.74	15.37	n.a.	4	Conair 22 (1)
											Clairol 12 (2)
											Sassoon 8 (3)
Cordless vacuums	n.a.	n.a.	n.a.	n.a.	38	38	n.a.	n.a.	25.70	1	Douglas 8 (2)
											Sears 8 (2)
											Norelco 7 (4)
Lighting products	65	57	38	n.a.	44	36	n.a.	n.a.	21.10	1	First Alert 25 (2)
											Sunspot 5 (3)
											Norelco 4 (4)

than the lower-price ranges. In the fall of 1984, the average retail price of a B&D small appliance was 16% higher than the average for non-B&D appliances.[7] The B&D retail price premium varied across product categories as follows:

Food preparation[8]	15%	Cleaning (Dustbuster)	10%
Ovening	26%	Lighting (Spotliter)	6%
Garment care	5%	Smoke alarms	9%
Personal care	16%		

Some B&D executives were concerned that the price umbrella in some categories left B&D vulnerable to lower-priced competition. They advocated price decreases on some models for 1985. Other executives, noting that B&D/GE housewares prices had increased on average by only 10% between 1980 and 1984, believed that price increases were necessary to maintain margins.[9] However, all agreed that despite B&D's share leadership position, competitive brands did not appear to set their prices in relation to B&D's prices.

B&D's price premium in the food preparation category was partly due to the premium-priced Spacemaker line of under-the-cabinet kitchen appliances. Launched in 1982 with a can opener, the Spacemaker line was expanded in 1983 to include a toaster oven, drip coffeemaker, mixer, and electric knife. The Spacemaker line attracted first-time purchasers into these five categories but, more important, persuaded current owners to trade up. While the Spacemaker line at first reversed GE's share erosion in these categories, lower-priced imitations were soon introduced. GE's standard countertop version of the Spacemaker appliances lost share as GE's competitors slashed prices to maintain their sales volumes in countertop models. Nevertheless, Spacemaker models were expected to account for about 40% of B&D/GE's 1984 unit sales in the five product categories they competed in.

Competition

B&D's principal competitors in the housewares market were Sunbeam (a subsidiary of Allegheny International), Proctor-Silex (Wesray), Hamilton-Beach (Scovill), and Norelco (Philips). Few offered as broad a line as B&D, but all four competed against B&D in at least six categories. In addition, B&D had to contend with specialty competitors in each product category. For example, Cuisinart was the market share leader in food processors as was Mr. Coffee in drip coffeemakers. European manufacturers such as Krups were increasingly penetrating and helping to expand the premium-price segment in some categories. Their higher-margin products were welcomed by department stores seeking ways to continue to compete with mass merchandisers in housewares. Japanese manufacturers were not a factor in the U.S. small-appliance market, except for small, dual-voltage travel irons.

---

[7]The value of consumer mail-in rebates was factored into this comparison.

[8]Coffeemakers and percolators were included with food preparation appliances in this calculation.

[9]The contribution margin on B&D small appliances, after variable costs, averaged 40%. The percentage margin was higher on premium models such as the Spacemaker products.

Following the acquisition announcement, B&D's housewares competitors saw the imminent demise of the strongest brand name in the housewares market as an opportunity to increase their market shares. Hence, prices on some existing models were reduced, price increases announced for 1985 were minimal, and promotional and merchandising allowances escalated. The timing of new product introductions was accelerated and, in some cases, manufacturers decided to enter new product categories. Norelco and West Bend, for example, both announced that they would launch a line of irons.

Sunbeam was especially aggressive, heavily advertising two new products in the fall of 1984, the Monitor automatic shut-off iron and the Oskar compact food processor. Both were introduced at premium rather than penetration price levels. In addition, Sunbeam announced a $43 million marketing budget for 1985, including $25 million for national advertising, $10 million for cooperative advertising, and $8 million for sales promotion. The 1985 budget was more than Sunbeam had spent in the previous five years combined.

In addition to competition from GE's long-standing competitors, B&D also had to contend with imitators of B&D's cordless vacuums and lights. Believing that the newly acquired product lines would divert management attention and resources, they redoubled their efforts to capture market share from B&D.

Distribution

Small electric appliances were distributed through a variety of channels. The following table shows the percentages of 1984 industry dollar sales accounted for by each of seven channels.

	Industry
Catalog showrooms	15%
Mass merchandisers	28
Department stores	9
Drug stores	6
Hardware stores	5
Discount stores	8
Other*	29

*Includes sales through stamp and incentive programs, premiums, and military sales.

Mass merchandisers, such as Montgomery Ward and discount stores, such as K mart had gained share in recent years, mainly at the expense of department stores. Catalog showrooms such as Service Merchandise carried the broadest line of small appliances whereas other channels tended to cherrypick the faster-moving items. GE had built a disproportionately strong share position with volume retailers, notably catalog showrooms and mass merchandisers. B&D was traditionally strong in hardware stores. In the fall of 1984, B&D accounts carried, on average, 30 B&D stockkeeping units (SKUs).[10]

[10]A stockkeeping unit was an individual model or item in the product line.

Small appliances were not viewed as especially profitable by most retailers. Retail margins averaged 15–20% though promotional merchandise was typically sold near cost. Hence, the space allocated to housewares by most chains remained stable, despite an increasing proliferation of new products. As a result, manufacturers were under more pressure than ever to secure shelf space through merchandising and promotion incentives.

Housewares and hardware buyers at B&D's major accounts determined twice a year which models they would specify as "basics." These selected models were carried in distribution for the following six months, usually in all the stores of a chain. Other models not specified as basics might occasionally be stocked but only in response to temporary promotion offers.

Basics were typically specified in January and May. Retail sales of small appliances peaked prior to Mother's Day and Christmas. Twenty-one percent of retail sales occurred in the first calendar quarter, 21% in the second, 17% in the third and 41% in the fourth. Manufacturers and retailers scheduled their advertising and promotion efforts accordingly.

Consumer Behavior

Consumers shopping for small appliances were often characterized as having low information needs, low-perceived interbrand differentiation and high price-sensitivity. A 1984 B&D survey concluded:

☐ Two out of three consumers bought their last housewares appliance on sale and/or with a rebate. The highest percentages of products bought on sale were countertop drip coffeemakers, mixers, and can openers.

☐ Two out of three consumers compared the prices of different brands and checked to see which brands were on sale.

☐ Fewer than one out of three consumers was willing to wait until a specific brand went on sale.

☐ Almost three out of four consumers were willing to switch from their current brands when they purchased replacements. However, fewer than one out of four consumers were indifferent to brand names.

A follow-up study of buying behavior for irons found that most consumers, when they needed a replacement, would not wait for a sale but would check to see if a store sale was on. Fifty percent bought a replacement within seven days. Only 10% of irons were bought as gifts.[11] Forty-two percent of purchasers had a specific brand in mind when they set off for the store, and 85% of these ended up buying that brand. Thirty-eight percent were attracted to a particular store by a store advertisement, and most bought in the first store they shopped. Half of all purchasers bought their irons on sale and/or with a rebate.

---

[11]The percentage bought as gifts, and therefore the seasonality of retail sales, varied widely from one product category to another. Gift purchases of food processors, for example, accounted for 40% of sales.

PLANNING THE BRAND TRANSITION

Once the acquisition was completed, the principal challenge facing B&D executives was determining how to transfer the B&D name to the GE small-appliance line without losing market share. One group argued that the name change should be executed across the entire product line as soon as possible to demonstrate B&D's commitment to the trade. At the other extreme, a second group, skeptical about the likely pulling power of the B&D brand in housewares compared to the GE name, proposed that B&D should delay the name transfer until the end of the three-year period. Other executives supported a gradual transition whereby all the items in one or two product categories would be reintroduced under the B&D name in successive six-month periods. A further option was to execute the name change first on the premium quality items in several product categories, to be followed later by the remaining lower-priced items in each product line. One manager argued that the transition schedule should be linked to a new product development program, and the name change would only be implemented in a category after the product line and packaging had been redesigned and/or when B&D could offer a new product with enhanced features.

Consumer Research

To aid transition planning, B&D surveyed 600 men and women, 18 to 49 years old, in four geographically representative cities during July, 1984. The survey first probed consumers' awareness of ten housewares manufacturers, their ownership of small appliances by each manufacturer and the degree to which their overall image ratings of each manufacturer were favorable or unfavorable. These results are summarized in Exhibit 2.

Next, respondents were asked to rate each manufacturer on a variety of attributes using a 100-point scale. Averaging all responses, the researchers identified

EXHIBIT 2   Consumer research on major housewares manufacturers

	Aided corporate awareness (%)	Product ownership (%)	Corporate image ranking	
			Men	Women
General Electric	100%	91%	2	1
Black & Decker	99	67	1	2
Mr. Coffee	99	51	4	5
Conair	79	43	9	8
Hamilton Beach	93	43	5	6
Norelco	98	54	3	4
Proctor-Silex	80	28	8	7
Rival	56	19	10	10
Sunbeam	96	48	6	3
Toastmaster	92	41	7	9

B&D's strengths and weaknesses compared to GE and to its main housewares competitors (GE excluded) as follows.

	Black & Decker advantage vs. closest competitor*	Black & Decker difference vs. GE
Black & Decker Strengths		
Has high quality workmanship	+24	+5
Makes durable products	+23	+4
Makes reliable products	+20	+1
Leader in making innovative products	+18	−7
Black & Decker Vulnerabilities		
Makes products that can be easily serviced	+7	−17
Makes products most people would consider buying	+7	−12
Makes attractive, good-looking products	+6	−8
Makes products that are generally priced lower	+5	−9
Makes products that are easily found	+2	−9

*Other than GE.

The survey asked respondents whether they currently perceived B&D favorably or unfavorably as a manufacturer of each of 16 products. The percentages answering "very favorably" on a four-point scale were:

Smoke alarms	62%	Irons	18%
Flashlights	60	Portable mixers	17
Vacuums	48	Toasters	17
Grills/griddles	29	Food processors	16
Electric knives	25	Coffeemakers	13
Can openers	24	Skillets	12
Scales	22	Curling irons	11
Toaster ovens	21	Hair dryers	9

Qualitative research indicated that consumers considered B&D a suitable manufacturer of these products, but they were largely unaware that B&D already participated in them.

1985 Product Plans

Since these data suggested that the difficulty of implementing the brand name transition varied by product category, B&D executives decided on a gradual transition. They weighed the difficulty of the task along with the sales and profits at risk in the transition of each category to determine the order. Exhibit 3 shows the sequence in which various GE product lines were scheduled to undergo the name change. A standard PERT chart involving 140 steps to be completed over 14 weeks was developed to facilitate the transition of each product category. Plans for 1985, announced at the October, 1984 Housewares Show, included the following.

☐ The B&D name would first be applied to GE's highly successful Spacemaker line of under-the-cabinet appliances. This would establish the B&D name in

EXHIBIT 3   Brand transition plan by product category

	January 1985	April 1985	January 1986	April 1986
Food preparation				
Food processors	1 Spacemaker	–	–	All others (2)
Portable mixers	1 cordless	–	–	All others (1)
Knives	1 Spacemaker	1 Spacemaker	–	All others (4)
Can openers	1 Spacemaker	1 Spacemaker	–	All others (3)
Drip coffeemakers	3 Spacemaker	2 countertop	All others (6)	–
Ovening				
Toaster ovens	1 Spacemaker	1 slant-front model	–	All others (7)
Toasters	–	–	–	All models (5)
Electric skillets	–	–	–	All models (3)
Grills/griddles	–	–	–	All models (3)
Garment care				
Irons	1 Stowaway	1 The Auto Shut-off	All others (16)	–
Personal care				
Hair dryers	2 Stowaway, 4 Black Tie	3 The Performers	–	All others (5)
Curling brush/irons	1 Stowaway	2 The Performers	–	All others (1)
Other				
Scales	–	–	All models (2)	–
Security alarms	–	–	All models (2)	–

five kitchen appliance categories and hopefully associate it, in the eyes of consumers and the trade, with leading-edge, premium-quality housewares. GE's Spacemaker appliances were redesigned by B&D to look sturdier and more compact, and the edges were rounded for additional safety.

☐   B&D also planned the transition of the hair care product line in 1985. GE's market share position in this category had been relatively weak. Because of its low profitability, some executives argued that the line should be discontinued. However, others argued that doing so would detract from B&D's efforts to establish itself as the dominant housewares manufacturer. In addition, one manager argued: "If we can make the transition work in hair care, we can make it work in all other product categories." To execute the transition, B&D planned to launch the Black Tie™ line of "men's grooming tools." Priced at a 15% price premium over the existing hair care line, they were to be positioned as gifts for men. The established line of GE hair care appliances would be relaunched as the B&D Performers.

☐   B&D announced a new subbrand in October, 1984, the Stowaway line of dual-voltage travel appliances. The line included a folding iron, hair dryer, and curling irons. Just as the Spacemaker trademark cut across several categories of kitchen appliances, the Stowaway line aimed to do the same for B&D in personal care appliances.

☐   B&D planned to launch, in January, 1985, the first extension of its cordless technology to a kitchen appliance—the Handymixer™ cordless beater.

☐   An automatic shut-off iron introduced under the GE brand in the fall of 1984 was expected to become one of B&D/GE's top-selling models. However, it was quickly matched by Sunbeam, which promoted its version aggressively. Because the GE name was especially well established in irons, B&D had hoped to execute the transition of the iron product line later rather than sooner. Sunbeam's new product launch, however, required B&D to take action to avoid having its market position in irons preempted. Hence, B&D executives decided to accelerate the transition and announced the launch, for the spring of 1985, of a B&D automatic shut-off iron that would be marketed for its first year alongside the existing GE iron line.[12] One manager commented:

> We wanted to avoid dual branding in any category to prevent consumer confusion at the point-of-sale. In this case, though, we had no choice. We'll be placing transition hang tags on the B&D iron to explain its part of the GE line.

To convey the appearance of a product "family," all small appliances launched or relaunched under the B&D name were to be packaged in similar cartons carrying B&D's corporate colors, black and orange.[13] Lucite display fixtures were developed to carry the Spacemaker and Stowaway lines. They were to be offered free to trade accounts that carried the full subbrand line and ran qualifying feature advertisements during peak retail selling periods. B&D contracted with a detailing organization to set up and replenish these displays, and ensure they were used for B&D products.[14] Finally, to emphasize B&D's commitment to quality and service, management had decided that all B&D brand housewares, whether new products or relaunches, should carry a two-year warranty, double the industry standard one-year warranty GE had offered.

Advertising

Exhibits 4 and 5 summarize the advertising, promotion, and merchandising expenditures for GE's housewares and B&D's household products for 1983 and 1984. Details of the 1985 plan are also provided. Increased expenditures in 1985 were believed necessary to bolster consumer brand loyalties in the face of more aggressive competition. Sales for GE housewares were expected to increase only slightly in 1985 over 1984 levels.

Historically, GE housewares had benefited from advertising for other GE products. In 1984, the GE consumer businesses in total spent $40 million on media advertising, including $25 million on the corporate "We bring good things to life" campaign. B&D's announced media expenditures for the brand transition campaign were $100 million.

With the launch of several B&D appliances near at hand, the issue of how to handle the brand transition in advertising was still debated. Some executives

[12]Unlike the Sunbeam model, this B&D iron beeped to let the consumer know it had been left on.

[13]Fortunately for B&D, consumer research indicated that the color black was especially associated with a "high-tech" image.

[14]B&D expected to place 9,000 displays, each costing $125, by the end of 1985.

EXHIBIT 4 Advertising and merchandising expenditures for GE housewares
(percentage of net sales billed)

	1983	1984	1985 (est.)
Push programs			
Flexible funds (off-invoice)	3.5%	4.5%	–
Retail incentive plan*	2.8	2.9	2.5%
Cash discounts	–	–	–
Subtotal	6.3	7.4	2.5
Pull programs			
National advertising	1.7	3.3	6.8
Co-op advertising	5.2	5.1	5.4
Consumer rebates	2.6	1.9	3.0
Consumer promotions	0.3	0.2	0.1
Sales promotion materials	0.6	0.3	0.7
Press relations	0.2	0.2	0.2
Exhibits	0.2	0.2	0.2
Functional support expenses	0.3	0.3	0.4
Corporate promotion assessment	–	–	–
Basics plus†	–	–	1.0
In-store merchandising	–	–	0.7
Subtotal	11.1	11.5	18.5
Total merchandising expenditures	17.4	18.9	21.0

Note: 1984 and 1985 figures continue to separate the former GE housewares line from the former B&D household products line for ease of comparison. Total 1985 B&D Household Products Group expenditures can be calculated by using the last columns in Exhibits 4 and 5.

*Includes volume rebate and volume plus programs.

†Includes advertising promotion costs and program administration. Costs of basics plus media advertising are included in co-op advertising above.

believed that B&D should focus its advertising on innovative flagship products that offered the consumer distinctive benefits. Advertising for new product lines such as the Stowaway and Black Tie series would, of course, include no reference to GE. Transition products like the Spacemaker line would also include no reference to GE, but could temporarily carry the tag "now by B&D" before eventually being referred to as "the B&D Spacemaker line." However, B&D's advertising agency argued against any tag lines. Exhibit 6 shows a proposed 1985 television advertisement for the Spacemaker line, and Exhibit 7 shows a proposed 1985 Spotliter advertisement that represented a continuation of the 1984 campaign.

Other executives believed that explicit references to GE in B&D's advertising were necessary to maintain market share during the transition, especially in those categories where GE's brand name equity was strong. An immediate problem of this nature was how to present the new B&D automatic shut-off iron. One manager argued that if sales of the GE models were to be helped by this innovation, a transition statement such as "designed by GE, built by B&D" would have to be included in

EXHIBIT 5   Advertising and merchandising expenditures for Black & Decker household products* (percentage of net sales billed)

	1983	1984	1985 (est.)
Push programs			
Flexible funds (off-invoice)	–	–	–
Retail incentive plan	–	–	0.6
Cash discounts	0.9	0.9	0.9
Subtotal	0.9	0.9	1.5
Pull programs			
National advertising	8.9	9.2	11.0
Co-op advertising	2.0	2.4	4.3
Consumer rebates	–	1.7	6.9
Consumer promotions	–	–	–
Sales promotion materials	–	1.2	0.8
Press relations	–	–	–
Exhibits	–	0.1	0.2
Functional support expenses	–	0.1	0.2
Corporate promotion assessment	–	0.8	1.2
Basics plus	–	–	–
In-store merchandising	–	–	–
Subtotal	11.4	15.5	24.6
Total merchandising expenditures	12.3	16.4	26.1

*Dustbuster Vac, Spotliter, and Scrub Brusher.

advertising and on hang-tags at the point-of-purchase. Critics of this approach argued that it would confuse consumers and simply sustain the GE franchise.

Apart from the content of the advertising, there was also debate regarding how much, if any, of the national advertising budget should be allocated to corporate-type advertisements for the entire Household Products line, to advertisements for subbrands such as Spacemaker, and to advertisements for specific product lines or models. In addition, discussions continued about how much national advertising support should be given to those lines that still carried the GE name.

MERCHANDISING AND PROMOTION PROGRAMS

To explain the acquisition to the trade, B&D's CEO addressed a special meeting in Chicago in February, 1984 to which the presidents of 200 key accounts were invited. This was followed by meetings with key retail buyers at the March, 1984 Housewares Show and the development of a monthly transition newsletter for retail buyers.

However, despite assurances to the contrary, some trade accounts remained concerned that GE's merchandising programs, which were regarded as more generous than B&D's, would be curtailed. Competitive housewares manufacturers did all

EXHIBIT 6   Proposed 1985 Spacemaker advertisement

(SFX: TRAFFIC)
ANNCR: (VO) One of the most densely
populated places on earth

is your kitchen counter. So crowded, the
only place to go is up.

Presenting Black & Decker Spacemaker
Appliances.

Coffeemaker,

mixer,

toaster oven,

electric knife

and can opener. The only completely
coordinated line of under-the-cabinet
appliances.

(SFX: BIRDS CHIRPING)
They return your counter

to a more natural state.

The Spacemaker line

from Black & Decker. Ideas at work.

EXHIBIT 7 Proposed 1985 Spotliter advertisement

(SFX: Electronic High Tension)
ANNCR: (VO) It splits the dark with a powerful beam.

Spotliter rechargeable light from Black & Decker.

A light built so strong

it can survive a drop of 6 feet.

Spotliter stores all the power you need in its own recharging base.

So on a moment's notice

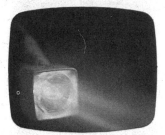

It gives you light.

Light for your safety. . .and peace of mind.

It's one utility light that does more than just shine.

Spotliter.

One of the many lights

in the lighting series. From Black & Decker. Ideas at work.

they could to cultivate this concern in an effort to secure additional basics listings and shelf space for their own products.

There were program differences. For example, B&D offered a 2% cash discount, GE did not. GE offered a volume rebate, B&D did not. There were three reasons for the differences. First, B&D's merchandising programs were tailored to hardware rather than housewares buyers. Almost by historical accident, different programs were common to different product categories. Second, B&D's housewares products, notably the Dustbuster Vac, had been on allocation to the trade because consumer demand exceeded supply. Hence, there was less need for generous merchandising programs and consumer promotions.

Third, the different merchandising programs reflected different distribution systems. Eighty percent of B&D's shipments were made from a single distribution center to the warehouses of major chains, and B&D charged higher unit prices for an order less than a pallet quantity.[15] In contrast, 80% of GE housewares were shipped from five distribution centers direct to individual retail outlets, supposedly because of their low bulk-to-value ratio.

The following sections discuss each of the major merchandising and promotion programs that B&D inherited. For competitive reasons, it was not possible in most cases to make substantial changes in 1984. However, B&D executives wished to reevaluate these programs for 1985. As previously noted, Exhibits 4 and 5 summarize 1983, 1984, and anticipated 1985 expenditures on a variety of merchandising and promotion programs for GE housewares and, separately, for B&D's three housewares products.

Purchase Allowances and Flexible Funds

During the 1970s, GE had initiated purchase allowances (PAs) on selected models against orders paid for during the first two months after Christmas and Mother's Day, the peak retail selling periods. Over time, PAs came to be offered on orders placed beyond these two-month periods. By 1983, 90% of shipments included an off-invoice PA. One executive commented:

> PAs were originally seen as a flexible tool to adjust our price premium over competition on selected models. However, because the price gaps between different models in any one of our product lines are so narrow, a PA on one model could quickly disrupt the pricing structure of the whole line. As a result, PAs quickly spread to other models and the trade began to regard them as an entitlement.

In 1984, GE replaced PAs with a new flexible funds (FF) program in order to add merchandising performance requirements to its off-invoice allowances. Under the FF program, two-thirds of the allowances were deducted from the invoice when an account placed an early order during one of the two two-month periods. The remaining third was paid if and when the account ran a feature advertisement for the product during the subsequent peak retail selling period.

---

[15]Equivalent to 288 Dustbuster Vacs.

As a result of these restrictions, the percentage of shipments qualifying for FF allowances fell from 90% to 60% during the first half of 1984. The sales force expressed concern and the clerical cost of checking account compliance with the feature advertising requirement proved onerous. Hence, the FF program for the second half of 1984 permitted an account to receive all of its funds off-invoice at the time of the order if the account promised to run a feature advertisement for the product later. The percentage of shipments qualifying returned to 90%.

Management, however, was not satisfied. B&D executives were considering discontinuing the FF program in 1985 and passing through the allowances in the form of a proportionate reduction in manufacturer list prices. On some models, higher prices were scheduled for early 1985 so, in these cases, the equivalent of the FF allowances would be used to cushion price increases rather than permit price reductions.

Volume Rebates

GE operated a Volume Rebate Program (VRP) that offered trade accounts a year-end refund of up to 4 % of their net purchases during the year. In 1983, this program cost the Housewares Division 2.9% of sales. One executive explained the origins of the program:

> After the end of fair trade in 1973, retailers began using GE small appliances as traffic builders because of the pulling power of the GE name.[16] Price competition among outlets reduced each retailer's unit margin. GE initiated the VRP to reward those accounts that continued to sell large quantities of GE small appliances rather than encouraging their customers to switch to other higher margin brands.
>
> In addition, the VRP was preferred over simple cash discounts by many retail buyers because they could apply year-end rebates, but not discounts, to the profit margin figures on which they were evaluated. They could always count on their year-end rebate checks no matter how close their retail selling prices were to cost.

GE's VRP was not computed on the basis of total GE shipments to an account but on GE's shipments to each of the 20,000 stores that carried GE's small appliances. To qualify for the minimum volume rebate, a store had to take shipment of at least $7,000 worth of small appliances over 12 months. For legal reasons, GE was concerned that all breaks in the quantity discount schedule be cost justified and that even small accounts be able to qualify for some level of rebate.[17] As a result, many large accounts were easily able to qualify for the maximum $4\frac{1}{2}$% rebate.

Early in 1984, GE resolved to attach performance requirements to the VRP. One executive commented on the implementation of this kind of change:

> In my view, it's a good idea to change a merchandising program every couple of years. If you keep the same program in place for too long, the trade buyers figure out how

---

[16]The end of fair trade meant that manufacturers could no longer require their trade accounts to maintain particular retail prices for their goods.

[17]For similar reasons, GE shipped any order over $500 freight prepaid.

to make it work for them rather than you. And when you make a change, it's easier to launch a new program under a new name rather than attempting to explain why you're modifying an existing program.

B&D worked with managers from the acquired GE Housewares Division to formulate a new Growth Rebate Program (GRP). Under this program, each account qualified for various percentage rebates according to the degree to which its purchases increased over those of the previous year. There were two other features of the GRP. First, it was computed on an account's total purchases rather than separately for each shipping point. Second, it attempted to maintain the total number of SKUs by requiring a dealer to have incremental sales in four of six defined product groups to earn the maximum rebate.

Following the acquisition, B&D was especially concerned about holding its share of shelf space and feature advertisements during the 1984 Christmas season. One B&D marketing manager commented:

> We needed an exciting, innovative program that could be run on a one-shot basis without the trade feeling that they were entitled to a repeat the following year.

The result was the Basics Plus Program (BPP) whereby B&D focused $3 million against the 175 accounts that represented 85% of B&D's housewares business. To qualify, an account had to agree to carry at least the same number of GE SKUs in its basics line-up for the second half of 1984 as it had in the second half of 1983.[18] Each qualifying account then received an allocation of the $3 million according to its relative 1983 GE housewares purchases to buy spot television advertising time between September and December 1984. Each spot included eight-second vignettes on three GE small appliances with the remaining six seconds being used for the store tag line.[19] B&D sales executives developed a proposed media schedule for each account though the accounts themselves made the final decision on which spots they wanted to run and in which markets. An additional clause in the BPP offered each account 5% more spots than its initial allotment for each extra SKU it added to its 1984 basics over 1983, up to a maximum of 50%.

The BPP was well received. Almost all 175 accounts participated. The average account increased its basics SKU count by 5%. A total of 20,000 television spots were run. Many larger chains that had been pressing B&D for cooperative broadcast advertising funds especially welcomed the BPP and ran extra feature advertisements for B&D/GE products in their store flyers to tie in with the television spots. Only two problems emerged. First, an account with stores in high media cost markets could not purchase as many spots with its allocated funds as an equivalent account doing business in low media cost markets. Second, highly valued accounts—principally, the catalog houses—that already carried many GE SKUs in their basics claimed that it was harder for them to take advantage of the bonus offer for adding SKUs than accounts which had been cherrypicking the line.

---

[18]The BPP did not apply to the B&D Dustbuster Vac, Spotliter, and Scrub Brusher.

[19]B&D developed eight-second video vignettes on 65 SKUs at a cost of $750 each.

For 1985, B&D management planned to integrate elements of the BPP into a new Volume Plus Program (VPP). Accounts would be permitted to earn an annual rebate of up to 3% of net sales per shipping point. However, the purchase quantities needed to qualify for each rebate level were significantly higher than those in the former VRP. The VPP also permitted each account to earn additional discounts if it maintained or increased from one year to the next its total purchases, its total basics SKU count, and/or its basics SKU counts on specific product lines.

Dating Discounts

Dating involved allowing customers to pay for goods after they were shipped and received. Dating encouraged trade accounts to place early orders for goods that they did not have to pay for immediately. The seasonality of retail sales, the desire of trade accounts to avoid holding high bulk-to-value small appliances in their own warehouses, and the long lead times required for manufacturing small appliances offshore made dating programs a necessity in the small appliance industry.[20] Production planning and scheduling could become more efficient if a trade account placed early orders at the same time that it decided which SKUs to specify for its basics line-up.

GE Housewares Division's standard terms required full payment by the tenth of the month following an order, plus 45 days. The dating program permitted an account to place an order in May and June for shipment before September 1 and payment by December 10.[21] A second dating program required payment by May 10 on orders placed in December and January. A schedule of anticipation allowances rewarded accounts for payment of invoices before the dating program due date. GE's purchase allowance and dating programs together permitted accounts to "pay less and pay later."

After the acquisition, B&D continued to offer these same dating terms. The May–June dating program ensured that house orders for the Christmas season were placed well ahead of the end of B&D's fiscal year on September 30. However, several B&D executives had reservations about the biannual dating programs. First, the B&D programs, like those of competitive companies, included no order cancellation penalties. As a result, many trade buyers, uncertain of which small appliances would prove most popular on the retail shelves six months later, often over-ordered from three or four suppliers. Up to 30% of Christmas orders of some models were canceled in 1984, resulting in industry overproduction and further pressure on manufacturer prices.

A second concern was the degree to which trade buyers cherrypicked the product line in placing advance orders. Not wishing to be left with overstocks at the end of a season, which would reduce the overall margins on which they were

---

[20]A five-month lag between placement of a production order and delivery of the goods to retail stores was required in the case of small appliances sourced offshore.

[21]Half the order was for immediate delivery, and delivery of the second half had to occur before September 1.

evaluated, trade buyers were more willing to place advance orders on mature products rather than newer or more marginal items. A third problem was raised over the planned discontinuation of the flexible funds program in January, 1985. If discounts for early season orders were curtailed, would the dating program alone be sufficient to secure the placement of early orders, especially in an economy in which interest rates were declining?

Stock Balancing

GE's Housewares Division offered a stock balancing service to its accounts, B&D did not. The GE program permitted an account to exchange merchandise still in the product line and in salable condition that had been held by the retailer for at least four months. Overall, 2 % of GE sales were subject to stock balancing in 1983. Stock balancing was believed to encourage retailers to carry more merchandise than they otherwise would.

Following the acquisition, B&D executives decided to retain the GE stock balancing program, at least in the short term. Special arrangements were developed to replace GE merchandise with B&D merchandise as items in the GE line made the transition. One executive commented on the implementation challenge of changing retail stocks:

> Once the transition was underway, we were surprised how quickly the trade wanted to switch over. They'd say, "If you're going to advertise B&D, that's what I want in stock." Some catalog houses caught us by surprise and wanted to switch mid-year and highlight new B&D housewares in supplementary catalogs. As a result, we had more GE inventory than we expected. We unloaded it, at minimal loss, through selected customers who wanted to continue promoting the GE brand. Fortunately, for us, the excess inventory was quickly sold through and without the embarrassment of rock-bottom prices on GE appliances being advertised in the local newspaper.

Distribution and Backhaul Allowances

Following the acquisition, several major chains asked B&D to ship bulk quantities of B&D housewares to their warehouses rather than to individual stores. B&D was considering these requests. If accepted, B&D expected accounts to request additional discounts of around 2–4%. In addition, B&D executives tried to persuade other accounts, especially drug chains, that sold few units per store to receive shipments at their warehouses. B&D executives argued that, as a result, these accounts would be better able than B&D to track their inventories and control against out-of-stocks. At the same time, B&D executives believed that increased warehouse deliveries would enable them to reduce the number of distribution points and would reduce B&D's vulnerability to being caught with substantial inventories of appliances that proved faddish or that were rendered obsolete by competitive product entries.

In addition to soliciting warehouse shipments, some accounts were also pressing B&D for backhauling allowances. Backhauling involved a trade account's trucks picking up merchandise at a supplier's factory or warehouse as they returned empty from making store deliveries to the account's warehouses. For three reasons B&D was reluctant to accommodate these requests. First, most accounts' estimates of the appropriate discount for their transporting the merchandise to their warehouses were higher than B&D's. Second, a logistics problem could arise if trucks from several accounts all pulled into a B&D warehouse on the same day to make pick-ups. Third, the prices B&D received from its trucking subcontractors could be in jeopardy if significant quantities of its merchandise began being backhauled.

Cooperative Advertising

GE's Housewares Division had long offered trade accounts a cooperative advertising program. Accounts accrued 3% of their net purchases in a rolling 12-month cooperative advertising fund.[22] Accounts could draw on these accruals to subsidize the cost of retail advertising that featured GE products. GE paid the full cost of qualifying advertising, but sometimes only partially charged accounts' accrual funds if they featured particularly profitable premium-priced products such as items in the Spacemaker line, if they ran advertisements featuring multiple GE items, or if they timed their advertising to coincide with flights of GE national advertising. Some executives argued that, in 1985, B&D should offer additional incentives for advertising models and subbrands that had made the transition and for including in their advertisements specific copy points developed by B&D to facilitate the transition.

Most cooperative advertising funds were applied to run-of-press newspaper advertisements, store flyers delivered in the mail, and free-standing store inserts in Sunday newspapers. The larger chains, particularly department stores, invariably used up most of their co-op funds and were increasingly interested in using them to subsidize radio and television advertising. The importance of cooperative advertising in driving retail sales was reinforced by consumer research showing that one in four purchasers of small appliances in one major chain visited the housewares department with a store flyer or free-standing insert in hand. Feature advertisements were believed to be especially important in driving retail sales of the lower-priced items in small appliance product lines.

The cooperative advertising program applied to B&D housewares prior to the acquisition differed from the GE program. The B&D program was based on allocation rather than accrual. B&D set its cooperative advertising budget at 4% of sales and then allocated each account a portion of this fund based on its share of forecast sales. An account that purchased more than forecast sales did not receive any more cooperative advertising funds. However, as long as B&D's principal housewares product, the Dustbuster Vac, was on allocation as demand exceeded supply, this drawback was of little practical consequence.

Following the acquisition, the GE cooperative advertising program was retained and extended to include the B&D housewares line. Other housewares manufacturers offered similar programs. Clairol alone was unique in tying its program to its dating

---

[22]Allowances accrued more than 12 months previously that had not been spent were forfeited.

terms. An account that paid by the tenth of the month following an order, plus 30 days, qualified for a 9% accrual on the value of that particular order. Payment within 60 days qualified for a 6% accrual and payment within 90 days qualified for a 3% accrual. Some executives believed that B&D should shift to a similar system in 1985. Others argued that integrating dating with cooperative advertising was "mixing apples and oranges."

Some B&D executives wondered at what level they should continue cooperative advertising in 1985. Another cooperative advertising issue was how to respond to requests from club discount warehouse stores that did not advertise that they be given the equivalent value of cooperative advertising allowances on an off-invoice basis.[23] Some of B&D's housewares competitors had accommodated these requests. However, the instinct of B&D management was to stand firm.

Consumer Rebates

Initiated in the 1970s to help sell through slower-moving models, consumer rebates had become endemic to the housewares category by the early 1980s. By 1983, almost all list price increases were cushioned with rebates and three-quarters of all feature advertisements for GE housewares included reference to manufacturer rebate offers. Top-of-the-line models, including the Spacemaker line, had not been rebated. While many consumers had come to expect a rebate on any small appliance they bought, rebates caused problems for some trade accounts. The shelf clutter in the housewares section caused by tear-off pads with rebate claim forms had prompted some chains to require that they be posted instead on bulletin boards at the front of each store and that manufacturers pay a fee for this service.

Nevertheless, rebates did offer manufacturers some advantages. First, unlike purchase allowances, pass-through to the end consumer was assured. Second, only a fraction of all rebates were claimed by consumers entitled to them so the dollar value of any rebate offer was always greater than the equivalent reduction in selling price that would result from a reallocation of rebate program funds. Third, rebate program costs were fairly predictable. For example, a five-dollar rebate on a small appliance typically drew claims from 50% of qualified purchasers. The predictability of claim levels was important since they were usually received and paid in the financial quarter after an offer was made.

Although housewares manufacturers would have preferred to offer rebates only during selected time periods such as the peak gift-purchasing periods, the growing importance of catalog houses as a distribution channel prevented them from doing so. Catalog houses printed annual catalogs and wanted to include manufacturer rebate information next to the price of each item. While it was possible for a manufacturer to restrict the dates when a rebate was available in a footnote, this inevitably caused consumer confusion. In recent years, catalog showrooms had begun supplementing their annual catalogs with periodic flyers and mini-catalogs. However, these merely

---

[23]Warehouse chains, such as Price Club, offered their members the opportunity to purchase brand name hard goods at rock-bottom prices in no-frills stores. They did no retail advertising.

resulted in manufacturers being pressed for additional flyer allowances and increasing rather than reducing the rebate offers in the basic catalogs.

The average value of housewares manufacturers' consumer rebates escalated as each tried to outdo the other. In an effort to lead the industry toward more realistic list pricing, GE in 1983 curtailed rebates on irons and toaster ovens, two categories in which it was the market share leader. Far from following GE's lead, competitors increased their rebate offers. As a result, GE's share declined six points in both categories within six months.

Rebates were reinstated in these two categories by B&D and offered on a total of 35 SKUs in 1984. Rebates on 57 SKUs were planned for 1985. One executive commented:

> We have tested the pulling power of other types of consumer promotions—cookbooks as premiums with our food processors and a tie-in sweepstakes with Procter & Gamble. We're also the exclusive housewares supplier to AT&T's Opportunity Calling program.[24] None of these promotions come close to consumer rebates in sales impact. We're stuck with them.

CONCLUSION

At the December 10 meeting, the following exchange occurred:

> *May:* In 1984, we agreed to emphasize continuity to address the concerns of the trade. I think 1985 is still too early to implement any radical changes in our promotion and merchandising programs.
>
> *Lessard:* We've made some progress in improving the productivity of these expenditures, but we could do more. Besides, regularly changing our merchandising programs keeps the trade off-balance and prevents them working our programs to their advantage.
>
> *Homa:* Before we discuss further changes, let's clarify the objectives of each of our current programs and the role they're playing in helping us to execute the brand transition.

---

[24]AT&T customers earned points for long distance calls which could be redeemed for a variety of merchandise and services from the Opportunity Calling catalog.

GENERAL ELECTRIC COMPANY: MAJOR APPLIANCE BUSINESS GROUP (D)

JOHN A. QUELCH
NEIL COLLINS

Stuart Dean, General Electric (GE) Major Appliance Business Group (MABG) manager of dishwasher marketing planning, had recently submitted his model-by-model sales and market share forecasts for the 1983 GE brand built-in dishwasher line. Pending final approval of these forecasts by William Tudor, MABG marketing vice president, Dean started work on developing a detailed 1983 budget of dishwasher advertising, promotion, and merchandising expenditures.

BACKGROUND

In 1982, GE expected to sell 196,600 built-in dishwashers through retail channels. A further 253,400 would be sold to contractors. GE brand led the contract market with a 26% share, partly because MABG could provide contractors with a full line of major appliances. In the retail market, GE brand ranked third in 1982 with a 17% unit share. MABG also sold the Hotpoint brand that held a 6% share in both the retail and contract markets. MABG's major competitors in the built-in dishwasher category were Whirlpool (12% and 20% retail and contract shares), KitchenAid (18% and 6%), Maytag (8% and 1%), and Sears' Kenmore brand (32% and 15%).

In the retail market, dishwashers were sold primarily through four channels. These were appliance chains such as Lechmere Sales and independent appliance specialty stores; general merchandise chains such as Sears, Roebuck and Co.; discount stores such as K mart; and kitchen remodelers that mainly sold higher-priced models. In 1981, these channels accounted for 31%, 33%, 13%, and 13%, respectively, of all built-in dishwasher unit sales and 46%, 0%, 25%, and 15% of GE brand sales.

Whereas GE and Maytag owned their wholesale distribution systems, half of all KitchenAid and Whirlpool models reached retailers through national networks of independent distributors. As a result, prices and promotional activity on particular models could vary widely from one region to another.

GE analysts segmented major appliance consumers into three groups on the basis of their buying patterns:

☐ High-end buyers sought information on alternative brands prior to shopping, decided which brand was best, and then purchased that brand. In 1981, high-end buyers paying $550 and above accounted for 19% of dishwasher retail unit sales.

☐ Mid-line buyers first identified the package of features they wanted in a dishwasher. They then shopped around and switched brands, as necessary, to achieve the best price-feature relationship. This segment, represented by price points between $300 and $549, accounted for 59% of retail unit sales.

☐ Low-end buyers were the most price-sensitive. They were apt to shop at only a single store, but one with a strong value reputation. Low-end buyers paid less than $300 and accounted for 22% of sales.

The 1983 GE brand dishwasher line would be much changed from 1982. Six of the seven models would be replaced. Three of the six new models (2800, 2600, and 2200), including the two most expensive, would feature electronic controls. Only the 1200, recognized in 1980 by *Consumer Reports* as the then best dishwasher on the market, would be retained in the line. Two new models would be phased in in March (600 and 900), three in May (500, 2600, and 2800) and one in September (2200).

The 1983 GE line was the culmination of a five-year effort to increase GE's share, especially in the higher-priced, higher-unit margin end of the market, through feature and quality improvements. During the 1970s, GE dishwashers developed a reputation for indifferent quality and durability. As a result, MABG committed to a $28 million investment in quality improvement and factory automation. This effort included, first, the use of a new material in all GE dishwasher tubs and door liners. This material was PermaTuf®,[1] a proprietary plastic compound backed by a ten-year warranty. Second, MABG invested more than any of its competitors in the development of electronic features to achieve product differentiation.

Exhibit 1 summarizes Dean's 1983 strategy for GE and Hotpoint dishwashers in the retail market. Exhibit 2 presents his sales and share forecasts. Dean was aiming to increase GE brand share in both the retail and contract markets to 20% and 28%, respectively. Hotpoint share in both markets was expected to remain stable in 1983.

---

[1]PermaTuf® and Potscrubber® were registered trademarks of the General Electric Company.

EXHIBIT 1   GE and Hotpoint built-in dishwashers: summary of marketing strategy

Retail price range	($550 and above)	($549–$400)	($399–$300)	($299 and less)
Consumer segment	High-End	Mid-Line	Mid-Line	Low-End
% industry, 1981	19%	28%	31%	22%
GE models: electronic / electromechanical	2800/2600	1200 2200 / 900	600 / 865	500
Hotpoint models		965	765	465
Primary target for volume/share improvement	←——— GENERAL ELECTRIC ———→		←——— HOTPOINT ———→	
Secondary target for volume/share improvement/maintenance	←——— GENERAL ELECTRIC		HOTPOINT ———— HOTPOINT ———→	
Primary competitors:	KitchenAid Maytag	KitchenAid Whirlpool	Whirlpool Sears	Sears

317

EXHIBIT 2 1983 GE dishwasher line unit sales forecasts (units in thousands)

New and retained models

	Electronic					Electromechanical		Total
	GSD2800	GSD2600	GSD2200	GSD1200	GSD900D	GSD600D	GSD500D	
Suggested retail selling price	$599	$549	$469	$499	$399	$349	$299	
Retail units	2.3	3.6	17.8	31.5	87.9	16.0	26.4	185.5
Contract units	–	1.6	6.4	8.8	11.7	55.6	106.4	190.6
Total	2.3	5.2	24.2	40.3	99.6	71.6	132.9	376.1

Models being phased out

	Electronic					Electromechanical	Total
	GSD2500	GSD1000	GSD900	GSD650	GSD551	GSD400	
Retail units	6.1	5.4	11.8	11.6	2.0	35.9	72.8
Contract units	1.1	2.1	9.0	0.9	8.7	121.7	143.5
Total	7.2	7.5	20.8	12.5	10.7	157.8	216.3

Core model forecast summary

	New line	Old line	Total
Retail	185.5	72.8	258.3
Contract	190.6	143.5	334.1
Total	376.1	216.3	592.4

GE projected brand total for 1983 = 608,400 units (16,000 = derivative models not shown).
Projected overall unit market share = 24.8% (based on 2.45 million market size).
Projected retail share = 20%. Projected contract share = 28%.

MABG DISHWASHER NATIONAL ADVERTISING

Most MABG marketers regarded national advertising as important to building GE's image in major appliances and to gaining a strong dealer sell-in, especially for new models. Accordingly, MABG had consistently supported the GE dishwasher line; the GE brand's share of category advertising had ranged from 19% to 37% in the last three years (see Exhibit 3). During this period, GE brand national advertising aimed to develop primary as well as selective demand. Product benefits such as convenience and wash performance were communicated in family settings similar to those used in other GE consumer advertising. Both the GE and Potscrubber® III names were displayed prominently together with the slogan "We Bring Good Things to Life," the unifying theme of all GE consumer sector advertising since 1979. This theme was intended to give GE products a younger, more modern, family-oriented, and user-friendly image. Exhibit 4 shows a typical 1980 television advertisement for GE dishwashers.

In 1981, after considerable debate, all GE dishwasher advertising focused on educating consumers about the electronic features of the new GSD2500. MABG executives believed that the electronics message would do more than a PermaTuf-based message to arouse consumer curiosity, distinctly differentiate GE dishwasher advertising from that of competitors, and enhance the company's reputation for technological leadership.

However, MABG executives faced the challenge of linking electronics to the basic benefit of washing performance. Their first effort (Exhibit 5) was designed to reflect the consumer sector advertising theme. It was subsequently replaced by the "Beep" execution (Exhibit 6), which implicitly stressed GE's leadership in dishwasher technology. This commercial had been originally produced for less than $50,000 as a sales training aid. Several MABG executives argued that the Beep execution was "too cold" and "inconsistent with the Good Things to Life campaign."

In 1982, the original GE dishwasher advertising budget of $3 million was cut to only $130,000 to protect dishwasher profits. These funds were devoted entirely to magazine advertising for the GSD2500 (see Exhibit 7). During 1982, MABG advertising expenditures for all products amounted to $3 million. Total GE advertising in 1982 reached $10.1 million.

The Hotpoint brand received far less national and local advertising support than the GE brand. First, Hotpoint models had fewer new features that could serve as a basis for exciting advertising copy. Second, Hotpoint was positioned as the MABG "value" brand, targeted at consumers who were believed to be less influenced by advertising than price. Third, Hotpoint's attractive retail prices meant that MABG margins were lower than on the GE brand, making advertising less affordable. Fourth, because its annual sales were only one-quarter those of the GE brand, Hotpoint could not afford to advertise at the minimal level necessary to have an impact on consumers. Finally, advertising of the Hotpoint brand name did nothing to reinforce the GE corporate image.

EXHIBIT 3 Dishwasher advertising expenditures by brand ($ thousands)

| | National Advertising | | | | | | | | Local/Co-op | |
| | 1979 | | 1980 | | 1981 | | 1982* | | 1981 | |
Brand	$	SOV	$	SOV	$	SOV	$	SOV	$	SOV
GE	$ 3,664	32.2%	$ 1,988	19.0%	$ 4,003	37.2%	$ 130	1.3%	$3,980	21.0%
—TV	1,472		1,284		2,367		0			
—Magazines	2,192		704		1,636		130			
Hotpoint	0	0.0	0	0.0	0	0.0	0	0.0	1,327	7.0
KitchenAid	2,700	22.1	2,996	28.7	2,184	20.3	3,888	39.9	3,601	19.0
Maytag	2,490	20.4	2,234	21.4	1,221	11.3	1,761	18.1	2,805	11.0
Whirlpool	2,134	17.5	1,740	16.7	1,731	16.1	3,969	40.7	1,894	10.0
Sears	381	3.1	216	2.1	474	4.4	0	0.0	4,169	22.0
Subtotal	11,369	95.3	9,174	87.9	9,613	89.3	9,748	100.0	17,056	90.0
Total category	$12,219	100.0%	$10,437	100.0%	$10,767	100.0%	$ 9,749	100.0%	$18,952	100.0%

Source: Advertising industry estimates.

Note: SOV = Share of voice.

*Projected.

EXHIBIT 4   1980 GE dishwasher TV spot

BBDO
Batten, Barton, Durstine & Osborn, Inc.

Client: GENERAL ELECTRIC		Time: 30 SECONDS
Product: POTSCRUBBER III	Title: "SIT AMERICA" - SECTOR VERSION	Comml. No.: GEMA 9063

ANNCR: (VO) The GE Potscrubber III cleans so well, things have changed.

DAUGHTER: Sit, I'll do the dishes.

SON: Sit, I'll do the dishes.

ANNCR: (VO) The GE Potscrubber III cleans dishes and pots so well, everybody wants to do the dishes.

It's powerful

three level

washing system directs streams of water

to get pots and dishes sparkling clean.

WOMAN: Sit, I'll do the dishes.

SINGERS: GE

We bring good things to life.

EXHIBIT 5   1981 GE dishwasher television commercial

BBDO
Batten, Barton, Durstine & Osborn, Inc.

Client:	GENERAL ELECTRIC		Time:	30 SECONDS
Product:	2500 DISHWASHER	Title: "LITTLE GIRL"	Comml. No.:	GEMA 1083

GIRL: Us Mommies have so much to do.

AVO: GE introduces a most sophisticated way to make dishwashing easy.

The GE 2500 dishwasher.

It provides the ease

. . .of advanced electronic controls. . .

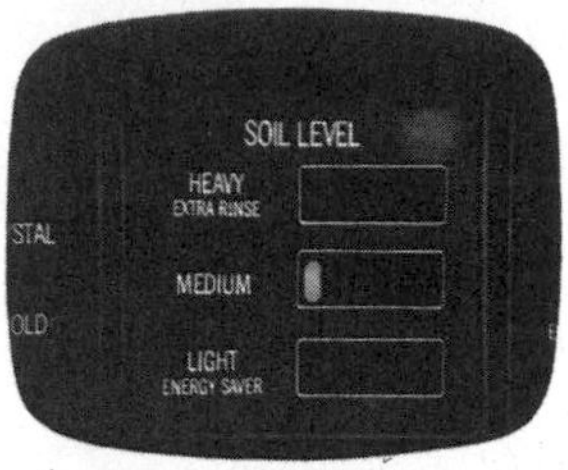

. . .computer memory

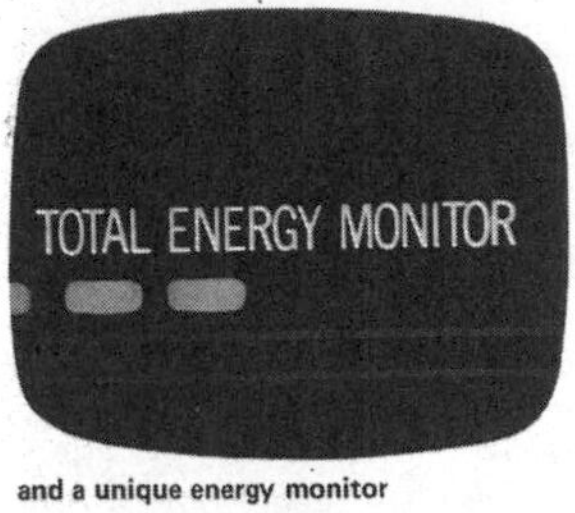

and a unique energy monitor

matched with GE's Potscrubber cleaning power.

GE Dishwashing made easy.

GIRL: See how hard I work for you?

SONG: GE

We bring good things to life.

EXHIBIT 6   1981 GE dishwasher television commercial

BBDO
Batten, Barton, Durstine & Osborn, Inc

Client:	GENERAL ELECTRIC	Time:	30 SECONDS
Product:	2500 DISHWASHER	Title: "BEEP"	Comml. No: GEMA 1053

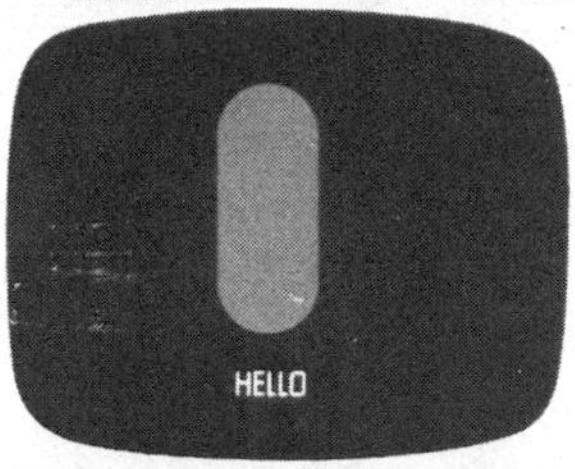

HELLO

(MUSIC & BEEP SOUNDS)

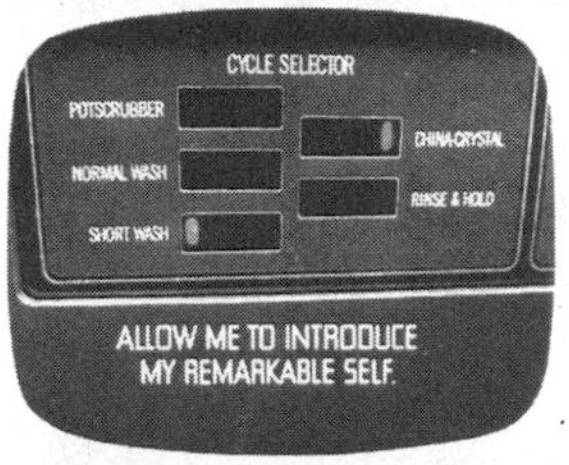

CYCLE SELECTOR

POTSCRUBBER   CHINA-CRYSTAL

NORMAL WASH   RINSE & HOLD

SHORT WASH

ALLOW ME TO INTRODUCE
MY REMARKABLE SELF.

(MUSIC & BEEP SOUNDS)

I AM THE NEW
GE 2500 DISHWASHER.

(MUSIC & BEEP SOUNDS)

I HAVE A COMPUTER
FOR A BRAIN.

(MUSIC & BEEP SOUNDS)

I CAN PUT 25 CLEANING CYCLES
AT YOUR FINGERTIPS.

(MUSIC & BEEP SOUNDS)

POTSCRUBBER

I CAN CLEAN YOUR POTS

(MUSIC & BEEP SOUNDS)

CHINA-CRYSTAL

...PAMPER YOUR CHINA

(MUSIC & BEEP SOUNDS)

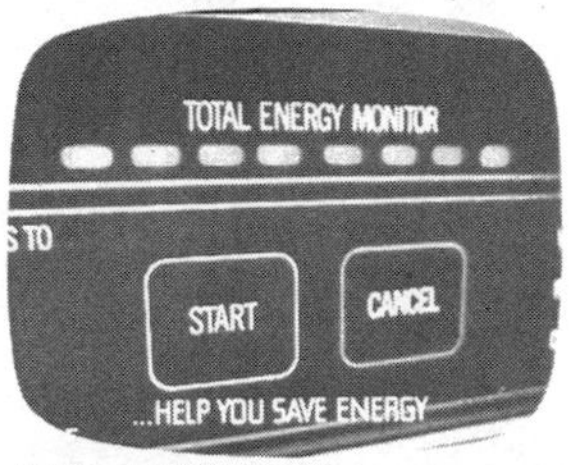

TOTAL ENERGY MONITOR

START   CANCEL

...HELP YOU SAVE ENERGY

(MUSIC & BEEP SOUNDS)

MINUTES TO

START

END OF CYCLE

...AND TELL YOU WHEN
YOUR DISHES WILL BE CLEAN.

(MUSIC & BEEP SOUNDS)

(MUSIC)
VO: The GE 2500. It can do almost everything but talk.

GENERAL ELECTRIC

SINGERS: GE. We bring good things to life.

We bring good things to life.
GENERAL ELECTRIC

BEEP! BEEP!

EXHIBIT 7   1981–82 GE dishwasher print advertisement

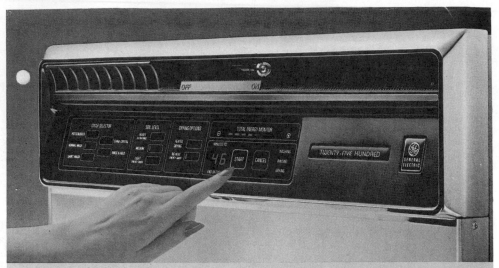

LET A BRIGHT DISHWASHER MAKE A DULL JOB EASY.

THE 2500 DISHWASHER FROM GE.

The advanced solid-state controls on the 2500 Dishwasher are so smart they make dishwashing easy. Here's what a dishwasher this bright can do for you.

The Outside Story. Fingertip electronic controls give you almost unlimited control over cleaning levels and energy use. First, touch the pad next to the washing cycle you want. Then the dishwasher automatically selects a soil level and sets a drying option that are right for most loads. It has an exclusive energy monitor. And it shows you exactly when your dishes will be clean. That's how easy it is.

But that's not all. The GE 2500 is even bright enough to warn you if certain things have gone wrong (like a household power failure or a plugged drain) and if you can fix it yourself.

The Inside Story. The 2500 has an exclusive Multi-Orbit™ washing system with a powerful Potscrubber® cycle that lets you get all kinds of dishes—from delicate crystal

to pots with baked-on foods—sparkling clean.

And the 2500 is as tough as it is bright. Just ask your dealer about our exclusive PermaTuf® tub and its fully written warranty against cracking, peeling, rusting, or leaking for 10 years, in normal use.

For your nearest GE dishwasher dealer, call toll free (800) 447-2882. In Illinois only, call (800) 322-4400.

The 2500 Dishwasher from GE. The dishwasher that's so bright it can make a dull job easy.

WE BRING GOOD THINGS TO LIFE.

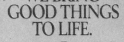

OTHER DISHWASHER MARKETING PROGRAMS

MABG used three forms of advertising besides national advertising and many other promotion and merchandising programs to support its major appliance lines. MABG executives believed that a mix of push and pull programs with each addressing different communications objectives was the essence of effective major appliance marketing. Exhibit 8 summarizes GE's expenditures on these programs for dishwashers in 1982.

Cooperative advertising dollars were accrued by dealers at the rate of 2% of their net purchases from MABG. Dealers were reimbursed from their accrued allowances for 75% of the cost of any advertising they placed featuring GE major appliances. Both the accrual and reimbursement rates varied somewhat across markets according to competitive conditions.

Allowances did not have to be spent on the product categories on which they were accrued. However, co-op advertising costs were allocated to each product category according to the value of advertising placed. If a product category was consistently underadvertised, a marketing planning manager could institute a temporary bonus co-op allowance tied to the advertising of his or her product line.

Research indicated that GE's share of local cooperative advertising for dishwashers matched its market share. In 1982, dealers used almost all of their accrued co-op funds.

Almost all co-op advertisements were in print and approximately 70% of them were based on MABG ad slicks.[2] These slicks typically showed specific models in several major appliance categories, highlighted key product features, announced consumer rebates, and left space for dealers to insert their own retail prices. A typical co-op ad slick is presented as Exhibit 9.

Key-city advertising was created and placed by MABG or its regional sales offices in the highly competitive key urban markets. MABG usually recouped 15% of the cost of this advertising by charging its dealers a fee for "tagging" ads with their store names and locations. Unlike co-op advertising, key-city advertising gave MABG tight control over message content and timing while permitting for tailoring to local market conditions.

By featuring particular models in key-city advertising, MABG could encourage its dealers to carry them. Key-city advertising was also used to announce consumer rebates to ensure that such offers stimulated incremental dealer traffic rather than merely giving a price break to consumers who would have purchased anyway. An example of a key-city advertisement is presented as Exhibit 10.

Some MABG executives believed that the funds used for key-city advertising would be better spent on increased co-op advertising. They argued that, if MABG reimbursed 100% instead of 75% of the co-op advertising cost, MABG's control over

---

[2]In New York City, individual dealers could not afford television advertising because rates were so high. Hence, they pooled half of their accrued co-op allowances in a common fund that was used to purchase commercial airtime. Participating dealers were "tagged" at the end of each advertisement.

EXHIBIT 8 MABG dishwasher projected marketing expenditures for 1982 ($ millions and % of NSB)

Marketing plan element	Retail Channel				Contract Channel			
	GE brand		Hotpoint		GE brand		Hotpoint	
	$	%	$	%	$	%	$	%
Net sales billed (NSB)	$49.49	100.0%	$17.36	100.0%	$61.70	100.0%	$14.22	100.0%
"Pull" programs								
National advertising	.54*	1.0	.03†	0.2	–	–	–	–
Key-city advertising	.48	1.0	.01	0.1	–	–	–	–
Local/co-op advertising	1.68	3.4	.59	3.9	.06	0.1	–	–
Consumer rebates	.67	1.4	.30	1.7	–	–	–	–
Market research	.09	0.2	–	–	–	–	–	–
Subtotal	3.45	7.0	0.88	5.9	.06	0.1	–	–
"Push" programs								
Trade advertising	.03	0.1	.01	0.1	.14	0.3	–	–
Sales campaigns and promotions	1.49	3.0	.26	1.8	.15	0.3	.03	0.3
Volume rebates/order size discounts	1.27	2.6	.45	3.1	.48	0.9	.04	0.4
Inventory financing	1.74	3.5	.44	3.0	.24	0.5	.06	0.5
Displays, printed point-of-purchase and sales materials	.39	0.8	.09	0.6	.02	–	.01	0.1
Other materials	.37	0.8	.09	0.6	.04	0.1	.02	0.1
Trade shows	–	–	–	–	.20	0.3	.05	0.4
Preview events	–	–	–	–	–	–	–	–
Subtotal	5.28	10.7	1.35	9.2	1.25	2.4	.21	1.8
Total	$8.73	17.6%	$ 2.23	15.1%	$ 1.31	2.5%	$ .21	1.8%

Source: Company records.

*Includes $130,000 devoted to dishwasher-specific advertising and a $500,000 allocation of advertising promoting the entire GE major appliance line.

† Dishwasher product category allocation of advertising promoting the entire Hotpoint major appliance line.

EXHIBIT 9　Cooperative advertising slick

EXHIBIT 10 Key-city advertising slick

the quality and content of dealer advertising would be greatly increased. Most MABG competitors used national and cooperative advertising, but not key-city advertising.

Trade advertising promoted GE dishwashers to retail dealers, contract dealers, and contractors in magazines such as *Home Furnishings Daily* and *Professional Builder*. Most trade advertisements served one or more of four purposes. First, they could present details of the manufacturer's marketing support, such as the planned national advertising budget. Second, they could present the features of a product that made it easy to sell. Third, they could announce a change in the positioning of a model. Fourth, they could alert dealers to new product introductions.

Consumer rebates of $25–$75 on medium- and higher-priced models were advertised to consumers for 30 to 60 days, often prior to Christmas and Mother's Day. Rebate certificates were distributed by dealers to purchasers. Rebates were used to accelerate the timing of consumer purchases, to move inventory of slower selling models, or to trade consumers up toward higher-end models. To ensure that rebated models would be readily available, MABG typically advertised the rebate and offered dealers a temporary 5% price discount during the 30 days prior to the consumer rebate period. However, 67% of consumers who claimed a GE dishwasher rebate reported that they first found out about it on the dealer sales floor.

Volume rebates and order size discounts applied collectively to dealer purchases of most MABG products. These discounts were available to dealers based upon order size and annual volume. Some regions also ran temporary "buy and get" promotions whereby, for example, a dealer who bought ten units of a certain popular model at full price could purchase two units of a less popular model for $75 each. Such a promotion could increase distribution of the less popular model. There was debate over whether the cost of such a promotion should include lost unit contribution as well as the gap between the $75 and the unit variable cost.

Purchase allowances were offered to dealers on one or more models every quarter in the promotion calendar. Usually, mid-line and high-end models other than the best-selling 1200 were promoted. GE's low-end models, the 500 and 600, were expected to command attractive retail price points, specifically $299 and $349, without being promoted. GE encouraged its dealers to include at least one of these "price impression models" in their co-op advertisements. Reflecting regional differences in market share, competitive pricing, and consumer preferences, regional sales offices could decide to offer higher or lower purchase allowances on different models than those suggested by Dean.

Floor plans usually offered dealers industry standard payment terms of 90 days after shipment of goods. Floor plan terms varied among markets according to competitive conditions. Sometimes extended floor plans of 120 or 150 days were offered. Each year the dishwasher marketing budget was charged an amount that was the product of the average outstanding dishwasher payables balance for the year and GE's average cost of debt financing.

Displays and point-of-purchase materials. MABG aimed to develop attention-getting displays that could effectively educate the consumer about product benefits, that could not be used to display competitors' machines, and that would help to expand GE's share of dealer floor space. Displays were essential for built-in dishwashers since they lacked counter tops and side walls. All MABG displays had sloping tops to prevent dealers from displaying other merchandise on top of them.

In 1982, MABG offered two display structures. One held four models side by side under a riser card headlined "General Electric Quality Built-In Dishwashers." Beneath this headline, four panels illustrated the general benefits of the GE line—guaranteed durability, Potscrubber performance, big load capacity, and quiet operation. Individual product features were described on the door interiors of each model. The second GE display was a single unit housing for the electronic GSD2500. The riser card explained the machine's many electronic features.

Dealers could purchase these displays at MABG cost (around $150 for a four-unit display). To encourage more widespread use, MABG operated a Display Dealer Program. Dealers who displayed four GE models, including two PermaTuf models, throughout the year received a price break of about 2% per unit over and above any purchase allowance.[3] A similar program existed for Hotpoint dealers. Participating dealers also received an 80% discount on the price of the display. In 1981, about 50% of GE built-in dishwasher sales were made by the 30% of GE dealers who participated in the display program.

Other materials. Over two million copies of catalogs describing all models in the product line were printed and distributed annually through mailing lists and through GE and Hotpoint dealers.

Trade shows for contractors permitted MABG to show off new models and maintain its market presence. There were no national trade shows for retail appliance dealers.

Preview events were held in Louisville in February and June to educate MABG sales counselors about new models and features, the role of each model in the line, and MABG marketing support programs.

Sales force incentives included payments (usually $5 or $10) by manufacturers to dealer salespeople on a "per machine sold" basis and sales contests that offered substantial prizes (often vacations) to the salespeople selling the most units. MABG believed such programs did little to enhance the brand franchise with either dealers or consumers. Larger volume dealers also objected to manufacturers trying to influence their salespeople through incentives. MABG's use of sales incentives was below the industry average.

COMPETITORS' MARKETING PROGRAMS

In developing his marketing budget, Dean reviewed the marketing programs of MABG's dishwasher competitors.

Whirlpool generally promoted models in the middle of its line, using trade promotions more often than consumer rebates. It shunned dealer sales incentives. Whirlpool's co-op advertising program and point-of-purchase display support were

---

[3]These display discounts were accounted for in average realized factory prices.

believed to be less generous than MABG's. In 1982, Whirlpool increased its national advertising despite the recession. Its advertising focused on product features for its electromechanical models and its new electronic model (see Exhibit 11). For ten years, Whirlpool had consistently used the same creative format, a dark background highlighting a specific model with an emphasis on features.

KitchenAid's 71 independent distributors frequently offered dealers price discounts for quantity orders or purchases of specific model mixes. KitchenAid distributors were also heavy users of dealer sales force incentives. KitchenAid supported its distributors and dealers with excellent point-of-purchase displays and consumer literature, and with outstanding training programs for dealer salespeople on how to sell its models. The company also occasionally offered consumer rebates, replacement allowances, detergent give-aways, savings bonds, and premiums. Unlike MABG, KitchenAid had increased its commitment to national advertising during the recent recession. Its advertising (see Exhibit 12) focused on the superior durability and energy-saving features of its models.

Maytag was the third largest dishwasher advertiser. Its advertising emphasized the themes of quality and dependability for both its dishwashers and its laundry equipment. Since Maytag sold directly to its dealers rather than through wholesalers, it was able to control its trade allowances tightly, preferring to use consumer rebates that ensured pass-through of any price reduction to the purchaser. The company was trying to shift some local advertising dollars from co-op to key-city programs. Maytag was aiming to increase share in the contract channel and was advertising heavily in contract trade periodicals using the headline, "Maytag quality, plus builder pricing."

Sears often ran price promotions on its popular mid-line models, although it was believed to be trying to reduce the percentage of units sold on promotion, while holding share. Sears' Kenmore brand was the most heavily advertised locally, but was rarely advertised in national media.

THE 1983 MARKETING PLAN FOR THE GE BUILT-IN DISHWASHER LINE

Like the marketing planning managers for other MABG product categories, Dean developed his sales promotion plans in conjunction with the MABG manager of Merchandising Programs (MMP) and the manager of Brand Merchandising (MBM). The MMP was responsible for working up the schedule of national umbrella promotion events under which all MABG product categories were promoted. He also developed "shelf promotions" that regional sales offices could quickly access and implement as needed.

The MBM was a former zone manager and acted as the liaison between headquarters and the merchandising managers in MABG's 20 regional sales offices. The regions were evaluated against volume and share objectives by product line and an overall profit margin objective covering all MABG product lines. Given this profit responsibility, the regions were charged the costs of their sales promotion activities.

EXHIBIT 11   1982 Whirlpool print advertisement

EXHIBIT 12   1982 KitchenAid print advertisement

THE KITCHENAID CHALLENGE.

Find another dishwasher with all these quality features, and KitchenAid will buy it for you.

It's no gimmick. Check these features against any other dishwasher brand. If you find one with all of these dishscrubbing and long lasting features found in the KitchenAid KD-20 dishwashers, we'll buy it for you. Nothing truly compares to a KitchenAid.
Offer expires December 31, 1982.

Extra-Clean Dishscrubbing Features.

☐ **High Pressure Multi-Level Wash System.**
KitchenAid dishscrubbing power is greater than all major dishwasher brands because our wash system delivers more water under greater pressure.

☐ **100% Usable Large Capacity Racks with ChinaGuard.**
No lost loading space because there are no cutouts in the lower rack. Exclusive ChinaGuard protects dishes against chipping.

☐ **Sure-Temp Water Heating.**
Insures sanitized cleaning every time. Automatically heats water to approximately 150°F in every complete cycle.

☐ **Built-In Soft Food Disposer.**
Assures sparkling clean dishes without pre-rinsing. Grinds soft foods during drain.

☐ **Gentle Forced Air Drying.**
It's safe. With no hot spots on dishes, pots or pans. Unlike other dishwashers, there's no exposed heating element in the KitchenAid dishwasher.

Long-Life Durability Features.

☐ **Porcelain and Steel Construction.**
To protect from scratches, stains, and odors, KitchenAid uses a full steel wash tank with two coats of tough, chip-resistant TriDura® porcelain plus an overglaze.

☐ **Heavy Duty ½ Horsepower Motor.**
Most others use a ⅓ horsepower or less. Since a stronger motor strains less, it's a lot less likely to wear out.

☐ **Reversible Front Panels.**
You can change panels with the stainless steel trim kit with four decorator colors provided. Choose from six optional solid and edged colors for unmatched flexibility.

☐ **Overflow Protection Twin Fill Valve.**
You don't have to worry about overflowing water. If one valve fails, the other continues to operate and normal dishwasher operation is maintained.

☐ **Triple Protection Warranty.**
A 1-Year parts and labor Full Warranty on the complete dishwasher. A 5-Year Limited Warranty on the motor. And a 10-Year Limited Warranty on the porcelain tank and inner door.

KitchenAid. Don't settle for less.

Hobart Corporation, Troy, Ohio 45374   KitchenAid and TriDura are registered trademarks of Hobart Corporation

EXHIBIT 13 MABG dishwasher marketing expenditures for proposed 1983 budget ($ millions and % of NSB)

Marketing plan element	Retail Channel				Contract Channel			
	GE brand		Hotpoint		GE brand		Hotpoint	
	$	%	$	%	$	%	$	%
Net sales billed (NSB)	$68.02	100.0%	$15.70	100.0%	$81.51	100.0%	$18.30	100.0%
"Pull" programs								
National advertising	3.10*	4.6	.21	1.4	–	–	–	–
Key-city advertising	1.23	1.8	.04	0.3	–	–	–	–
Local/co-op advertising	2.19	3.2	.56	3.6	.09	0.1	.04	0.3
Consumer rebates	.48	0.7	.17	1.1	–	–	–	–
Market research	.17	0.3	–	–	–	–	–	–
Subtotal	7.17	10.6	.99	6.4	.09	0.1	.04	0.3
"Push" programs								
Trade advertising	.14	0.2	.03	0.2	.17	0.2	.12	0.8
Sales campaigns and promotions	.68	1.0	.12	0.8	.17	0.2	.85	0.5
Volume rebates	1.52	2.2	.35	2.2	.84	1.2	.08	0.5
Inventory financing	2.18	3.2	.47	3.0	.31	0.5	.03	0.2
Displays, printed point-of-purchase and sales materials	.43	0.6	.14	0.9	.03	0.1	.03	0.2
Other materials	.40	0.6	.14	0.9	.03	0.1	.01	0.1
Trade shows	–	–	–	–	.08	0.1	–	–
Preview events	.08	0.1	–	–	.02	0.0	–	–
Subtotal	5.44	8.0	1.25	8.0	1.66	2.4	.34	2.2
Total	$12.61	18.6%	$ 2.24	14.2%	$ 1.75	2.5%	$ .38	2.5%

Source: Company records.

*Includes $3.05 million budgeted for dishwasher specific advertising and a $600,000 allocation of advertising promoting the entire GE major appliance line.

EXHIBIT 14   Proposed dishwasher advertisement

EXHIBIT 15 Brochure explaining GE electronic dishwasher display

EXHIBIT 15   (continued)

DISPLAY THEM RIGHT.

GET MORE DISHWASHER FOR YOUR MONEY

General Electric Touch Control dishwashers give you more options, more performance and more protection than ever before. They're the best dishwashers General Electric has ever made!

DELAY START

Allows you to delay the start of the dishwashing cycle from 1 to 9 hours. You can add late-night snack dishes before going to bed, run dishwasher at night when hot water demand is lowest, or take advantage of "off peak" utility rates available in many areas.

ENERGY MONITOR

Shows you the amount of energy used by each cycle and makes it easier for you to select the cycle you need that uses the least amount of energy.

TIME-TO-END-OF-CYCLE

Shows the amount of time, in minutes, to the end of the programmed cycle. Lets you plan other activities to coincide with the end of the dishwashing cycle.

CYCLE PHASE INDICATOR

Lets you know exactly where your dishwasher is in the cleaning cycle. You can add a dish while it's still washing. Or remove a pot right after the final rinse. It will also tell you when the dishes are clean.

EXCLUSIVE GENERAL ELECTRIC WARRANTY PACKAGE...FULL ONE-YEAR WARRANTY*
Guarantees parts and labor to repair any part of the dishwasher that fails because of a manufacturing defect within one year from date of purchase.

LIMITED SECOND-YEAR WARRANTY*
Guarantees replacement parts, but not labor, for any part of the water distribution system that fails due to a manufacturing defect within the second year from date of purchase.

EXCLUSIVE FULL TEN-YEAR WARRANTY*
Guarantees that this Perma-Tuf® tub and door liner won't leak from cracking, chipping, peeling or rusting for 10 years after you buy it, or GE will replace or repair the liner without charge for parts or labor.
See warranty for full details.

ENERGY MESSAGES
General Electric Touch Control Dishwashers offer a variety of energy-saving options suited to our energy-conscious age. Lighted energy messages aid you in choosing the most energy-wise cycles suited to your individual load.

The best way to display General Electric electronic touch control dishwashers is with the new GE "TOUCH ME" Display. This attractive, "hands-on" display demonstrates the ease and versatility of electronic touch controls and allows the performance, dependability and "easy-to-use" story to be told through the use of visually-appealing display panels. Simulated control panels are designed to facilitate demonstration, both by you *and* your customers!

EXHIBIT 15   (continued)

FOR MAXIMUM SALES

TOUCH ME...

First touch one of the five WASH CYCLE options (Potscrubber, Normal, etc.,) -- it will answer with a beep and light up.

Now touch one of the three SOIL LEVEL options (Heavy, Medium, or Light) --again it will answer with a light and a beep.

Then touch ENERGY-SAVER DRY, or HEATED DRY option.

Touch SANI option on -- if you want to heat the final rinse to 145° F. (Potscrubber, Normal cycles only).

Notice how the TIME-TO-END-OF-CYCLE and RELATIVE

ENERGY MONITOR vary with each different cycle selected.

SYSTEMS MONITOR also shows you whether you have chosen an energy-saving cycle.

Keep touching the DELAY START pad to delay the start of dishwashing up to nine hours. Then touch CLEAR/RESET...

Touch the START pad -- see how the Systems Monitor shows you that the dishwasher is in the "Washing" mode.

After you have touched START, the Systems Monitor

begins to count down time; after 2 minutes...the SYSTEMS MONITOR will simulate the display for "BLOCKED WASH ARM" -- this indicates that something has stopped the wash arm from rotating. Now touch CLEAR/RESET and start all over again.

This demonstrator panel is not hooked up to a dishwasher; therefore it can not show you all its extensive performance monitoring capabilities. Panels to your right and left show you more of the performance and protection features that General Electric Touch Control Dishwashers offer.

CREATE A BEAUTIFUL KITCHEN

A General Electric Touch Control Dishwasher can help you create a beautiful kitchen. Their uncluttered good looks and reversible color panels make them the ideal complement for any kitchen decor, from Early American to Contemporary to Futuristic. You can even use ¼" paneling inserts in the door and access panel, to match your kitchen cabinets. And, the Touch Control panels are easy to clean. General Electric Electronic Dishwasher also offer:
● Potscrubber® Washing Performance
● PermaTuf® Durability
● Large Loading Capacity
● General Electric Electronic Reliability
Ask your salesman about the specifics.

WE BRING GOOD THINGS TO LIFE.

After your customer has started a cycle, use this time to explain the various features to your customer, such as DETERGENT CUP OPEN and BLOCKED DRAIN sensors. After two minutes, the SYSTEMS MONITOR will display "BLOCKED WASH ARM". At this point, you have a natural transition to talk about the advantages of a diagnostic dishwasher system, and can say such things as, "Possibly a pot or pan is blocking the arm, or the dishwasher is not getting enough water to the arm to allow it to spin. Thus, the machine signals you back to make necessary corrections to the load."

EXHIBIT 15   (continued)

POTENTIAL—TODAY!

THE BEST SURPRISE IS NO SURPRISE AT ALL

General Electric Touch Control Dishwashers feature a high-performance wash system that produces sparkling clean dishes.

TEMPERATURE SENSOR SYSTEM

WASHING

HEATING

Hot water is necessary to get the best performance from your dishwasher. The GE Temperature Sensor System senses the water temperature and automatically heats it to the proper wash temperature, thereby avoiding the unpleasant surprise of unclean dishes at the end of the cycle.

BLOCKED WASH ARM

BLOCKED WASH ARM

A dislodged utensil that is blocking the bottom wash arm can prevent your dishes from getting clean. The Systems Monitor senses this condition and sends you this message (blinking and beeping) so that you can readjust the load to avoid the unpleasant surprise of unclean dishes at the end of the cycle.

DETERGENT CUP OPEN

CUP OPEN

An open detergent cup, which can occur when you fail to add detergent or when you forget to close the cup, can cause poor dishwashing performance. Systems Monitor senses this condition and prompts you to close the cup to avoid the unpleasant surprise of unclean dishes at the end of the cycle.

BLOCKED DRAIN

SEE DOOR LABEL   BLOCKED   DRAIN

A blocked drain results in poor dishwashing performance. The Systems Monitor senses this situation and prompts you to fix it to avoid the unpleasant surprise of unclean dishes or an unnecessary service call.

CYCLE MEMORY

A General Electric Touch Control Dishwasher automatically remembers the last cycle you programmed, and will run it again unless you want to change it. So all you have to do is touch START. This can be a real time and work saver.

CONTROL LOCKED

To prevent children from accidently starting or changing the cycle on your dishwasher, you can lock in the program you've chosen with the touch of your finger.

The GE Answer Center®
800.626.2000

QUESTIONS

about your General Electric dishwasher or other consumer products? Call the GE Answer Center™, toll-free, 24 hours a day, 7 days a week.

With the two-unit "TOUCH ME" Display from General Electric, the step up to the "No-Surprises" Dishwashers is an easy . . . and profitable one to make!

S.A.

They were, therefore, permitted to alter the promotions proposed by the headquarters marketing planning managers as they saw fit.

The MMP had already established MABG's overall objectives for co-op advertising and volume rebate programs as well as its inventory financing terms for 1983. MABG's objective was to reduce the percentage of sales paid out through these programs. MABG executives had decided to try to reduce co-op advertising expenditures on the GE brand from 3.4% to 3.2% of sales. Key-city advertising expenditures were to be increased to ensure greater consistency between local and national advertising.

In the sales promotion area, Dean recommended that $50 consumer rebates be offered on both the GSD2800 and GSD1200 during 1983. He budgeted a reduction in sales force incentives. He believed them to be less necessary given the outstanding quality of the new product line and forecasts of improved economic conditions.

Dean's proposed 1983 marketing budget is shown in Exhibit 13. Working with the MABG advertising manager, Dean planned a major increase in national advertising, most of which was to be spent in the third and fourth quarters. By then, the complete new model line would be in dealer showrooms. A new advertising message would emphasize the GE "family of electronic dishwashers" and focus on the "affordable" GSD2200. Dean thought this message would attract the attention of the broad range of consumers that GE needed to achieve its objective of increasing its share of high-end and mid-line models, while focusing on the line's most exciting and differentiating feature—electronics. However, he believed that Tudor might prefer to focus the campaign on the top-of-the-line GSD2800, using copy similar to the 1981 "Beep" execution for the GSD2500 (see Exhibit 14 for proposed advertisement). Dean had also considered a comparison advertising campaign versus KitchenAid based on performance and durability claims, but had decided to wait until the new line was established before pursuing this option further.

Dean also learned that MABG management was interested in funding an aggressive public relations campaign in 1983 to publicize the dishwasher plant renovation and automation. Dean argued that these funds could be spent more productively on product-specific advertising.

One outstanding issue was how many and which models GE dealers should have to display year-round to qualify for the display program. Should a dealer have to display five models instead of four to obtain the 2% display discount? Should a dealer have to display one or two of GE's electronic models, and on a separate stand from GE's electromechanical models? If so, would a dealer have to make room for two GE displays to qualify for the discount? Work was almost complete on a new display structure for two electronic models that would include an interactive electronic touch panel to capture consumer interest. Dean had just received proofs of a four-page brochure (reproduced as Exhibit 15) he had developed to explain to dealers how to use this interactive display.

IN DEFENSE
OF PRICE
PROMOTION

PAUL W. FARRIS
JOHN A. QUELCH

The increasing use of price promotions has aroused strong concern among many marketers. They argue that price promotions reduce the potential of other elements of the marketing mix by bleeding the advertising budget, decreasing brand loyalty, increasing consumer price sensitivity, and contributing to an excessive managerial focus on short-term sales and earnings.

We believe that some of these trends are inherent in today's marketplace, and that interest in price promotions is a *response* to them, not their cause. Price promotions—short-term incentives directed at the trade and/or the end consumers—can offer marketers substantial benefits, some of them not available through other marketing tools. Used effectively, they can enable small companies to challenge large competitors, reduce the risk of first-time purchase for consumers and retailers, and stimulate consumer demand. Perhaps most important, price promotions allow manufacturers to adjust to supply and demand fluctuations by using demand pricing (charging different market segments different prices for the same product).

Price promotion is being heavily criticized partly because accounting procedures typically exaggerate its costs and undervalue its contribution. This paper will focus on the general characteristics of price promotions, the specific value of demand pricing, and the proper evaluation of price promotion costs.

THE PROMOTION DEBATE

There is no doubt that the use of price promotions has increased more rapidly than the use of advertising in recent years.[1] Forces causing the growth include the following.

[1]R.D. Bowman, "Seventh Annual Advertising and Sales Promotion Report," *Marketing Communications,* August 1986, pp. 7–12.

☐ Slow population growth, combined with excess manufacturing and retail capacity, has intensified competition for market share. Promotions can achieve short-term increases in sales, market share, and capacity utilization.

☐ Fragmented consumer audiences and media-cost inflation have made advertising harder to manage.

☐ As product categories mature, opportunities for product differentiation decrease, good advertising copy becomes harder to develop, the quality gap between private labels and national brands narrows, and pressure for price promotions increases.

☐ Regional trade concentration, computerized sales data collected at the point-of-sale, and the increasing professionalism of retail management are adding to the trade's power and putting pressure on manufacturers for more deals.

☐ Mergers, acquisitions, and the securities industry have placed more pressure on top management to focus on short-term earnings. Price promotions boost short-term sales more assuredly than advertising does.

The airline industry is a good example of these forces at work. In 1985, 86% of all seats sold by the 12 major U.S. carriers were sold at a discount (average discount—44%), compared to only 56% in 1980. Excess capacity following deregulation resulted in only 62% of all seats being filled in 1985. Falling fuel prices, high fixed costs, and the inherent inability to inventory excess seats further encourage discounting. Computerized reservation systems can quickly implement fare changes and make it easy for competitors to respond.

The airline example also shows how the growth in promotion expenditures is partly artificial. A large proportion of promotion expenditures in the airline industry represents adjustments to artificially high list prices rather than genuine merchandising efforts.

Yet promotion continues to be seen as a *cause* of problems rather than a *symptom,* particularly by advertising executives who see the growth of promotion as a threat. Very often, promotion is blamed for the following trends.

☐ *Decreasing brand loyalty.* The inability of manufacturers to develop truly differentiated products and the proliferation of me-too products and line extensions are more basic causes of brand switching than promotion. The auto industry is a good example.

☐ *Increasing price sensitivity.* Although consumer responsiveness to promotions has been found to correlate with price sensitivity, this is a chicken and egg question.[2] The recessions of the 1970s and the early 1980s were at least as responsible as the proliferation of manufacturers' deals for programming many consumers to buy only on deal.

☐ *Detracting from a quality image.* So many products are now offered on deal that a product's image is unlikely to be hurt by promotion, particularly if

[2]C. Narasimhan, "A Price Discrimination Theory of Coupons," *Marketing Science* 3 (Spring 1984): 128–47.

the regular list price is recognized as artificially high; if the promotion is an annual event accepted by consumers, such as a year-end clearance sale; if the other elements of the marketing mix (such as the advertising, packaging, and distribution channels) testify to product quality; and if independent sources such as *Consumer Reports* give the product high marks.

☐ *Focusing management on the short term.* In fact, a short-term orientation, driven by top management's emphasis on quarterly results, is the *cause* rather than the result of promotions used to boost sales. A recent study indicated that 90% of product managers would rather spend less time on short-term promotion and more time on franchise-building advertising, but the top-rated managers were those who spent more time on promotion, indicating that senior management is rewarding a short-term orientation.[3]

BENEFITS OF PROMOTIONS

Not only are the cause-and-effect relationships between these four trends and price promotions often confused, but there are also many benefits of price promotions for manufacturers, retail trade, and consumers that are often overlooked. These include the following.

☐ Price promotions enable manufacturers to adjust to variations in supply and demand without changing list prices. Often price promotions can help even out peaks and valleys in consumer demand to lower average operating costs. In addition, list prices are often set high as a defense against price controls, rapid increases in commodity prices, and to test "how high is up" in sustainable price levels.

☐ Because price promotion costs are variable with volume, they enable small, regional businesses to compete against brands with large advertising budgets. The same "pay as you go" aspect of promotions permits the survival of new products targeted at segments too small to warrant mass media advertising.

☐ By inducing consumer trial of new products and clearing retail inventories of obsolete products, price promotions reduce the retailer's risk in stocking new brands. This fact allows these brands to get consumer exposure faster than otherwise would be the case (though promotions can also help marketers of existing products defend against new brands by loading inventories).

☐ Price promotions encourage different retail formats, thereby increasing consumer choice. Because different items are on promotion weekly, consumer choice is enhanced, and shopping for otherwise mundane products becomes more exciting.

☐ Price promotions may increase consumer demand by encouraging trial in new categories and by improving the attention-getting power of advertising. Many

[3]J.A. Quelch, P.W. Farris, and J. Olver, "The Product Management Audit," *Harvard Business Review* (March–April 1987): 30–36.

promotions, especially coupons and premiums, convey product benefits as well as price information. Awareness and knowledge of prices may be improved by price promotion activity.

☐ Buying on deal is a simple rule for time-pressured consumers; many of them derive satisfaction from being smart shoppers, taking advantage of price specials, and redeeming coupons.

PRICE PROMOTION AS DEMAND PRICING

An additional benefit of promotion—one that has received more attention from academics than from managers and is the focus of the remainder of this paper—is its value in implementing demand pricing.[4] *Demand pricing* means charging different market segments different prices for the same product or service. In this context, segments can mean different groups of purchasers as well as different purchasing situations with respect to time, place, and conditions of sale.

There are three reasons that demand pricing is an increasingly important aspect of price promotion.

☐ There is increasing *segmentation* in consumer markets. Thesse segments differ in their price and promotion sensitivities. A segment of price-insensitive dual-income households can be contrasted to a segment of price-sensitive and deal-prone consumers in fixed-income households whose purchasing power is not rising nearly as fast.

☐ This consumer segmentation is reflected in the proliferation of *new retail formats,* ranging from limited-assortment club warehouse stores to gourmet superstores, each with a different price-quality positioning. Demand pricing can be directed at classes of trade and individual trade accounts as well as at consumers.

☐ The emergence of *specialized media* vehicles such as regional magazines and focused cable TV, as well as direct mail, permits promotions to be targeted at specific segments with less leakage.

The concept of demand pricing applies to both "permanent" pricing structures and "temporary" price promotions. For example, early payment discounts are a permanent feature of pricing policies that offer lower prices to those paying promptly. Quantity discounts are also permanent pricing policies that may offer lower prices to one segment than to another.

Charging different prices to different segments will not be more profitable than charging everyone a single price unless the following conditions apply.

☐ The segments must be separated, or separable to some degree. For example, charging lower telephone rates on weekends encourages consumers to place more personal calls on weekends and also helps telephone companies to even

[4]A review of some of the academic discussion can be found in Narasimhan, op. cit.

out demand. However, business and personal callers are not perfectly separated; some consumers continue to place personal calls during peak hours, and others would have called on weekends anyway at the peak rate.

☐   The segments must have different price elasticities and/or different variable costs (or opportunity costs). Segments will have different optimal prices if either price-quantity relationships are different and the variable costs are the same, or vice versa. (If *both* elasticities and costs are different, the effects could cancel or amplify each other. For example, refrigerators may be worth less to Eskimos, but if it costs more to ship refrigerators a great distance, then you could still be forced to charge Eskimos more than you would mainland customers.)

Under comparable circumstances, demand pricing is more profitable when it is difficult for customers in one segment to buy at the price offered to another segment—in other words, when there is minimal "leakage."[5] Therefore, services that cannot be inventoried and are difficult to transfer, such as hotel rooms, can have widely different prices. On the other hand, most products can be inventoried and resold, so when manufacturers run regional price promotions, it is possible for trade customers to buy more than they need and divert the excess to other markets. Other examples of leakage are mistargeting in direct-mail coupon drops and broker trading in airline coupons that enables business travelers to take advantage of rates intended for vacationers.

A major benefit of price promotions to marketers is the ability to price discriminate (in the economic sense of the word) among segments on a temporary basis. Whether a price promotion can *separate markets* is key to its profitability, however. Natural separation of markets occurs as a result of geographic distance between segments, lack of communication between segments, the passage of time, and, in international markets, different taxes and duties. Marketers increase or decrease the separation of markets with slight product modifications, separate sales forces, policies with respect to freight charges, and other pricing decisions.[6]

Passive vs. Active Price Discrimination

Passive price discrimination occurs when a lower price is available to a purchaser, but the purchaser chooses not to expend the effort to take advantage of it. We do not question the right to a slightly better "deal" on a Porsche if someone is willing to travel to Germany, buy the car, and cope with shipping it back to the United States. In the same way, we acknowledge that consumers who go to the trouble of clipping, saving, and redeeming coupons should receive a price break.

Active price discrimination occurs when marketers restrict the availability of a special price to a certain occasion or group of consumers. Examples of active price discrimination include senior citizen discounts and regional price promotions.

---

[5]E. Gerstner and D. Holthausen, "Profitable Pricing When Market Segments Overlap," *Marketing Science* 5 (Winter 1986): 55–69.

[6]For example, quoting "delivered" instead of FOB prices can make it harder to compare net prices.

Two-Step Price Discrimination

In the case of trade discounts that may or may not be passed along to consumers, the distinction between active and passive price discrimination is even more difficult to make. Such discounts, although offered to the trade, not the consumer, can result in more price-sensitive consumers being offered lower retail prices through a two-step process.

Certain trade accounts buy more than their normal inventory to take advantage of manufacturer deals (forward buy) and thereby achieve lower average prices than accounts that do not. Some trade accounts—notably warehouse stores and club stores—forgo continuity of assortment in favor of buying *only* deal merchandise. The result is that some chains buy a larger percentage of their total merchandise on deal than do others. Many of these stores appeal to the more price-sensitive consumers in their local trading areas. Thus *temporary* trade discounts can allow stores with the most price-sensitive customers to achieve the lowest average prices over the entire year and permit demand pricing at the consumer level.

Even though equivalent prices may be offered to all trade accounts, passive price discrimination at both the trade and consumer levels occurs because not all retailers choose to take advantage of trade deals and not all consumers choose to shop at the chains that offer the lowest prices.

Profit Gains from Demand Pricing

Demand pricing can increase profits even when only "leaky" forms of market separation are possible. Calculating the profitability of demand pricing is a conceptually simple process that requires specific assumptions about the following:

☐ the marginal cost (principally variable cost) of supplying each segment;
☐ the demand function (price versus quantity relationships) of each segment;
☐ the degree to which leakage occurs; and
☐ the cost of the separation (such as the costs of printing and distributing coupons and of implementing trade promotions, rebates, and similar programs).

Standard spreadsheet models can be used for the analysis, even with a variety of assumptions about the four factors. In the next example only two segments are considered, but there is no reason either in theory or practice that more could not be analyzed using the same process.

Table 1 shows disguised data for a shampoo brand targeted at two distinct consumer segments. The list-price segment—the adult market—is relatively price insensitive and the promotion segment—the teenager market—is price sensitive. The variable cost of supplying each unit is $.80 per unit. The optimal price for the list-price segment, if one could perfectly separate it from the promotion segment, would be $2.00, and the optimal price for the promotion segment would be $1.40. If the segments could not be separated, the optimal single price would be $1.60.

Column 1 assumes a single-price strategy. Column 2 shows the expected contribution for a "perfect" or zero leakage dual-price strategy. Column 3 allows

TABLE 1   Contribution from price promotion strategy vs. single-price strategy

	Column 1	Column 2		Column 3	
	Single-price	Dual-price leakage = 0		Dual-price leakage = 20%	
	List	List	Promotion	List	Promotion
Price	$1.60	$2.00	$1.40	$2.00	$1.40
Units	140.00	70.00	90.00	56.00	89.00
Average unit price	$1.60	$1.63		$1.61	
Unit variable cost	.80	.80		.80	
Average unit margin	.80	.83		.81	
Total number of units	140.00	160.00		145.00	
Total contribution	$112.00	$138.00		$120.60	
Promotion administration (2%)	.00	($6.50)		($5.80)	
Net contribution	$112.00	$131.50		$114.80	
Gain from promotion	–	$19.50		$2.80	
Advertising	$20.00	$20.00		$20.00	
Promotion/gross sales	0%	21%		19%	
Advertising/gross sales	9%	7%		6%	
Advertising/promotion	100:0	25:75		25:75	

for 20% leakage and calculates volume and contribution for a dual-price strategy. The "units" line reflects the fact that the number of units sold will go up as prices go down.

To illustrate "leakage," we have assumed that 20% of the list-price segment would buy 17 units at the promotion price of $1.40 (20% of 85 = 17) and that 80% of the promotion-price segment would buy 72 units (80% of 90 = 72) at the promotion price.[7] Sales at list price would come only from the list-price segment (80% of 70 = 56) because, at the list price of $2.00, demand in the promotion-price-segment would be zero. Total promotion unit sales are 89 (17 + 72) and list-price unit sales are 56 (56 + 0). The unit sales to each segment at a given price are shown in Table 2.

Controlling Leakage

Leakage reduces profits when consumers who are not targeted to receive a promotion price manage to take advantage of it or when those who should have received a promotion price do not. However, as Column 2 in Table 1 illustrates, the net effect of price promotions on contribution to profit can still be positive even with substantial leakage. Nevertheless, managers should do the following to reduce leakage.

☐   Research the price sensitivities and the variable costs of serving various market segments and analyze the differences.

[7]The remaining 20% of the promotion price segment is not aware of the promotion price.

TABLE 2 Price, quantity, and contribution* relationships for list-price and promotion-price segments

Price	List-price segment		Promotion-price segment		Total market (list + promotion)	
	Units	Contribution†	Units	Contribution	Units	Contribution
$2.00	70.0	$84.00	0	$.00	70.0	$84.00
1.90	72.5	79.75	15.0	16.50	87.5	96.25
1.80	75.0	75.00	30.0	30.00	105.0	105.00
1.70	77.5	69.75	45.0	40.50	122.5	110.25
1.60	80.0	64.00	60.0	48.00	140.0	112.00
1.50	82.5	57.75	75.0	52.50	157.5	110.25
1.40	85.0	51.00	90.0	54.00	175.0	105.00

*Contribution based on variable unit cost of $.80.

†To be read: At a price of $2.00, the list-price segment would buy 70 units, producing a contribution of $84.00 (= 70 units × [2.00 − .80]).

☐ Take a "rifle-shot" approach to targeting announcements of price discounts through media that will selectively reach more price-sensitive consumers or those for whom the variable costs (sometimes opportunity costs) are lowest. Direct-mail delivery of consumer promotion offers is especially appropriate.

☐ Attach restrictions and qualifiers to promotions offering the larger discounts, as the airlines do, so that only the most price-sensitive consumers will expend the effort to obtain them.

☐ Enforce merchandising performance requirements that assure pass-through of trade allowances to consumers and minimize the leakage that results from forward buying by retailers and from the diversion of goods to other geographic markets or discounters.

Improving Price Promotion Costing

A few years ago—when price promotion expenditures amounted to only 1% of sales—assessing the profitability of promotions, calculating the level of leakage, and choosing costing procedures for promotions were relatively unimportant. However, now that promotion expenditures are often ten times that amount, managers need to understand the methods used to assess the cost of price promotions. We believe that many companies are using costing methods heavily biased against price promotions in situations where demand-pricing effects are substantial. The bias stems from using artificially high list prices for cost calculations.

The current method of calculating the amount spent for price promotions is as follows:

The discount offered per unit from list price is multiplied by the number of units sold on promotion. To this figure is added the costs of implementing the promotion, such as printing coupons, manufacturing special packages, and, in some cases, advertising the promotion. Summing these costs for each trade and consumer promotion yields the total amount allocated to price promotions.

List price for such calculations is typically the highest price charged. In our example, the costing process would show high costs of price promotions as a percentage of sales, and more than half of all units would be sold on deal. However, the effect of price promotions on profits would be positive, not negative.

Estimating the "cost" of promotions in this way assumes that the *optimal list price would be just as high if promotions were not run.* However, this assumption is not valid when price promotions help separate the market into price-sensitive and less price-sensitive segments. Under these circumstances, the optimal list prices when promotions can be offered is higher than the list price under a single-price policy. We believe that in calculating the cost of promotions, the appropriate list price to use is the price that *would be charged* under a no-promotion policy.

Using the example in Table 1, if price discounts were not offered, the optimal price would be $1.60. The cost of price discounts should be calculated against the $1.60 price. The $2.00 price should be charged only if promotions are used. Using the higher list prices makes promotions appear to cost more. Also, the budget should receive "credits" for sales at prices "higher than list" ($2.00 − $1.60 = +$.40 per unit). In some situations, the net effect of running a price promotion could be a credit, not a debit.

In fact, such a situation applies in our example. The actual average price received is higher with price promotions than without. Of course, not all situations yield such a result. Notice that the average price obtained is higher per unit *and* that more units are sold with price promotions than without. How, then, can a cost be associated with the price promotions?

The cost of administering promotions in marketing management and sales force time may be significant. In addition, there are incremental production and logistics costs to consider. Combined, these may amount to as much as 2% of sales. The more complicated the promotion policy, the higher the administration costs. However, the costs of a one-price strategy may be higher in terms of opportunities forgone. Also, well-executed price promotions will have less leakage across segments and, therefore, more profitability.

Managers should avoid using incorrect costing procedures for price promotions because they can have the following undesirable consequences.

☐ Artificial concern is generated over apparently increasing expenditures for promotion; and, by comparison, advertising appears to suffer. In fact, advertising expenditures may not have changed.

☐ If the budgeting process is to establish first the size of the marketing budget and then allocate shares to advertising and promotion, promotion costs could be overestimated and advertising could be *wrongly* reduced as a result.

☐ If sales figures are based on list prices, increasing promotion would cause gross sales to increase faster than either unit sales or net sales after promotion discounts. Of course, such increases would be mainly accounting artifacts.

IMPLICATIONS

Price promotions are a symptom, not the cause, of the many phenomena for which they are blamed. We believe that the current emphasis on returning to pull marketing risks overlooking the many benefits of price promotions. One key benefit is promotion's use in implementing demand pricing or price discrimination policies that generate long-term volume and profits. We believe that this benefit is being undervalued by the use of inappropriate costing practices that make promotions appear more expensive than they are, reduce the incentive to use them, and inflate their apparent share of the marketing budget. When variations in marginal costs, administrative costs of promotions, relative price elasticity of the segments, and "leakage" between segments are all considered, the use of price promotions will frequently be more profitable than a single-price policy.